W9-CKM-058

SEATTLE

Pacific Gem

◆ GREG PROBST / HILLSTROM STOCK PHOTO

◆ JIM CORWIN

By Jim French *and* Jim Bates ■ *Profiles in Excellence by* Teresa J. Taylor

SEATTLE

PACIFIC GEM

Captions by LYNN MUCKEN ■ *Art Direction by* BRIAN GROPPE

Library of Congress Cataloging-in-Publication Data

French, Jim, 1928-
Seattle—Pacific gem / by Jim French and Jim Bates ; profiles in excellence by Teresa J. Taylor.
p. cm. — (Urban tapestry series)
Includes index.
ISBN 1-881096-45-9 (alk. paper)
1. Seattle (Wash.)—Civilization. 2. Seattle (Wash.)—Pictorial works. 3. Business enterprises—Washington (State)—Seattle. 4. Seattle (Wash.)—Economic conditions. I. Bates, Jim, 1949- II. Taylor, Teresa J. (Teresa Joy), 1959- III. Title. IV. Series.
F899.S45F73 1997
979.7'772—dc21 97-26166

Towery Publishing, Inc.
1835 Union Avenue
Memphis, TN 38104

Publisher: J. Robert Towery
Executive Publisher: Jenny McDowell
National Sales Manager: Stephen Hung
Regional Sales Manager: Michele Sylvestro
Marketing Director: Carol Culpepper
Project Directors: Liz Bourland, Linda Frank

Executive Editor: David B. Dawson
Managing Editor: Michael C. James
Senior Editors: Lynn Conlee, Carlisle Hacker
Editor/Profile Manager: Jana Files
Editors: Mary Jane Adams, Lori Bond
Assistant Editors: Jennifer C. Pyron, Allison Ring

Profile Designers: Jennifer Baugher, Laurie Lewis, Kelley Pratt, Ann Ward
Digital Color Supervisor: Brenda Pattat
Production Assistants: Geoffrey Ellis, Enrique Espinosa, Jeff McDonald, Robin McGehee
Print Coordinator: Beverly Thompson

Urban Tapestry Series
Towery Publishing, Inc.

▲ Jim Corwin

◆ JIM CORWIN

OZ

By Jim French

▲ TOM REESE

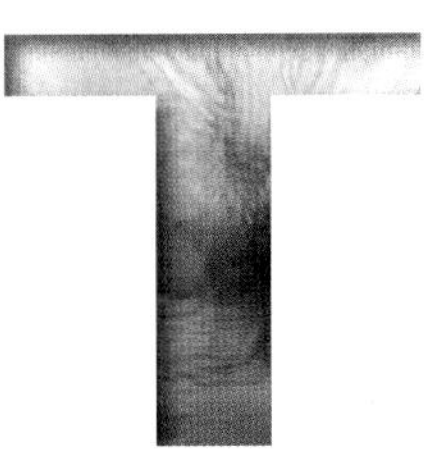

HE STORY OF SEATTLE IS A TALE OF TWO CITIES. THERE'S THE old Seattle, founded in 1851 by a small knot of hardy pioneers from the East who landed at Alki Point, unpacked their Bibles, and raised a few cabins. Then there's the Seattle of today, discovered in 1962 by a large contingent of tourists from California who landed at Sea-Tac International Airport, unpacked their money, and raised our taxes. Or so many a native Seattleite will tell you.

Being a migrant Californian myself (arriving circa 1953), I lived through the civic metamorphosis that began in 1962 and made Seattle a very different town than it was when I first arrived. Why 1962? That was the year of the Seattle World's Fair, which reshaped the Queen City of old into the Emerald City of today—the capital of the northwest rain forest; a mecca for digitized, creative subcultures; and home to the country's best assortment of coffee emporiums.

The World's Fair also gave Seattle its enduring logo, the Space Needle. Privately owned (both then and now), this wasp-waisted obelisk provides the city with a visual reference point, replacing quaint postcard images of ferryboats and the Smith Tower. Its very existence is a metaphor for what happened—and is still happening—to Seattle.

The fair, I can attest, was a lulu. Not only did it leave the city a legacy of useful civic buildings that encompass science, the arts, and high-altitude sight-seeing, but it also attracted thousands of people who had never been to Seattle before and who thought of the city as an untamed northern outpost—if they thought of it at all. But after the World's Fair, the secret was out and Seattle was thus discovered. Soon after, Elvis Presley came here to make the movie *It Happened at the World's Fair*, and Namu the killer whale abided for a while just across the bay.

Except for L.C. Smith's funky white monument to the typewriter that made him rich, to that point, we hadn't had a skyscraper to our name. Built in 1914, the 42-story Smith Tower was—until the Needle—the tallest building west of the Mississippi River. (It will tell you so in a bronze plaque by its Second Avenue entrance.)

But since the World's Fair, Seattle's skyline has metamorphosed into something reminiscent of Dorothy's view of Oz at the end of the yellow brick road. Glittering shafts of steel and granite cluster together and shoot higher and higher into the sky above narrow downtown canyons. Chisel-topped, domed, or spiked with communications towers, Seattle's bundle of brawny buildings today envelops the few graceful and ornate art deco edifices of the 1930s that remain.

Why are there so few of these architectural gems left? Because Seattle needed big new hotels, a new art museum, a new symphony hall, and more office space. And, unfortunately, there was no room left in which to expand. See, downtown Seattle is pinched by water on the left and a hill on the right, and a freeway runs right through the middle of it. When progress came calling, the bulldozers had to work overtime to make room for all the necessary new buildings.

So, down came the elegant old theaters, department stores, and office buildings. And up went biotech research centers and world headquarters buildings for a score of major industries that didn't exist when the Space Needle was brand-new. In a nutshell, Seattle completely rebuilt itself.

▲ SEATTLE TIMES / JOHNNY CLOSS

▲ SEATTLE TIMES

▲ SEATTLE TIMES

While Kansas may be nice, most locals agree that there's no place like home. Providing a magical backdrop for the city's many cultural and entertainment opportunities is downtown Seattle, anchored by the widely recognized Space Needle. The 600-foot-tall structure was built for the 1962 World's Fair, an event that attracted large crowds, innovative machinery, and prominent celebrities to the Emerald City.

▲ CHRIS BENNION

▲ SEATTLE TIMES

DAN LAMONT

FOR DISTANT
VIEWING

TOM REESE

LOOKING BACK TO THE REAL BEGINNINGS OF SEATTLE, THIS BUSINESS of pushing real estate around doesn't seem so new. Although the city was—and is—blessed by nature with an improbably beautiful setting, Seattle's earliest promoters carved up the landscape in order to accommodate commerce. For starters, they filled in the swampy land on Elliott Bay so that the proper dockage for ocean vessels could be provided at the foot of the bustling little town.

This move proved to be provident: In 1875, six years after Seattle was incorporated as a city, the first regular steamship service between Seattle and San Francisco was inaugurated. Even though Seattle's piers were a hundred miles from the ocean in a bay on Puget Sound, the city's northern location made it a vibrant threshold for trade with the Orient, thereby bringing it all the blessings and curses of a seaport town.

Back in 1889, when a glue pot started a blaze that the city's fire brigade couldn't quench before it had wiped out most of downtown, the cluster of shacks, false-front stores, and dens of iniquity that had sprouted like mushrooms around the town's core was laid to waste. As a result, mendicants, merchants, and madams had to set up shop under tents until a new and better Seattle could be built—this time, under the city's strict architectural regulations. When it was finished, a new epoch of brave civic development shifted into high gear, filling in sloughs and sluicing down inconvenient hills.

When gold was discovered in the Yukon in 1896, Seattle became the natural springboard for those adventurous souls who wanted a piece of the action. The city supplied all of the things that Alaska could not, and prospectors set out for the goldfields on Seattle-owned vessels, loaded with Seattle-bought tools, and even wearing Seattle-made boots and heavy-weather gear. And when the first ton of gold was scraped out of Alaska and put aboard a ship, naturally, the first port of call was Seattle. In a fitting reversal of accepted business methodology, we got 'em going and coming.

Today's Seattle bears little evidence of this lusty past. Oh, there's Pioneer Square, which is rich with old rococo buildings that have been refurbished into trendy shops and upscale apartments. And beneath the square's sidewalks are a few unique blocks of storefronts from the 1890s, which were once on street level before city engineers instigated another massive waterfront fill-in. But at the southern edge of downtown, the depression-era shantytown (called, like so many others around the country, Hooverville by its destitute denizens) has long since been bulldozed to make way for commerce. All that flat acreage, reclaimed from the stumpy swamp of yore, is now a storage yard for cargo containers, and the Kingdome is its neighbor.

SEATTLE TIMES / MARK HARRISON

Modern-day Seattle bears little resemblance to its pioneer beginnings. Following a devastating fire in 1889, the city began to rebuild under much stricter architectural regulations. Today, the burgeoning business district continues to reach new heights, as do Seattle's firefighters and preservationists, who use technology and plenty of hard work to avoid the destruction of the past.

SEATTLE TIMES

SEATTLE TIMES

SEATTLE TIMES

JIM CORVIN

DAHL-FERGUSON

Seattle is a city of hills and water, with Puget Sound on the west and Lake Washington on the east. Countless streams meander among the city's diverse neighborhoods, which are stitched together with some 1,200 bridges ranging from a 10-story span over Lake Union to three freeway bridges that literally float in Lake Washington. These structures serve as gateways to Seattle's communities, each of which has its own distinct personality.

Take the Ballard Bridge over the Ship Canal, which arcs from the western flats at the foot of Queen Anne Hill, creeps out across mast-choked Fisherman's Terminal, and lands you squarely in the Scandinavian stronghold of Ballard. Fishermen and shipwrights from Norway, Finland, Sweden, and Denmark, who must have felt a familiar tang in the salt air and brisk breeze off the Sound, settled this notch between Sunset Hill on the west and Fremont on the east. Originally a separate town, Ballard eventually fell prey to the growth of Seattle but, like most of the city's districts, is still very much its own community.

Speaking of individuality, take Fremont. And take care that you don't call it the Fremont district to anyone who lives there. Fremont is Fremont, and on occasion, it has campaigned to secede from Seattle. This relatively small neighborhood, which can be reached from the Queen Anne district by its own drawbridge, is called "the center of the known universe" by its residents. You'll especially know this to be true if you talk with Suzie Burke, the daughter of pioneer Fremont businesspeople, who controls much of the commercial property along the northern bank of the Ship Canal.

◀ JIM BATES

◀ JIM CORWIN

A stroll around the city reveals beauty in unexpected places, whether it's eclectic mannequins outside a colorful shop, the much-decorated *Waiting for the Interurban*, the 18-foot-tall *Troll* in Fremont, or the whisper of a rainbow over Bellevue's Downtown Park. But few sights, if any, equal a view of Mount Rainier at sunrise as it looms over Lake Washington.

◆ JIM CORWI

Fremont is home to a mixed bag of artists and creative retailers who make and sell countless items you won't find at such mainstays as Nordstrom. The town is a feast for the eyes for its handmade signs and graphics, and a treat for the palate for its Bohemian fare and minuscule cafés. To find Fremont, just look for the pastel drawbridge and a piece of sidewalk art called *Waiting for the Interurban*. This life-size sculpture of a stoic group is much loved by

▶ JIM BATES

Fremonters, who clothe the patient cement commuters in scarves and caps in the winter. They, like many of us, are waiting for Seattle to solve its transportation problems, but the statues will have a long wait before the old Interurban trolley cars roll again.

Fremont is not the only free-spirited neighborhood in town. West Seattle thinks of itself as a distinct community, and in personality, it is. Pointing a jutting peninsula straight at Ballard across Elliott Bay, West Seattle sniffs at being thought of as a borough of the big city. Regardless, it has one of the best views of the breathtaking spikes of downtown, and some residents are fortunate enough to live in cliffside homes that look onto nearby Vashon Island or northwest into the misty reaches of Puget Sound.

In West Seattle, there are long beaches where sunbathers gather, a rugged shoreline that is beloved by painters and naturalists, an ancient lighthouse that guards the entrance to the harbor, and plenty of older homes that are lovingly restored and maintained. As in other parts of the city, West Seattle's respect for its 60-, 70-, and even 80-year-old dwellings goes against the grain of other West Coast communities: Young people here seem to like living with the handicraft of the past.

Nowhere is Seattle's diverse population more evident than on Capitol Hill. You'll find everyone from leather-clad punks to old-money mainstays to members of two dozen ethnic groups in this colorful community east of downtown. And if you understand how these distinct groups can live happily as neighbors, you'll understand Seattle, a city of unique communities where everyone can find a home.

▶ SEATTLE TIMES / TERESA TAMURA

In a blur of light and color, commuters wind their way to and from downtown and over the Evergreen Point Floating Bridge (PAGES 18 AND 19).

▼ JIM CORWIN

GOV. A. D. ROSELLINI
BRIDGE
EVERGREEN POINT
MOTOR
VEHICLES
ONLY

▲ JIM CORWIN

SEATTLE'S CULTURAL AND COMMERCIAL COMMUNITIES ARE EQUALLY diverse and interesting. For example, in recent years, the city has become a trendsetter in the arts. Numerous movies and television shows are filmed here each year, and Seattle has been the point of origin for at least two recent big waves in rock music culture. In addition, it is hot property for the stage, with a vast number of theaters in the region.

Perhaps the short, dark days of winter are the reason we read so much here, but booksellers agree that Seattle is one of the best markets for books of all kinds. We do have a plethora of snazzy bookstores, as well as a wide range of smaller specialty shops, and Seattle can boast a sizable number of famous writers who have chosen to work and live here.

One sure sign of the city's coming of age is its major-league sports franchises. Seattle has gone so crazy for its Mariners, Seahawks, and SuperSonics that the teams are outgrowing their venues. After the NBA had to call a game because the 30-year-old Seattle Center Coliseum had sprung a leak on a rainy day, the building underwent a complete refurbishment and emerged as the KeyArena. Now, the Sonics and their fans have no complaints about wet seats. The Mariners will soon be playing ball in a new park with a wide-open view of the sky instead of a concrete ceiling. And not to be outdone, the Seahawks, purchased by local billionaire Paul Allen, are building a new stadium to replace their present home, the Kingdome.

▼ PACIFIC NORTHWEST BALLET / BEN KERNS

▼ JIM BATES

A dancer performs a grand jeté during the Pacific Northwest Ballet's production of *Cinderella*, while footballers demonstrate a few fancy steps of their own at the annual Apple Cup contest between the Washington State University Cougars and the University of Washington Huskies.

Allen—a partner of Bill Gates in founding Microsoft, the computer software empire headquartered across the lake in Redmond—is only one of many local businesspeople with a world-class reputation for their acumen. It hardly needs mentioning that the Nordstrom empire sprang from a small, family-owned Seattle shoe store, or that the Starbucks coffee chain is headquartered here,

▼ DAVID SAILORS

as are SBC (Seattle's Best Coffee) and more than a dozen other retail chains.

But by far the oldest, largest, and most influential Seattle enterprise is The Boeing Company. It's still true that the ups and downs of the Boeing payroll can control the economic vitality of the whole region. In a city of less than half a million people, the loss (or gain) of Boeing jobs has a ripple effect that touches every business in the area. Of course, Boeing isn't the only giant hereabouts; the aforementioned Microsoft dynasty feeds Seattle's prosperity too, as do the many high-tech and biotech industries located up and down the technology corridor. The University of Washington is internationally acclaimed in science and medicine, and the Fred Hutchinson Cancer Research Center and a number of other cutting-edge medical technology centers make their homes in Seattle.

All of the area's commercial development, coupled with the rapid growth of suburban communities, has challenged Seattle and the Puget Sound region to maintain the values that attracted so many people here in the first place. A lot of attention has been paid to the permitting process when developers want to open new neighborhoods or build commercial buildings in formerly pristine areas, but with each new arrival come more cars to a freeway system that is already choked. Soon, there may well be a fourth floating bridge on Lake Washington, serving commuters between the burgeoning Eastside communities of Bellevue, Kirkland, Issaquah, Redmond, and Woodinville. And north and south traffic on Interstate 5 between Everett and Tacoma is concentrated in the middle—which is to say, smack inside the Seattle city limits.

An alternative to the single-occupant private car is long overdue, but into the last half of the 1990s, the only agreed-upon solutions have been high-occupancy lanes on freeways and an ongoing advertising campaign urging people to take the bus. Seattle's Metro Transit and similar bus systems in neighboring Snohomish and Pierce counties are good, but they still haven't lured enough drivers out of their cars to make any noticeable improvement on the highways and byways. Some combination of rail and bus transit is expected to go into operation before the end of the century.

ALEX WATERHOUSE-HAYWARD

CHRIS BENNION

TOM REESE

When you're one of the 18 million or so commuters who use the Washington State Ferry System each year, nothing gives you a lift like a strong cup of coffee. Unless, of course, it's a production of Tony Kushner's Tony Award-winning epic, *Angels in America*, at the Intiman Playhouse. The run was the venue's most successful production ever—playing to more than 63,000 patrons.

PIKE PLACE
we pack fish to keep fresh
YES, WE HAVE SMOKED SALMON
HOME DELIVERIES
NOW AVIALABLE
PLS. ASK FOR MORE INFO
FREE!
TO ALL
DOWNTOWN
FRESH WASHINGTON COAST DUNGENESS CRAB
EXTRA FANCY SALMON CAVIAR $15.00 JAR
FRESH LING COD $4.99 lb
LIVE MAINE

GARY GREENE

CO.
hours
WE PACK FISH TO GO
IN 48 HOUR ICE PACKS
WE ALSO SHIP FISH ANYWHERE
IN THE U.S.A. VIA FEDERAL X-PRESS
CAUTION!
LOW flying FISH
PIKE PLACE FISH T-SHIRTS $15.00 ea.
915
Reynolds
FILM
FRESH! CHILEAN SEA BASS $7.99 LB.
FRESH! HALIBUT FILLETS $7.99
FRESH! STEELHEAD $4.99 LB.
FRESH! KING SALMON FILLETS $7.99 LB.
FRESH HALIBUT $6.99 LB.
FRESH! KING SALMON STEAKS $6.99 LB.
PACKING TO FLY
18 HR FREE
24 HR $2.00
48 HR $7.00
PICKLED HERRING $4.49 LB.

LIKE THE SPACE NEEDLE, THE PIKE PLACE MARKET IS A SYMBOL OF the city—in this case, Seattle's resilience and fervor. On every visitor's must-see list, the Market isn't just a walk-through visual; it's a multimedia, multisensory experience. In 1963, it almost got bulldozed in favor of a slick, new development, but fortunately, wiser heads prevailed before this irreplaceable splinter of history could be obliterated.

The Market got its start in 1907, when local farmers rebelled at having to sell their produce to middlemen before the public could enjoy it. As a result, a few of them hooked up their teams and hauled dewy-fresh vegetables from their Kent Valley farms to a section of land at the foot of Pike Street and sold their wares out of their wagons. The next weekend, more farmers showed up, and such was the beginning of what has become one of the most distinctive parts of this decidedly unique city.

The Market was even politically prescient; Seattle just didn't like fat cats or bossism. About the time the Market began to thrive, labor reformers drummed into town and recruited longshoremen, stevedores, teamsters, loggers, and fishermen. In the end, just about all of the trades got into the act in one way or another. A disdainful writer once called the state the Soviet of Washington.

By way of contrast to the noisy Pike Place Market, we have the University of Washington Arboretum, a tranquil preserve of gorgeous greenery in the midst of the city. Paths and a two-lane avenue link woodsy grottoes, rolling lawns, and a Japanese garden with ponds and rustic bridges. There's no doubt about the value of homes in nearby Broadmoor, a walled, private community that backs onto the Arboretum. But you don't have to live in an exclusive enclave to enjoy what grows around here. When I first came to Seattle, it looked to me as if everyone were living in a national park, what with all the big, black-green trees and the lakes and the mountains. Today, it still pretty much does.

But for everything, there is a price, and the price Seattle pays for its lush foliage is rain. In this temperate climate, it seldom gets really, really cold and almost never gets really, really hot. In fact, when our mercury falls to 10 above or soars to 90 degrees, it makes headlines. Figure on five snowy days each winter, and the same number

◂ SEATTLE TIMES / ALAN BERNER

◂ SEATTLE TIMES / ALAN BERNER

Seattle boasts its fair share of recognizable landmarks. Among the most notable is Pike Place Market, which offers fresh produce, meat, and seafood, as well as interesting artwork and the usual tourist trinkets (PAGES 22 AND 23). Here, a local "hand delivers" a salmon (LEFT), while a congratulatory hand is presented to native son Gary Locke, the first Asian-American governor of a U.S. state outside Hawaii (RIGHT).

◆ TOM REESE

of 80-plus days in the summer. But the fact is, and you've heard this before, Seattle is a very rainy city. Statistically, we may get less rain than, say, New York City, Chicago, Philadelphia, or Washington, D.C., in measured inches of annual rainfall. The difference is that our 40 to 60 inches per year aren't dumped on us in a handful of dramatic cloudbursts that are spaced throughout the year; our rain comes drifting down for six months at a stretch with very little letup.

But people keep moving to Seattle, rain or no. Which brings up the tricky question: What's a Seattleite like? And today, the answer often is "someone who moved here from somewhere else." Ours is one of the most diverse cities in America. Despite their relatively small population, a fair number of African-American citizens are running the government, including the offices of mayor and fire chief. Asians make up an increasing share of Seattle's

TOM REESE

Songs like Perry Como's musical tribute to our blue skies were obviously written by a tunesmith who sacrificed reality for rhyme, or who happened to visit here on a clear day. The skies over Seattle are most often gray, but when the sun *does* come out and the clouds go away, there is no more splendid place on earth. My theory is that Seattleites appreciate sunshine much more than most other folks because it's so rare. How else do you explain the fact that, per capita, more sunglasses are sold in Seattle than in any other U.S. city?

demographics, and have been welcomed into politics and business. There are also smaller but growing numbers of Hispanics and other ethnic groups.

Seattle's laid-back attitude long ago got a double-tall shot of caffeine, and not just from the multitudes of latte stands that enliven the city's sidewalks. There are as many overachievers and type A personalities around here as in any other city west of Manhattan. The big difference is that in the afternoon, knock-'em-dead entrepreneurs can be found sailing on the Sound, whacking handballs and pumping iron, water or snow skiing, climbing nearby mountains, working in the garden, and generally making use of the beauty around them.

At one time, Seattleites had a decided inferiority complex that seemed to say, "Never mind that we're way out of the mainstream, last on the coast to pick up on any national trend; we're content up here in our little corner of the country, and if you don't like us,

TOM REESE

go home." Well, a lot of that has changed. Seattle now sets trends. We are the future, and we've become a magnet for outsiders.

The trick for us all will be to enjoy the gorgeous beauty around us without destroying it, and to temper our love of freedom in this expansive region with responsible stewardship, so that the Emerald City will continue to be a place of delight for generations, and the Space Needle's trajectory will forever symbolize the aspirations of those who live in its shadow.

Locals find many ways to enjoy a sunny day on the area's abundant waterways, from diving off a platform at Madison Park and Beach to rowing silently across Lake Washington. With a relatively high number of rainy days, however, many folks choose to do their tanning indoors.

JIM CORWIN

▼ JIM BATES

▲ JIM BATES

▼ NATALIE FOBES ▲ BENJAMIN BENSCHNEIDER

As the city's most enduring symbol, the Space Needle maintains a presence in all things Seattle, whether it's stretching high above the International Fountain at Seattle Center (page 26) or playing a rare second fiddle to a festive fireworks display (page 27).

▲ COURTESY SEATTLE SYMPHONY / ROBIN BARTHOLICK

A FEAST FOR THE EYES AND ears, Seattle is always in motion, from a drummer keeping the rhythm at a Tulalip Indian ceremony to a trail of stars over majestic Mount Rainier to a musical flourish from Maestro Gerard Schwarz and the Seattle Symphony.

▼ JIM BATES

ART IMITATING ART: A character in the Pacific Northwest Ballet's performance of *The Nutcracker* (OPPOSITE) unknowingly mimics Duane Pasco's *Tsonaqua: The Wild Woman of the Woods*, which stands in Pioneer Square's Occidental Park (ABOVE).

▲ PACIFIC NORTHWEST BALLET / RICK DEAN

Interesting works of art abound in and around Seattle. Though unintentional, a "still life" on the waterfront in Ballard exudes as much character as the 300-year-old rock carvings found near Cape Alava or the ferocious face of a totem pole on the Seattle waterfront (pages 32 and 33).

▼ TOM REESE

▼ NATALIE FOBES

▲ SUSAN ALWORTH

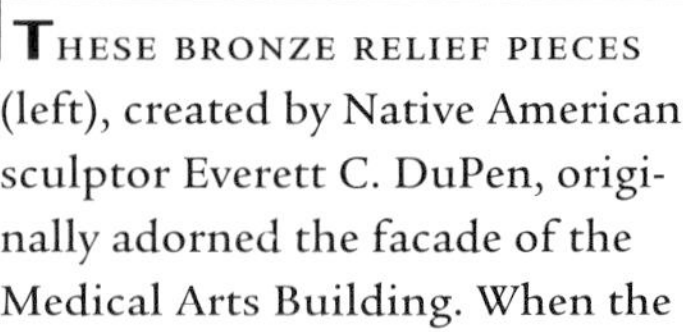

JIM BATES

GARY HAYES

THESE BRONZE RELIEF PIECES (left), created by Native American sculptor Everett C. DuPen, originally adorned the facade of the Medical Arts Building. When the structure was razed and replaced by the Washington Bank Building, the unique pieces were preserved and incorporated into the new edifice.

JIM BATES

JIM BATES

JIM BATES

Adorning a dental office building in the University District, the stone face of a man in agony beckons anyone who feels his pain to step inside (LEFT), while a row of walrus heads that stare down the Arctic Building probably leave some passersby feeling a toothache coming on (RIGHT). Proudly bearing *its* pearly whites is a totem pole outside the Thomas Burke Memorial Washington State Museum, located on the University of Washington campus (OPPOSITE RIGHT).

JIM BATES

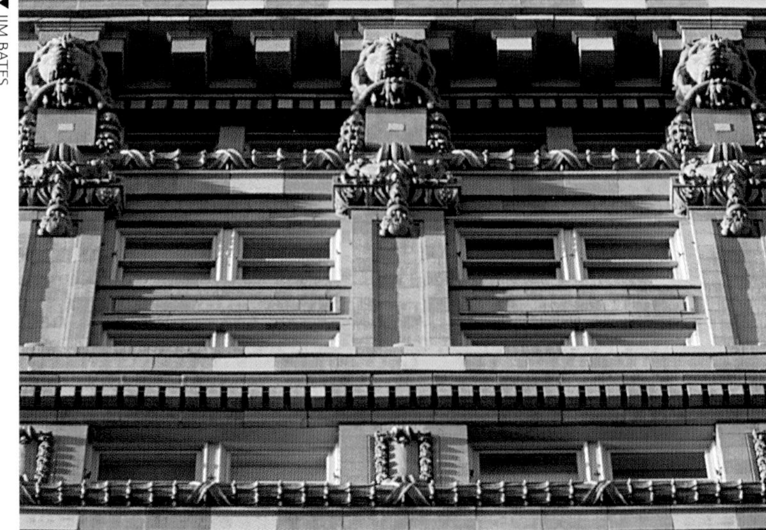

JIM BATES

SUSAN ALWORTH

BENJAMIN BENSCHNEIDER

THE WIDESPREAD INFLUENCE of Native American culture on the Pacific Northwest can be found in local art and architecture, from details on the terra-cotta Cobb Building downtown (TOP LEFT) to a totem pole in Occidental Park (BOTTOM LEFT). Other architectural elements demonstrate the impact diverse cultures have had on Seattle, especially in Pioneer Square, where such delights as historic stone ornamentation (TOP RIGHT) and remnants of Underground Seattle (BOTTOM RIGHT) greet you at every turn.

▲ FRED LYON

JUST A FEW BLOCKS FROM EACH other in Pioneer Square are two unique structures built in the early 1900s. A cast-iron pergola, installed in 1909, provides shelter to pedestrians in the shadow of the landmark Smith Tower, opened in 1914.

THE 42-STORY SMITH TOWER, funded by businessman Lyman Smith, was Seattle's first fireproof steel structure and the tallest building west of the Mississippi River until 1969. The tower features the only manually operated elevators on the West Coast, as well as the unusual Chinese Room, which contains a Wishing Chair for single women hoping to get married.

◄ HERMINE DREYFUSS

ALEX WATERHOUSE-HAYWARD

ALEX WATERHOUSE-HAYWARD

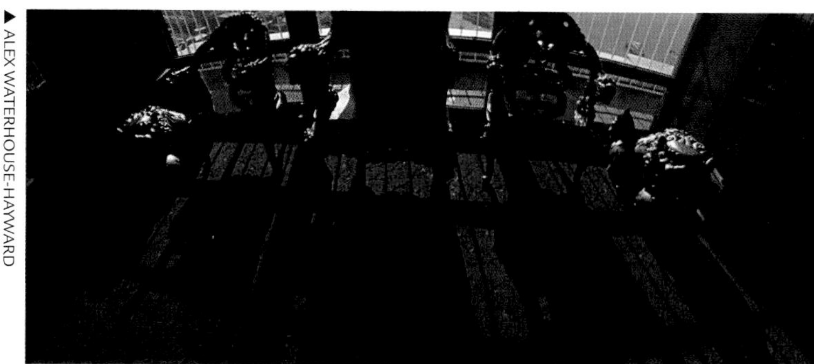

ALEX WATERHOUSE-HAYWARD

ALEX WATERHOUSE-HAYWARD

▼ RICHARD T. NOWITZ

▲ JIM BATES

▲ GARY GREENE

▲ JIM BATES

Nestled between downtown and the sports complexes where the NFL Seahawks and American League Mariners play, the Pioneer Square historic district draws countless visitors to stroll among its Romanesque buildings, complemented by an abundance of green trees and street lamps that tell time. There are also plenty of opportunities to take a break, including the Waterfall Garden at Second and Main (center) and the Merchants Cafe, which has welcomed Seattleites since 1890 (bottom right). On the northeast corner of Pioneer Square is another longtime local resident, the Alaska Building, which opened in 1904 (top right).

Art lovers gravitate to Pioneer Square on the first Thursday of every month for Art Walk, during which galleries and shops extend their hours to show off their new displays (top and opposite top).

▼ SEATTLE TIMES / GARY SETTLE

▼ SEATTLE TIMES / BENJAMIN BENSCHNEIDER

▲ SEATTLE TIMES / ALAN BERNER

SUPERB MUSEUMS, SCATTERED throughout the city, offer patrons the chance to appreciate diverse genres. The Frye Art Museum, featuring primarily 19th-century European salon paintings, is housed in an International Style building that is a masterpiece in and of itself (BOTTOM). Located on the University of Washington campus, the Carl Gould-designed Henry Art Gallery contains such unique pieces as this enormous mud circle, painted by Richard Long (OPPOSITE BOTTOM).

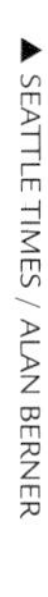

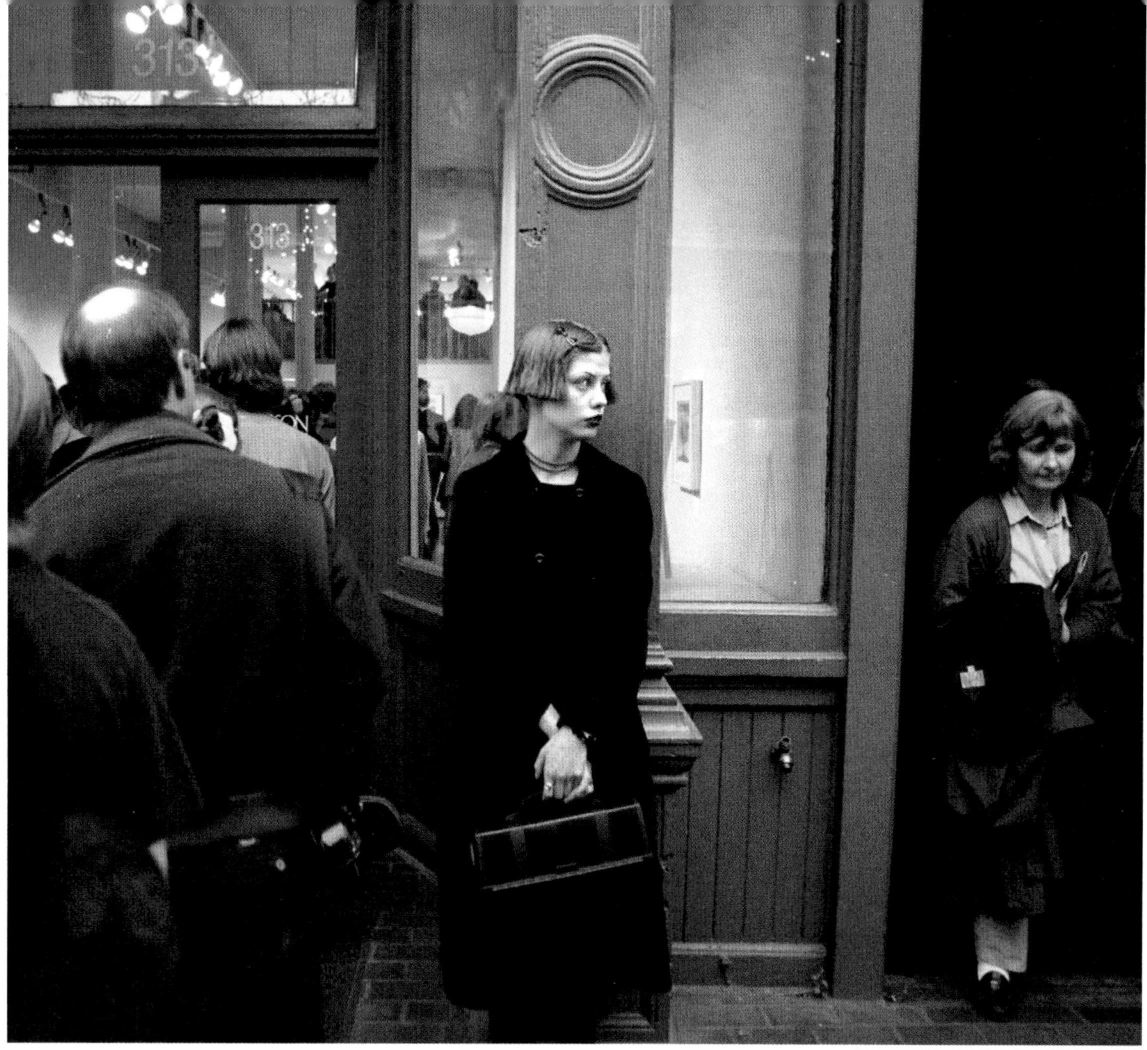

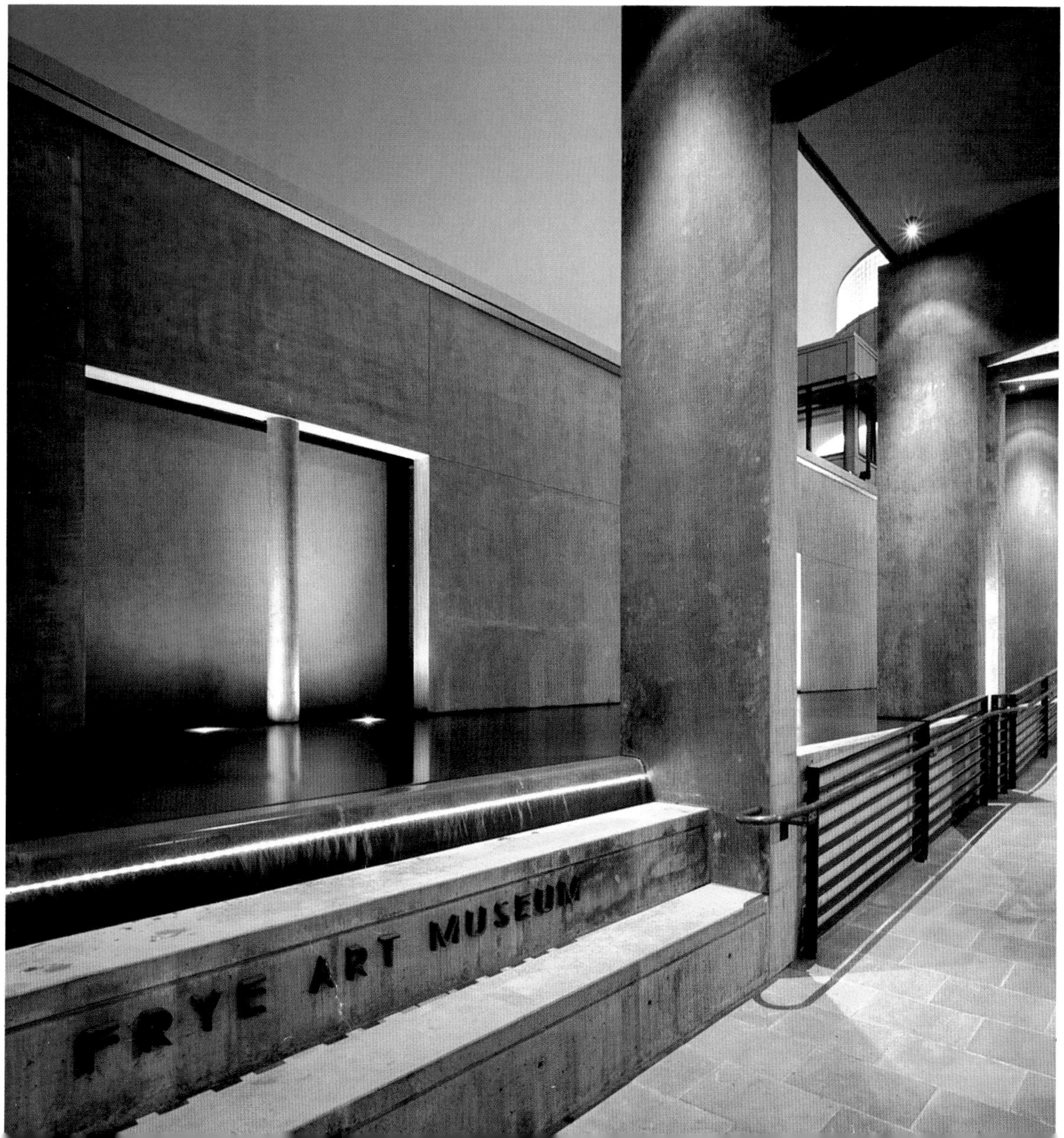

▲ SEATTLE TIMES / BENJAMIN BENSCHNEIDER

JIM CORWIN

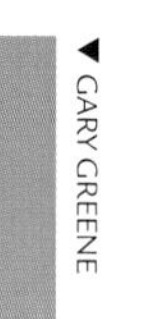

GARY GREENE

ALTHOUGH THE CRITICS TEND to hate it, plenty of Seattleites love Jonathan Borofsky's *Hammering Man*, a 48-foot-tall, mechanical sculpture that pounds away constantly outside the Seattle Art Museum. The 11-ton steel structure, which collapsed once during its installation, has been the subject of several pranks: On Labor Day in 1993, an artists' group attached a ball and chain to the statue's legs.

SEATTLE ART MUSEUM
INSIDE
TAILOR · CLEANER
▲ GARY GREENE
▲ SEATTLE TIMES / TOM REESE
▼ JOHN STAMETS

▼ JOHN STAMETS

▼ JOHN STAMETS

▶ JOHN STAMETS

▶ JOHN STAMETS

THE PIKE PLACE MARKET, located above the waterfront on the north edge of downtown, is the nation's oldest continuously operating farmers' market, and a purveyor of all things touristy. The Public Market, as it is also called, draws nearly 40,000 people daily.

▼ JIM CORWIN

▼ SUSAN ALWORTH

▼ ALEX WATERHOUSE-HAYWARD

▼ ALEX WATERHOUSE-HAYWARD

▶ ALEX WATERHOUSE-HAYWARD

▶ ALEX WATERHOUSE-HAYWARD

▶ KEVIN MCGOWAN / STRODE PHOTOGRAPHERS

▶ JIM BATES

WHETHER YOU'RE CRAVING handpicked fruit and vegetables, fresh fish, colorful wind socks, or spicy peppers, you can find it all at the Pike Place Market.

SEATTLE TIMES / TOM REESE

WHILE THE EMERALD CITY HAS for years been a popular location for movies, it was the 1993 hit *Sleepless in Seattle*, featuring Tom Hanks and Rob Reiner (ABOVE), as well as the city's famous houseboats (OPPOSITE), that made so many Americans fall in love with the town.

▲ TOM REESE

▼ NATALIE FOBES

OPTING FOR A LESS TRADI-tional marriage ceremony, this couple exchange vows aboard the classic schooner *Zodiac*.

▲ JIM CORWIN

▲ NATALIE FOBES

AS HOME TO MUCH OF THE FLEET that works Pacific and Alaskan waters, Seattle remembers its fishing heritage with several traditions. Each May, a ceremony to bless the fleet takes place in front of the bronze-and-concrete Seattle Fishermen's Memorial at the Ballard Fishermen's Terminal (LEFT). Here, a local mariner gives a kiss for good luck to the first salmon of the season (RIGHT).

▲ NATALIE FOBES

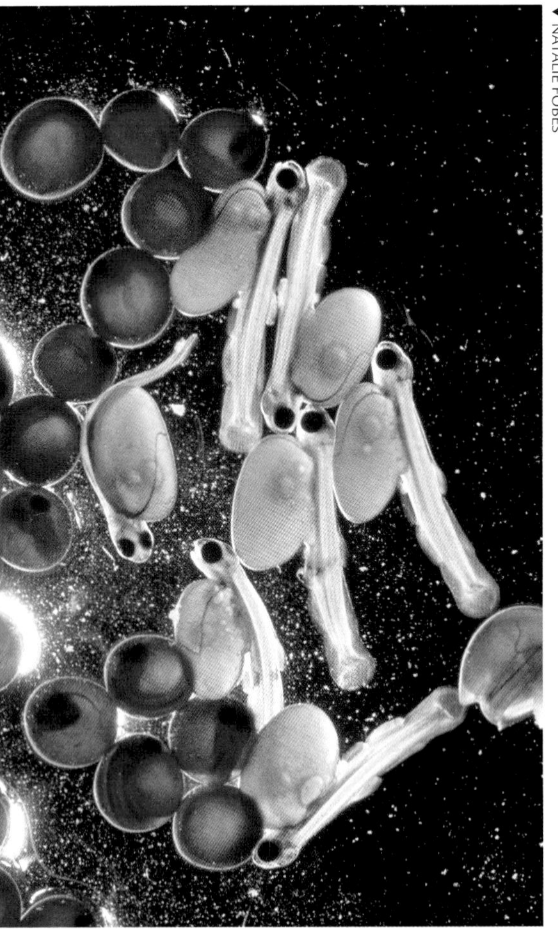

▲ NATALIE FOBES

▲ NATALIE FOBES

▶ NATALIE FOBES

▶ SEATTLE TIMES / MERYL SCHENKER

SALMON REMAIN THE LIFEBLOOD of the Northwest fishing industry. A landmark court ruling gives Native Americans a share of the catch, while hatcheries and fish ladders use modern technology in an effort to preserve the dwindling fish runs.

WHERE THERE'S WATER, THERE must be bridges. After a smaller predecessor was put out of commission when it was struck by a passing ship, the West Seattle Bridge today arches high over the Duwamish Waterway, ensuring a sufficient pathway for large freighters.

◀ KEVIN MCGOWAN / STRODE PHOTOGRAPHERS

▶ JOHN COULTER GOSSETT

▶ KEVIN MCGOWAN / STRODE PHOTOGRAPHERS

THE LAKE WASHINGTON SHIP Canal supports all manner of water traffic, but for land-loving commuters, the canal's bridges are the way to go. Although the Fremont Bridge, with its neon Rapunzel, allows the right-of-way to passing boats (TOP RIGHT), the larger Aurora Bridge promises uninterrupted travel, not to mention a great view of Lake Union (BOTTOM). On the opposite side of Lake Union is the University Bridge, which opened in 1919 and is registered as a city historic landmark (TOP LEFT).

▶ FRED LYON

▶ KEVIN MCGOWAN / STRODE PHOTOGRAPHERS

▼ KURT THORSON

▼ JIM CORWIN

KEVIN MCGOWAN / STRODE PHOTOGRAPHERS

NO MATTER THE SIZE OF YOUR boat, the water is a great way to get from point A to point B. Here, a ferry steams across Puget Sound, a crew competes in a high-energy race on Montlake Cut, and a couple and their dog drift lazily in a canoe on Union Bay.

▼ TOM REESE

▼ JIM BATES

▼ KEVIN MCGOWAN / STRODE PHOTOGRAPHERS

▼ JIM BATES

ANY WAY YOU LOOK AT IT, THE Emerald City is a kid-friendly town. At the Seattle Aquarium, youngsters can immerse themselves in the marine life of the region (TOP AND BOTTOM RIGHT). Located on the waterfront, the facility boasts an interactive exhibit where children can touch starfish and look through microscopes.

SEATTLE TIMES / MERYL SCHENKER

FRED LYON

JIM BATES

SEATTLE TIMES / BETTY UDESEN

PLAYFUL OTTERS FROLIC AT THE Seattle Aquarium (TOP LEFT), while migrating salmon make their way through the Ballard Locks fish ladder (BOTTOM LEFT). Ladders like this help fish reach the higher waters of inland lakes, a service that the area's locks provide for both commercial and recreational vessels (TOP RIGHT). Moving at its own pace, Tom Jay's traveling sockeye sculpture entices children wherever it stops (BOTTOM RIGHT).

▲ KEVIN MCGOWAN / STRODE PHOTOGRAPHERS

▶ CHRIS BENNION

▶ SEATTLE TIMES / RON WURZER

The Emerald City's thriving theater scene offers everything from Stephen Sondheim's *Sunday in the Park with George* at the Seattle Repertory Theatre (top) to an umbrella dance by UMO, a guerrilla theater troupe (bottom). Performed around the International Fountain during the Bumbershoot arts and music festival, held each year over the Labor Day weekend, the umbrella dance provides inspiration to kids of all ages.

▼ SEATTLE TIMES / MERYL SCHENKER

ART IS IN THE EYE OF THE beholder. "Mooing" at hot-air balloons in the sky over the eastern suburb of Redmond is this 12-foot-tall cow, created by welder Gary Vig out of used 300-gallon diesel fuel tanks.

SEATTLE TIMES / JIMI LOTT

SEATTLE TIMES / MIKE SIEGEL

Lenin and Liberty: This 16-foot, 8.5-ton statue of the late Soviet leader, posing here with local luminary Suzie Burke, was retrieved from a town dump in Slovakia after the fall of the Soviet Union and reerected in funky Fremont (left). Meanwhile, a giant balloon version of the Statue of Liberty watches over Gas Works Park on the Fourth of July (right).

FROM LANDSCAPED DINOSAURS at the Pacific Science Center (TOP) to a happy hippo at the Woodland Park Zoo (OPPOSITE), Seattle is a fountain of inspiration for local humorist Gary Larson (BOTTOM), who has gained millions of fans with his popular cartoon, *The Far Side*.

▼ JIM BATES

▼ SEATTLE TIMES / NICK GUNDERSON

▲ JIM BATES

When the sun comes out in Seattle, everybody—and his dog—puts on a pair of shades.

Living large, a proud pooch eclipses downtown Seattle from its position in Gas Works Park (opposite top).

GARY GREENE

▲ TERESA TAMURA

▲ SEATTLE TIMES / JIMI LOTT

As THE SAYING GOES, IT TAKES two to tango. These ostriches find a home on a Bothell farm, but pairs of Bengal tigers, plains zebras, and brown bears prefer the near-natural settings of the Woodland Park Zoo. Visitors to the zoo's gift shop can take an ark full of memories home with them.

▼ SEATTLE TIMES / JIMI LOTT

▲ JIM BATES

▲ JIM CORWIN

If you're in Seattle, chances are it *is* raining, *was* raining, or *will be* raining again soon, and the diminutive drops leave their mark throughout the city. But these poncho-clad youngsters in Woodland Park are prepared for fun, no matter what the skies hold (bottom).

RAINDROPS ON WINDSHIELDS and showers on infants: While cloudbursts may not be everyone's favorite thing, Seattle's watery weather makes for lush landscapes. Each year, it rains approximately 42 inches in the Emerald City, less than in Charleston, South Carolina; Columbus, Ohio; Houston; Knoxville; and Atlanta.

▼ SEATTLE TIMES / ALAN BERNER

▼ SEATTLE TIMES / ALAN BERNER

▼ SEATTLE TIMES / ALAN BERNER

▲ BRIAN GROPPE

Olympic National Park, located west of Seattle on the Olympic Peninsula, is famous for its dense rain forests (TOP AND OPPOSITE), created by a temperate climate and clouds that dump most of their moisture as they bounce against the Olympic Mountains. On the opposite side of the city, meandering through Washington's extensive network of national forests, is the 2,600-mile Pacific Crest National Scenic Trail, which runs from Canada to Mexico (BOTTOM).

▲ GREGORY WILLIAMS
▼ BENJAMIN BENSCHNEIDER

▼ JIM BATES

▼ BRIAN GROPPE

If there's anything you can depend on in the Pacific Northwest, it's clouds and mountains. Seattle is flanked by the Olympics to the west and the Cascades to the east.

▲ TOM REESE

IT MAY BE CALLED THE WILDERNESS Beach Hike, but the trail system along the coast of Olympic National Park is well developed and well maintained, drawing countless nature lovers each year to hike its paths.

▲ TOM REESE

▼ TIM J. JOHNSON / STRODE PHOTOGRAPHERS

▲ JIM CORWIN

Seattleites don't have to go far to commune with nature in its many forms. The hiking trails of the Cascade Mountains are less than an hour east of the city; red-tailed hawks can be spotted flying over Laurelhurst, an upscale community within the city limits; and breathtaking waterfalls tumble down at scenic points throughout the area.

▼ DEAN RUTZ

YOU CAN TAKE YOUR PICK AT Snoqualmie Falls just east of Seattle: Stay in the comfort of the Salish Lodge on top or trek down the path to the rocky basin 270 feet below. Either way, the view is gauranteed to please.

▶ DEAN RUTZ

Looming over North Bend, located east of Seattle along Interstate 90, is the massive Mount Si, where the popular 4.5-mile hike attracts nature lovers year-round.

IN RECENT YEARS, THE TELEvision industry has found the Northwest to be a perfect setting for several popular programs. Here, director David Lynch films a scene for the now-defunct *Twin Peaks* in North Bend (RIGHT). During *its* successful run, *Northern Exposure* turned the Cascade foothills town of Roslyn into Cicely, Alaska, home of the show's trademark moose (OPPOSITE).

▼ SEATTLE TIMES / HARLEY SOLTES

▲ ROBERT FRIED

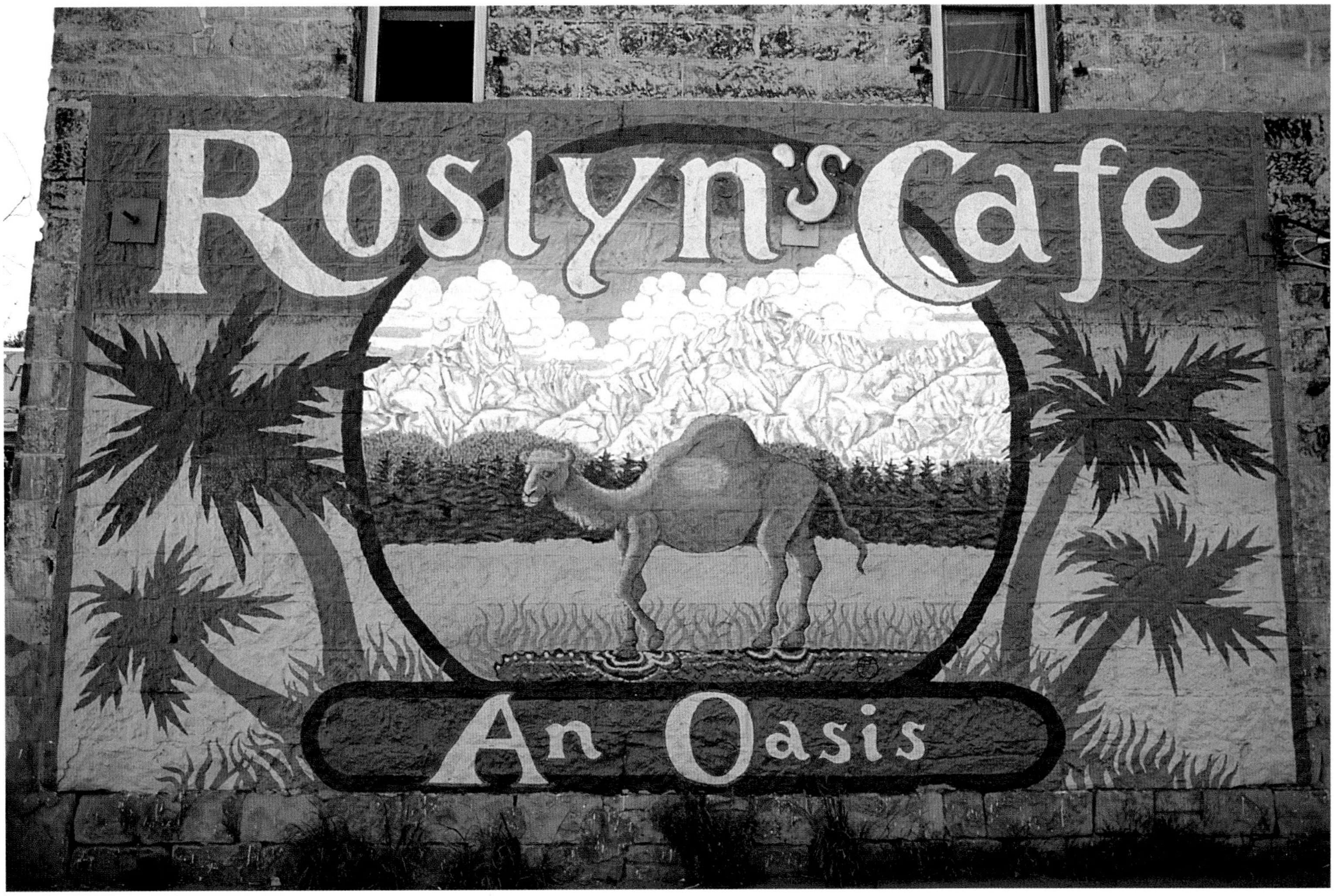

▲ JIM BATES

▼ TOM REESE

TOM REESE

NATALIE FOBES

NATALIE FOBES

JIM CORWIN

An industry that helped build the Pacific Northwest, logging is still a primary economic force, thanks to the forested hills of the Olympic and Cascade mountains.

ROBERT ESPOSITO

WHEN NATURE IS INVOLVED, there are few straight lines. A tug weaves a raft of logs through Deception Pass north of Seattle (ABOVE), mimicking the curling flow of the Skykomish River and nearby train tracks as they pattern the landscape near Everett (OPPOSITE LEFT).

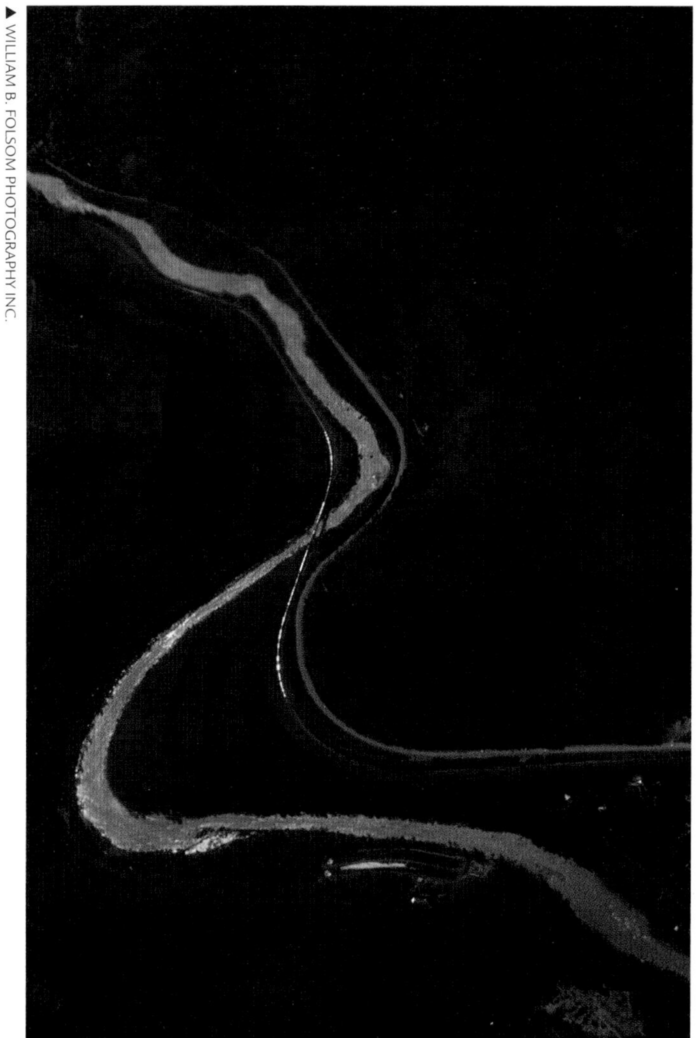

▶ WILLIAM B. FOLSOM PHOTOGRAPHY INC.

▶ ALEX WATERHOUSE-HAYWARD

JONATHAN RABAN (RIGHT) IS a transplanted Seattleite who migrated from England on a travel assignment and never left. In his recent novel *Bad Land*, acclaimed by the *New York Times* and winner of a 1997 National Book Critics Circle award, Raban wove an intriguing tale of farmers in 19th-century Montana.

▼ JANICE BELL

As it takes a dramatic, 50-foot plunge, Christine Falls aptly illustrates the beauty of Mount Rainier National Park, which offers a wonderland of trees and glaciers less than two hours from the city.

▶ SUSAN ALWORTH

THE BALD EAGLE, AMERICA'S national symbol, is a relatively common sight in Seattle. While a few of these majestic birds make their home in the Woodland Park Zoo (ABOVE), others can be seen in the wild, nesting in Discovery Park on the city's western edge and flying to Green Lake for a meal.

LOCAL BIRD-WATCHERS FIND ample opportunity to enjoy the sights. Snow geese fill the sky around Mount Baker near the Canadian border (TOP) and float serenely on Union Bay (BOTTOM). A group of blue herons prepare to leave their nests along Mercer Slough, on the east side of Lake Washington (OPPOSITE).

▶ JIM CORWIN

▶ TOM REESE

▲ JIM BATES

▼ JIM CORWIN

JIM CORWIN

Mother Nature marks the passage of time at North Seattle's Evergreen Washelli Cemetery, the final resting place of war veterans, political representatives, and everyday citizens.

GARY GREENE

ONE OF SEATTLE'S IN-CITY gems is the Volunteer Park Conservatory, modeled after the old Crystal Palace exhibition hall in London. Located on Capitol Hill, the conservatory was restored in the early 1980s, and an etched-glass canopy of flowers, called *Homage in Green*, was added over the entrance.

▲ GARY GREENE

TUCKED AMID THE RESIDENTIAL neighborhoods of Capitol Hill, the Washington Park Arboretum is a 200-acre woodland designed by the Olmsted brothers. Visitors to the arboretum are treated to a variety of native flora, as well as a Japanese tea garden and Azalea Way, a three-quarter-mile path that features dogwoods, cherry trees, and azaleas.

At 14,410 feet, Mount Rainier is the highest summit in the Cascade mountain range (**right and opposite**). Called Tahoma by area tribes, the dormant volcano is a majestic presence to all who live in the region.

◀ DEAN RUTZ

▲ STEVE WARBLE

THE SETTING SUN SPOTLIGHTS the snowcapped Mount Shuksan, located approximately 100 miles north of Seattle near the Canadian border. At 9,100-plus feet, the peak ranks as the 13th largest in the state and is a standout amid the massive Cascade range (PAGES 100 AND 101).

JIM CORWIN

▼ JIM CORWIN

STEVE WARBLE

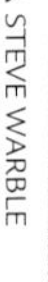

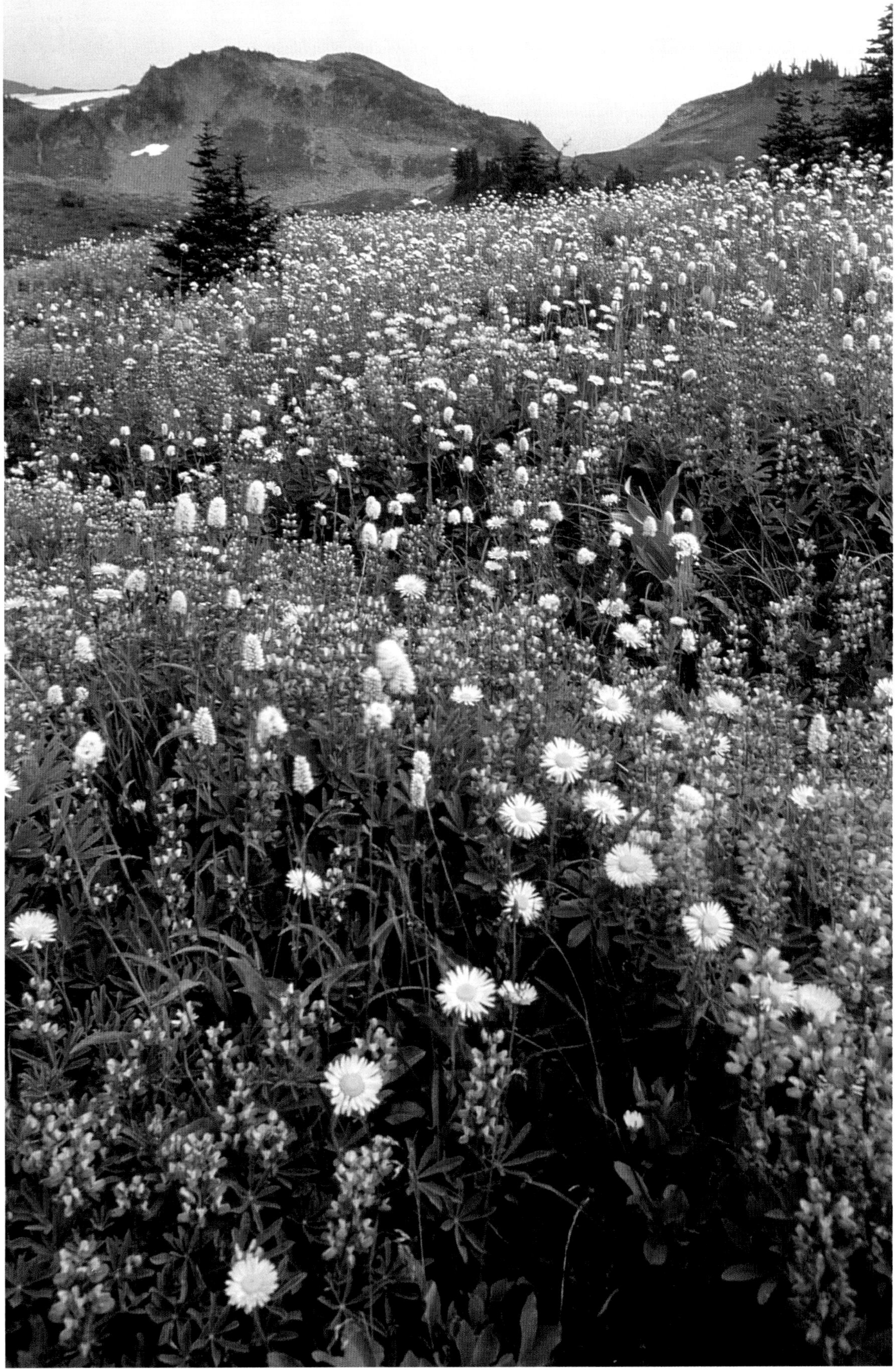

DEVASTATED BY AN ERUPTION in 1980, the area surrounding Mount St. Helens, southeast of the city of Olympia, has only recently begun supporting plants and wildlife again (OPPOSITE). Flora and fauna flourish, however, at nearby Mount Rainier National Park (LEFT), where the perpetually snowcapped volcano that gave the park its name is dormant.

▼ TOM REESE

▲ TIM J. JOHNSON / STRODE PHOTOGRAPHERS

WITH MILES OF ROCKY TERRAIN, hikers are given ample opportunity to trek the Pacific Northwest, from climbing the flanks of Mount Rainier along the Puyallup Glacier (ABOVE) to traversing the Cascade Mountains along the Pacific Crest National Scenic Trail (OPPOSITE).

Seattleites aren't afraid of a little bit of snow on the ground. Families frolic in the powder at Paradise on Mount Rainier (this page), while skiers prepare to glide down the slopes at Stevens Pass Ski Area (opposite). Several quality ski facilities, including Crystal Mountain, Mount Baker, Snoqualmie Pass, and White Pass, are within a few hours' drive of the city.

▼ TOM REESE

▼ KEVIN MCGOWAN / STRODE PHOTOGRAPHERS

▲ TOM REESE

WHETHER YOU'RE OUT FOR some cross-country skiing or merely enjoying nature's canopy, the Pacific Northwest can accommodate. An intrepid sportsman glides across the white expanse of Mount Rainier (PAGE 108), and a wall of evergreens blankets an area of the Olympic Peninsula (PAGE 109).

◆ TOM REESE

JIM CORWIN

▲ ANTHONY P. BOLANTE

▲ ANTHONY P. BOLANTE

A GOOD CLIMB IS WHEREVER you find it. Plenty of folks get their fill in the relative safety of the Stone Gardens facility in Seattle (OPPOSITE). Other dare-devils prefer the steep Deception Crags area in the Snoqualmie Valley (LEFT).

▲ ANTHONY P. BOLANTE

▲ TOM REESE

No matter your destination, there's usually an interesting way to get there. Bikers head down a winding road in the semirural suburb of Woodinville (above), but it takes more than wheels to make your way skyward in the Deception Crags area (opposite).

▼ TOM REESE

▲ TOM REESE

A PATH OF WOODEN PLANKS through the overgrown portions of Olympic National Park (OPPOSITE), displays a man-made order that seldom imposes itself on the mountains of driftwood awaiting visitors to one of the park's wilderness beaches (ABOVE).

BOTH FUN TO CATCH AND FUN to eat, clams are a regular feature at many restaurants in this "waterlogged" town. Here, small butter clams are extracted from the rocky shores of Puget Sound (TOP) and Hood Canal (BOTTOM), while large razor clams are harvested by the sackful along many Pacific beaches (OPPOSITE).

◄ TOM REESE

◄ TOM REESE

▲ SEATTLE TIMES / STEVE RINGMAN

AT MORE THAN 10,770 FEET, Mount Baker towers over the scenic San Juan Islands. The northeasternmost peak in the Cascade Mountains, the volcano, which last showed signs of activity in 1975, is visible for miles.

▲ SEATTLE TIMES / TOM REESE

SINCE 1966, DR. ROBERT Paine, an ecologist at the University of Washington and past president of the Ecological Society of America, has studied the complex ecosystem on the tidal fringe of Tatoosh Island, located off Washington's northwest coast. By removing all starfish from the island, Paine discovered that the entire ecosystem was disrupted, a phenomenon he called the "keystone effect."

THIS "SEA SCULPTURE," CREATED by sun-bleached seashells and concrete pilings (BOTTOM LEFT), serves as a reminder of Seattle's marine location. At Alki Beach in West Seattle, a veritable melting pot of visitors enjoy the sun, sand, and scuba diving (TOP AND OPPOSITE). Nearby, a pile of driftwood points the way to the Alki Point Light Station, which stands at the southern entrance to Elliott Bay (BOTTOM RIGHT). The tower has served as a beacon to ships since the mid-1870s.

◀ KEVIN MCCOWAN / STRODE PHOTOGRAPHERS

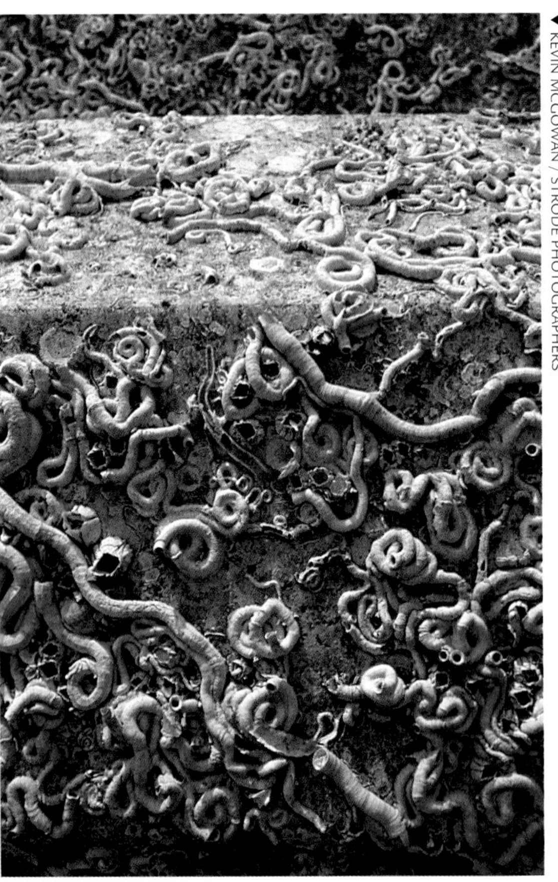

◀ KEVIN MCCOWAN / STRODE PHOTOGRAPHERS

◀ FRED LYON

▲ KEVIN MCGOWAN / STRODE PHOTOGRAPHERS

Artists have their work cut out for them when it comes to capturing the region's natural beauty. As a group of women seek inspiration from the Okanogan National Park in northern Washington (top), a landscape painter puts the final touches on his rendition of Capitol Hill (bottom). Sometimes, the finished product becomes public art, as evidenced by this flying orca whale created by local artist James Crespinel (opposite).

▼ NATALIE FORES

▼ TOM REESE

▶ JIM BATES

WITH THE EXCEPTION OF Miami, Seattle has more boats per capita than any other city in the United States. Graceful sailing vessels are plentiful in both rural and urban settings, from the waters below Mount Shuksan (PAGE 124) to Lake Union, where the Seattle skyline forms its own lofty backdrop (PAGE 125).

◆ JIM CORWIN

JIM CORWIN

▼ SEATTLE TIMES / TERESA TAMURA

SEATTLE TIMES / GREG GILBERT

A BIRD'S-EYE VIEW OF THE Emerald City reveals the diverse ways Seattleites get from here to there. Kayakers paddle their way through the Washington Park Arboretum, while a floatplane glides over the Evergreen Point Floating Bridge across Lake Washington.

ALTHOUGH CITY RESIDENTS ARE accustomed to seeing Elephant Car Wash signs around town, many commuters were awestruck when the Ringling Bros. and Barnum & Bailey Circus paraded live elephants down Fourth Avenue on their way to KeyArena.

▼ JIM CORWIN

▼ SEATTLE TIMES / JIMI LOTT

▲ KEVIN MCGOWAN / STRODE PHOTOGRAPHERS

TOWING CAN BE FUN: AT LEAST that's the philosophy Lincoln's Toe Truck tries to live by.

▼ JIM CORWIN

▼ KEVIN MCGOWAN / STRODE PHOTOGRAPHERS

▼ KEVIN MCGOWAN / STRODE PHOTOGRAPHERS

▼ CHRIS BENNION

Locals learn early on about recycling and bettering the environment, but the actors in a Seattle Repertory Theatre production of Samuel Beckett's *Endgame* (bottom right) seem to have a different view of garbage.

▲ SEATTLE TIMES / HARLEY SOLTES

Bill Nye, a former engineer for The Boeing Company, turned his dream of crossbreeding comedy and science into a network TV gig as *Bill Nye The Science Guy*.

▲ SEATTLE TIMES / GREG GILBERT

▲ STEVE RINGMAN

▲ SEATTLE TIMES / GREG GILBERT

▲ SEATTLE TIMES / GREG GILBERT

▲ SEATTLE TIMES / HARLEY SOLTES

▲ SEATTLE TIMES / GREG GILBERT

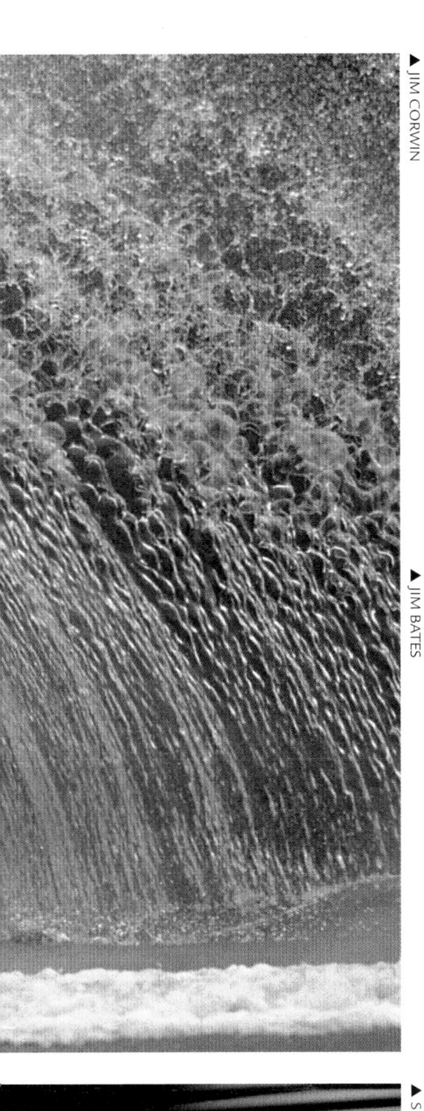

▲ JIM CORVWIN

▲ JIM BATES

▲ SEATTLE TIMES / BENJAMIN BENSCHNEIDER

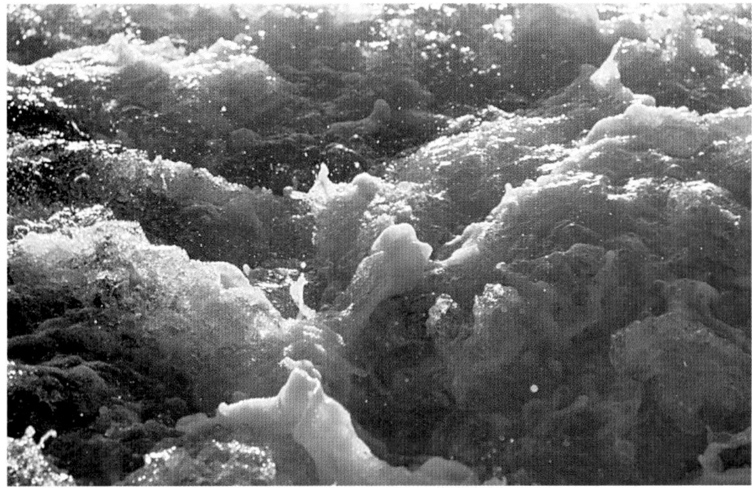

▲ KEVIN MCGOWAN / STRODE PHOTOGRAPHERS

THE BUDWEISER HYDROPLANE takes an ugly spill during a 1994 test run for Seafair. Making waves of their own are a daring water-skier, a group of river rafters, and some intrepid souls at Alki Beach. Assisted by the "catapult of science," Bill Nye demonstrates *his* version of tossing water on television's *Almost Live!*

▼ JIM BATES

▼ SEATTLE TIMES / BENJAMIN BENSCHNEIDER

▲ CHRIS BENNION

THE EMERALD CITY BOASTS several characters who seem to defy gravity, from Port Townsend's Flying Karamazov Brothers (ABOVE) to a cycler at the Pacific Science Center (OPPOSITE LEFT) to Project Bandaloop dancers, practicing the routine they will perform during the Bumbershoot festival (OPPOSITE RIGHT).

▲ JOHN STAMETS

▲ JOHN STAMETS

WASHINGTON RESIDENTS VOTED in 1997 to tear down the 21-year-old Kingdome, which has hosted everything from NFL and Major League Baseball games to a Billy Graham crusade, a Rolling Stones concert, and a Promise Keepers convention. Among the facility's more "ferocious" events have been the Monsters of Rock concert (TOP) and numerous monster truck shows (BOTTOM).

▼ JIM BATES

▼ SEATTLE TIMES / GREG GILBERT

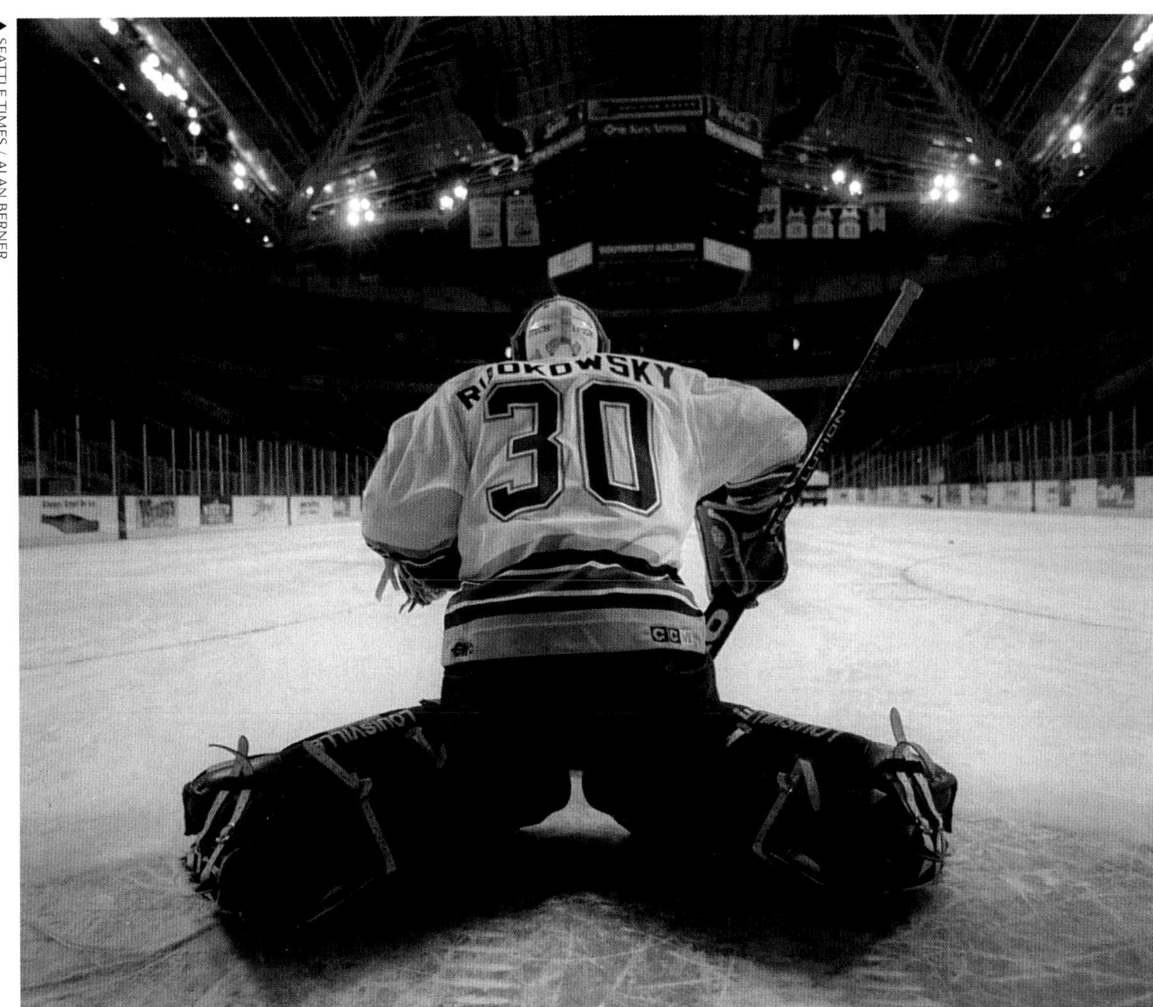

▲ SEATTLE TIMES / ALAN BERNER

▲ SEATTLE TIMES / MARK HARRISON

FOR TOP-NOTCH SPORTING events, the KeyArena is the place to be. Home to the NBA-champion SuperSonics (OPPOSITE BOTTOM), the venue also hosts the Western Hockey League's Seattle Thunderbirds (THIS PAGE).

▼ JIM CORWIN

▼ JIM BATES

▼ SEATTLE TIMES / ALAN BERNER

PERHAPS IT'S HUSKY STADIUM'S scenic location on Lake Washington that draws crowds to University of Washington (UW) football games, but more likely it's the team's winning record. The Huskies are among the few college clubs to outdraw the pros for attendance. One of the biggest games each year is the Apple Cup matchup between UW and Washington State (BOTTOM LEFT).

▶ TOM REESE

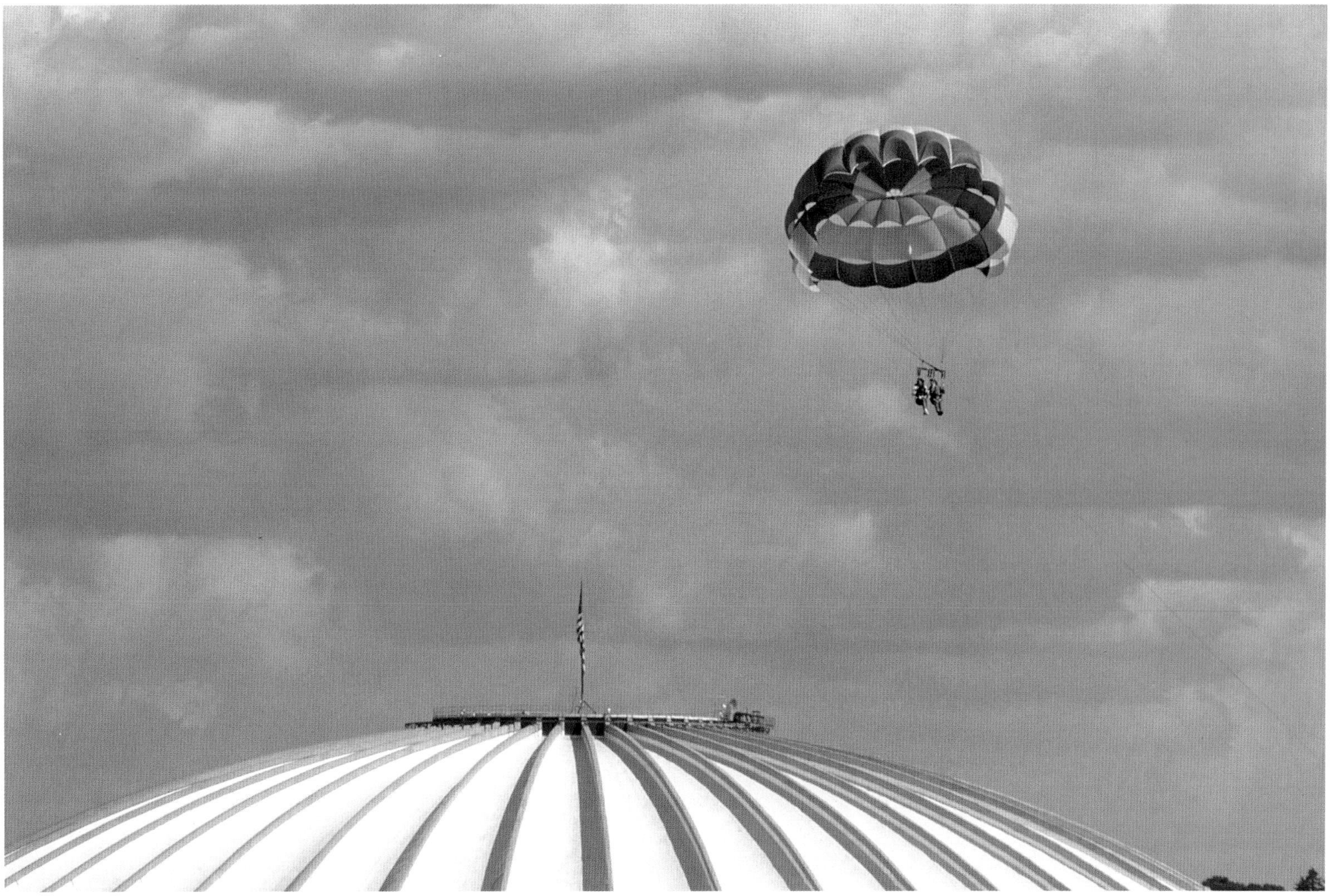

▶ SEATTLE TIMES / STEVE RINGMAN

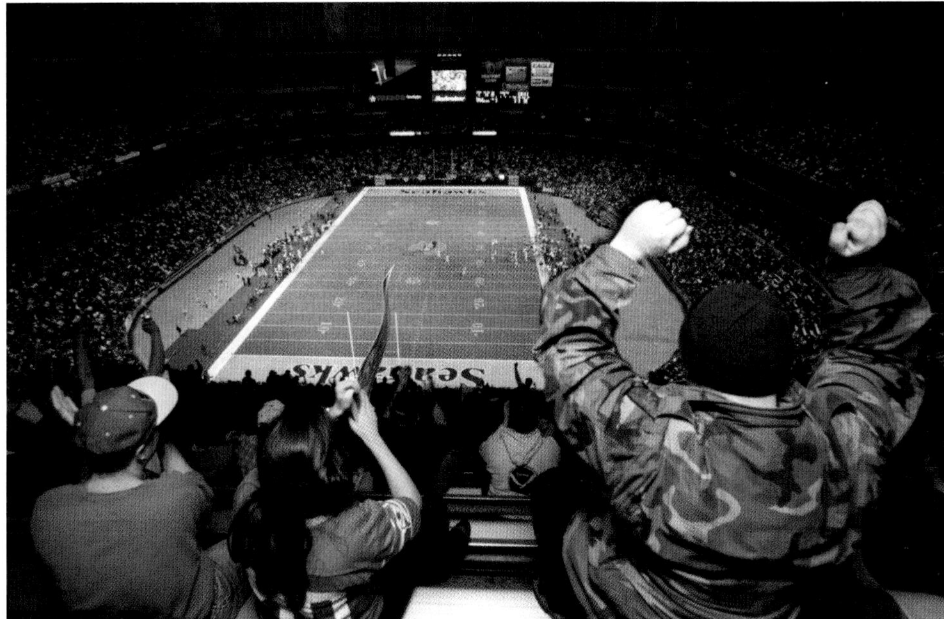

▶ SEATTLE TIMES / ROD MAR

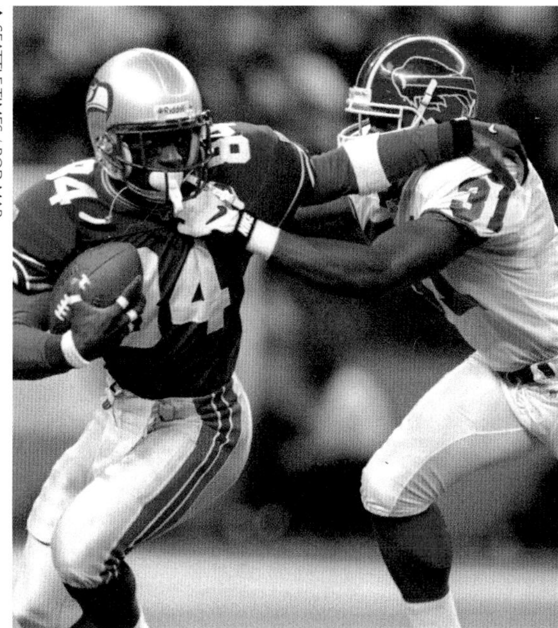

LONG SCORNED AS AN UNATTRACTIVE addition to Seattle's skyline, the Kingdome can nonetheless claim the world's largest single-span concrete roof. The facility has also hosted plenty of exciting football, thanks to the Seahawks, who started playing there in 1976. In the near future, the Seahawks and their "dome-mates," the Mariners, will move to their own new stadiums nearby.

In part publicly-subsidized, of course.

Ken Griffey Jr.'s home-run hitting and spectacular defense for the Seattle Mariners (right and opposite, bottom left) have inspired baseball historians to place him in a class with Joe DiMaggio, Mickey Mantle, and Willie Mays. LPGA sensation Karrie Webb follows Griffey's lead by blasting a drive at suburban Meridian Valley Country Club (opposite, bottom right). Not to be outdone, the U.S. Navy's Blue Angels try to best them both with a high-flying routine of their own (opposite top).

◄ SEATTLE TIMES / PEDRO PEREZ

▶ SEATTLE TIMES / JIM BATES

▶ SEATTLE TIMES / MARK HARRISON

▶ SEATTLE TIMES / BENJAMIN BENSCHNEIDER

Current and former members of the nation's armed services show their patriotic stripes in Seattle, which boasts major military bases to the north, west, and south. The Blue Angels soar over Lake Washington as part of the annual Seafair celebration (top), while World War II vet Art Carlson stands among the various flags of the United States at a Veterans Day ceremony (center). Showing their ability to combine work and play, these sailors waste no time making plans during their shore leave (bottom). Back on the job, a solitary seaman enjoys a peaceful, moonlit night from an aircraft carrier (opposite).

▲ JIM CORWIN
▼ JIM BATES

▼ SEATTLE TIMES / ALAN BERNER

▼ SEATTLE TIMES / JIM BATES

▼ SEATTLE TIMES / BENJAMIN BENSCHNEIDER

▲ ROBERT ESPOSITO

A FULL-SIZE REPLICA OF THE ship Robert Gray used to explore Northwest waters in the late 1700s, *Lady Washington* offers three-hour tours of the Seattle waterfront, complete with a crew dressed in period attire. The official goodwill ambassador of Washington, the boat was built in time for the state's centennial celebration.

▲ SEATTLE TIMES / BENJAMIN BENSCHNEIDER

▼ SEATTLE TIMES / LINDA COAN

CHARGING ASHORE AT ALKI Beach are the brawny Seafair Pirates. The pirates, whose landing marks the official opening of the annual Seafair festival, have toned down their performance in recent years after it was pointed out that kissing pretty young women and threatening children with swords were no longer politically correct.

▲ JIM CORWIN

▲ SEATTLE TIMES / MARK HARRISON

▲ SEATTLE TIMES / STEPHANIE BOYAR

THE AREA'S MEDIEVAL FESTIVALS and Renaissance performances are popular ways to celebrate the past. Here, a storyteller captivates his audience at the Canterbury Faire in Kent; several "ironclad" jousters put on a show at the Camlann Medieval Faire in Carnation; and a group of actors perform *Love's Labours Lost* during the Shakespeare in the Park series.

WHETHER IT'S A PLUMED HELMET at the Canterbury Faire, a colorful headdress at Kent Cornucopia Days, or a spectacular mask at Pioneer Square's Fat Tuesday celebration, Seattleites know how to strut their stuff.

◀ JIM CORWIN

◀ JIM CORWIN

◀ JIM BATES

▲ ALAN BERNER

▲ ALAN BERNER

EACH SEPTEMBER, SEATTLE'S Native American residents pow-wow along the waterfront as part of the Salmon Homecoming Celebration. The event honors the cultural, spiritual, and economic influence of salmon on the Pacific Northwest.

SUSAN ALWORTH

JIM CORWIN

JIM CORWIN

THE INTERNATIONAL DISTRICT is home to much of Seattle's Asian population, whose influence on local culture can be seen in this outdoor mural on the old Bush Hotel in Hing Hay Park (LEFT), a performance by the Chinese Girls Drill Team during the Chinatown Seafair Parade (RIGHT), and the annual Chinese New Year celebration (OPPOSITE).

▲ SEATTLE TIMES / BARRY WONG

MODELED AFTER AN 11TH-century garden in Kyoto, the 3.5-acre Japanese Tea Garden in the Washington Park Arboretum is considered one of the most authentic Japanese gardens outside of Japan itself (PAGES 154 AND 155). Its lush panoramas, originally created in 1960, incorporate more than 500 enormous boulders brought from the Cascade Mountains.

GARY GREENE

▲ JIM BATES

▲ JIM CORWIN

▲ SEATTLE TIMES / BENJAMIN BENSCHNEIDER

A VERITABLE MELTING POT OF ethnic groups, Seattle spends much of the year celebrating its diversity. A group of Russian dancers perform at the Seattle Center (TOP LEFT), some patriotic souls celebrate Norwegian Constitution Day in downtown Ballard (TOP RIGHT), the Keith Highlanders Pipe Band marches across the 18th hole at the Safeco Classic golf tournament (BOTTOM), and a couple of young immigrants play the bandura for Kent's Ukrainian Independence Day (OPPOSITE).

▲ SEATTLE TIMES / JIM BATES

▼ TERESA TAMURA

▶ JIM BATES

MUSIC IS A COMMON THEME IN everyday Seattle, from this large Asian banjo at a Thai festival (OPPOSITE) to the giant guitar at the Pacific Science Center (LEFT).

SEATTLE TIMES / BARRY WONG

SEATTLE TIMES / TOM REESE

JIM BATES

▲ JIM BATES

THANKS TO A HOST OF FESTIVALS and a number of local bands that have made it on the national scene, Seattle is a music lover's paradise. Good seats often are hard to come by for Summer Nights at the Pier, a series of big-name concerts on the downtown waterfront (OPPOSITE RIGHT), while the Northwest Folklife Festival, held over Memorial Day weekend, is guaranteed to get your toes tappin' (ABOVE). With the help of other local groups like Nirvana and Soundgarden, Pearl Jam and its lead singer Eddie Vedder (OPPOSITE LEFT) have put Seattle on the music map in the 1990s.

GARY GREENE

JIM BATES

SKAGIT VALLEY, LOCATED SOME 60 minutes north of Seattle, is the nation's leading producer of tulips, boasting 1,500 acres of beautiful blooms (PAGES 162 AND 163). Each April, thousands of visitors travel to the area for the Skagit Valley Tulip Festival.

▶ JIM BATES

▶ SEATTLE TIMES / HARLEY SOLTES

LOCAL GUITAR LEGEND JIMI Hendrix, who died of a drug overdose in 1970, lives on in a statue on Broadway and in the procession of fans who trek to his grave in Renton's Greenwood Cemetery.

JIM CORWIN

JIM BATES

RON WURZER

RON WURZER

PART OF SEATTLE'S CHARM IS its niche neighborhoods, unique in their population and in their landmarks. The University District boasts a number of bookstores, boutiques, and cafés, as well as the Blue Moon Tavern (TOP LEFT); Fremont increasingly caters to the microbrew crowd (TOP RIGHT); and Capitol Hill is home to the Comet Tavern, with its "please post bills" facade (BOTTOM LEFT) and a diverse crowd that includes gays, aging hippies, and tons of kids.

▶ RON WURZER

PROVIDING HEALTHY FOOD choices in an over-the-top, futuristic setting, the Gravity Bar is located in the Broadway Market, which has served residents of Capitol Hill since 1928.

KEVIN MCGOWAN / STRODE PHOTOGRAPHERS

ALEX WATERHOUSE-HAYWARD

SEATTLEITES ARE AMONG THE nation's leading consumers of reading material, whether it's something light from The Comic Stand in the University District (LEFT) or a cult first edition at Ed Leimbacher's MisterE Books in the Pike Place Market (RIGHT).

▶ SEATTLE TIMES / HARLEY SOLTES

▶ JIM CORWIN

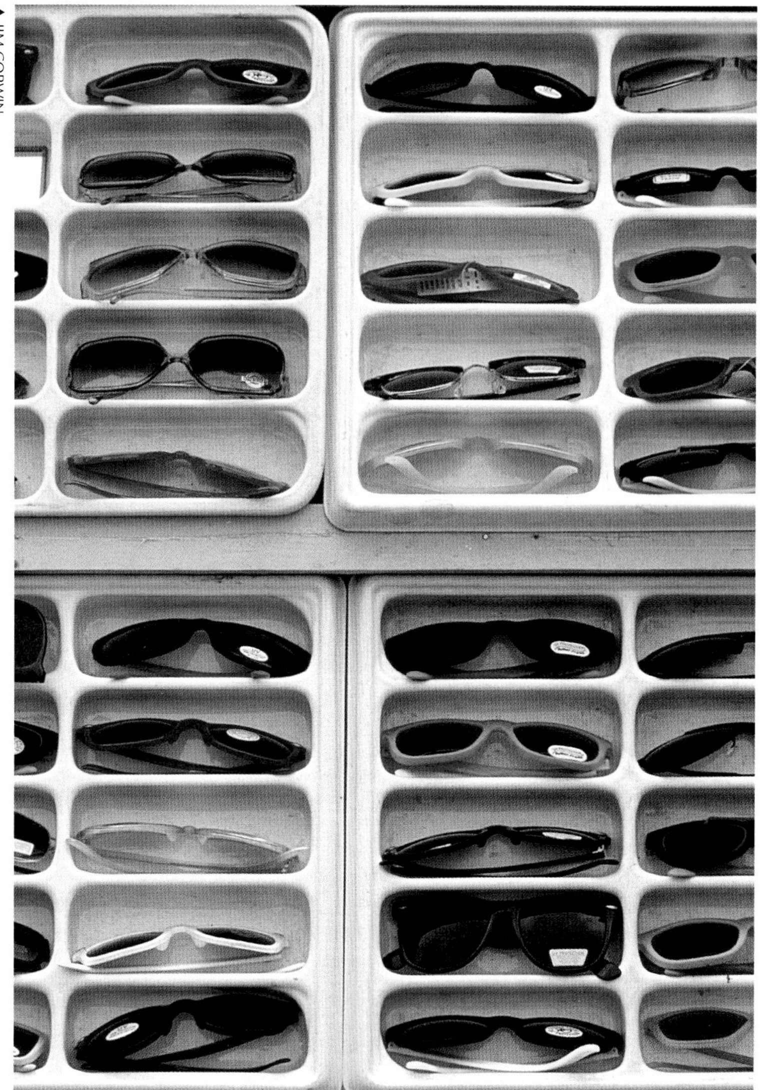

SEATTLE-AREA AUTHOR TOM Robbins not only pens novels (*Even Cowgirls Get the Blues* and *Still Life with Woodpecker*), but also makes wry observations on Northwest life, such as "Eating a raw oyster is like French-kissing a mermaid." Robbins, like most northwesterners, is quick to don a pair of shades anytime the cloud layer thins.

JIM CORWIN

The ornate Suzzallo/Allen Library on the University of Washington campus is one of the best-known works of architect Carl F. Gould, who designed 18 other buildings on the campus.

◄ JIM CORWIN

▲ ALEX WATERHOUSE-HAYWARD

The mystical fog along Lake Washington Boulevard may be what attracted British transplant Michael Dibdin (above) to Seattle, where he authored a critically acclaimed novel, *Dark Specter*, about a serial murderer.

◀ SEATTLE TIMES / GARY SETTLE

▶ JIM BATES

▶ SUSAN ALWORTH

▶ SEATTLE TIMES / BARRY WONG

STARBUCKS CEO HOWARD Schultz (OPPOSITE), who helped make Seattle the coffee-consuming capital of the United States, now seems destined to conquer the rest of the world. Of course, java in its many forms isn't the city's only vice, as evidenced by this man strolling in front of a mural at a downtown construction site (BOTTOM).

SEATTLE TIMES / BETTY UDESEN

SEATTLE TIMES / GARY SETTLE

JIM CORWIN

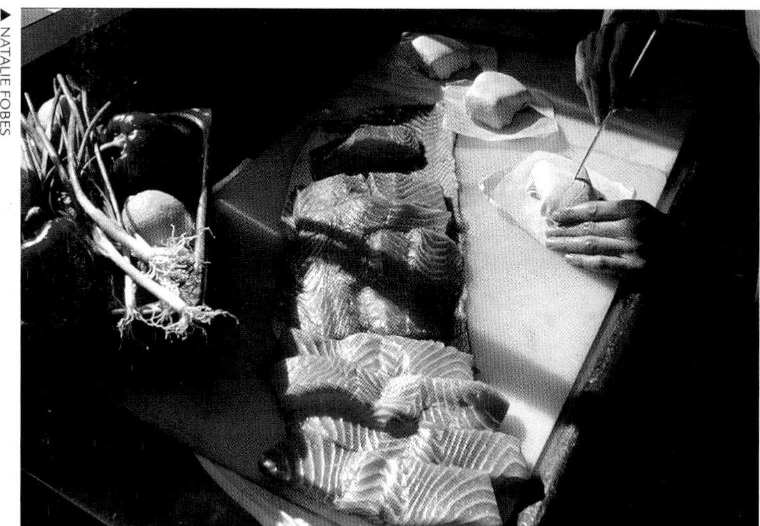

NATALIE FOBES

NATALIE FOBES

JIM BATES

SEAFOOD IS A STAPLE OF LIFE IN this Pacific Northwest town, which proudly takes its place as Washington's largest seaport. Each day, the area's rivers, as well as Puget Sound and the nearby Pacific Ocean, provide local chefs with fresh supplies of lobster, salmon, striped bass, oysters, and countless other fruits of the sea.

▼ ALEX WATERHOUSE-HAYWARD ▲ JIM BATES

▲ KEVIN MCGOWAN / STRODE PHOTOGRAPHERS

NOT ALL CULTURE IS HIGHBROW, and Seattle has more than its share of kitsch, including a life-like chicken on a permanent roost (OPPOSITE) and a ceramic monk inscribed with an ironic commandment at the Fremont Sunday Market (RIGHT). One of the city's more unusual sights is Western Avenue's Jell-O Mold Building, which offers some 400 ideas for shaping this well-loved gelatin dessert (CENTER).

JIM BATES

JIM CORWIN

▶ JIM CORWIN

▶ MICHAEL J. GLAZE

There are plenty of ways to "grab" a person's attention, whether it's the Dahlia Lounge's neon chef, who beckons passersby in Seattle's business district; the work of neon artist Jeff Becker; the friendly gnome on Market Street in Ballard; or a temporary sand sculpture on Alki Beach.

▼ JIM BATES

▲ JIM CORWIN

▲ JIM CORWIN

ON THE FIRST SATURDAY IN May, rain or shine, sailors arrive early to celebrate the opening day of yachting season (OPPOSITE). Meanwhile, these wooden mariners, battened down in Snohomish, don't seem to mind missing the excitement (ABOVE).

▼ JIM CORWIN

▲ DEAN RUTZ

As a city that claims one boat for every 12 people, Seattle sees its fair share of floating vessels, from wooden rowboats along the south shore of Lake Union (opposite) to *Dancer*, dry-docked at Fisherman's Terminal in Ballard (above).

▼ GARY GREENE

LOCATED ON SALMON BAY, Fisherman's Terminal has been owned by the Port of Seattle since 1913 (ABOVE AND OPPOSITE). It is the home port of more than 700 commercial fishing vessels, including much of the Alaskan fleet.

GARY GREENE

ACCOMMODATING SOME 1,200 boats and yachts, Elliott Bay Marina in Magnolia is among the dozens of local facilities that cater to the sailing and recreational-boating crowd (PAGES 188 AND 189).

◆ GARY GREENE

MERICAN SEAFOODS COMPANY
AMERICAN DYNASTY

▼ TOM REESE ▲ GARY GREENE

▼ KURT THORSON

WITH SO MANY SPECTACULAR views in the Emerald City, it's easy to think you're in paradise. Seattle boasts dozens of outstanding vantage points, including (CLOCKWISE FROM OPPOSITE TOP) Queen Anne Hill, which overlooks Puget Sound and the Olympic Mountains; Magnolia Park, which affords a tree-framed panorama of downtown Seattle; and the houses on Lake Washington, which have a front-row view of waterfront activity.

▼ SEATTLE TIMES / TOM REESE

GARY GREENE

Everywhere you turn in Seattle, you're greeted by majestic peaks. Southeast of the lighthouse on Vashon Island is the snow-capped Mount Rainier (above), while a westward glance over the shipping lanes of Puget Sound is met by a view of the serene Olympic Mountains (opposite).

▼ TOM REESE

▲ JIM CORWIN

LINKS TO THE PAST AND THE future: Seattle's working ports offer reminders of the city's rich maritime history, as well as the promise of continued economic prosperity.

THIS 90-METRIC-TON PROPELLER, made of solid brass, undergoes repairs at Todd Pacific Shipyards in Seattle. The propeller belongs to the 902-foot *Hyundai Emperor*, the heaviest ship ever to be drydocked in Puget Sound.

◀ SEATTLE TIMES / STEPHANIE BOYAR

▲ JIM BATES

▲ SEATTLE TIMES / GREG GILBERT

WITH ALL THE TALK ABOUT water transportation, people may forget that Seattle is also an international center for aviation, thanks in part to The Boeing Company. One of the world's leading manufacturers of airplanes, the company is known for its innovative products, including the 737-700 business jet, introduced in 1997 (BOTTOM). Among the many popular exhibits at Boeing's Museum of Flight is the Lockheed SR-71 Blackbird, the fastest jet in the world (TOP).

▲ SEATTLE TIMES / JIMI LOTT

▲ KEVIN MCGOWAN / STRODE PHOTOGRAPHERS

All things big and small: The cargo ship *Hyundai Liberty* is unloaded at Harbor Island, while a much smaller pleasure craft slips past Gas Works Park on Lake Union.

▼ KEVIN MCGOWAN / STRODE PHOTOGRAPHERS

KEVIN MCGOWAN / STRODE PHOTOGRAPHERS

SEATTLE TIMES / RON WURZER

Gas Works Park on the northern edge of Lake Union attracts visitors with its huge sundial (opposite) and ample breezes that make kite and model-plane flying easy (top). Microsoft, with an ever expanding campus in suburban Redmond (bottom), attracts *its* share of attention. Founded in 1975, the corporate giant is the world's leading software provider.

▲ TOM REESE
◀ JIM CORWIN

▲ SEATTLE TIMES / BARRY WONG

Power of one sort or another is a common theme in the Emerald City. Here, a worker does his duty at the electrical station in Ballard (opposite), Seattle City Light employees brave the heights to make repairs (top), and Microsoft founder Bill Gates explains his grand vision for the future (bottom).

▲ JIM CORWIN

▶ JIM CORWIN

▶ JIM CORWIN

Seattle offers a number of colorful opportunities when the sun goes down, including countless views of the Space Needle, where you can also enjoy a rollicking ride on the Tilt-a-Whirl at the Fun Forest Amusement Park.

▲ JIM BATES
◀ BENJAMIN BENSCHNEIDER

▲ SEATTLE TIMES / BENJAMIN BENSCHNEIDER

▲ SEATTLE TIMES / BENJAMIN BENSCHNEIDER

FOR DECADES NOW, SEATTLE has dared to reach for the top. Although it's no longer the tallest structure in town, the Space Needle has provided inspiration for other local architecture, including the Seattle Temple of the Church of Jesus Christ of Latter-Day Saints (TOP) and the Fremont Rocket (BOTTOM LEFT).

▼ BOB BROOKS

▼ JIM CORWIN

▼ BOB BROOKS

SEATTLE MAY NOT BE KNOWN for its white Christmases, but the entire city lights up each year with the holiday spirit. Shopping districts downtown decorate with festive Christmas trees and other eye-catching adornments, while Santa and his reindeer ride high above the shores of Lake Washington.

GARY GREENE

CHATEAU STE. MICHELLE IN suburban Woodinville is more than just a winery; with its concerts and festivals, the beautiful estate has become one of the area's cultural centers.

Local youngsters start early in their study of dance, with dreams of one day becoming prima ballerinas. These students (bottom) display a range of emotions as they wait to audition for bit parts in the annual holiday presentation of *The Nutcracker*, performed by the Pacific Northwest Ballet (top).

▼ PACIFIC NORTHWEST BALLET / DAVID COOPER

▼ SEATTLE TIMES / BENJAMIN BENSCHNEIDER

▲ STEVE RINGMAN

▼ SUSAN ALWORTH

▼ JIM BATES

▲ WILLIAM B. FOLSOM PHOTOGRAPHY INC.

It's the size of your imagination, not your horse, that counts. Whether you're riding the merry-go-round at Seattle Center, or participating in the Evergreen Classic at suburban Marymoor Park, it's always a thrill to cross the finish line.

▼ JIM BATES

THE GENERAL PETROLEUM Museum on Capitol Hill may be one of the Emerald City's lesser-known attractions, but its collection of service-station pumps and products—the largest in the country—draws its fair share of visitors. Housed in a former Ford truck agency, the facility boasts a neon pegasus rescued from an old Mobil station.

▶ GARY GREENE

▶ JIM CORWIN

▶ GARY GREENE

▶ TOM REESE

Autumn promises all manner of delights, from farm-fresh produce to fun-filled Ferris wheels. Each September, the Western Washington Fair brings cotton candy, country music, and carnival rides to town (top and bottom left).

▼ TOM REESE

▲ SEATTLE TIMES / RON WURZER

▲ SEATTLE TIMES / JIMI LOTT

WHILE SOME SEATTLEITES ARE content to stand back and admire the beauty of area rivers and lakes, others prefer to hop on in. An unused freeway ramp near the Washington Park Arboretum is a popular jumping-off point for many teenagers (TOP).

▼ SEATTLE TIMES / MARK HARRISON

▲ GARY GREENE

THE LIVIN' MAY BE EASY FOR some horses, but these equines (OPPOSITE) get a vigorous early morning workout before a day of competition at Marymoor Park.

▼ JIM CORWIN

▲ JIM CORWIN

On a foggy morning in Seattle, city and country don't seem so different after all. Here, the steeples of St. James Cathedral bookend the Columbia Seafirst Center (above), while three turrets crown a barn in Snohomish (opposite).

▼ SEATTLE TIMES / GARY SETTLE

▲ JIM BATES

▲ SEATTLE TIMES / HARLEY SOLTES

SOMETIMES LIFE IN THE CITY demands a little solitude and a touch of greenery. Other times, it just requires lots of energy and a frontal attack.

▼ JIM BATES

▼ JIM BATES

▶ SEATTLE TIMES / JIMI LOTT

▶ SEATTLE TIMES / TERESA TAMURA

WHETHER IT'S AN OLYMPIC bicycle trial, a spirited equestrian competition, a well-attended run, or simply the usual rat race, in Seattle, it's sure to draw a crowd. While cyclers charge forth in the Microsoft Grand Prix and a couple of ponies make strides at Emerald Downs, pedestrians clog the streets of downtown and joggers compete in the Beat the Bridge Run.

▼ JIM CORWIN

▼ SEATTLE TIMES / HARLEY SOLTES

FOLKS WHO EQUATE SEATTLE with gridlock have forgotten the city's transportation network. The bus tunnel (BOTTOM) runs from the north edge of downtown to a station in the International District (TOP), the waterfront trolley scoots tourists along the shore (CENTER), and Amtrak brings trains into its station tucked between Pioneer Square and the International District (OPPOSITE).

▼ GARY GREENE ▲ ALEX WATERHOUSE-HAYWARD

◀ JIM BATES

◀ TIM J. JOHNSON / STRODE PHOTOGRAPHERS

◀ TOM REESE

SEATTLE TIMES / JIM BATES

A NEW 777 TAKING OFF FROM Boeing Field, located south of downtown on Interstate 5, promises a lofty ride. If you prefer transportation that is a little more down to earth, Amtrak and the Washington State Ferry System are happy to oblige. Seattle's ferries even accommodate commuters who don't want to leave their cars behind.

▼ SEATTLE TIMES / STEVE RINGMAN

▶ NATALIE FOBES

NO MATTER YOUR VANTAGE point, the Olympic Mountains are gorgeous in their coat of fog.

▼ SEATTLE TIMES / RON WURZER

▼ SEATTLE TIMES / RON WURZER

▶ SEATTLE TIMES / BENJAMIN BENSCHNEIDER

BIRD'S-EYE VIEWS OF DOWNTOWN and its distinctive architecture reveal the ambitious nature that has made Seattle the gem of the Pacific Northwest.

© STEFAN SCHULHOF

GREG PROBST / HILLSTROM STOCK PHOTO

GREG PROBST / HILLSTROM STOCK PHOTO

SEATTLE

Profiles in Excellence

A look at the corporations, businesses, professional groups, and community service organizations that have made this book possible. Their stories—offering an informal chronicle of the local business community—are arranged according to the date they were established in Seattle.

AlliedSignal Inc. ■ Aon Risk Services, Inc. of Washington ■ ARIS Corporation ■ AT&T Wireless Services ■ Baugh Enterprises ■ Benaroya Capital Company ■ Bob Bridge Auto Center ■ The Boeing Company ■ Boullioun Aviation Services, Inc. ■ Cavanaugh's on Fifth Avenue ■ Cegelec ESCA Corporation ■ Chateau Ste. Michelle Vineyards & Winery ■ Children's Hospital and Medical Center ■ Continental Savings Bank ■ Costco Wholesale ■ Covenant Shores Retirement Community ■ The Crowne Plaza Hotel-Seattle ■ Dames & Moore ■ Eddie Bauer ■ Expeditors International of Washington, Inc. ■ The 5th Avenue Theatre ■ Fisher Radio Seattle ■ Four Seasons Olympic Hotel ■ Fred Hutchinson Cancer Research Center ■ Garvey, Schubert & Barer ■ Graham and James LLP/Riddell Williams P.S. ■ Group Health Cooperative of Puget Sound ■ Harbor Properties, Inc. ■ Heartstream Inc. ■ Holland America Line-Westours Inc. ■ Illinova Energy Partners ■ Insignia Corporate Establishments (U.S.), Inc. ■ Insulate Industries, LLC ■ Johnson & Higgins ■ Mikron Industries ■ Northern Life Insurance Company ■ Oberto Sausage Company ■ O'Brien International Inc. ■ Overlake Hospital Medical Center ■ PEMCO Financial Services (PFS) ■ Phil Smart, Inc. ■ Pike Place Market ■ Pinnacle Realty Management Company ■ Providence Health System, Puget Sound ■ Ryan, Swanson & Cleveland, PLLC ■ Sabey Corporation ■ Seattle Center ■ Seattle City Light ■ Seattle Pacific University ■ Seattle Public Utilities ■ The Seattle Times ■ Seattle Wash, Inc. ■ Seed and Berry, LLP ■ Shannon Electronics ■ Skyway Luggage Company ■ Sorrento Hotel ■ Southwest Airlines ■ Starbucks Coffee Company ■ Swedish Medical Center ■ United Airlines ■ The University of Washington ■ University of Washington Academic Medical Center ■ URS Greiner, Inc. ■ U.S. Bank of Washington ■ U S WEST Communications ■ Virginia Mason Medical Center ■ Visio Corporation ■ Wall Data Incorporated ■ Washington Athletic Club ■ Watts-Silverstein and Associates ■ Wells Fargo ■

1859-1920

1859 Wells Fargo

1861 The University of Washington

University of Washington Academic Medical Center (1946)

1877 Providence Health System, Puget Sound

1883 U S WEST Communications

1889 U.S. Bank of Washington

1891 Seattle Pacific University

1891 URS Greiner, Inc.

1895 Seattle Public Utilities

1896 The Seattle Times

1897 Ryan, Swanson & Cleveland, PLLC

1899 Woodland Park Zoological Gardens

1906 Graham and James LLP/Riddell Williams P.S.

1906 Northern Life Insurance Company

1907 Children's Hospital and Medical Center

1907 Pike Place Market

1909 Sorrento Hotel

1910 Seattle City Light

1910 Skyway Luggage Company

1910 Swedish Medical Center

1912 Johnson & Higgins

1916 The Boeing Company

1918 Oberto Sausage Company

1918 Seed and Berry, LLP

1920 Eddie Bauer

1920 Virginia Mason Medical Center

GARY GREENE

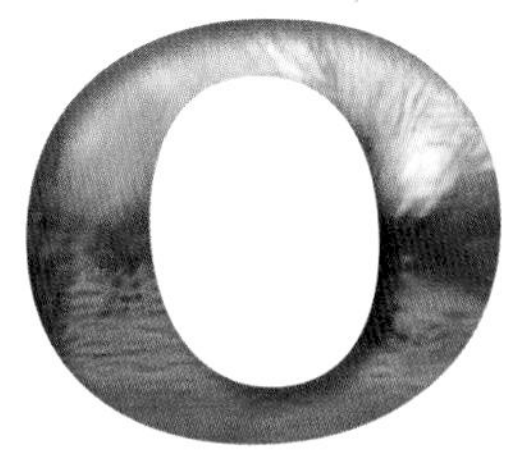

One of the largest banks in the United States, Wells Fargo provides Seattle-area residents with the most comprehensive, up-to-date banking products and services available anywhere. As part of its vigorous commitment to meeting customers' needs, the bank offers a wide variety of account choices and strives to deliver superior customer service.

Anytime, Anywhere Banking

Because Wells Fargo offers so many ways to bank, customers can choose the options that are most convenient for their lifestyles. And they can access their account information any time of the day or night from just about anywhere in the world.

Wells Fargo Express ATMs located throughout the Puget Sound area make banking fast and easy. Bank-by-mail, telephone banking, Internet banking, and branches inside supermarkets are other convenient choices. Wells Fargo was the first bank in the country to offer on-line banking, which lets customers download their account information onto their personal software and conduct transactions using their personal computers. For customers who choose the traditional method of banking, Wells Fargo has many conveniently located branches with extended hours and friendly, knowledgeable agents.

A Colorful Past

It was this same commitment to serving customers that led to the establishment of Wells Fargo back in 1852. The company was founded in San Francisco by Henry Wells and William Fargo to provide banking and express services to western pioneers during the gold rush. Wells Fargo quickly grew, offering essential banking services, reliable transportation of gold and goods, and dependable mail delivery to miners, merchants, loggers, and farmers.

Wells Fargo was founded in 1852 to provide banking and express services to western pioneers during the gold rush.

Wells Fargo began serving Washington in 1857 in the Puget Sound logging towns of Olympia, Port Townsend, and Bellingham. The first Seattle office opened in 1859. When the Klondike gold rush struck, some $40 million in Alaskan gold passed through Seattle with the help of Wells Fargo. The expanding enterprise helped connect and build a growing nation up until 1918, when the U.S. government, as a wartime measure, nationalized the country's express companies into a single federal entity. Wells Fargo had to sell its express horses, stagecoaches, and office overnight, ending its presence in Washington for nearly 80 years.

In 1996, Wells Fargo returned to Seattle when it merged with First Interstate Bancorp in the largest bank merger in U.S. history. Residents of the Evergreen State can now take advantage of Wells Fargo's century-and-a-half-long dedication to coming through for its customers.

An Exciting Future

Today, Wells Fargo boasts more than 4,200 ATMs and nearly 2,000 locations throughout its 10-state region. With $108.9 billion in assets, the company is a solid financial institution offering a full range of banking services to individual, corporate, commercial, and real estate customers in Seattle, throughout Washington, and across the country. In fact, Wells Fargo is one of the nation's leading small-business lenders.

Wells Fargo is also one of the country's leading managers of personal trust accounts and mutual funds. Wells Fargo Securities Inc., a subsidiary of Wells Fargo, offers a variety of investment solutions for retirement planning, a college education, or a major purchase. Licensed financial consultants provide professional financial planning services and, using Prodigy software and a Wells Fargo brokerage account, customers can trade their own stocks, bonds, and options on the Internet.

Following in the tradition of its legendary frontier agents, who were renowned for their integrity and enthusiasm in helping customers, Wells Fargo's personal bankers are dedicated to understanding their customers' needs and meeting them with state-of-the-art services and superior customer care.

▸ Special Collections, Univ. of Washington Libraries, #UW 12514

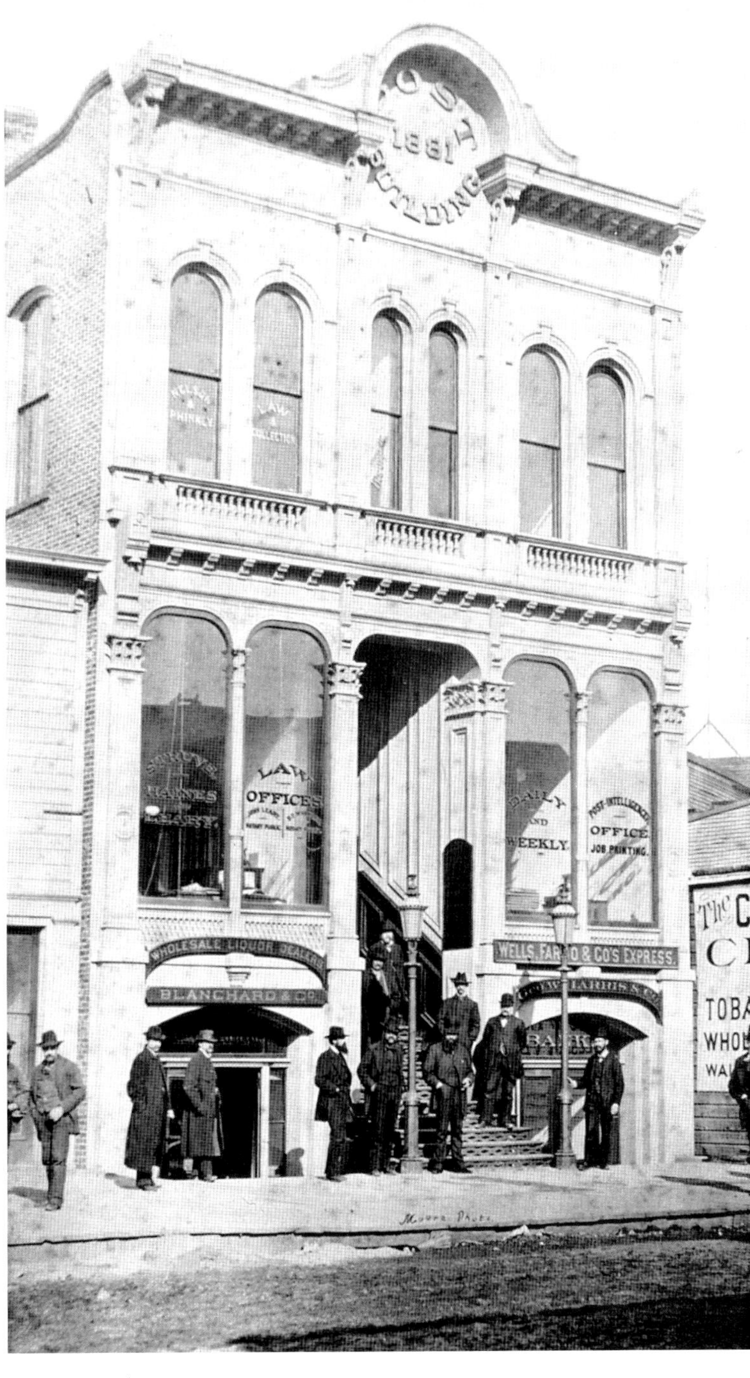

As a leader in banking technology, Wells Fargo offers customers convenient banking choices to fit their lifestyles.

On left: Wells Fargo office, Mill Street, Seattle, c. 1882

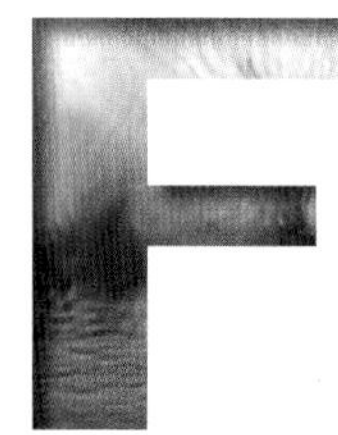

Founded in 1861, the University of Washington has long been a leading institution of higher learning in the Pacific Northwest. With 16 schools and colleges located on its main campus in Seattle and new campuses in Bothell and Tacoma, the University of Washington has many programs that are among the best in the country—from aeronautics and drama to medicine, computer science, and zoology. In programs that stress broad-based education, students enjoy the benefits of a major research university: faculty at the forefront of their fields, a dynamic curriculum, opportunities for direct research experience, and extensive library collections. The university operates such state-of-the-art research centers as the Friday Harbor Laboratories, widely acknowledged as the world's leading center for teaching and research in invertebrate animals.

Each year since 1974, the university has won more federal research funds than any other public university in the country, and it now ranks second among all universities in federal funding. This distinction reflects the quality and competitiveness of the university's faculty, which includes 35 members of the National Academy of Sciences, 26 fellows of the American Academy of Arts and Sciences, and four Nobel laureates.

JEFF ZARUBA

JEFF ZARUBA

Clockwise from top:
Founded in 1861, the University of Washington has long been a leading institution of higher learning in the Pacific Northwest.

The Physics/Astronomy Building was dedicated in September 1994. The chance to work on the cutting edge of scientific research draws almost 8,000 graduate students annually to University of Washington programs.

The Kenneth S. Allen Library was dedicated in February 1991.

World-Class Graduate Programs

The University of Washington has earned a world-class reputation for the quality of its graduate programs, which places it among a handful of elite institutions. The chance to work on the cutting edge of scientific and scholarly research draws almost 8,000 graduate students to University of Washington programs, which include more than 90 special research centers and 25 field sites. Students learn, teach, and conduct research in some of the nation's top-ranked programs, including nursing, oceanography, dentistry, public health, bioengineering, social work, and geography.

Many of the graduate programs cross traditional disciplinary boundaries. For example, the Ph.D. program in molecular and cellular biology incorporates faculty from all the biological sciences as well as the Fred Hutchinson Cancer Research Center. The business school's management program gives MBA students rigorous training in the economic, scientific, legal, and public policy aspects of environmental management. Students in urban planning and design, forestry, and numerous other programs benefit from similar interdisciplinary training.

Adding to the rich diversity in graduate programs, about 1,400 students pursue professional degrees in dentistry, law, medicine, and pharmacy at the university. Once in the workforce, professionals in these and other fields rely on the university for continuing professional education.

For decades, the university has been recognized as one of the nation's premier centers for Asian studies. The department of Asian languages and literature is renowned, and the Henry M. Jackson School of International Studies offers special expertise in Japanese politics, Southeast Asian development, and the Chinese economy. The Asian law program has one of the largest concentrations of American legal specialists on Japan, and the most extensive collection of Japanese legal material in the United States.

LOYD C. HEATH

The Liberal Arts Quadrangle, rimmed with blooming cherry trees, adds to the beauty of the campus (top).

The Broken Obelisk by artist Barnett Newman stands in front of the Suzzallo Library (bottom).

The international dimension of the university, however, extends beyond the Pacific Rim. The Jackson School, for example, offers 10 major regional studies programs. Virtually all University of Washington schools and colleges include programs with an international focus, and six schools—business, law, forest resources, public health, public affairs, and marine affairs—offer master's programs developed jointly with the Jackson School.

Working with the government, private organizations, and individuals to fashion a better society is an essential part of the university's mission. The study of human behavior at the university has led to research and problem solving across a broad spectrum—from developing and testing a violence prevention program to conducting the largest ever survey of commuter behavior in order to design tomorrow's "intelligent" highway systems.

Cultural and Economic Benefits

The university helps shape the identity of the Pacific Northwest. University of Washington faculty and graduates helped launch Seattle's now thriving theater scene, and the university continues to enrich local culture and support the arts with its two museums, three theaters, and more than 450 performances each year. Plays, concerts, exhibits, and lectures draw thousands of visitors to the main campus annually. For sports fans, there are football games in Husky Stadium and events in 22 additional Husky sports.

The university also bolsters the region's economy. First, it contributes high-quality workers to the labor force. Each year, 70 percent of its approximately 9,000 graduates remain in the state and add their skills to the economy. The university also generates some 35,000 jobs in the state beyond the 20,000 people it employs directly.

The University of Washington produces the entrepreneurs of tomorrow. It is a source of cutting-edge developments in technology and promotes the transfer of technologies to the commercial sector. New ideas and inventions spawned in biotechnology, computer software, manufacturing processes, and dozens of other fields fuel economic growth throughout the state. In the past five years alone, two dozen new Washington companies were formed to commercialize technologies developed at the university.

LOYD C. HEATH

The range and distinction of its programs have made the University of Washington one of the nation's leading institutions of higher learning, and one of the state's most valuable resources.

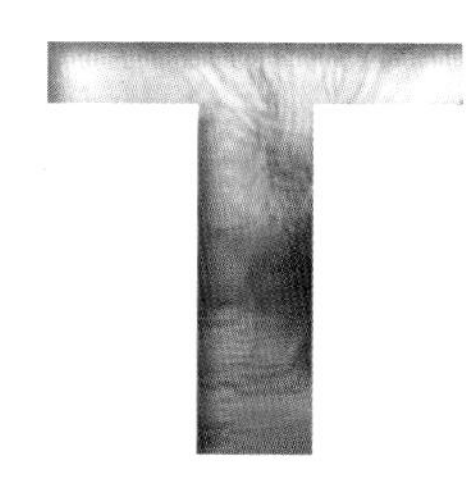

THE UNIVERSITY OF WASHINGTON (UW) ACADEMIC MEDICAL Center trains health care professionals, provides world-class health care, and is also a leading force in biomedical research. Composed of the UW School of Medicine, University of Washington Medical Center (UWMC), Harborview Medical Center (HMC), and affiliated services, the Academic Medical Center provides region-wide medical excellence for residents of Washington, Wyoming, Alaska, Montana, and Idaho. In addition, the UW Physicians Network increases access to primary care services at clinics throughout King County. The UW Academic Medical Center has established a World Wide Web site at http://www.washington.edu/medical.

UNIVERSITY OF WASHINGTON SCHOOL OF MEDICINE

Established in 1946, the UW School of Medicine has experienced remarkable success in balancing the human and the high-tech, making it an international model for medical education. For four years running, *U.S. News & World Report* has rated it as the nation's best school for the training of primary care physicians. The school's strength rests in its outstanding faculty, which includes many world-renowned leaders representing virtually all fields of patient care and research.

The UW School of Medicine is ranked first nationally among public medical schools in federal research funding and is a leader in biomedical research. Its discoveries have improved the lives of people around the world and opened avenues to promising new fields of scientific inquiry in areas such as molecular biotechnology, AIDS, and cardiovascular research. The school also places great value on teaching research skills to medical students and is one of only a handful of medical schools nationwide that require every student to complete a research project before graduating.

While it excels in research, the school is also recognized nationally for its clinical and community programs. It prepares more than half of its graduates for primary care practice, more than double the national average. Through affiliations across the Pacific Northwest, students can train in more than 170 communities, including remote villages in Alaska and other rural areas.

As the only medical school serving the five states of Washington, Wyoming, Alaska, Montana, and Idaho, the UW School of Medicine has formal arrangements with their legislatures to provide students with medical training. Students complete their first year of classes in their home state, and can do much of their clinical training in their own state and elsewhere in the region.

UNIVERSITY OF WASHINGTON MEDICAL CENTER

University of Washington Medical Center is the region's preferred resource for specialty care and serves patients from all over the world. An in-house interpreter service is available for non-English-speaking patients. UWMC is located on the University of Washington campus and is an integral component of UW's Warren G. Magnuson Health Sciences Center, which includes the schools of dentistry, medicine, nursing, pharmacy, public health and com-

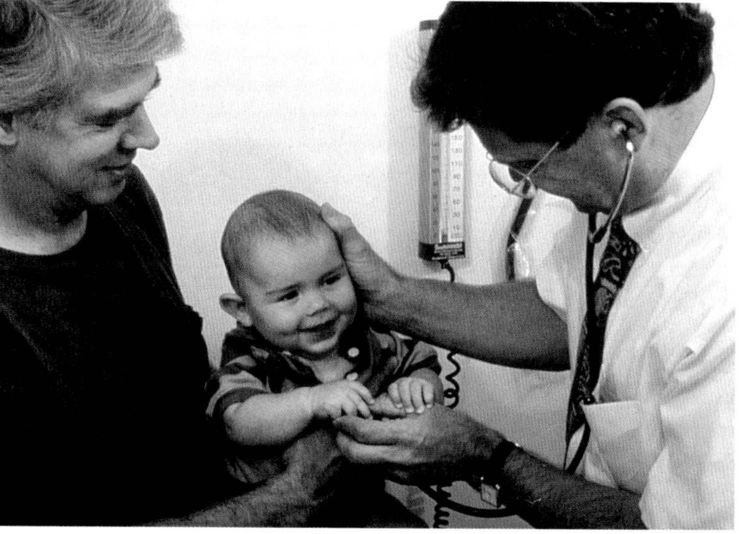

JORDAN REHM

Clockwise from top:
All of the more than 1,200 attending physicians who teach and practice at University of Washington Medical Center and Harborview Medical Center are faculty members of the UW School of Medicine, one of the top-ranked medical schools in the country.

Among the many programs at HMC, located near downtown Seattle, is the Harborview Injury Prevention and Research Center, which has led efforts to require helmets for bicyclists and equestrians, and to reduce acts of violence through researching and publicizing the public costs of gunshot wounds.

University of Washington Medical Center, licensed for 450 beds, also offers more than 80 outpatient clinics, and multidisciplinary specialty centers in cancer and pain.

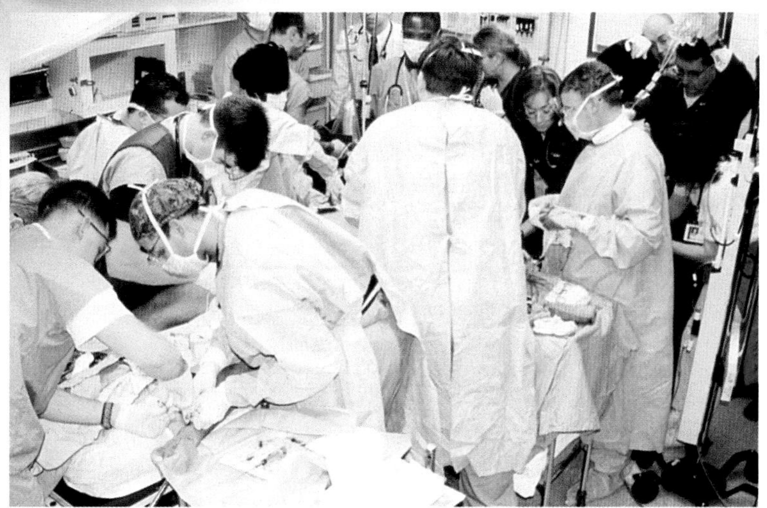

ROXANNE EBERHART

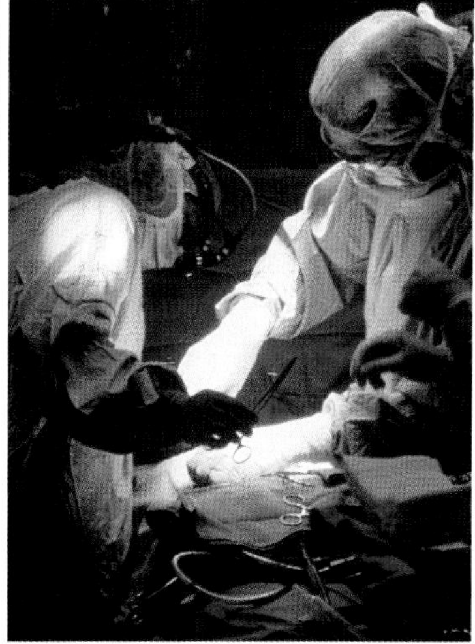

JORDAN REHM

DOUG PLUMMER

Clockwise from top left: Harborview Medical Center's recent expansion doubled the size of its emergency and trauma facilities.

University of Washington Medical Center contributes to advances in such areas as cardiology and cardiac surgery, genetics, brain mapping, kidney dialysis, breast cancer, organ transplantation, rehabilitation, and high-risk maternity and newborn intensive care.

In Whitefish, Montana, a University of Washington medical student trains under the supervision of a local family doctor. Community-based teaching is an integral part of the medical school's five-state regionalized medical education program.

munity medicine, and social work.

Established in 1959, UWMC provides comprehensive primary and specialty care for area residents, and is a regional referral and treatment center, with special expertise in the diagnosis and treatment of bone and joint problems, cancer, cardiac conditions, infertility, and obstetrics. UWMC is ranked as one of the best hospitals in the country by *U.S. News & World Report,* and is recognized for its excellence in bone marrow and organ transplantation, rehabilitation medicine, and many other surgical and medical specialties. UWMC is a founding member of Airlift Northwest, which provides access to UWMC for patients who require critical care in flight. The medical center also sponsors programs in health education and community outreach, including tours for schoolchildren, health talks, and patient information on the World Wide Web.

As a major component of the UW Academic Medical Center's teaching and research programs, University of Washington Medical Center contributes to advances in clinical research, and conducts pioneering diagnostic and treatment programs through its Clinical Research Center, funded by the National Institutes of Health.

Harborview Medical Center

Founded in 1877, Harborview Medical Center is owned by the citizens of King County and has been managed under contract by the University of Washington since 1967. Harborview's mission is to serve the community's poor and disenfranchised while providing the highest level of emergency, trauma, and burn care to residents from Washington, Alaska, Montana, and Idaho.

Harborview houses the only level I adult and pediatric trauma center and regional burn center in the four-state region. To meet the community's growing need for its services, the medical center recently expanded with a new, 440,000-square-foot facility.

Harborview provides advanced treatment for epilepsy, difficult pulmonary problems, orthopedics, and complicated neurosurgical problems such as cerebral aneurysms, in addition to specialized diagnostic and treatment programs. The medical center leads the nation in advanced burn treatment, including pain control, wound management, and reconstructive plastic surgery.

Harborview has also been involved in developing premier programs in pre-hospital care. Seattle's Medic One program, recognized and emulated worldwide, was founded at Harborview. Paramedics throughout the region are trained through a Harborview-based program. Airlift Northwest, the region's helicopter and fixed-wing air ambulance service, provides in-flight critical care to patients who need services provided by Harborview and other Seattle-area hospitals. Harborview, University of Washington Medical Center, Children's Hospital and Medical Center, and Providence Medical Center are the original partners that founded this critical community service.

Together, University of Washington Medical Center, Harborview Medical Center, and the UW School of Medicine fulfill the university's mission to provide outstanding programs in teaching, research, and public service to people in a region encompassing more than one quarter of the land mass of the United States.

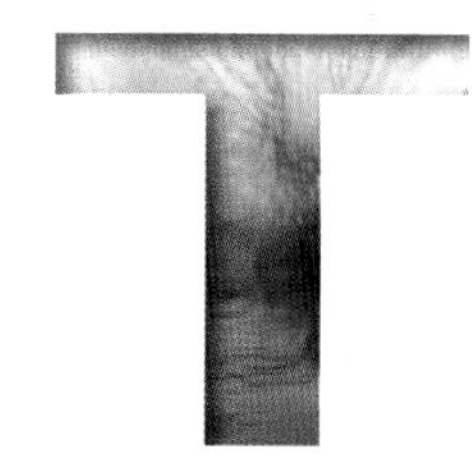

The Providence Health System was founded by a pioneering Catholic sister named Mother Joseph, who, along with four other sisters, came from Montreal to the Pacific Northwest in 1856. Crisscrossing the Washington Territory, they established schools, hospitals, orphanages, and other institutions to serve those in need. In 1877, they arrived in Seattle to take possession of the King County Poor Farm and start a hospital that eventually became Providence Seattle Medical Center.

Today, Providence Health System provides a comprehensive range of health services in Alaska, Washington, Oregon, and California. In the Puget Sound region, the Providence Health System consists of Providence Health Plans, Medalia HealthCare, Providence Seattle Medical Center, Providence Home Services, and two long-term-care facilities—Providence Mount St. Vincent and Providence Marianwood. There are Providence facilities in Everett, Olympia, Centralia, Chehalis, and Yakima, as well.

Providence Health System, Puget Sound is a partnership of services organized to meet the health needs of the community. As part of a Catholic system with a long tradition of service, the people of Providence care for patients and work with each other in a way that reflects the organization's core values: respect for the individual, care for the whole person, compassion for those in need, advocacy for social justice, and dedication to professional excellence. Providence's individual and collaborative commitment is to improve the health and well-being of the Puget Sound community.

Comprehensive Services

Providence's comprehensiveness makes it unique in the market. Providence Health Plans is the umbrella name for three divisions: Good Health Plan of Washington, Providence Health Care, and Sound Health. Providence's managed care programs offer a single source of coordinated coverage over a broad geographical area, serving more than 1.1 million members in Washington and Oregon.

Medalia HealthCare is a family of 330 doctors and other health care professionals. Sponsored by the Providence and Franciscan Health Systems, Medalia has 48 clinics throughout Puget Sound, including Seattle, the Eastside, Everett, Monroe, Gig Harbor, Tacoma, Bainbridge Island, and Enumclaw. Medalia doctors accept most major insurance plans and, should hospitalization ever be necessary, deliver care for patients in hospitals located in the local community. Most Medalia clinics are open during regular business hours, and many offer extended hours—both early in the morning and into the evening.

Providence Seattle Medical Center is a 436-bed hospital offer-

The first Providence Hospital was located at Fifth and Madison in Seattle.

TERRY REED

ROD HULING

ROD HULING

The people of Providence care for patients and work with each other in a way that reflects the organization's core values: respect for the individual, care for the whole person, compassion for those in need, advocacy for social justice, and dedication to professional excellence (top left and right).

Providence Health System provides a comprehensive range of health services in Alaska, Washington, Oregon, and California (bottom).

ing general and intensive medical-surgical services in more than 30 specialties, subspecialties, and outpatient programs. The hospital is a medical training facility affiliated with the University of Washington School of Medicine and several schools of nursing. The comprehensiveness of its programs, high-tech facilities, and research affiliations have attracted a top-notch medical staff from some of the best medical schools and institutions across the nation. The medical center is especially renowned for its Heart Center. Started in 1960, it is the oldest and largest heart program in the region, performing more than 1,000 open-heart surgeries and more than 3,000 diagnostic/therapeutic procedures each year.

Providence Home Services consists of Providence Homecare, Hospice of Seattle, and Home Infusion. Providence Homecare provides a wide range of at-home services by registered nurses, home health aides, therapists, medical social workers, and volunteers. Hospice of Seattle offers care at home to individuals and families with a member experiencing a life-limiting illness. Hospice focuses on comfort care, not cure, and works to ease the pain and discomfort of illness. Home Infusion provides intravenous medications in the home or at an ambulatory infusion center. These services are also offered statewide through the Providence Home Services Network.

The elderly have held a special place in the heart of the Sisters of Providence since the 1840s, when founder Madame Emilie Gamelin sheltered a 102-year-old woman and others in need in her Montreal home. In the Puget Sound area, subacute care (a transition between hospital and home) is provided at Providence Seattle Medical Center, Providence Mount St. Vincent in West Seattle, and Providence Marianwood in Issaquah. Mount St. Vincent and Marianwood offer skilled nursing care, as well. Other long-term-care and community-based services for seniors are provided through Providence ElderPlace, Heritage House at the Market, and Vincent House.

Through Providence Partners, Providence Health System is building collaborative relationships with community organizations, assessing the health needs of Puget Sound residents, and supporting programs to provide greater health for individuals and the community. This includes working to improve societal conditions not normally directly associated with health care, such as domestic abuse, street violence, poverty, and homelessness.

Since its founding more than 100 years ago, the Providence Health System in Puget Sound has grown from one hospital to a comprehensive system of health services providing a continuum of care. "The integrated system of care that we're building at Providence has lasting benefits for the community," says Raymond Crerand, CEO of the Puget Sound Service Area. "By working collaboratively in a coordinated fashion, we are developing a mission-driven and customer-oriented health system that seeks to control costs, improve quality, and find ways to keep people healthy."

S WEST Communications packages and delivers an array of communication products and services to more than 25 million customers in 14 western and midwestern states. The company offers basic local telephone services, long-distance services, and network access services for long-distance and wireless companies. U S WEST Communications is part of U S WEST, Inc. A separate unit, U S WEST Media Group, offers domestic and international cable and telephony, wireless communications, and directory and information services.

Formerly known as Pacific Northwest Bell, the company became part of U S WEST in 1984 and has provided high-quality phone service continuously for more than 100 years. "It's a local company with a long tradition of serving a diverse customer base," says Kirk Nelson, Washington general manager of local markets. "We know the local telecommunications markets better than anyone."

Linking the Global Community

With its local telephone network growing rapidly—both in the number of customers it serves and the information content it carries—U S WEST Communications has enhanced the value of its basic telephone service by offering new products with advanced features. In 1992, it became the first regional Bell company to offer high-speed data networking services. The company also provides telecommunications and data networking equipment and services to business customers and government agencies nationwide.

"The future of telecommunications is about more than push-button phones and a dial tone. It's about linking all of us together in one community—a telecommunity," says Solomon D. Trujillo, president and CEO of U S WEST Communications. "We work with customers to tailor new technologies in ways that fit their lifestyles. Customers won't have to settle for one-size-fits-all service."

Today, U S WEST is working to offer customers one-stop shopping with complete integrated solutions to meet all their communications needs, and services few could have imagined years ago. For home offices, U S WEST offers packages for customers ranging from business start-ups to mobile business owners. For its residential customers, U S WEST offers packages that can log calls and handle conference calling. Customers with teenagers in the home can combine paging, custom ringing, and a second line.

U S WEST has made service its top priority. Customer-focused, market-driven, and performance-based, U S WEST's strategy is to earn its customers' business by knowing exactly what they want and then providing full-service solutions to meet their communications needs. More than 50,000 employees, including 7,000 employees in Washington State alone, work to package and deliver convenient, affordable communications products and services to customers.

Providing extensive capabilities as a Fortune 500 company,

Offering an integrated slate of high-speed data networking devices and meeting businesses' needs is the focus of U S WEST's !NTERPRISE division. Preparation and planning by skilled !NTERPRISE staff means quick deployment of services. U S WEST was the first company in the nation to offer DSL (digital subscriber line) technology (left).

Customers depend on state-of-the-art services such as frame relay, which sends packets of data at speeds between six and 1,600 times faster than standard data networks. Testing and configuring data transport equipment to meet customer requirements is a priority at U S WEST (right).

U S WEST Communications serves a region that includes seven of the 10 fastest-growing states in the country. The $10 billion company serves customers from multiple locations, and multiyear contracts with many major corporate headquarters in the region speak to the confidence these companies have in U S WEST.

New Technology, New Solutions

In addition to delivering innovative services for complex applications, such as distance learning and teleradiology, U S WEST has captured a significant share of the high-speed data networking markets through its !NTERPRISE Networking Services division. The division offers businesses an intranet solutions package, which includes bundling services, high-bandwidth lines, electronic mail, firewall security software, and full customer support.

Building on those successes, U S WEST is pursuing new opportunities to offer state-of-the-art paging, wireless, and cable-television services. By early 1998, the firm plans to enter the regional long-distance market with a program to bundle local and long-distance calling services and features into one easy-to-use package for both business and residential customers. In 1997, U S WEST launched its wireless personal communications service (PCS) in selected markets. This technology integrates the company's existing network of wireless services by allowing users to connect cellular phones with computers, fax machines, pagers, and even traditional wired phones from any location.

Part of the Northwest Community

Dedicated to the Northwest community, the U S WEST Foundation and U S WEST Communications invest millions of dollars each year to ensure a healthy education system. The foundation's total giving in Washington adds up to $4 million a year. In 1996, the foundation launched Washington Teacher Network, which, funded at $1.7 million over three years, trains teachers in integrating technology into teaching and learning. The project involves 296 school districts in the state and more than 6,200 teachers.

U S WEST's support for high-quality education and the long-term capabilities of Washington State institutions is evident in the Connecting Teachers with Technology program, which provides funding for grassroots projects. In one instance, a team of teachers from Silverdale was awarded a $12,000 grant to implement a project translating stories written by K-12 students into braille by inmates of the Washington Correctional Facility.

U S WEST underwrites the use of multimedia in training high school and college faculty, while Connected Schools™ provides schools with Internet access, home-page hosting, and a range of other telecommunications services. U S WEST also facilitates distance learning for both education-at-home and work-at-home capabilities. And the economic growth in rural areas in the region continues to create demands for new services from U S WEST.

U S WEST's community involvement and hometown spirit also include sponsoring Seattle's basketball teams—the NBA's Sonics and the ABL's Seattle Reign—plus the Spokane Indians baseball team. And U S WEST has joined with KING-TV to sponsor Education in Action.

Spending more than $1 million per work day to meet service needs and bring new technologies to the market, U S WEST is continuing its long history of success in the Northwest.

▸ DAVID ROBBINS

▸ DAVID EVANS

▸ KATHY SAUBER

Clockwise from top:
U S WEST and Wells Fargo Bank worked together to successfully implement a packaged solution for the conversion of 1,400 branch and ATM locations in Washington and seven other western states. Multiple technologies were installed, using diverse routing, to meet the bank's reliability and backup criteria.

Dedicated to being part of the Northwest community, U S WEST takes pride in its gold-level sponsorship of the Seattle Reign of the American Basketball League.

U S WEST Communications personnel keep customers connected to their worlds, whether in their businesses or at home. U S WEST packages and delivers an array of communications products and services—all aimed at simplifying customers' lives.

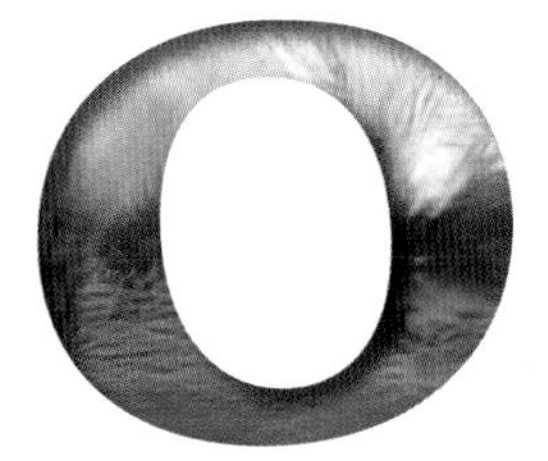

PERATING IN ONE OF THE FASTEST-GROWING REGIONS IN THE country, where population, employment, and personal income growth exceed the national average, U.S. Bancorp offers the unique combination of a community-oriented bank's personal attentiveness and the resources of a national financial services leader.

When U.S. Bank of Washington opened as Peoples Savings Bank in 1889, it was the second savings bank in Seattle. Today, its parent company, U.S. Bancorp, with assets of $33 billion; more than 600 branches; and the largest combined commercial and industrial loan portfolio in Oregon, Washington, and Idaho, leads the region in supporting the growth of businesses.

Committed to Business

U.S. Bank is the state's third-largest commercial bank, with assets of $10 billion and almost 200 branches. It has carved a niche for itself as the state's second-largest small-business lender, and is a preferred Small Business Administration (SBA) lender and state leader in SBA lending loan volume.

With a 38 percent market share, U.S. Bank is also the second-largest corporate lender in the state, offering a wide array of solutions to meet the needs of businesses and providing excellent customer service. Its international banking offices in Seattle and Tacoma house specialists with language skills and expertise in doing business in the Pacific Rim, Latin America, Europe, and Canada, and provide access to a network of global contacts.

U.S. Bancorp also offers leasing expertise in 25 states across the United States, and has helped businesses in the Northwest raise capital for growth through its Corporate Finance Group. Its Structured Finance Team provides businesses with low-cost access to capital markets through commercial paper and receivable security products.

As regional bankers, U.S. Bank representatives know the ins and outs of the region's industries, including commercial real estate development, wireless communications, high technology, and natural-resource-based industries.

As the leading agricultural lender in Washington, the bank provides loans for one-half of all hop financing and one-third of the financing for the state's wine grapes, apples, and potatoes; accounts for 40 percent of all financing for apple-packing companies and wineries; and provides nearly one-third of the financing for onion-packing operations in the state.

U.S. Bank's commitment to the agricultural community has made it one of the three largest agricultural lenders in the nation.

Innovative Banking Services

U.S. Bank has built a solid reputation as a leader in high-tech and convenience banking by creating innovative products and services. Customers enjoy shortened loan applications and quick loan decisions, easier access to credit, 24-hour-a-day telephone banking, the ability to pay bills and obtain loans by phone, and the convenience of using debit cards to make long-distance phone calls.

In addition, U.S. Bancorp offers a family of proprietary

◄ C. Bruce Forster

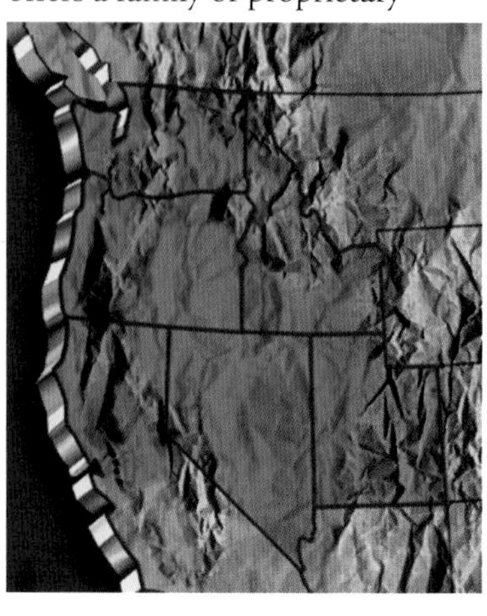

Using UBANK ON-Line®, customers can access their accounts and manage their finances via personal computer, and may also access accounts via the Internet (left).

Today, U.S. Bancorp, with assets of $33 billion; more than 600 branches; and the largest combined commercial and industrial loan portfolio in Oregon, Washington, and Idaho, leads the region in supporting the growth of businesses (right).

▲ MUSTAFA BILAL

U.S. Bank employees volunteer for various community projects, including United Way's Day of Caring.

mutual funds that are managed by the bank's affiliate, Qualivest Capital Management. Through products such as its Dynamic Allocation Series, which lets customers invest in a range of mutual funds with one targeted investment, the bank meets customer demands for simplified investment options. Qualivest was named the nation's best bank-managed fund in 1995 by *Bank Investment Product News*.

U.S. Bank was the first financial services company in Washington to offer customers on-line banking using off-the-shelf software. Using UBANK ON-Line®, customers can access their accounts and manage their finances via personal computer, and may also access accounts via the Internet.

"We have to earn our customers' business each and every day," says Phyllis J. Campbell, U.S. Bank of Washington president and CEO. "To do this, we must provide people with the ability to choose when and where to do their banking— as well as the services people want, need, and deserve."

Dedicated to the Community

U.S. Bank takes its role as a corporate citizen to heart, underwriting programs for youth,

▲ J.F. HOUSEL

Located in the U.S. Bank Centre overlooking Elliott Bay, U.S. Bank offers the unique combination of a community-oriented bank's personal attentiveness and the resources of a national financial services leader.

education, health and human services, and the arts. In 1996, the bank made more than $1.8 million in charitable contributions to such civic and cultural organizations as Mothers Against Violence in America (MAVIA), Habitat for Humanity, YMCA, United Way, and the Corporate Council for the Arts.

Several outstanding bank programs support students of all ages statewide. In 1991, with a goal of increasing minority participation in the workplace, U.S. Bank established an ongoing college scholarship program and an internship program for ethnic minorities. U.S. Bank also sponsors a high school internship and mentoring program at Seattle's Garfield High School, and contributes more than $240,000 per year in support of four homework hot lines across the state.

U.S. Bank is also a leader in developing products, services, and programs that meet the credit needs of low- and moderate-income families, and has been rated outstanding by federal regulators for its commitment to the Community Reinvestment Act. One area in which U.S. Bank has been particularly proactive is in creating, financing, and supporting programs and initiatives aimed at the development of affordable housing. The bank also offers several programs for first-time and low- to moderate-income home buyers.

On March 20, 1997, First Bank System, Inc. of Minneapolis announced the signing of a definitive agreement to acquire U.S. Bancorp, a transaction which is expected to close in the third quarter of 1997. The combined organization, which will use the U.S. Bancorp name and will be headquartered in Minneapolis, will provide customers with banking services in 17 states in the West, Rocky Mountain states, and Midwest.

OUNDED IN 1891 WITH ONLY A HANDFUL OF STUDENTS, SEATTLE Pacific University (SPU) is now a flourishing liberal arts university with a strong Christian heritage. Recognized for its academic quality, SPU is rated one of America's best colleges in the West. The university draws its 3,300 students from 36 states, the majority coming from Washington, Oregon, and California. In addition, students come from 51 foreign countries including Korea, Japan and other Asian nations, Canada, and the Middle East.

SPU is governed by the Free Methodist Church of North America, which founded it with an open vision for a nonsectarian school. The university has evolved over the past century to include a variety of denominations, and today its faculty, staff, and student body represent a rich tapestry of Christian faith traditions.

Seattle Pacific University sits on 35 acres in northern Queen Anne. The original building, constructed in 1893 in classic turn-of-the-century architecture, is still in use today. It shares the campus with a dozen more modern buildings, including a $10 million state-of-the-art library built in 1994. SPU also owns a 965-acre wilderness campus on Blakley Island, and a 150-acre camp on Whidbey Island, where it holds conferences, retreats, and a variety of student functions.

The university is comprehensive for its size. With a $50 million operating budget, it has a faculty of 200 and a support staff of 300. Although it focuses primarily on undergraduate students, SPU also offers nine master's degrees in fields including education, business, and nursing, and doctoral degrees in education and clinical psychology.

A Sense of Community and Academic Excellence

"What's great about SPU, students tell us, is the sense of community it gives them and the relationships they form while in school," says Philip Eaton, president of Seattle Pacific University.

Students give two main reasons for choosing to study at SPU—the integration of faith and learning it offers, and the academic quality of the programs. In all, 85 percent of the faculty hold doctoral degrees or the highest degrees in their field; the faculty is well-known for both its quality and its dedication to the education of students.

The university is reengineering its operations to hold down costs and tuition. Besides adding classrooms and meeting space, SPU uses advanced technology to streamline administrative work and deliver education to where people live, including to the some 2,000 students taking continuing education courses via distance learning. Opportunities abound for students to develop leadership skills in clubs, student government, and service organizations, and through peer leadership in residence halls. SPU's dynamic intramural program offers 65 sports and recreational activities, such as volleyball, bowling, Ping-Pong, and basketball. SPU is also proud of having one of the premier soccer teams in the NCAA Division II, the winner of five national titles.

Championing the idea of the city as a classroom, a high percentage of students complete internships with businesses and social agencies. SPU students also volunteer a total of 20,000 hours a year, working in nursing homes and shelters, and with civic organizations. Altogether, SPU's impact is widely felt in the community.

The academic heart of SPU's campus is its new, $10 million library complete with the latest in on-line technology for information search and retrieval (left).

SPU's 35-acre campus features a blend of historic and modern buildings in a parklike setting just minutes from the heart of downtown Seattle (right).

◄ JON WARREN

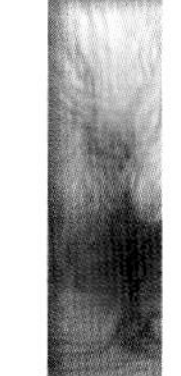

Inspired by the Italian Renaissance and reminiscent of a fine residence, the Sorrento Hotel has exemplified the stately elegance and old-world charm of a European hotel since its opening in 1909. Today, the lobby's Honduran mahogany paneling and the fireside lounge create warmth and comfort, no matter what the season.

The Sorrento is proud to be rated by readers of *Condé Nast Traveler* as one of the top 25 hotels in the country in 1996. The Sorrento offers guests a choice of 76 rooms, including 42 suites, each styled in traditional European furnishings and offering a unique configuration and cityscape view. In suites, French doors close off the living area where the couch folds out for extra guests. Windows open in every room to let in a fresh breeze.

Luxurious Details Make the Difference

It's the attention to small details in such pleasurable surroundings that keeps guests returning. Every morning, guests greet the day with their choice of four daily papers. Bed warmers are tucked under the covers on chilly nights, and guests enjoy the Sorrento's complimentary Towncar service. Each room has a two-line phone with voice mail and data port. A fax machine prints the day's menu from the award-winning Hunt Club, one of Seattle's most romantic restaurants. Guests can work out on state-of-the-art Nautilus equipment in the 24-hour fitness center or enjoy a relaxing shiatsu massage.

Special Treatment

The Sorrento's concierge is happy to arrange special requests, from a round of golf to a hydroplane ride across Puget Sound; a private, chauffeured tour of the Emerald City; airport pickup and drop off; late night champagne delivered to the room; or secretarial services for the business traveler.

The seventh-floor meeting rooms are used for executive board retreats, sales meetings, dinner functions, and other events of five to 200 people. As part of its corporate giving, the Sorrento hosts benefit events in the Top of the Town, which can serve 100 people reception-style. Large windows bathe the octagonal room in natural light, and provide beautiful views of the city and the Sound beyond.

The Hunt Club continues its tradition of specializing in superb regional cuisine. The hotel chef frequently hosts evenings of fine dining with wine pairings that showcase Washington and Oregon wines. From July to September the Piazza Capri serves cocktails, appetizers, and lighter Italian fare. Year-round, appetizers and cocktails are served in the Fireside Room.

Featuring some of the best Seattle has to offer, the Sorrento Hotel has a long history of satisfied visitors.

▲▼ MIDWEST PHOTO CO.

▲▼ MIDWEST PHOTO CO.

Clockwise from top left:
Guests of the Sorrento Hotel can enjoy tea or after dinner drinks in the Fireside Room, which is richly paneled with Honduran mahogany.

Guests can conduct a private reception or business conference in the spacious Top of the Town or The Sorrento Room.

The Hunt Club is famous for award-winning cuisine ranging from innovative Northwest dishes to traditional American fare.

Antique furnishings enhance sitting and dressing rooms, and such amenities as goose down pillows, bathrobes, and oversize bath towels contribute to the atmosphere of intrinsic comfort.

URS Greiner, Inc. (URSG) is one of the oldest engineering firms in Seattle. Founded in 1891 as Stixtrud & Naston, the firm surveyed such noteworthy projects as sections of the original University of Washington campus, the Seattle Tide Lands, the Cedar River pipeline, and a myriad of roadway, residential, commercial, and industrial projects.

In 1971, the *Seattle Daily Journal of Commerce* published an article celebrating the company's 80th anniversary and referred to it as "a pioneer engineering firm." Although URSG was founded on land surveying services, the company played a pivotal role in designing many of Washington State's major infrastructure improvements and environmental programs. For example, in the 1940s, URSG served as adviser and engineer to many of the districts created to serve Seattle's burgeoning suburbs. Additionally, the efforts of the company's earliest leaders led to the state's first sewer district laws. These endeavors laid the groundwork for many of the firm's longstanding client relationships.

Long-Standing Relationships

"The heartbeat of the Seattle office has always been its longstanding relationships. Repeat business accounts for over half of our annual assignments, and we are very proud of the relationships we have nurtured with our clients over the years," says Vice President of Northwest Operations John E. Butts.

Since 1942, URSG has designed numerous multidisciplinary street improvement, water distribution/supply, and sewer projects for the City of Oak Harbor, Washington. URSG has subsequently prepared the city's first comprehensive sewage plan, designed the primary and secondary treatment plants and various water supply and distribution projects, and performed environmental assessments. URSG is currently preparing a five-year update to the city's 20-year comprehensive sewage plan to accommodate predicted growth in its service area.

In 1946, URSG helped to form the Midway Sewer District in the Des Moines, Washington, area and then to expand its boundaries through annexation to its present size of 12 square miles. The firm designed all of the district's primary and secondary treatment plants, including upgrades, and performed numerous environmental assessments, such as the Des Moines Creek Trunk and Outfall Pipelines Environmental Impact Statement that was completed in 1996. Today, URSG is performing shellfish resource (geoduck) and eelgrass surveys to assist in the design and permitting of a new marine outfall—consisting of 48-inch-diameter pipe extending approximately 1,800 feet—expected to be in operation by early 1999.

Today

URS Greiner was created in April 1996 when URS Consultants, Inc. acquired Greiner Engineering, Inc., a nationally recognized leader in air and surface transportation. With 60 offices nationwide and abroad, URSG has expanded its technical expertise, resources, and geographic presence to offer a broad range of planning, design, and program and construction management services to public- and private-sector clients. The synergy created by joining the two firms boasts record revenues

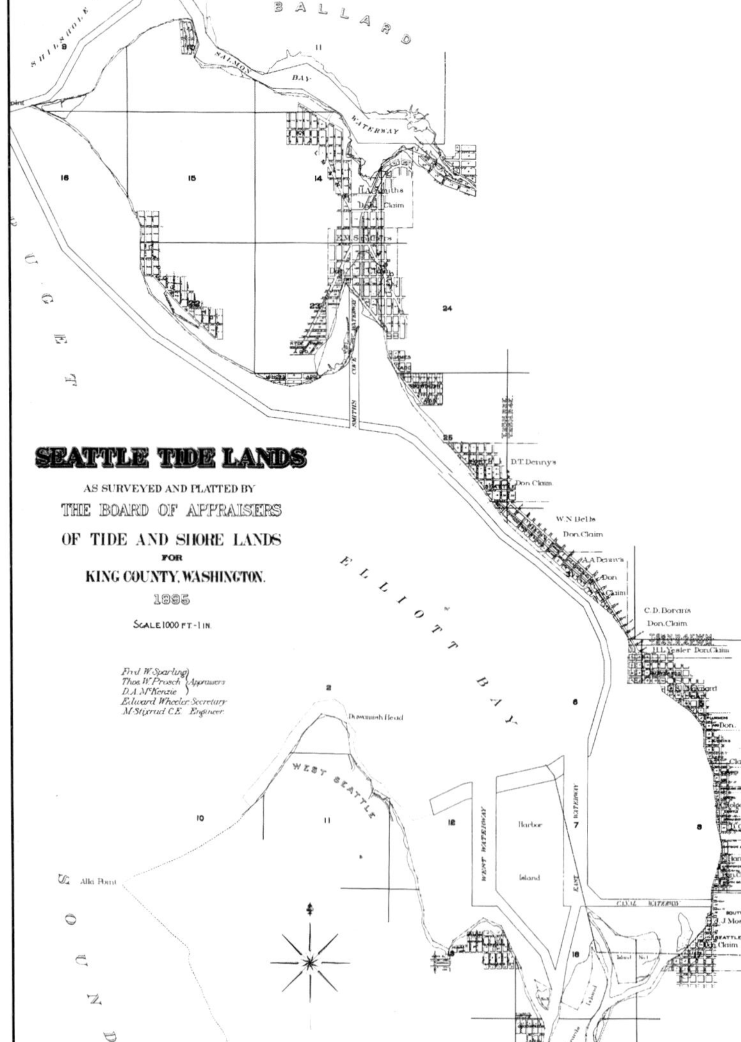

URS Greiner was founded in 1891 as Stixtrud & Naston and surveyed such noteworthy projects as the Seattle Tide Lands (left).

The Seattle office was awarded a Comprehensive Long-Term Environmental Action, Navy (CLEAN) contract—a 10-year, $166 million project to assist the U.S. Navy in the investigation and remediation of naval activities in the Pacific Northwest (right).

of $363 million in 1996, with $695 million in backlog. URSG is ranked as the fourth-largest transportation firm and 17th-largest design firm in the United States.

URSG Seattle specializes in the engineering of wastewater collection and treatment; water supply, distribution, and treatment systems; surface and air transportation; marinas and ports; hazardous and toxic waste remediation; planning and community relations; program and construction management; and all facets of environmental engineering. Of particular interest, the Seattle office was awarded a Comprehensive Long-Term Environmental Action, Navy (CLEAN) contract—a 10-year, $166 million project to assist the U.S. Navy in the investigation and remediation of naval activities in the Pacific Northwest. Similar services are being provided for the Environmental Protection Agency (EPA) under the Alternative Remedial Contract Strategy program to support the EPA's responsibilities under Superfund.

The Seattle office has more than 160 employees and can pool the nationwide resources of the firm to meet the needs of large, complex, multifaceted programs. URSG employs more than 3,000 engineers, architects, planners, environmental scientists, construction specialists, technicians, and support personnel to meet any combination of specialized project requirements.

In the last six years alone, URSG has provided professional services to support public and private clients in the management of complex facilities programs in the Pacific Northwest with a cumulative value approaching $1 billion. URSG staff blend with in-house client resources to form an integrated team to manage many of the Northwest's most challenging programs, particularly those requiring integration of diverse elements and innovative approaches. Clients include some of the region's most prominent organizations, such as major universities, ports, transportation agencies, retail organizations, public school systems, high-tech companies, and local, state, and federal agencies.

URSG continues to be a recognized industry leader in surface and air transportation. Locally, the Seattle office was part of the team awarded the contract for the expansion of Concourse A at Seattle-Tacoma International Airport. Seattle office staff are also working on projects for international airports in Orlando; Midway (Chicago); Greater Buffalo; Vancouver, British Columbia; and Sydney, Australia, among others. The Airport Services Group is performing multidisciplinary services, ranging from feasibility and environmental studies and project planning to the design of terminals, baggage handling systems, and other airport systems, to construction administration.

Recent surface transportation projects include the SR 101/Black Lake Boulevard Urban Interchange in Olympia, 700 Avenue West and Heller Roadway Widening/Intersection Improvements for the City of Oak Harbor, and roadway improvements and widening projects at several intersections of Military Road South for the City of Federal Way.

"We pride ourselves in being an efficient, high-quality, cost-effective provider," says Butts. "Our goal over the next five years is to be among the top 10 engineering firms in the country, and the provider of choice for our many valued clients."

▶ JOHN KNOBBS

▶ WALTER HODGES

▶ VINCE STREANO

Clockwise from top:
The Oak Harbor Secondary Wastewater Treatment Plant was originally designed in 1972. Currently, URSG is performing design and construction management services to upgrade the facility.

At the University of Washington, the firm has provided project management and contract administration services for many projects, including the renovation of the historic Suzallo Library.

The outfall of the Renton Effluent Transfer System extends 9,500 feet into Puget Sound at a depth of 600 feet.

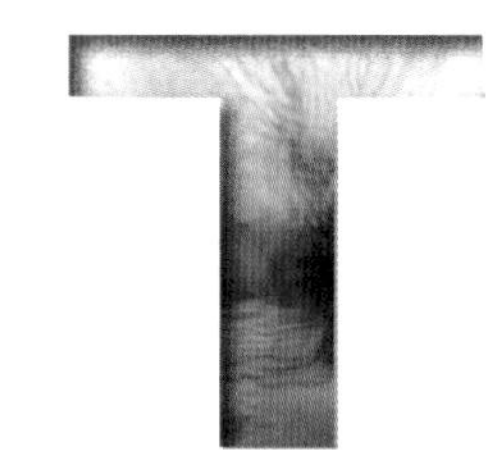

HE HISTORY OF SEATTLE'S WATER AND ENGINEERING utilities is the history of Seattle itself. For more than 100 years, Seattle has grown outward and upward on the roads, bridges, watersheds, seawalls, sewers, and drainage, garbage, and electrical systems built by its water and engineering departments.

Seattle was founded in 1865 as a frontier outpost of wooded hills, salmon-filled waters, and 350 hardy residents. The new community grew, and so did the problems already known to other 19th-century towns. The beautiful hills were an impediment to commerce. Water supplies were uncertain and unhealthy. Garbage piled up in streets and alleys.

Between 1885 and 1889, Seattle's population increased from 10,000 to 40,000. Without a public sewage system or reliable water supply, the problems increased, too. Seattle had an unhappy reputation as one of the country's most unhealthy towns.

Two crises in 1889 challenged public officials and pushed the fledgling city forward. Already hit by cholera epidemics, Seattle suffered a typhoid outbreak from sewage-polluted water in Lake Union. Health, engineering, and water officials convinced Seattle's city council of the need for separate systems for sewage and drinking water. They began to build sewers and storm drains, and to remove the rotting, wood-planked road system. And they began to develop a protected water supply, high in the Cascade Mountains, with a system of pipelines and reservoirs owned and operated by the city.

The second crisis of 1889 changed Seattle's skyline forever. The Great Fire of that summer eliminated the 64-acre business district. From the ashes, the city rebuilt itself with a new image. Seattle was no longer a makeshift frontier town, but a city of substance and permanence with the beginnings of the infrastructure it still uses today.

Seattle was pushed and pulled into the 20th century by its water and engineering departments. When a new supply of power and water was needed for a growing population, city engineers delivered water from the Cedar River. By 1909, water and sewage systems were in place, and Seattle boasted of being the world's healthiest city.

During these early days, Denny Hill and Jackson Street were regraded, and the city's parks system was mapped out with the help of the Olmsted brothers—the sons of Frederick Law Olmsted, who designed New York City's Central Park. City streets were paved, and garbage was collected. Rivers were straightened to prevent flooding, and swamplands were filled to add harbor and industrial areas.

Between 1911 and 1922, more than a dozen viaducts and bridges were built, allowing maritime and

Clockwise from top:
The 90,000-acre Cedar River Watershed provides two-thirds of the drinking water for 1.3 million people in the Seattle region. It is also a vast protected wildlife preserve.

The 6,100-foot Alaskan Way Seawall, completed in 1936 at a cost of $1.4 million, transformed an area plagued by a soft foundation and a 16-foot tidal range into one of Seattle's most important municipal assets.

Seattle's original water pipeline from the mountain reservoirs to the city was constructed of wood. Some wood-stave pipeline was still in use in the 1990s.

The West Seattle Low-Level Bridge—the world's only hydraulically operated double-leaf concrete swing bridge—has won seven major awards since its completion in 1991.

commercial traffic to expand beyond Seattle's natural borders. Two more dams, the Diablo in 1930 and the Tolt River in 1964, were built to accommodate a growing need for fresh water and electricity. After World War II, the Alaskan Way Viaduct and Battery Street Tunnel became the basis of Seattle's inner-city highway system.

For 100 years, the Seattle Water Department and Seattle Engineering Department planned, designed, constructed, and maintained Seattle's infrastructure and utility services. For a century they worked with pride, skill, and dedication to help Seattle grow from a frontier town of 350 into a world-class city of 535,000.

World-Class Utility Services in a New Century

Today, new challenges face Seattle and the Puget Sound region. In 1997, Seattle Public Utilities was created to meet those challenges. The new department consolidates functions of the Water Department and Engineering Department, including engineering services, solid waste utility, and drainage and wastewater utility. A century-old tradition of excellence in infrastructure and utility management has been joined with a new, stronger focus on seamless customer service, environmental stewardship, and integrated planning and operations. The consolidation has given Seattle residents one-stop shopping for all city utility services: water, sewage, flood control, and electricity, as well as garbage, recycling, and yard waste collection.

Once considered an infinite commodity, fresh water now is valued as a precious regional resource. Today, 28 suburban cities and special districts purchase water from Seattle's regional supply system, which serves a total of 1.25 million area residents and businesses. Seattle Public Utilities ensures customers have sufficient supplies of high-quality drinking water, despite what nature may have in store for the Pacific Northwest.

In 1996, Seattle completed a land exchange agreement with the U.S. Forest Service that gives it control of 99.9 percent of the Cedar River watershed, the vast natural area in the Cascade Mountains that supplies two-thirds of the system's water. Seattle Public Utilities' comprehensive habitat conservation plan for the Cedar Watershed ensures a steady supply of water for the region while continuing to protect fish, animals, and habitat.

In the next decade, Seattle Public Utilities will complete major projects that include an innovative DBO (design, build, operate) project for filtration of drinking water from the Tolt River and an ozonation project on the Cedar.

Sewer and drainage systems safeguard public health, control flooding, and protect Seattle's streams, lakes, and bays. Over the last 30 years, investments in pollution control and flood prevention facilities have been made in every neighborhood. Preventive maintenance is standard in the department, and robots and other "trenchless technologies" are used to find and repair problems in sewers without tearing up streets or disrupting daily life. Hundreds of millions of dollars have been invested in controlling sewer overflow problems and storm-water-related pollution, and in cleaning up historical contamination.

The department's construction engineers meet challenges posed by Seattle's hills, shorelines, and waterways. They design, construct, and maintain streets, curbs, sidewalks, seismic retrofittings, new wetlands, bicycle and pedestrian trails, and more than 150 bridges throughout the city. Additionally, Seattle Public Utilities works on capital projects for the Seattle Transportation Department and neighboring jurisdictions such

In addition to removing graffiti from public property , the Graffiti Rangers teach community groups about safe cleanup and removal techniques (top).

A model conservation home proved that a home can be attractive, affordable, and environmentally friendly (bottom).

as Metropolitan King County, Washington State Department of Transportation, Washington State Department of Ecology, and the University of Washington.

Solid waste management, including an internationally recognized recycling program, rounds out the department's integrated utility services. Seattle's management of the reduction, collection, and disposal of solid, recyclable, and household hazardous wastes stands as a model. In 1995, Seattle residents recycled 48 percent of their solid waste and, at 45 percent, businesses weren't far behind. Variable can rates for garbage service are key to curbside recycling collection. Customers are charged by the size garbage can they choose. More than 90 percent of residents subscribe to one-can (32-gallon) service or less.

While Seattle's goal is to recycle 60 percent of its solid waste, its vision for the future is to make less waste altogether. Through education and community outreach, the city gives residents the know-how to shop smart, compost, reduce bulk mail, reuse goods and materials, and do other things that will reduce the total amount of waste that must be collected and disposed of.

By managing water, sewer and drainage, infrastructure, and solid waste collection and disposal services all in one place, Seattle Public Utilities offers customers a single contact for utility services, and ensures that the planning and operation of the services are bound together in a common concern and respect for Seattle's urban and regional environment.

Urban Environmentalism and Education

Seattle is a leader in pioneering an urban environmental agenda, due in great part to the strong environmental ethic of its residents.

Environmental programs for children are an important part of this agenda. Every year, Seattle Public Utilities sponsors visits by some 6,000 students to the Seattle Aquarium, where they learn about the life cycle of salmon and the human role in providing conditions that help them to thrive.

Seattle has helped restore salmon runs to urban creeks through rehabilitation of creek habitat. In 1990, the city started the Salmon in the Classroom Program to teach stewardship values. Today, some 20,000 students from 105 schools raise salmon fry (juvenile salmon) from eggs in their classrooms and release them into city creeks in the spring. Salmon are returning to those creeks for the first time in generations. Tours to the Cedar River Basin teach thousands of children each year about water quality and watershed management. At Denny Middle School, students, teachers, parents, and a local nursery and chamber of commerce collaborated with the department to create a low-water garden in the courtyard that taught students firsthand about water conservation.

Other programs to increase salmon populations on Washington's rivers have reaped rewards, including the Cedar River Interim Sockeye Salmon Hatchery and projects on the Tolt River, where summer steelhead are returning in growing numbers.

Seattle Public Utilities continues to make outdoor water use more efficient, principally through conservation. Most residential water consumption is in yard care, so the city creates educational programs to promote effective, efficient lawn care. Soundscape, a lawn demonstration and research site aimed at large-scale irrigators, has been expanded. Other efforts that promise big benefits are water audits of schools, parks, cemeteries and multifamily properties, and training sessions for landscape architects and grounds keepers.

Programs for sustainable building and reuse or recycling of construction debris are growing. A model conservation home built in partnership with a nonprofit housing corporation shows that recycled and energy efficient products can be affordable. Recycled and salvaged materials, low-water landscaping, appliances that use low energy and water, and innovative design were showcased during public tours before the house was sold.

Partnerships with Communities and Customers

Seattle Public Utilities meets its conservation, waste reduction, and recycling goals by forging partnerships with Seattle residents and businesses. In curbside recycling, for example, customers are asked to remove labels from cans and tops from bottles, separate materials, and place recyclables three feet from the curb on collection day. Recycling participation is high and contamination is low because a visible and well-funded public education program uses market research and targeted materials to reach Seattle's diverse population, giving residents information they need to make recycling work.

Volunteer programs are popular, and thousands of residents participate in Friends of Recycling, Master Composters, and other green programs. More than 140 Adopt-A-Street groups clean up litter and graffiti in their neighborhoods. With Less Is More grants, groups and individuals try out ideas for waste reduction projects. Stewardship Through Environmental Partnerships (STEP) supports community-based water quality protection and awareness projects. STEP projects range from 1,500 Student Conservation Association volunteers cleaning creeks on Earth Day to residents installing rain barrels to provide relief sewers and irrigate gardens. Grants help teachers develop environmental projects in schools. One second-grade class made a quilt with squares that carried environmental messages; other classes have performed plays with environmental themes. And throughout the city, residents have responded enthusiastically to a water conservation initiative that retrofits homes with low-volume showerheads, faucet flow restrictors, and toilet tank displacement devices.

Partnerships create ways for residents and businesses to reach goals in their neighborhoods and business districts. Free paint to cover graffiti is available from the household hazardous waste collection sites, saving individuals the cost of buying paint and saving the city the cost of disposing of it. The city's Graffiti Rangers paint out graffiti on public facilities, and help community and school groups prepare walls for mural projects.

The success of these progressive volunteer programs reflects the civic-mindedness of the citizenry of Seattle, which remains ahead of the curve nationally in successful environmental efforts. Seattle is a city of people who get involved. Recognizing this incredible asset, Seattle Public Utilities continually seeks ways to strengthen communication with the residents and businesses it serves, and to empower them to carry out programs that benefit their neighborhoods and the environment.

As Seattle moves into the 21st century, employees of Seattle Public Utilities are bringing world-class utility services to their neighbors through partnerships with communities and customers, respect for the environment, and unequaled customer service.

The Recyclettes teach the three Rs of reduce, reuse, and recycle at community and school events (top).

During the 1995-96 school year, some 3,500 elementary students from 59 schools raised chum salmon fingerlings and released them into local streams. As a result of Seattle Public Utilities' Salmon in the Classroom program, mature chum salmon have begun to return to Seattle's waterways (bottom).

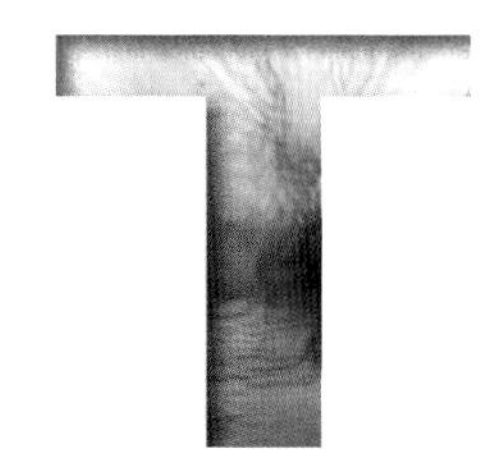

The Seattle Times IS ONE OF THE FEW REMAINING FAMILY-OWNED metropolitan newspapers in America. It is the only locally owned daily newspaper in the Puget Sound area. ■ When Colonel Alden J. Blethen made his way to the frontier city of Seattle in 1896, he was 50 years old and broke. The Colonel borrowed $3,000 from relatives to purchase a small, failing newspaper, the *Seattle Daily Times*.

With the 1897 Klondike Gold Rush as a catalyst, Blethen quickly turned the *Times* into Seattle's leading and most successful newspaper. In a newspaper era of loud headlines and strident personalities, Blethen and the *Times* became part and parcel of Seattle's growth, development, and personality. The Colonel remained one of the most visible, controversial, and dominant Seattle figures until his death in 1915. Blethen's philosophy was summed up in his famous quote, "Raise hell and sell newspapers."

Blethen's legacies of journalistic commitment, community service, and local family ownership are carried on today by the fourth generation of the family.

Growth and Dominance

With more than 1 million Sunday and 500,000 daily readers, *The Seattle Times* is the largest newspaper and dominant source of information in Washington State.

Over the past decade, the *Times* has gone through an unprecedented period of growth and investment. During this period, more than $250 million was spent to build the nation's most modern and sophisticated printing plant, located in suburban Bothell, and to build the sophisticated computer infrastructure now required by a modern metropolitan newspaper.

Part of that growth has been through traditional print journalism and part through new electronic information delivery. In 1991, the *Times* bought the 40,000-circulation *Yakima Herald-Republic*. In 1972, it bought the 15,000-circulation *Walla Walla Union-Bulletin*.

More recently, the *Times* has developed a sophisticated World Wide Web site to complement its journalistic mission and business focus. The site can be accessed at http://www.seatimes.com.

Says Frank Blethen, *The Seattle Times* publisher, "Our biggest challenge is the same one we've faced since our beginnings: Dealing with and adapting to change, particularly the ever increasing pace of technological change and information delivery. The traditional role in gathering and producing news won't change. The only question is delivery of the product. I think it will always be paper, but 100 years from now it may be paper printed in your own home."

Quality

The *Times'* commitment to excellence is seen throughout the organization.

Local ownership has enabled a level of commitment to journalistic excellence and community service that is rarely seen today.

Clockwise from top:
Colonel Alden J. Blethen purchased the *Seattle Daily Times* in 1896 and quickly turned it into Seattle's leading and most successful newspaper.

After publishing the *Times* in a Yesler Way printing shop, Blethen moved the business into larger quarters at Second Avenue and Columbia Street.

C.B. Blethen (second from right) took over as publisher of *The Seattle Times* upon his father's death in 1915.

This is underscored by the *Times'* national recognition as the nation's best regional newspaper. Winner of seven of the eight Pulitzer prizes ever awarded to Northwest newspapers, the *Times* has won the University of Missouri lifestyle award five of the past 10 years.

The *Times*-owned *Walla Walla Union-Bulletin* has also won significant national recognition, including two Sigma Delta Chi public service awards. The *Union-Bulletin* is widely recognized as the best small newspaper in the Pacific Northwest and one of the best in the country.

Cutting Edge

The *Times'* commitment to quality, values, and community service is evident in several other areas where it is considered both a local and a national leader. Most notable has been the *Times'* commitment to a family-friendly workplace and to workplace diversity.

In 1987, the *Times* became one of the few newspapers in the country to sponsor an on-site day care center. For six consecutive years since 1991, the *Times* has been listed on *Working Mother* magazine's top 100 list for best places for mothers to work. Until recently, the *Times* was the only Northwest company on the list and the only newspaper. This is typical of the *Times'* wide recognition as one of the country's most progressive and sensitive workplaces.

Because of the *Times'* commitment to gender equity and racial diversity, it has become a model in the newspaper industry. Its newsroom has been among the half dozen most diverse in the country for several years, and the number and level of women in significant senior management roles is one of the highest in the country.

Family Tradition and Values

Bucking the trend of media consolidation, the *Times* is committed to remaining family owned, local, independent, and private. Along with his name, Alden Blethen's legacy has been handed down to five fourth-generation shareholders, including Frank Blethen and cousins Robert Blethen, corporate marketing director, and William Blethen, treasurer, both of whom serve on the company's board of directors. Another cousin, John Blethen, also is a company director. Three members of the fifth generation already work full-time at the newspaper.

"It hasn't been easy keeping the newspaper in the Blethen family all these years," says Frank Blethen. "It's taken moxie, hard work, and sheer good luck to fight off local competitors and national newspaper chains." He adds, "I'm continually struck by two constants in our 100-year history: dynamic change and adhering to core values. We've put everything in motion for the paper to continue for the next 100 years. There's no doubt the Seattle area will continue to grow in both numbers and influence."

As a sophisticated, innovative, and professionally operated newspaper and knowledge company, *The Seattle Times* has also become a national model for successful multigenerational family businesses. It is a values-driven company that operates around four core values: to remain family owned, private, and independent; serve the community through quality journalism; maximize the workplace satisfaction of all employees; and be the country's best regional newspaper.

The *Times* operates the nation's most modern and sophisticated printing plant, located in suburban Bothell, Washington.

Fourth-generation Blethens who are majority shareholders in *The Seattle Times* include (from left), Alden J. Blethen, Robert C. Blethen, John P. Blethen, Frank A. Blethen and William K. Blethen (insert).

John Ryan Sr. opened his Seattle law practice in 1897, and dedicated himself to providing outstanding legal services for a reasonable fee. One hundred years later, his practice continues in the firm that still bears his family name: Ryan, Swanson & Cleveland. ■ Ryan took on his first partner, Grover Desmond, in 1914, and by 1926, he was joined by his son, John Ryan Jr. After his father's death, John Ryan Jr. took over the firm and added former Washington Supreme Court Justice William Askren as a partner.

John Ryan Jr. served as managing partner of the firm for 49 years, until his death in 1982. Ryan was passionately devoted to his family, community, and profession, and was known for his warmth and generosity. During his tenure, the Ryan firm not only grew in size and stature, but in many ways, began to reflect his personality.

Ryan excelled at the human aspect of the legal profession, and always sought to give his clients personal attention as well as sound advice. He also made sure the lawyers who worked with him shared his philosophy. Ryan's ideals continue to motivate the firm today.

Ryan, Swanson & Cleveland bears the names of two other longtime partners, Ray Swanson and Dick Cleveland. Both practiced with the Ryan firm for nearly 40 years before their recent retirements.

A Diversity of Services

From its modest beginnings, Ryan, Swanson & Cleveland has grown to a midsize, full-service law firm located in the heart of downtown Seattle, offering a wide range of legal services. The Ryan firm has always placed a strong emphasis on helping local businesses, small and large, with business formations, contracts, financing, taxes, employment, real estate issues, and other business concerns. The firm has several lawyers who are qualified in all areas of dispute resolution as well: jury and nonjury trials, appeals, arbitration and mediation, and regulatory proceedings. Other areas of expertise include bankruptcy, immigration, securities offerings, estate planning, and probate. The firm is particularly well versed in issues unique to the insurance, health care, and retail industries.

A Commitment to Values

Ryan, Swanson & Cleveland adopted a credo in 1987 embodying its core values and articulating the firm's aspirations. The credo has been a widely publicized model, emulated by other law firms.

The credo commits the Ryan firm's lawyers to provide their clients with the full benefit of their knowledge, ability, and effort. The credo recognizes that the shared goal is to be the best law firm possible, not necessarily the biggest or most profitable.

The credo acknowledges that success requires investment in human and technical resources, and that the firm must strive to enable all employees to grow to their highest potential. The credo also recognizes the obligations each

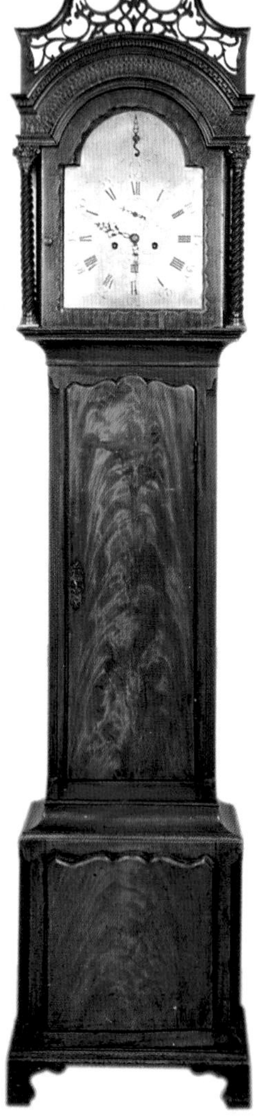

Huntoon Photography

This clock stands in Ryan, Swanson & Cleveland's reception area. Handcrafted in 1770, the clock is a symbol of the firm's tradition of excellence and its rich heritage of client services (top).

Lawyer Roger Kindley and secretary Dawn Krause are an example of the Ryan firm's commitment to teamwork (right).

employee has to his or her family and community, and commits the firm to support and encourage those obligations.

The Ryan firm's commitment to its credo is ongoing. The firm continually endeavors to offer a welcoming environment for clients, and to enhance the quality of life for its employees. The Ryan firm regularly celebrates personal and legal achievements, and has a sabbatical program for staff as well as for attorneys. The firm also makes annual contributions to the volunteer organizations its employees support.

To ensure excellence, the Ryan firm continues to expand its practice and develop new areas of expertise to keep pace with changing laws and client needs. The Ryan firm stays abreast of technology, offering advanced telecommunication capabilities, the latest in computer services support, and extensive legal research capabilities. Every Ryan lawyer utilizes a personal computer.

▶ HUNTOON PHOTOGRAPHY

A Centennial Milestone

For its 100th anniversary, Ryan, Swanson & Cleveland dedicated 1997 to giving thanks to its community through special donations and contributions: in March, delivering 100 blankets to the homeless; in April, participating in the Christmas in April program by renovating a homeless shelter; in May, planting 100 trees through Mountains to Sound Greenway; in June, contributing 100 books to Washington Literacy; in July, donating 100 teddy bears to the Teddy Bear Patrol; in August, delivering 100 balloons to the Children's AIDS ward at Harborview Hospital; in September, volunteering 100 hours of its members' time to various community service groups; in October, rendering 100 hours of free legal advice coordinated through the Allied Arts Foundation; in November, sponsoring a family at Thanksgiving and donating 100 pounds of food to them; and in December, fulfilling a child's wish through the Make-A-Wish Foundation.

A View to the Future

The growth and success of the Ryan firm is a monument to its clients, its community, and the dozens of men and women who have devoted their careers to serving others. Given its history and commitment, Ryan, Swanson & Cleveland is uniquely positioned to continue its progress into its second century.

Clockwise from top:
The Ryan firm represents clients ranging from individuals to international corporations, and its expansive practice includes everything from real estate to health care .

The Washington Mutual Tower is home to Ryan, Swanson & Cleveland.

Receptionist Beverly Wilson greets clients in the firm's main lobby.

In 1899, the City of Seattle purchased Woodland Park Zoo from the former estate of land developer Guy Phinney. A jewel in the crown of the Puget Sound community, Woodland Park Zoo spills over the crest of Phinney Ridge, offering a natural garden setting where families and individuals can escape from the pressures of modern life and experience a rare intimacy with nature.

Woodland Park Zoo is one of the most modern and successful in the country. In 1985, with the promise of nearly $43 million in public and private funds, the zoo began a dramatic redevelopment program. This resulted in a series of expanded and upgraded exhibits that have virtually changed the face of more than three-quarters of the zoo's 92 acres. Since that time, the zoo has become a world-renowned leader in designing and building naturalistic exhibits that approximate various bioclimatic zones of the world. It has received numerous Best New Exhibit awards from the American Zoo and Aquarium Association, with winners including the Northern Trail, Tropical Rain Forest, Elephant Forest, and African Savanna exhibits.

Pioneering Design, Research, and Education

Visiting Woodland Park Zoo is an adventure in discovery. More than 300 animal species, accompanied by an enormous number of plant species, thrive in settings carefully designed to re-create their indigenous environments. Creative use of native plants, natural land formations, artificial rock and plant work, temperature controls, and cultural props lends authenticity to the experience. In addition, paths and viewing points are designed to immerse the visitor in nature by hiding barriers and support areas, and presenting animals at eye level.

Woodland Park Zoo's mission is to help create a sustainable future for wildlife. Through research, captive breeding, the promotion of environmental management, and conservation education, Woodland Park Zoo has contributed to preserving numerous endangered species. Success stories include lion-tailed macaques, snow leopards, western lowland gorillas, Malayan sun bears, and, closer to home, western pond turtles. In addition, the Trail of Vines exhibit almost exclusively features endangered primates, including siamangs, lion-tailed macaques, and, the greatest attraction, a family of highly intelligent orangutans. These "people of the forest," as the name signifies in their Indonesian homeland, flourish in a rain forest canopy, complete with high rock walls and rushing streams.

While most of Woodland Park Zoo's animals were born on the premises, it frequently plays the role of rescuer. Over the past 25

AGNES OVERBAUGH

LARRY SAMMONS

LARRY SAMMONS

KEVIN SCHAFER

Clockwise from top left:
A siamang ape demonstrates its amazing acrobatic abilities in the lush, natural surroundings of the Tropical Asia exhibit.

An endangered orangutan explores its "tropical" home. In order to re-create a tropical rain forest in Seattle, zoo horticulturists deftly incorporated temperate look-alikes into the exhibit.

Concealed by a cloak of lush foliage, an ocelot awaits its prey in the award-winning Tropical Rain Forest exhibit.

A young child marvels at a river otter and a mountain goat, residents of the award-winning Northern Trail exhibit.

years, the zoo has received more than 175 sick or injured bald and golden eagles for rehabilitation. Those capable of surviving are returned to the wild and the rest are either relocated to other zoos or incorporated into public educational programs where they become ambassadors for their species.

Educating children about animals in nature is a thrust of Woodland Park Zoo's activities. The educational experience includes public programs that offer close-up encounters with animals and zoo staff, interactive exhibit signs, and an interpretive program featuring a number of tactile connections with works of art. Children can touch life-size bronze sculptures of otters, ravens, gorillas, and even a baby elephant—making a visit to the zoo more than just a visual experience. They can explore a bear cave, climb into a wolf den, or scramble on a giant spiderweb. Kids can also ride ponies; touch sheep, goats, and other domestic animals at the Family Farm; examine smaller creatures, including insects, in other zoo facilities; and have hands-on wildlife experiences at the Discovery Room.

Things to Do at the Zoo

Visitors can watch elephant keepers bathe their charges every morning in the Thai-designed Elephant House, watch raptors soar overhead at the Raptor Center, or touch a snake at one of the regularly scheduled public programs. In addition, new events happen all the time at the zoo, and schedules are listed at zoo gates, at Guest Services, or in the Seattle Rotary Education Center.

Year-round, gardeners can buy a high-grade bulk compost called Zoo Doo, a sweet-smelling blend of straw bedding and the generous manure contributions of elephants, ponies, hippos, elk, wallaroos, and other herbivores. With zoo animals generating 50 tons of manure each month, the program raises $25,000 annually while saving the zoo nearly $60,000 in disposal fees every year.

During the popular weekly ZooTunes summer concert series, which kicks off in July, locals relax to music while enjoying a picnic in the North Meadow. The Rain Forest Cafe and its indoor and outdoor food court serve specialty foods from national franchises, as well as cater or host private parties, corporate events, and weddings. To raise money, the zoo sponsors the Jungle Party auction every July, where it auctions unusual art, including paintings by elephants, to some 800 invited guests.

"It takes a whole community to make a zoo," says Zoo Director Dave Towne. "A strong partnership of government, civic groups, businesses, and individuals generously supports the zoo's mission to promote wildlife conservation, education, research, and recreation." The zoo enjoys the broadest base of support of any attraction in the region, with more than 40,000 household members and some 1.2 million visitors each year.

▶ GERRY ELLIS

▶ CAROL BEACH

▶ KEVIN SCHAFER

Clockwise from top:
A keeper demonstrates the supreme beauty and flight capabilities of our national bird—the bald eagle—at an on-site raptor demonstration.

A lion relaxes in the tall grasses of the African Savanna exhibit, which also features zebras, red-crowned cranes, and giraffes.

A small herd of Asian elephants congregates at the entrance to their impressive indoor accommodations, architecturally inspired by the great temples of Thailand.

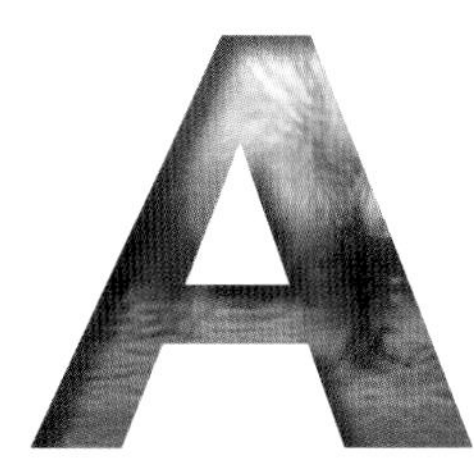

long-standing citizen of the Seattle community, Graham & James traces its roots in the Pacific Northwest back to 1906, when the late Charles Riddell began his practice in Seattle. Richard Riddell joined his father in the practice in 1941, which led to the partnership of Riddell, Williams, Bullitt & Walkinshaw. In January 1996, the firm merged with Graham & James, a leading international law firm with more than 30 offices throughout the United States, Asia, Europe, Australia, and the Middle East. The combined firm has the largest network of international law offices of any firm in the Northwest, enabling it to serve clients wherever they do business.

Graham & James concentrates its practice in the areas of trade, technology, and finance. Approximately 50 percent of the practice is in corporate and commercial matters, with litigation and alternative dispute resolution making up the other half. Working with leading American and multinational companies to pioneer markets and uncover opportunities, the firm serves clients across a broad spectrum of industries, including electronics and telecommunications, hotel and recreational properties, real estate, retail, energy, transportation, manufacturing, entertainment, and insurance.

With offices in the world's predominant business and financial centers, Graham & James' substantial national and international legal practice includes more than 400 attorneys in eight domestic offices, including New York, Washington, D.C., Los Angeles, San Francisco, and Seattle, plus foreign offices in Tokyo, Beijing, London, and Milan. Through a global network of affiliate offices, clients have access to an additional 1,000 lawyers practicing in virtually every area of the law.

Among American law firms, Graham & James has one of the leading Asian practices and the most extensive Japan practice, going back to 1955 when it established its office in Tokyo. The firm was helping American, European, and Japanese clients with interests in China even before it opened its Beijing office in 1979, as one of three original American law firms authorized to operate in China. The firm also has built a strong presence in the fast-growing economies of Southeast Asia.

Graham & James values diversity in the firm. Its team of attorneys and staff, among whom some 20 languages are spoken, is rich in ethnicity, nationality, and business experience, and is sensitive to the cultural nuances that make or break a deal. These qualities benefit the firm's clients worldwide.

A Strong Northwest Presence

As a gateway to the Pacific Rim and the dominant business center in the Northwest, Seattle is home to Graham & James' second-largest office, which employs more

Graham & James' office is located in the heart of Seattle's financial district in the 1001 Fourth Avenue Plaza Building.

FRED HOUSEL, PHOTOGRAPHY

JOEL SACKETT

than 80 lawyers. The firm has one of the largest and fastest-growing finance groups in the Pacific Northwest, handling all types of financial matters, from organizing and financing new ventures to initial public offerings, mergers and acquisitions, and municipal finance.

Graham & James also boasts the largest intellectual property practice of any full-service firm on the West Coast, with more than 40 patent attorneys who use their backgrounds in science and engineering to provide advice on the protection of intellectual property through patents, trademarks, and copyrights.

Clients such as Active Voice Corp., Airborne Freight Corporation, Emerson Electric Co., Redhook Ale Brewery, Inc., and WestCoast Hotels, Inc. reflect the diversity of businesses served by the Seattle office. The firm serves a range of clients from individual entrepreneurs and start-up businesses to large publicly traded companies.

"Our lawyers serve as business savvy advisers, not just legal technicians, guiding clients through a complex legal world," says Karen Jones, principal and chairman of the marketing group in the Seattle office. "We know the ins and outs of our clients' business and take a long-term view to support their business development."

Locally, Graham & James is well known for partnering with companies to nurture their growth. Airborne Freight Corporation, familiar to most as Airborne Express, was founded in Seattle in 1949. The firm has provided legal counsel to Airborne for more than 45 years, helping guide the company from five employees to a worldwide organization rated as the third-largest overnight air express company in the nation.

CHRIS BENNION

The firm's work with Redhook Ale Brewery began with the brewery's incorporation in 1981, shortly before it began operations in a converted muffler shop. Redhook is credited with launching the craft beer industry in the Pacific Northwest, the nation's most developed market for craft beer. Graham & James has guided Redhook from capitalization to distribution. The firm helped the brewery raise $12 million in venture capital, establish an unprecedented distribution alliance with Anheuser-Busch, Inc., and conduct a public offering. Today, Redhook is one of the leading brewers of craft beers in the country, with distribution in 47 states and breweries on both coasts.

Rooted in the Community

Bolstering a rich tradition of community involvement, pro bono work is a strong cultural component of Graham & James. Attorneys are involved with more than 100 civic, environmental, social services, arts, legal, and political organizations in the Puget Sound area.

One long-time example is the firm's involvement with A Contemporary Theatre (ACT), which the firm helped found. In recent years, the firm provided legal advice to help ACT acquire and remodel the historic Eagles building, as well as obtain financing, develop low-income housing on-site, and sell ACT's former building.

Clockwise from top left:
Every night Airborne Express processes more than a million shipments at its central sort facility in Wilmington, Ohio.

Redhook Ale Brewery combines state-of-the-art brewing technology with innovative architecture to create a popular visitor destination. Guests can observe the entire brewing and packaging process and then sample the full lines of distinctive beers.

Kreielsheimer Place, A Contemporary Theatre's new, $30.4 million facility in downtown Seattle, holds two main theaters and a third, smaller cabaret space.

Since its founding in Seattle in 1906 by brothers D.B. and T.M. Morgan, Northern Life Insurance Company's central mission has been to provide the best long-term financial security possible for its customers. ■ Today, Northern Life serves clients in 49 states and the District of Columbia. It focuses on helping K-12 educators and other employees of nonprofit organizations understand their risks and opportunities, and plan for a secure financial future. In addition, it holds seminars on state retirement benefits, Social Security, and planning for retirement. Northern Life's field force is perfect for the task: Approximately 75 percent of its agents are former teachers, which gives them a special insight into their customers' needs.

Northern Life President and CEO Michael Dubes, CLU, ChFC, CFP, LLIF

Delivering an Important Message

Unfortunately, retirement is one of the last things that crosses many educators' minds. That's a glaring oversight when one considers that waiting just a single year to start putting money aside can mean thousands of dollars less on hand at retirement. Furthermore, according to the American Council of Life Insurers, the average 55-year-old has only approximately $10,000 in personal funds outside of employer contributions to his or her pension funds—far too little to finance a comfortable retirement. That's why Northern Life works tirelessly to spread the word about the need to provide for retirement.

A TSA Pioneer

In 1973, Northern was one of the first companies to market an internal revenue code (IRC) Section 403(b) tax-sheltered annuity (TSA), a retirement funding account designed especially for educators and employees of eligible nonprofit organizations. A TSA has important advantages over a taxable account. First, contributions are not taxed until they're withdrawn, reducing a client's current income taxes. Second, interest also accumulates tax-free until withdrawals are made. This leads to rapid accumulation compared to a taxable account. Then, at retirement, the client can receive income from the TSA in a variety of ways.

For more than 20 years, Northern Life's products have stood the test of time. This performance has made the company one of the country's three leading providers of TSAs to educators in K-12 school districts. Professionals in higher education, government agencies, and qualifying nonprofit organizations round out the client base. In addition to 403(b) TSAs, Northern Life also markets IRA and IRC 457 annuities, as well as nonqualified annuities funded by after-tax contributions.

Northern Life is proud of its community commitment, supporting such organizations as the United Way and partnering with school districts to support education.

Commonsense Investing—Superior Performance

Northern Life carefully diversifies its investment portfolio by investment type, region, and industry to insulate its clients' money from downturns in specific markets. Consequently, even in a challenging market, Northern Life has continued to demonstrate superior performance and record-breaking growth. TSA premiums shot from roughly $50 million in 1985 to $494 million at year-end 1995, while statutory assets surged from approximately $700 million to nearly $5 billion.

As a member of the Minneapolis-based ReliaStar Financial Corp. (NYSE:RLR), Northern Life can leverage a full range of benefits and services to its customers, including mortgage and credit card services.

Community Support

Throughout its 91-year history, Northern Life has established a strong tradition of community support. It customarily devotes 2 percent of its pretax profits to charitable giving and has won awards from the United Way for employee participation.

Northern Life reaches out to young people through the Urban Scholar program, in which eight to 10 at-risk 11th graders spend their summers learning job skills and job preparedness, including a weeklong computer training camp. At the end of the summer, the participants interview at a job fair and are hired by local firms.

Other examples of Northern Life's community involvement include Partners in Public Education, a program that pairs private companies with public schools in a cooperative relationship; United Way; March of Dimes; Northwest AIDS Foundation; Pacific Science Center; Corporate Council for the Arts; a selection of children's programs on the Public Broadcasting System; and *All Things Considered* on National Public Radio. Northern Life also supports a program that educates battered women so they can return to the mainstream population. In addition, a company-sponsored program through the Seattle Symphony gives every fifth grader in the Seattle area the opportunity to attend a concert and brings symphony members into the classroom to introduce children to music and musical instruments.

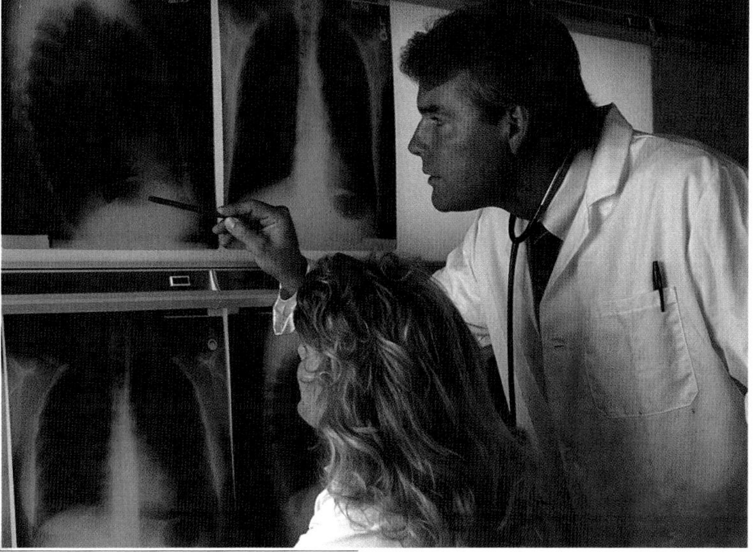

Northern Life's client base includes professionals in higher education, government agencies, and qualifying nonprofit organizations.

Support for Educators

Several years ago, Northern Life established the Educators' Advisory board, a group of outstanding educators and administrators from around the country, to help it focus more clearly on the financial needs of its main customers. Then, in 1996, it launched the Education's Unsung Heroes Award, a scholarship program that awarded a total of $200,000 to 80 K-12 educators across the nation who demonstrated innovation and originality in teaching. In addition to the standard $2,000 scholarship, the top three winners were recognized with additional awards of $5,000, $10,000, and $25,000 to be used to further their projects.

Northern Life's Education's Unsung Heroes Award has generated considerable excitement. "You have no idea what this award means to educators who struggle for every dollar and resource to do their jobs," says Northern Life President and CEO Michael Dubes, CLU, ChFC, CFP, LLIF. "We're giving them the resources to pursue their creative talents and incorporate new ideas into teaching. The outcome has been tremendous."

Whether by ensuring financial security or supporting charitable organizations, for nearly a century, Northern Life Insurance Company has displayed its commitment to helping people. Carrying on that commitment, the company stands ready to serve the Puget Sound community, its clients, and members of the educational community for years to come.

Northern Life focuses on helping K-12 educators and other employees of nonprofit organizations understand their risks and opportunities, and plan for a secure financial future.

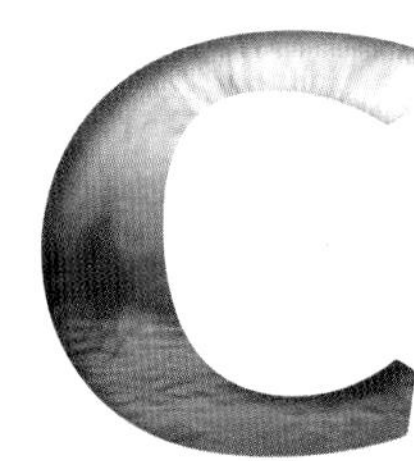ELEBRATING ITS 90TH ANNIVERSARY IN 1997, CHILDREN'S Hospital and Medical Center greets the 21st century as the premier regional pediatric care center in the Pacific Northwest, with national prominence for its clinical expertise and affiliation with the University of Washington School of Medicine. Children's was founded in 1907 by a group of 24 women who shared a vision of a hospital that would provide care to any child in need. That vision continues today.

The hospital's mission is to serve children of the Pacific Northwest with the best medical care. Research and teaching are also important parts of Children's mission. A long-standing affiliation with the University of Washington has provided Children's the opportunity to develop into a renowned research center and to serve as an academic resource for future health care providers. The hospital's mission also includes child advocacy.

Of the 140,000 patient visits that occur at Children's each year, many are children whose families cannot cover the cost of health care. The hospital provides about $30 million in uncompensated care, a testimony to its founding mission.

Today, most children rarely require a hospital stay, but when they do, they often represent the most complex conditions and critical illnesses. The medical center also treats children whose illnesses may be less severe, requiring a short stay or day surgery. Children's serves as the regional pediatric referral center for health care providers in Washington, Alaska, Montana, and Idaho (WAMI). Coordinated regional care benefits the community by eliminating duplication of medical services, which leads to cost and use efficiencies. The core of Children's patient care commitment is represented by a medical staff of 200 full-time physicians on the faculty at the University of Washington. Children's pediatric specialists are recognized nationally for their expertise, representing a broad spectrum that includes cancer, heart disease and cardiovascular surgery, birth defects, nephrology, gastroenterology, infectious disease, pulmonary disease, plastic and reconstructive surgery, rehabilitation medicine, and urology, to name a few. Children's medical staff extends into the community, with about 1,000 physicians who refer and care for pediatric patients.

Not all patients come to Children's for their specialty care. Physicians from the hospital provide clinical services, training, and other resources throughout the

Providing the best care possible to children from the Pacific Northwest is a key mission of Children's Hospital and Medical Center, which was established in Seattle in 1907.

DON SEABROOK

MICHAEL RAMEY

WAMI region in coordination with local providers. In Alaska, for example, outreach visits by Children's ensures that care for children takes place where it will best serve them, preferably close to home or, if necessary, at the hospital.

In collaboration with the Fred Hutchinson Cancer Research Center, Children's treats patients with leukemia and tumors, and works closely with the State of Washington to develop programs for children with chronic illnesses.

The Seattle campus has 208 beds and 40 outpatient clinics, which provide specialty care from asthma to transplantation. Children's Bellevue on the Eastside provides a variety of specialty clinics, while Odessa Brown Children's Clinic in Seattle's central area offers primary medical, dental, and mental health services. Children's also oversees an extensive home health care program throughout the Pacific Northwest, with expertise in complex pediatric therapies for intravenous infusion and respiratory care, in-home nursing care, medical equipment, and short-term staffing for hospitals and clinics.

The Importance of Research and Teaching

More than 130 funded research projects at Children's pursue an array of clinical and laboratory investigations, with an emphasis on infectious disease, virology, gastroenterology, nephrology, surgery, and audiology. Several long-standing research programs have resulted in breakthroughs that contribute to the prevention of childhood illnesses and the overall well-being of children. New life-sustaining therapies for children with cystic fibrosis and *E. coli* infections, for example, stem directly from the hospital's clinical and laboratory investigations.

Nationally, Children's is recognized as a premier training center for pediatricians, surgeons, and other clinicians with a broad scope of regional outreach programs as part of its active training program.

A Healing Environment

The environment in which children heal has always been important at Children's. Landscaped gardens surround the hospital; in the lobbies, large aquariums with colorful fish await patients. Trains, rockets, whales, and balloons guide visitors down corridors flanked with artwork and murals.

There's an exceptional playroom that offers activities and entertainment for patients; a special recreation center for teens; a swimming pool for therapy; and a parent resource center complete with a resource library, chapel, a place to read and relax, and showers.

The staff at Children's believes that family support is critical in the healing process. To encourage parents to be with their children, accommodations for overnight stays are available in many of the inpatient rooms. In addition, two parent houses close by are also open to families.

In Touch with the Community

The medical center touches people's lives through educational programs that promote children's health and safety. The Children's Resource Line is staffed by nurses with pediatric expertise who are available daily, 7 a.m. to midnight, to answer questions about child health, child development, and parenting, as well as to provide referrals. The hospital also maintains a Web site with information about services and events.

Community support, whether through financial contributions or gifts of time, allows Children's to thrive and flourish. More than 450 guilds in the Seattle area and in the region offer opportunities for involvement. And there are about 850 volunteers throughout the year who donate their time, either at the hospital or for special events.

Throughout its 90-year commitment to serving the unique health care needs of children, Children's Hospital and Medical Center has distinguished itself as the pediatric referral center contributing to the overall quality of health care for children in Seattle, the surrounding communities, and the Pacific Northwest.

▶ FRED HOUSEL

▶ FRED HOUSEL

Children's Hospital and Medical Center serves as both a community and a regional source for health care providers for families from Washington, Alaska, Montana, and Idaho.

Seattle's historic Pike Place Market looks and operates like a small, busy city within a city. Often described as "the heart and soul of Seattle," the Market is truly a cultural crossroads, teeming with energy and diversity. ■ The task of caretaking the Market lies primarily with the Pike Place Market

Often described as "the heart and soul of Seattle," the Pike Place Market is truly a cultural crossroads, teeming with energy and diversity.

Preservation and Development Authority (PDA), a nonprofit public corporation chartered by the City of Seattle. Revenues for operating the Market are derived through tenant rents and other PDA property management activities. The Market is not tax supported or subsidized by city government.

The Market is a nine-acre labyrinth of streets, alleys, interior arcades, stairs, and walkways connecting hundreds of shops, open-air stalls, and residential apartments. The PDA owns, manages, and maintains about 80 percent of the properties within the Market.

Historic Firsts

The Pike Place Market is the first historic district in America created by a popular vote of the people. It is also the first in which traditional uses of space were preserved along with the historic architecture. The PDA is charged with maintaining the traditions, practices, and character of the Market as an authentic, working marketplace and as a residential neighborhood with community and social traditions.

The Market's heart is its farmer's market—a full-time, year-round sales arena that has operated continuously on the same ground since 1907. Maintaining and enhancing the Pike Place Market as a direct-sales outlet for local farmers is a primary purpose of the PDA. To this end, the PDA provides marketing and technical support programs to growers who sell at the Market, as well as actively advocating for the broader interests of small agriculture throughout Washington State.

Nearly all of the approximately 600 businesses that operate in the Market each year are independent, family-owned and -operated enterprises—from specialty merchandise retailers to farmers and craftspeople. PDA leasing and property management practices are geared specifically toward maintaining the Market as an incubator for start-up busi-

nesses. Chain stores and franchises are not allowed to lease space in the Market, although a number of businesses have grown from their Market beginnings to much larger success.

The Market Foundation

The PDA's charter also includes a commitment to support housing and human services for low-income and elderly residents in the downtown neighborhood. To accomplish these objectives, a private, nonprofit organization called the Market Foundation was formed in 1982. Through ongoing fund-raising efforts, the Market Foundation supports the work of a Market senior center, health clinic, child care center, and food bank. The Market Foundation also raises funds to help meet the capital needs of the Market's heavily used historic buildings, housing, and human services facilities.

Although Seattle's downtown residential population is growing, low-income housing is threatened. Part of the PDA's mission is to maintain low-income and affordable housing in the Market, which includes about 300 apartment units. The PDA participates in programs to support low-income residents and is a strong advocate for new programs on their behalf.

The Pike Place Market—Seattle's public market center—has thrived under public ownership. While remaining true to its century-old roots as a local shopper's market, today's Market is a highly diverse and dynamic retail center, generating approximately $75 million in sales each year, and fueling many millions more as Seattle's leading downtown attraction.

The PDA is proud of the role it has played in preserving and perpetuating what is widely recognized as one of the world's premier public markets and most successful downtown revitalization projects. The Pike Place Market stands as a vibrant example of the success that can be achieved when public and private interests cooperate in the spirit of true community building.

Clockwise from top left:
The Market's economy has always revolved around food. Through marketing and property management initiatives, the PDA constantly strives to improve the competitive strength of the Market as a premier food center for local shoppers.

The PDA operates programs for both adults and children to learn about the Market community and its resources. Elementary students learn firsthand about life and work as a street performer.

New residential buildings rise from the blocks surrounding the Pike Place Market. The Market has been a major catalyst for both residential and commercial redevelopment in downtown Seattle.

Seattle City Light is proud to have been publicly owned for 87 years. This long tradition in the Pacific Northwest gives the utility continuity and a larger role as a member of the community. As the electrical industry undergoes huge changes, Seattle City Light stands strong in its support of the Puget Sound area. In short, Seattle is a great place to live and to work, and Seattle City Light is committed to keeping it that way. The utility and the community are positioned to prosper in what promises to be a challenging and exciting future.

Through careful management of bold investments made in the past, Seattle City Light remains one of the lowest-cost and most reliable electric service providers in the nation. Seattle City Light is also proud of its environmental stewardship. The ability to provide clean, efficient, reliable, and low-priced electricity has helped make Seattle City Light one of the most successful publicly owned utilities in the nation.

A History of Success

In 1886, Seattle Electric Light Company launched the first lighting system west of the Rocky Mountains—providing streetlights just four years after Thomas Edison perfected the means of lighting a large area from a central source. In 1902, Seattle citizens had the forethought to pass a bond issue to develop the Cedar River as a source of hydroelectric power, which three years later became the nation's first municipally owned hydroelectric project.

In 1910, the City Council established Seattle City Light, formerly called Seattle Lighting Department, and in 1951, citizens voted to make the agency the city's sole supplier of electricity. Today, Seattle City Light operates seven hydroelectric generating stations and supplies electric power to a service area that stretches beyond the city limits.

With 20 percent of its customers residing outside the city, Seattle City Light strives to customize solutions to the energy needs of both residential and commercial users. It is also one of a handful of utilities nationwide to be recognized for exemplary demand-side management programs to reduce energy consumption. Customers receive innovative and cost-effective solutions that help them manage their energy use. As part of this program, Seattle City Light collaborated with The Boeing Company to make a major product line more energy efficient, and provided new, energy efficient lighting to the Paramount Theatre during its recent refurbishing. In addition, the agency participates in the design of buildings through its Energy Smart Design program.

Owned by the community, Seattle City Light also operates the most extensive program on the West Coast targeted to low-income residents. For this program,

Clockwise from top:
At night, Seattle is ablaze with light. As the provider of the lowest-cost, most reliable electricity in urban America, Seattle City Light is proud of its contribution to Seattle.

City Light played a major role in the growth of Seattle. The utility's headquarters were located at the intersection of Third and Spring for many years. One of the public utility's many responsibilities is maintaining street lights in its city.

First City Light's line crews restore power to their own customers. Then, shown here, they wait for a ferry to take them across the sound to help a neighboring utility restore power to its customers.

it provides power at half the normal rate, and has implemented a number of highly successful conservation strategies. The utility also coordinates tree plantings in the city and operates a tree trimming program that enhances system reliability while preserving Seattle's urban forest.

Seattle City Light manages its many environmental resources carefully. Not only is Diablo Dam a source of power, it is also a factor in the ecosystem of the Skagit River.

Fiscally and Environmentally Sound

Dedicated to keeping Seattle beautiful, Seattle City Light promotes long-term sustainability of the ecosystems it affects throughout its operations. The utility's environmental stewardship extends to how it manages its assets, contracts to purchase power, and makes resource acquisition decisions to meet this goal. In 1991, Seattle City Light made a commitment to meet all load growth by the year 2002 through energy conservation. To date, the utility has saved enough electricity to match the load growth—the ingenuity of utility employees saved more than $200,000 in one year—and is right on target in meeting this goal.

Through its new capital planning process, the agency has eliminated projects that are of less strategic or operational value—resulting in savings of $38 million in 1996, $31 million in 1998, and projected savings of $150 million by the year 2002.

Seattle City Light is a national model for its agreements with the Federal Energy Regulatory Commission to protect the environment and cultural resources within its jurisdiction. The agency has achieved spectacular success with increasing salmon populations below the Skagit Hydroelectric Project. Both 1994 and 1995 were banner years for returning salmon, demonstrating the payoff of the utility's operation of the Skagit dams on a salmon-protection-first policy. The utility is currently developing an environmental learning center on Diablo Lake devoted to the study of the North Cascade ecosystems. The purchase of 6,000 acres of wildlife habitat and the funding of a laboratory facility to research wildlife populations and behaviors are some of the ways in which Seattle City Light preserves the natural beauty of the Northwest.

Success with increased salmon populations is not lost on Seattle's public school kids, who come face-to-face with the spawning salmon as part of Seattle City Light's extensive public education outreach program. Students also learn about electrical safety, maintenance, and the distribution service through demonstrations at public schools by Hard Hat Heroes, who are members of the agency's line crews.

Seattle City Light is part of a very successful local government, reflected in part by the utility's location downtown in the city-owned, 62-floor Key Tower. The agency's success begins with its 1,800 employees, many of whom donate thousands of hours and dollars to charities, Annual Spring Clean, Earth Day projects, student tutoring, school boards, parent-teacher associations, food banks, social service agencies, and crisis intervention programs.

"Our customer partnerships encompass more than energy efficiency planning and neighborhood projects," says Mayor Norm Rice. Seattle City Light actively engages citizens in decision making in order to chart a course that solves today's diverse energy needs and leaves a healthy legacy for future generations.

The utility's dedication to diversity is one of its strengths. Today, women join men on Seattle City Light's line crews (left).

Students learn about electrical safety, maintenance, and the distribution service through demonstrations at public schools by Hard Hat Heroes, who are members of the agency's line crews (right).

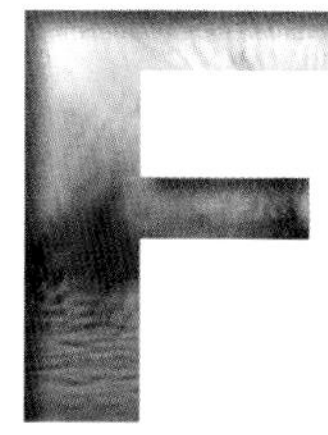

Founded in Seattle in 1910, Skyway Luggage Company's history has paralleled that of the city that continues to be its home. Like the city, Skyway was founded by an energetic youth—company founder A.J. Kotkins arrived from Lithuania as a teenager. And like the city, Skyway developed self-sufficiency to counter being located in a corner of the United States, far from eastern sources of supply and the East Coast population centers where customers for its products lived. But, just as Seattle has emerged as a prime gateway to "the Pacific Century," Skyway today considers its location as a key, sustainable advantage for the millennium to come.

Founder A.J. Kotkins behind the counter of his store circa 1910

A family-owned business originally called Seattle Suitcase Trunk and Bag Manufacturing Company, Skyway is today the largest independently owned luggage supplier in America. When Chairman Henry L. Kotkins Sr. took over the small business upon the death of his father in 1936, he decided to concentrate on making hand luggage instead of trunks, which were then the mainstay of the industry. Capitalizing on the romantic appeal of air travel, he gave up the company's original Bulldog brand name in favor of Skyway, which later became the company name as well.

Henry L. Kotkins Sr., chairman, Skyway Luggage Company

With close to 90 years of experience, Skyway has watched competitors come and go. The company has flourished because of a dedication to adapting to the changing needs of consumers. Skyway has always been committed to providing a highly functional "box" for the traveler, and doing so with lots of value and at a fair price. Driven by a continual search for improvement, Skyway pioneered color in luggage, chrome hardware, combination locks, performance fabrics, wheels, and many other innovations that have become industry standards. Always looking for functional improvements, the company's upright handle and wheel systems offer the greatest stability and packing capacity on the market. As the company has evolved from producing luggage solely in the United States to manufacturing in Pacific Rim countries, it retains its knowledge of luggage production, which sets it apart from other importers.

Just as in prior years, when the company was willing to invest in manufacturing equipment in order to better serve its customers, it is today constantly investing in software and hardware to more efficiently integrate with its customers. Skyway is committed to having the systems in place to meet its customers' needs. Today, the company operates a virtually seamless system with major retailers, together combining to minimize the time cycle from product sale to replenishment of the shelves.

A Broad Mix of Products

Skyway's product philosophy dictates that each item be on the top rung of quality for its product and value category—whether it is an inexpensive tote or a top-of-the-line garment bag. Within those parameters, Skyway offers a uniquely broad mix of luggage products, spanning most product categories and price ranges. It has long been the company's goal to offer products that are both durable and attractive in a style that's contemporary, but not trendy. With products that are always innovative, distinctive, and of great practical value, the company sells under several brand names, including Skyway Luggage, Ascot International Travel Goods, Northwest Trails, and Lewis & Hyde. Skyway is also the licensee for the American Airlines brand name and produces a private label for several select companies. The company sells to retailers in the United States, Canada, and Mexico, as well as Europe, the Middle East, Asia, South Africa, and South America.

A Long-Term Perspective

Skyway attributes its success to putting its customers first, industry leadership in product innovation, a savvy sense of the market, a commitment to offering an extremely strong price-value relationship, family ownership, and, most important, a high standard of ethics in all its dealings. "Skyway is a company steeped in a history of taking a long-term perspective and always doing what is right for our customers, our partners, our employees, and our community—no matter what the short-term costs," says Bill Wilhoit, executive vice president and chief operating officer.

This approach is evident in the way Skyway relates to its community. Seattle has a rich, multicultural fabric and an orientation toward innovation, high principles, and the environment, which the company has embraced in its business practices. Henry Kotkins Sr. has been recognized as a true civic leader, active in building international business for the region, promoting the local economy, and serving for 14 years as a commissioner of the Port of Seattle. The company embraced equal opportunity employment practices long before they were mandated. Skyway has had a wonderful no-strike relationship with its employee union for more than 50 years, and speaks with pride about each of its employees, some of whom have been at Skyway more than 40 years.

"Even though our Seattle location presented some real challenges when my father was growing the business from a regional to an international player, the opportunity to live and work in this wonderful city has always been extremely valuable to us," says Henry "Skip" Kotkins Jr., president and CEO of the company and grandson of the founder. "We believe that supporting and being involved with the civic, cultural, and educational institutions that make this city so special is an essential element of good corporate citizenship."

As one of the oldest family businesses in Seattle, Skyway Luggage Company is proud of its heritage in the Pacific Northwest. When the 14 Asia-Pacific Economic Cooperation Group (APEC) nations first met in Seattle in the early 1990s, Skyway noted that it had ongoing business relationships in all but one of those nations. This fact emphasizes that, with its location at the strategic crossroads of international trade, the company looks forward to many more years of successful business in a vibrant, successful community.

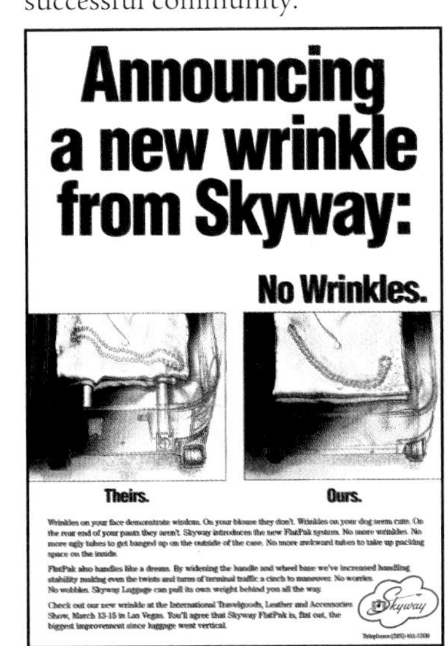

In its ninth decade, the company is still a products innovator.

Skyway Luggage Company's roots and understanding of manufacturing set it apart from its competitors—in the 1940s (shown at left) and today.

Swedish Medical Center opened in 1910 as a small, 24-bed facility called Swedish Hospital. It was the dream of immigrant Dr. Nils Johanson, who founded the hospital with loans of $1,000 each from 10 Swedish friends. Johanson led Swedish Hospital for its first 40 years, and his vision for the future has helped Swedish become the largest, most comprehensive medical center in the Pacific Northwest, with 1,900 physicians and nearly 4,000 employees.

For almost 90 years, Swedish has remained a nonprofit medical facility. It delivers more babies, treats more cancer and AIDS patients, and performs more surgeries than any other hospital in Washington State. Swedish's flagship campus, located on First Hill near downtown Seattle, spans 13 city blocks and serves approximately 600,000 patients each year. The 697-bed medical center is a regional referral center for several major medical specialties. Physicians throughout the Pacific Northwest and around the world refer patients to Swedish.

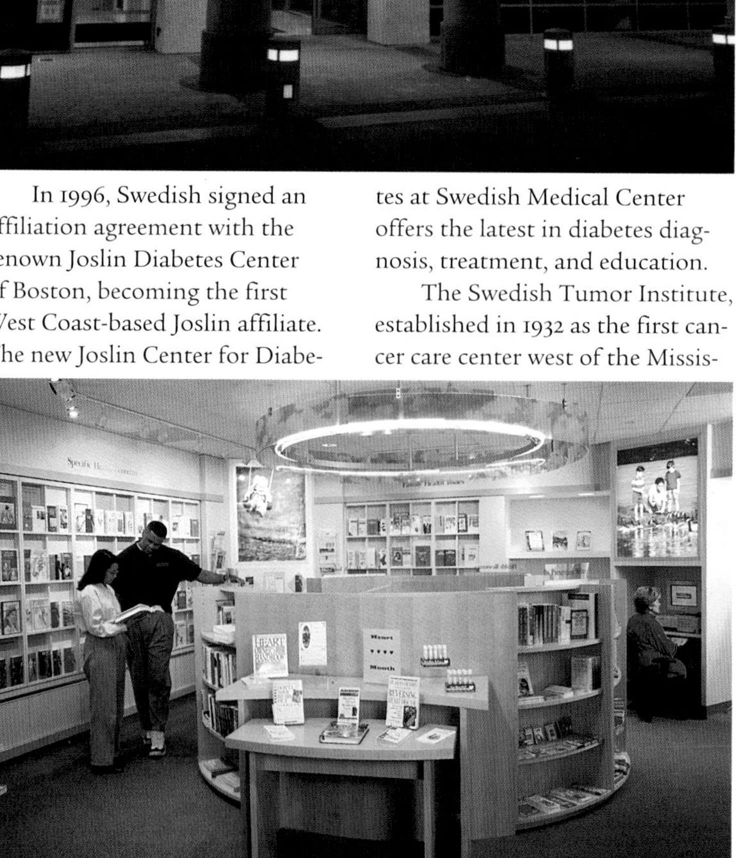

Innovative and Comprehensive Care

Swedish is proud if its many firsts in the medical field. The center's infertility program was the first in the Northwest to perform in vitro fertilization and the first to deliver in vitro twins. Swedish's Organ Transplant program was the first in the Northwest to perform a kidney transplant from an unrelated donor.

In 1996, Swedish signed an affiliation agreement with the renown Joslin Diabetes Center of Boston, becoming the first West Coast-based Joslin affiliate. The new Joslin Center for Diabetes at Swedish Medical Center offers the latest in diabetes diagnosis, treatment, and education.

The Swedish Tumor Institute, established in 1932 as the first cancer care center west of the Missis-

Clockwise from top:
Swedish's flagship campus, located on First Hill near downtown Seattle, spans 13 city blocks and serves approximately 600,000 patients each year.

With an eye to meeting community needs and making medical information more accessible, Swedish opened the Health Resource Center, which offers a wide range of health information for free or for purchase.

In addition to providing general medical and surgical care, Swedish Medical Center/Ballard boasts several special programs.

sippi, treats more patients each year for more types of cancer than any other facility in the Pacific Northwest. Each year, more than 75,000 patient visits are recorded, representing nearly 100 different types of cancer. In a long-standing partnership with the Fred Hutchinson Cancer Research Center, Swedish also provides hospital care for the the center's inpatient bone marrow transplants.

Swedish also specializes in high-risk pregnancies and newborn intensive care, in addition to delivering thousands of healthy babies each year. It operates one of only two level III neonatal intensive care units in the Seattle area. With one of the most active orthopedic programs in the country, Swedish performs more than 6,000 orthopedic surgeries each year. The Cardiac Services program at Swedish is also one of the most comprehensive in the Northwest, treating people with heart disease from as far away as Alaska.

The Neurodiagnostics program at Swedish treats patients with neurological disorders and head and back injuries, and those recovering from strokes and neurosurgery. Swedish's Pain Management Service provides consultations, evaluation, and treatment of difficult pain problems.

Swedish operates the largest hospital-based AIDS program in Washington, serving more than one-third of the approximately 2,000 AIDS patients in King County with inpatient, outpatient, and home care. Patients in the acute care unit are supported by an interdisciplinary team with extensive experience helping patients with the physical and emotional challenges of AIDS.

Partners in Caring

In 1992, Swedish merged with Ballard Community Hospital to add Swedish Medical Center/Ballard to the Swedish system. The 163-bed medical center, in addition to providing general medical and surgical care, boasts several special programs. Its Eating Disorders unit is the only hospital-based program in a five-state region that treats bulimia, anorexia, and compulsive overeating.

Some 40 million Americans suffer from one of 84 sleep disorders, yet only 5 percent are diagnosed. Since 1989, Swedish/Ballard has diagnosed and treated patients with sleep disorders and conducted sleep studies. Swedish/Ballard also operates an Addiction Recovery Services program offering detoxification and rehabilitation to inpatients and outpatients, as well as special programs for seniors and pregnant women. The Transitional Care Unit at Ballard fulfills a niche by offering cost-effective care for patients no longer needing intensive hospitalization but still requiring therapies and nursing care before returning home. Swedish also has a Home Health and Hospice program, which provides a full spectrum of health care services in the home.

In 1995, Swedish formed a partnership with Pacific Medical Center, a regional leader in outpatient services, managed care, and ambulatory care. Through Pacific Medical's collection of clinics, Swedish is finding new opportunities to help the medically underserved.

Charity care is an important part of Swedish's mission. The Paul Glaser Residents Clinic provides free and low-cost surgical care to approximately 800 patients each year. A maternity health clinic serves the prenatal and postnatal needs of uninsured and low-income women. And Swedish physicians and employees contribute free medical services to Healing the Children, a nonprofit organization that treats children from around the world.

With an eye to meeting community needs and making medical information more accessible, Swedish opened the Health Resource Center, which offers a wide range of health information for free or for purchase. Here, patients and their families can find a vast array of information on diseases and treatment alternatives in books and on CD-ROMs, computer databases, and videocassettes. The Health Resource Center is also open to the general public.

Swedish also sponsors free health education classes on topics ranging from birthing to risk assessment for heart disease, to nutrition and smoking cessation. Throughout the year, the medical center hosts free clinics providing vaccines, pregnancy testing, blood pressure checks, and numerous other services.

Since its beginnings as a 24-bed facility, Swedish Medical Center has grown along with Seattle, and continues to meet the changing health care needs of the region.

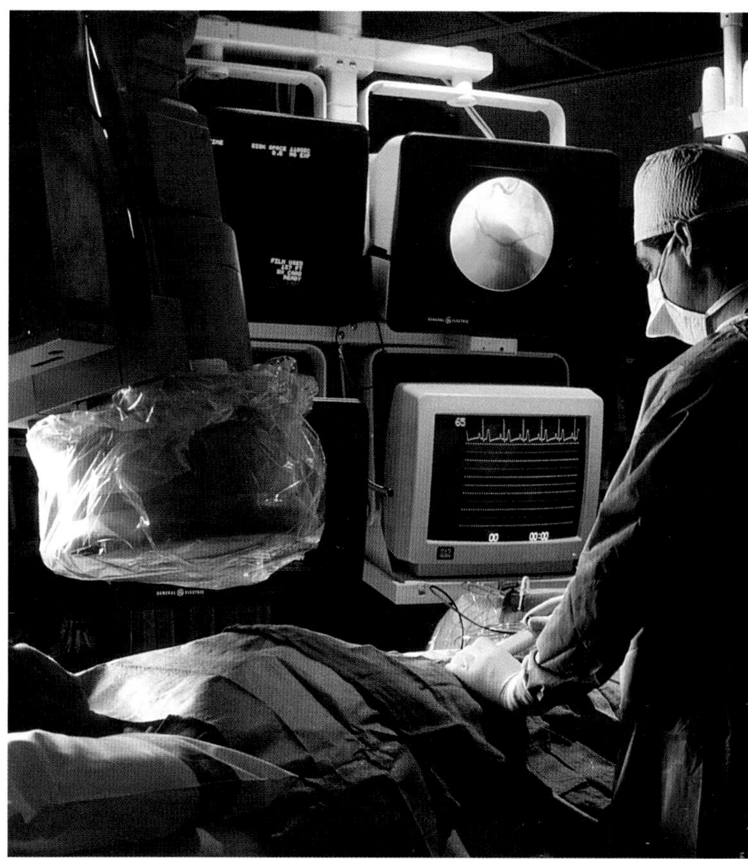

The Cardiac Services program at Swedish is one of the most comprehensive in the Northwest, treating people with heart disease from as far away as Alaska.

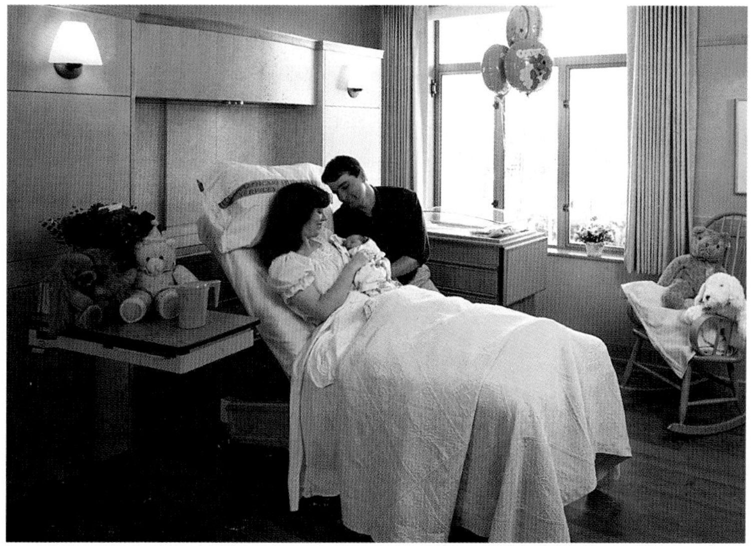

The Women and Infants Center at Swedish Medical Center provides prenatal and postnatal care in a comforting environment.

Few organizations in the United States have a tradition as long or as rich as that of Johnson & Higgins (J&H). Founded at the dawning of the great era of the Yankee clipper ships in 1845, J&H built a business on the New York City waterfront as marine insurance brokers and average adjusters—evaluating the risks faced by a ship's cargo (including pirates, storms, and spoilage) and assessing how to share the losses.

From tragedies like the Chicago fire in 1871 and the San Francisco earthquake in 1906, J&H has evolved with the times. Today, as the world leader in risk management consulting, the firm helps organizations reduce exposures, avoid losses, and limit adverse financial effects.

A Local Presence

J&H opened for business in Seattle in 1912, the same year the New York office was resolving claims on the ill-fated *Titanic*. The Seattle office specializes in risk management consulting, commercial property and casualty insurance brokerage, and employee benefit consulting. Clients in aviation, health care, energy, food, fishing, timber, and other sectors benefit from the expertise of the largest risk control staff in the Puget Sound area.

A team dedicated to Boeing arranges property and casualty insurance for each new generation of Boeing jetliners. The Seattle office has grown with Microsoft since the software giant was small, building its risk management portfolio to serve domestic and international needs. J&H also arranges property and casualty coverage for the Seattle Mariners as well as the Seahawks, and works with several local health care providers to find innovative and cost-effective insurance solutions.

Experienced Consultants

J&H personnel serve as an extension of a client's staff to offer objective advice on risk control. The firm draws on the expertise of structural engineers, claim consultants, industrial hygienists, lawyers, accountants, health care specialists, financial experts, and other professionals, along with an extensive network of brokers. J&H evaluates a client's risks, tailors risk management strategies to the organization, and adapts the program as the company grows and changes. J&H is constantly seeking new solutions beyond traditional boundaries.

A Corporate Citizen

J&H takes pride in its spirit of community leadership. The Seattle office devotes time and resources to Children's Hospital & Medical Center, Fred Hutchinson Cancer Research Center, Boys and Girls Clubs of King County, and United Way, among many other local nonprofit endeavors. A private initiative exposes Seattle public high school students to the world of business through visitor days and a summer internship program for InRoads students. Beginning in 1995, to celebrate the company's 150th anniversary,

Johnson & Higgins' Seattle office devotes resources to Children's Hospital & Medical Center, Fred Hutchinson Cancer Research Center, and United Way, among other nonprofit endeavors.

J&H began closing its offices worldwide for a day of community volunteerism.

An International Leader

The company's clientele spans the spectrum—from art museums to professional athletes, from Fortune 1,000 companies to the Navajo nation. J&H has placed coverage for Andrew Mellon's business properties, horse racing champion Secretariat, and the seven original Mercury astronauts. For the past four Olympic Games—in France, Spain, Norway, and Atlanta—J&H has placed coverage for the Olympic family of athletes, coaches, trainers, officials, and dignitaries, as well as such ancillary activities as new construction, security, transportation, crowd safety, and broadcast television rights. The firm will continue this tradition with the 1998 Winter Olympics in Japan.

J&H's global resources and personnel are at the service of every client. The firm partners with companies worldwide to place complex coverages and resolve local service issues. Business flows both ways in this arrangement, giving international firms unique access to the U.S. market.

Technology for Tomorrow

After a century and a half of new ideas, the pace of innovation is faster than ever. Employees around the globe are connected through InfoEdge, a sophisticated telecommunications network that links underwriters and clients with J&H databases worldwide. InfoEdge, in fact, earned J&H the 1993 *Computer World-Smithsonian* award for innovative information technology solutions, and contributed to its ranking in 1995 as the number one broker in the country by *Corporate Finance* magazine.

J&H's edge in technology has enabled it to develop advanced systems to help clients manage information and improve their ability to control risk and reduce costs.

▲ SEATTLE MARINERS / JOHN CORDES

Clockwise from top:
A team dedicated to Boeing arranges property and casualty insurance for each new generation of Boeing jetliners.

J&H also arranges property and casualty coverage for the Seattle Mariners as well as the Seahawks.

J&H works with several local health care providers, including Group Health, to find innovative and cost-effective solutions.

A New Partnership for the Future

In March 1997, Johnson & Higgins merged with Marsh & McLennan, another longtime industry leader. Begun in 1871, Marsh & McLennan Companies evolved into a worldwide professional services firm offering risk and insurance services, consulting, and investment management.

This joining of the top two companies in insurance services and human resources consulting created the premier firm in the industry. The companies' compatible cultures, talented professionals, and global operations, as well as their dedication to quality service and innovative technology and products, will provide the strength to respond to the increasing and more complex risks facing their clients. The company's new Seattle operation will harness the combined talents and expertise of more than 260 professionals.

The new company name, J&H Marsh & McLennan, Inc., embodies both firms' longstanding heritage of quality, integrity, and exceptional client service.

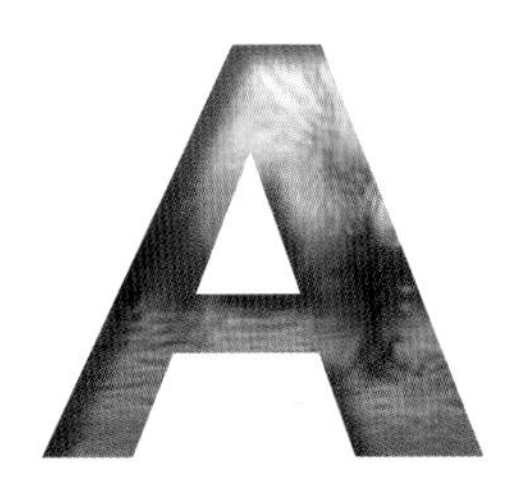

S THE WORLD'S LEADING MANUFACTURER OF COMMERCIAL airliners, The Boeing Company designs, produces, and supports commercial airplanes, defense systems, and defense and civil space systems. But the integrated aerospace company builds more than airplanes; it uses its role as a leader in the business community as a catalyst to build communities. And, just like building airplanes, Boeing believes this is a team effort.

"The job is far too big for any one entity to do alone—government, business, individuals, or nonprofits. It all boils down to people," says Phil Condit, chairman and chief executive officer. "The overwhelming generosity of our employees stems from their sense of community. We reinforce employee giving by valuing and supporting their community involvement, letting people know about opportunities to help, and then letting them fly."

Building Communities

Boeing views its contributions as integral to the health and well-being of people in communities where it does business. Despite the fact that it doesn't sell products to the community at large, it has a vested interest in maintaining the quality of life.

"We can't hope to attract and retain skilled and knowledgeable people in a cultural vacuum," says Condit. "That's why we support activities such as the symphony, the opera, and the zoo. And more important, we can't design and build our airplanes without a skilled and knowledgeable workforce. That's why we're so involved in education."

Boeing strategically focuses its corporate funding where it can do the most good. In 1996, gifts to nonprofit organizations totaled nearly $60 million, including more than $24 million in employee contributions. The single largest portion of corporate contributions, 42 percent in 1996, went to education, including K-12 schools, faculty fellowships, and historically African-American colleges and universities. The balance went to health and human services organizations, cultural organizations, and civic activities. And more than 30 years ago, Boeing created a "rainy day" trust to ensure that it could keep its commitments during the downtimes of its business cycles.

The Boeing Employees Good Neighbor Fund (BEGNF), started in 1951, is the largest employee-owned charitable fund in the world—and is second only to Boeing as the largest grant maker in the Pacific Northwest. While the company pays all administrative costs for BEGNF, an employee-elected board decides where contributed dollars go.

Employees launched the annual Food and Essentials Drive in 1983 after asking Boeing what they could do for the community in lieu of an annual Christmas party. In 1996, they donated more than 1 million pounds of food, an undertaking led by a grassroots team of employees from throughout the company.

Volunteerism is also a significant part of Boeing's culture of citizenship. Boeing employees, retirees (through a volunteer group named the Bluebills), and families of both employees and retirees donate their time and expertise to hundreds of nonprofit organizations in the Puget Sound area. Boeing volunteers serve on boards of directors, as chairs of fundraising for capital campaigns, as members of the BEGNF team projects, as one-on-one volunteers, and in many other ways.

In addition to being Washington State's largest private employer,

By supporting the Seattle Children's Theatre, Boeing helps make theater come alive for young audiences and people of all ages, as in this production of *Alice's Adventures in Wonderland* (left).

The Boeing 777, the world's largest twinjet, provides comfort preferred by passengers worldwide (right).

◀ CHRIS BENNION

Boeing contributes to many of the area's notable organizations. In the Puget Sound region, Boeing supports the Nature Conservancy, Children's Home Society, Seattle Children's Festival, Seattle Children's Theatre, Seattle Art Museum, Boeing Tropical Rainforest at Woodland Park Zoo, and more. Grants and seed money go to initiatives such as low-income dental clinics, Mountains to Sound Greenway, Pike Market Campaign, and Teen Link. Boeing also gives several million dollars to United Ways nationwide and makes multiyear commitments to cultural and arts campaigns.

"Boeing was instrumental in bringing to the Puget Sound the Local Initiatives Support Corporation (LISC), the nation's largest intermediary for community development, and remains our largest corporate funder," says Tom Lattimore, senior program director. "With Boeing's financial help and organizational guidance, LISC has financed approximately 4,000 units of affordable housing in the area."

But monetary contributions aren't enough. That's why Boeing lends employees to work on-site, full-time, to share their management skills with schools, arts organizations, social programs, and the United Way. In return, Boeing people gain a greater sense of how Boeing fits into the community and learn valuable team-building skills from the nonprofit sector.

"Boeing's critical role in developing our vibrant cultural life is very clear," says Peter Donnelly, president of the Corporate Council for the Arts. "Always our largest funder, Boeing leads important arts initiatives throughout the community with generous grants and high-level leadership."

"Boeing's involvement isn't just financial," says Deborah Card, executive director of the Seattle Symphony. "The company has provided visionary support and advice, as well as invaluable project management skills in overseeing the construction of Benaroya Hall, a gift worth an estimated $2 million."

"Four years ago, Boeing stepped forward with seed money to create the conservation career development program, which trains young women and youth of color for careers in conservation," says Marci Cornell, Northwest regional director of the Student Conservation Association. "Through its ongoing support, Boeing demonstrates its commitment to the region's environment."

Known for being involved without being invasive, and for thoroughly researching projects, Boeing does much more than just write a check. "First and foremost, Boeing has been involved in creating quality public schools," says Phil Bussey, president of the Washington Roundtable, an organization comprised of CEOs statewide that Boeing helped create in 1983 to address public policy challenges. "Boeing's leadership has dedicated unparalleled resources and personal time, both in local involvement and state policy. It's based more than on a desire to be a good neighbor. They see their role as a fundamental part of shaping our community and nation's educational future."

▶ JOHN FRASSANITO AND ASSOCIATES

Clockwise from top left:
Phil Condit, chairman and chief executive officer of Boeing, is greatly interested in preparing America's youth for success as future citizens and productive members of the workforce. In 1996, the largest portion of the company's contributions—more than $10.8 million—went to educational programs and projects.

Children from Puget Sound youth agencies experienced air travel for the first time on Kids' Flight, a special event hosted by Boeing and organized by employees through the Boeing Employees Good Neighbor Fund.

Boeing is the prime contractor for NASA on the design and development of the International Space Station, the largest peaceful international scientific endeavor ever undertaken. Scheduled for completion in 2002, the project includes participation by 11 members of the European Space Agency and by Canada, Japan, Russia, and the United States.

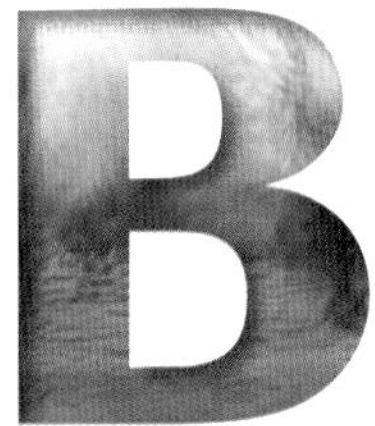

BEEF JERKY, ONCE A STAPLE OF THE OLD WEST COWBOY AND Native American diet, has reemerged as one of America's fastest-growing snacks. As the fat-free era has galloped into the 1990s, Oh Boy! Oberto's 97 percent fat-free Beef Jerky and 98 percent fat-free Turkey Jerky have leaped into the saddle of the snack food mainstream. No longer a male-only commodity, natural jerky's health appeal has lassoed kids and women too.

"Consumers love Oberto Turkey Jerky," says Laura Oberto, president and CEO of Oberto Sausage Company. "It's great tasting, 98 percent fat-free, preservative-free, and only 80 calories per serving. It's turning up in kids' lunches, purses, briefcases, and backpacks, as well as the kitchen pantry."

The company's modern-day version of the pioneer snack has come of age since Oberto's grandfather Constantino started the Oberto Sausage Company in 1918 in Seattle's Rainier Valley. He sold fresh Italian sausage and salami at busy truck stops, corner taverns and markets, and delicatessens. His son Art, who delivered the products as a youth from the sole company truck, assumed the company helm at the age of 16 upon his father's death and later introduced Oh Boy! Oberto natural beef jerky in response to consumer demand.

As the business continued to grow, so did Art's family circle. His wife, Dorothy, and his daughter and three sons have all shared involvement in and contributed to the growth of the Oberto Sausage Company over the years.

Art's daughter, Laura, has worked in virtually every facet of the family business since she was five years old, including spending four years in the jerky-processing plant. She holds a degree in finance from Seattle University. Under her leadership, company sales have tripled since she became president in 1991.

A Healthy Alternative

The meat company has evolved over the years from a small, family-run, entrepreneurial business to the nation's market leader in natural jerky and the second-largest meat snack producer, with a workforce 700 strong. The firm is the top meat snack supplier to the U.S. military and exports to such markets as Japan, Canada, Norway, and Mexico.

Under a no-sacred-cows directive, the company set out to discover what the public thought of its products. Oberto learned that consumers were largely unaware of the low-fat, high-nutritional value of its beef jerky. It began marketing its products to women and children, fine-tuning the drying process to further reduce the fat content, and modifying product ingredients to reflect consumer preference for fewer preservatives. All-natural Turkey Jerky, introduced in 1995, compares favorably with pretzels and low-fat frozen yogurt in nutritional content.

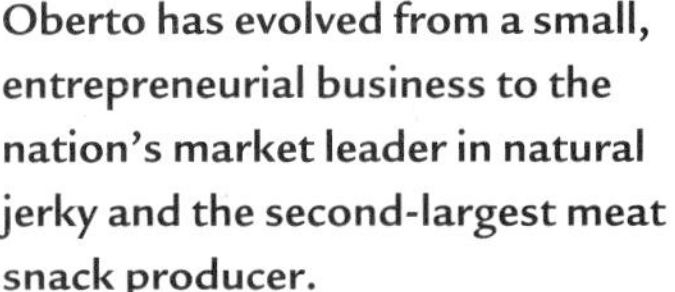

Oberto has evolved from a small, entrepreneurial business to the nation's market leader in natural jerky and the second-largest meat snack producer.

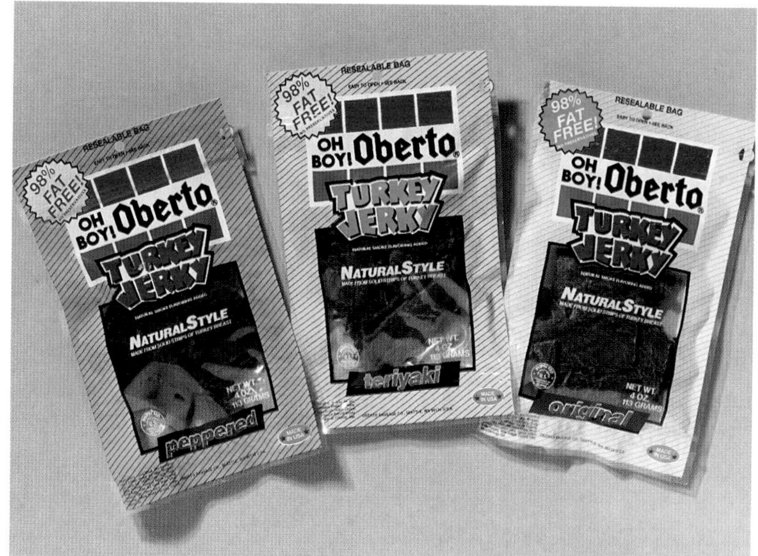

In 1994, Oberto Sausage Company acquired Curtice Burns Meat Snacks, the producer of Lowery's and SmokeCraft products. The $35 million acquisition doubled the company's sales and production capacity, while broadening its distribution and product mix with brands that specialize in cut-and-formed meat products. It also transformed the company into a national player in the food processing business.

Today, Oberto Sausage Company operates three plants in the Seattle area and a plant in Albany, Oregon. It sells natural beef jerky, turkey jerky, kippered beef steak, smoked sausage, salami, pepperoni, and other Italian specialty meats in supermarkets, convenience stores, mass merchandisers, and club warehouses. The firm dominates the western U.S. market, particularly the Pacific Northwest, where its meat snacks consistently rank a 97 percent or greater market share.

Oberto's record-setting growth in the competitive food snack industry is tied to how the company views its competition. "We don't consider ourselves competing with other meat snacks," Oberto says. "We're competing with other snack foods—the whole gamut."

To stay abreast of the competition, the company has invested millions of dollars in installing new equipment and upgrading facilities, including automating its smokehouse and drying equipment. It recently implemented an Enterprise Resource Planning (ERP) system to track all phases of a product, including production, inventories, distribution, and efficiencies.

"It's on the same magnitude as building a new plant," says Oberto, who was named 1996 Executive of the Year by *Snack Food* magazine. "It shows us the materials we've used compared to how much we should have used."

Preparing for the Future

Food safety and the safety of its employees are important issues to the company, which boasts a quality control program that exceeds USDA requirements. Safety and sanitation procedures for new employees are reinforced during 30-, 60-, and 90-day reviews, and a quality checkpoint has been established wherever there is a potential place for human error. The company rewards plants that go accident-free for 100 days by giving every plant employee a free lunch. Plants that are accident-free for one year celebrate with a company-sponsored steak and lobster dinner.

In recognizing the value of input from employees, the company created the Great Idea program, which awards $50 to any employee who proposes an idea that the company later implements. More than 100 ideas are generated every quarter in response to such questions as "How can we eliminate waste?" or "What would make us a better place to work?"

The company is constantly growing its base of products. Oberto recently launched a new line of kippered steaks under the Lowery's brand and has planned a new line of SmokeCraft products. In order to keep up with consumer demand, the company is building a 90,000-square-foot facility in Kent, Washington.

In the coming years, the company looks to strengthen its position in midwestern and eastern U.S. regions; increase sales to mass merchandisers and club warehouses, two key channels for future growth; and penetrate new export markets. Oberto constantly anticipates the future, growing the business while challenging herself to retain the family atmosphere that has made Oh Boy! Oberto the market leader it is today.

Clockwise from top left: Beef Jerky is one of America's fastest-growing snack categories.

Oh Boy! Oberto Turkey Jerky, which is 98 percent fat-free, was developed to meet consumer demand for great-tasting, low-fat, low-calorie snacks with no added preservatives.

Laura Oberto, company president since 1991, has seen the company's sales triple under her leadership.

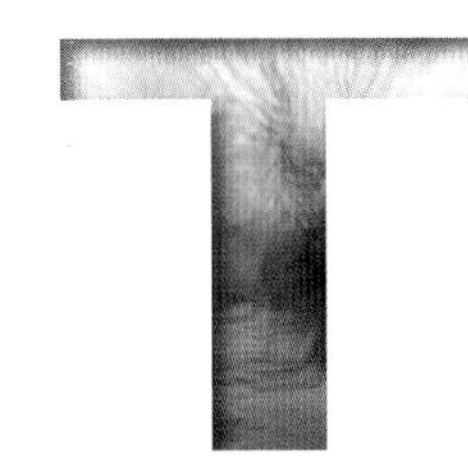HE FUTURE OF THE NATION DEPENDS . . . ON THE EFFICIENCY of industry, and the efficiency of industry depends . . . on the protection of intellectual property." ■ This 1991 quote from Judge J. Posner, Seventh Circuit Court, represents one informed opinion on how important intellectual property has always been to this country. Today, however, technological advances race along so fast that a company's intellectual property can be jeopardized in an instant—along with that company's future. Just one small piece of commercial information can make an enormous difference in protecting a trade secret for the next 20 years.

Seed and Berry's business is to keep one step ahead in this race, creating the best possible legal protection for its clients' intellectual property. The firm is frequently cited as the Northwest's premier intellectual property law firm, with clients ranging from industry giants like Microsoft and MCI to cutting-edge leaders in technology like Immunex and Micron, to household names like Nordstrom, StairMaster, and Red Robin.

"We make a concerted effort to stay focused on our areas of expertise, while continuing to grow," says Richard Seed, co-founder of the firm. Continuing to grow has been a constant for Seed and Berry, thanks in part to two powerful factors.

First, rapid advances in technology have enabled the firm to extend its expertise into a national and international business. A strong presence nationally, the firm has prosecuted patent, trademark, and copyright cases in more than 79 countries, and works with 130 international associates. Many Seed and Berry attorneys have strong foreign language skills, which are invaluable in protecting client interests in European and Asian markets.

The second factor is clearly visible from Seed and Berry's three-story headquarters in Seattle's Columbia Center, where the firm's 120 employees enjoy panoramic vistas of the mountains, sparkling bays, and lakes of their Seattle home. One of the fastest growing economic powerhouses in the country, Seattle's growth has also powered Seed and Berry, enabling the firm to further enhance its standing as a national leader in intellectual property protection.

Seed and Berry was formed in 1962, when Seed and Ben Berry merged two firms that traced their roots to the beginning of the century. Approaching the next century, Seed and Berry has grown into one of the largest intellectual property law firms in the nation for engineering, computer science, and biotechnology, with additional expertise in chemistry, including pharmaceuticals, clothing design

Seed and Berry, LLP is frequently cited as the Northwest's premier intellectual property law firm.

◀ SPIKE MAFFORD PHOTOGRAPHY

and manufacture, and artists' and authors' works, including publishing.

What Is Intellectual Property Law?

Trademarks, domain names, trade secrets, copyrights, patents, licenses and agreements, unfair competition—all these areas and more fall into the broad category of intellectual property.

Working in these highly specialized areas requires much more than technical expertise. Regardless of size, and whether counsel is sought for a technological innovation or a new logo, Seed and Berry attorneys can take the time to learn each client's business in detail and tailor a protection plan to fit the client's overall business strategy. The firm can also help companies develop and coordinate global strategies for products marketed abroad. In addition, they are able to perform competitive analyses, analyze the patentability of prospective products, and, in appropriate cases, guide clients in determining where to spend their research and development dollars. Further, the firm educates clients on maximizing protection for their intellectual property, especially patent litigation, addressing issues like basic patent law, patent procurement, and problem identification. A properly executed protection plan must be individually tailored, and will often require a combination of legal protection devices.

Seed and Berry's litigation practice includes 12 attorneys, each of whom is also highly specialized in a particular field of engineering or science. This outside experience enables Seed and Berry attorneys to spot issues quickly, such as particular problems that arise during a deposition with an inventor or nuances in the law that are critical for the client. The extremely complicated nature of this work also requires extensive experience in patent law, which places general practice litigators at a distinct disadvantage.

"One of the reasons we've been successful over the years is that we meld new ideas with time-tested experience, which benefits clients in the long run," says David Maki, a partner whose "outside" expertise is in molecular biology.

Maki's unique combined knowledge of patent law and science, and the similar double abilities of his colleagues, translates into better service and real cost advantages for Seed and Berry's clients. In fact, many of Seed and Berry's 42 attorneys hold advanced degrees in specialized technical areas and joined the firm from private industry.

All Seed and Berry attorneys round out their unique technical expertise with strong communication and legal skills—and they always work as a team. This team approach means attorneys with complementary experiences and skills work together to provide the most comprehensive, efficient, and cost-effective legal service possible.

As Seed and Berry continues to expand nationally and internationally, its attorneys must be available for clients thousands of miles away. To that end, the firm has invested in modern systems to enhance communications with clients. In addition to electronic mail, the firm now uses innovative tools like softboard, a technology that transfers images placed on a white board to a client's computer screen in real time. Further, attorneys and staff receive comprehensive, ongoing training to keep them up to date on all aspects of intellectual property.

Seed and Berry's excellence in the specialized field of intellectual property law is based on an ongoing commitment to innovation, providing quality service to the firm's clients, and ultimately enhancing the value of its clients' intellectual property.

▸ SPIKE MAFFORD PHOTOGRAPHY

▸ SPIKE MAFFORD PHOTOGRAPHY

Rapid advances in technology have enabled the firm to extend its expertise into a national and international business (top).

The firm's clients range from industry giants like Microsoft and MCI to cutting-edge leaders in technology like Immunex and Micron, to household names like Nordstrom, StairMaster, and Red Robin (bottom).

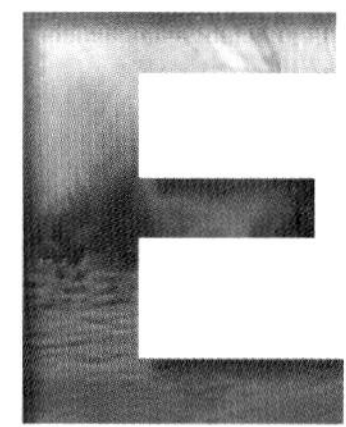

Ever since Eddie Bauer opened his first store in 1920 in downtown Seattle, the company has been a pioneer in the retail business. Within two years of opening, Eddie Bauer Sporting Goods set a new retail standard by creating one of the first unconditional guarantees—a guarantee that still lives today.

In 1927, Bauer introduced women's clothing into his inventory. And in 1935, the company manufactured and patented the first ever goose-down insulated garment.

During World War II, Eddie Bauer made 50,000 B-9 flight jackets for the U.S. Army Air Corps. When the pilots returned, their enthusiasm about the jacket's performance set off a national demand for the company's goose-down products, leading to the company's first mail-order catalog.

Bauer field-tested everything he sold. The company's goose-down products have been tested during numerous scientific and exploratory expeditions. That same attention to high quality applies to every Eddie Bauer garment made today. Each item sold is subjected to rigorous quality-assurance testing to be certain that every detail lives up to company standards.

Ever since Eddie Bauer opened his first store in 1920 in downtown Seattle, the company has been a pioneer in the retail business.

Diversification, Innovation, Growth

Today, Eddie Bauer has grown to more than 500 stores, mails catalogs to more than 100 million customers, and sells direct from its Web site (www.eddiebauer.com). The company is a leader in casual lifestyle products and offers the full spectrum of merchandise through its three divisions—Eddie Bauer Sportswear, A|K|A EDDIE BAUER™, and Eddie Bauer Home™. The company combines these three store concepts under one roof in some markets, and in its larger resource catalogs.

Eddie Bauer Sportswear offers seasonal collections of high-quality men's and women's sportswear, footwear, gear, and accessories. A natural extension of the sportswear and sports business, A|K|A EDDIE BAUER offers men's and women's dress sportswear, designed to take casual wear to the office and beyond.

The largest Eddie Bauer store to date opened on Michigan Avenue in Chicago in October 1996.

Eddie Bauer incorporates the company's expertise in textiles into home furnishings made exclusively for Eddie Bauer Home. The comfortable, casual furnishings and accessories are designed for every room in the house, with a special emphasis on bedrooms, great rooms, and bathrooms.

Innovation in both product and service delivery continues to be Eddie Bauer's hallmark. In 1996, it launched its EBTEK™ collection, which includes both daily active-wear and the EBTEK System of high-performance, interlocking outerwear.

Corporate sales represents an expanding direction for the company. Eddie Bauer offers special services to companies that need large quantities of clothing for uniforms, such as khaki pants or customized polo shirts for restaurant workers. Through its corporate licensing program, Eddie Bauer has developed partnerships with successful businesses such as Ford Motor Company, with whom it produces

the popular Eddie Bauer Ford Explorer and Eddie Bauer Ford Expedition, as well as Ambassador Travel, to offer adventure travel tours that are uniquely Eddie Bauer-oriented.

Internationally, Eddie Bauer has opened 21 stores in Japan since 1994. Planning to open stores in one European country at a time, Eddie Bauer now operates retail stores and catalogs in Germany and Great Britain.

"There is tremendous opportunity to grow further. We believe there is demand out there for several thousand stores," says Richard T. Fersch, company president.

▶ H. FRY

▶ PETER ROBBINS

A natural extension of the sportswear business, A|K|A EDDIE BAUER offers men's and women's dress sportswear, designed to take casual wear to the office and beyond (left).

Eddie Bauer Sportswear offers seasonal collections of high-quality men's and women's sportswear, footwear, gear, and accessories (right).

Roots in the Northwest

A forward-thinking company that has grown and benefited from a high-quality Pacific Northwest workforce, Eddie Bauer has developed a unique corporate culture and a progressive workplace. More than 20 new programs have been introduced since 1994 to make associates' lives easier—from on-site flu shots and Kid Care Backup to telecommuting, adoption assistance, discounted mortgage services, and even dry cleaning pickup and delivery. In 1996, Eddie Bauer added an extra paid day off, called Balance Day, for associates to use as they wish.

▶ ALAIN REDDER

Fabrics such as Gore-Tex®, Polartec® 200, and Premium Eddie Bauer Goose Down go beyond high performance. The pure comfort and styling of Eddie Bauer's EBTEK outerwear and active-wear make them clothes to live in.

The company has received widespread recognition for its leadership in the work and family arena from publications like *Business Week*, *Working Mother*, and *Parenting* magazines.

Eddie Bauer gives back to the communities in which it does business through environmental initiatives. It created the Eddie Bauer Global Releaf Tree Project, a joint effort with American Forests, to help damaged forests around North America. The program has led to the planting of more than 700,000 trees in the United States and Canada, working toward a goal of 2.5 million trees by the year 2000.

Eddie Bauer has a rich tradition, which is reflected today in its quality products, customer service, and corporate culture. And Eddie Bauer continues to grow and succeed by living up to its company creed, established in 1922: "To give you such outstanding quality, value, service and guarantee that we may be worthy of your high esteem."

Eddie Bauer incorporates the company's expertise in textiles into home furnishings made exclusively for Eddie Bauer Home.

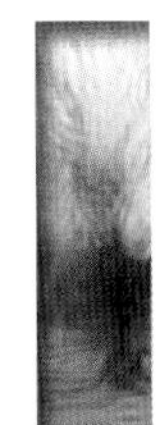

In 1920, Drs. James Tate Mason and John M. Blackford dreamed of creating a health care center where patients could receive coordinated, comprehensive care. Celebrating its 75th anniversary in 1995, the Virginia Mason Medical Center is the culmination of that dream. ■ Named for the daughters of its two founders, Virginia Mason is a regional and national leader in integrated patient care. Utilizing a team concept, each patient is placed under the supervision of a group of health care professionals who determine and then coordinate a plan of treatment. Among the many benefits of this team approach is the pooling of patient data so that doctors and medical technicians stay informed.

A Range of Quality Care

Licensed for 336 beds, Virginia Mason offers primary and tertiary care with a diverse, multispecialty group practice. Nearly 400 physicians practice in 45 different medical, surgical, and diagnostic areas; and about 180 physicians hold faculty appointments at the University of Washington. Virginia Mason is featured in *The Best Hospitals in America* for 1995 and 1996, a consumer guide to the 64 finest U.S. facilities chosen from approximately 6,000 hospitals.

Virginia Mason is a major referral center for hospitals and physicians in the five-state Northwest region for comprehensive services in diagnostic examination, treatment, and rehabilitation, with roughly 42 percent of its patients coming from outside the Seattle area. Airlift Northwest transports critically ill and injured patients in remote locations to Virginia Mason to receive specialized medical care.

To meet the needs of 827,000 annual patient visits, the medical center built a network of 21 neighborhood clinics to serve the Greater Seattle area, and outlying areas as far away as Port Angeles, Anacortes, and Enumclaw. A team of rotating physician specialists visits the clinics regularly, making a full spectrum of services—including obstetrics and tertiary care—more accessible to low-income individuals.

A History of Trail Blazing

Virginia Mason has blazed new trails in a number of critical areas. It was the first institution west of the Mississippi to use insulin to treat diabetic patients; the first to develop regional anesthesia; the first in the state to establish a midwifery program; and the first in the region to perform

Clockwise from top:
Virginia Mason has 21 satellite clinics located throughout the Puget Sound area. The satellite in Federal Way, located south of Seattle, provides office and ambulatory services for 34 physicians.

Virginia Mason Medical Center founders and staff pose in front of the original hospital entrance at Terry Avenue and Spring Street in 1929.

The original hospital building was constructed in 1920.

cochlear implantation, a procedure that enables deaf persons to hear again. It opened Bailey-Boushay House, the first nursing residence for AIDS patients; was the first to use the X-ray machine for deep therapy; and the first to use ultrasound to dissolve kidney stones.

Virginia Mason devotes significant resources to promoting medical research and education. The Research Center is internationally recognized for its programs in immunology, metabolic disorders, pharmacology, neuroscience, cardiopulmonary physiology, and health care delivery. Virginia Mason researchers attracted worldwide attention when they discovered genetic markers that indicate a likelihood for developing diabetes. Scientists at the Research Center also discovered a way to predict a person's risk for developing rheumatoid arthritis.

The Virginia Mason Cancer Center opened in the 1940s. Today, it treats nearly 5,000 new cancer patients each year and has three radiation oncology centers in the Puget Sound area. It participates in national clinical trials and conducts joint studies at the Fred Hutchinson Cancer Research Center so patients can benefit from the latest techniques and drugs to combat cancer.

Each year, specialists help more than 2,500 people at the Benaroya Diabetes Center, the largest and oldest diabetes program in the Northwest. The Buse Diabetes Teaching Center, established almost 60 years ago, was the first of its kind in the Northwest, and remains the most comprehensive. The Virginia Mason Heart Center is a national leader in applying sophisticated technology in a coordinated, multidisciplinary approach. The Center for Women's Health offers complete health services to care for women through all stages of life. The residency training program is the oldest in the state and sought by students nationally.

Virginia Mason is taking advantage of the burgeoning field of telemedicine—the use of communications technology in medical consultations and clinical teaching—to treat patients as far away as Homer, Alaska, and Kalispell, Montana. Virginia Mason's medical leadership also extends to Russia, where physicians participate in an exchange program, and dozens of patients needing specialized care come to Seattle each year.

The Virginia Mason Research Center was founded in 1956. The center has become internationally recognized for its programs in immunology, metabolic disorders, pharmacology, neuroscience, cardiopulmonary physiology, and health care delivery.

Meeting Community Needs

Virginia Mason offers a number of programs and services to meet targeted needs. Tender Loving Care is the Northwest's first day care center for mildly ill children. The Sports Medicine Clinic in downtown Seattle treats sports injuries and offers conditioning programs for school, recreational, and professional athletes. Virginia Mason Hospital owns and operates the Inn at Virginia Mason, which exists for the convenience of patients and their families visiting Seattle.

In addition to providing extensive charity care—typically more than $10 million per year—Virginia Mason has formed partnerships to address the pressing health needs of, and provide educational/vocational support to, at-risk youth in the community. Employees of the medical center are also committed to these efforts: Their annual Sweet Charity Auction has raised more than $500,000 for uncompensated care and charitable projects.

With an eye on the future, Virginia Mason is expanding its regional referral sources and participating in provider networks. It formed an alliance with Group Health Cooperative in 1993 to share equipment, expertise, and resources. Virginia Mason continues to provide access for patients by participating with a large number of insurance carriers and health plans.

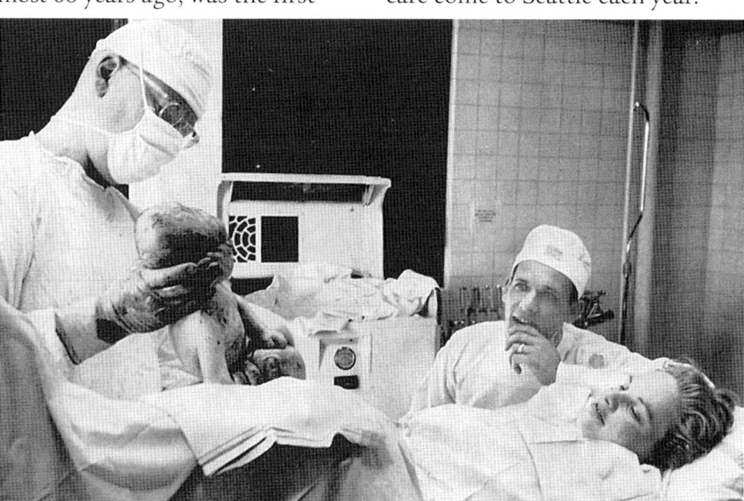

Virginia Mason was one of the first hospitals in the nation to allow fathers in the delivery room.

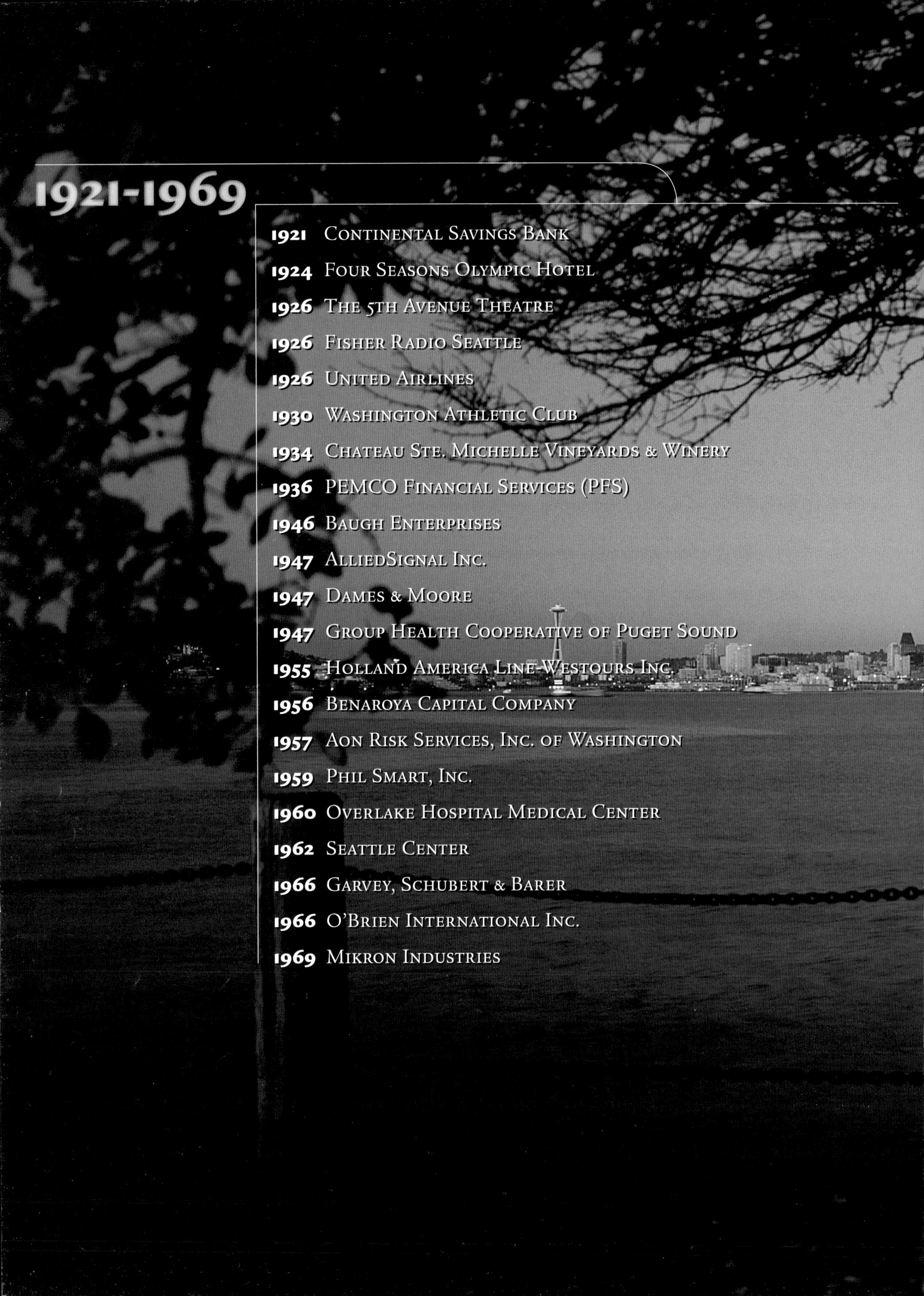

1921-1969

1921 Continental Savings Bank

1924 Four Seasons Olympic Hotel

1926 The 5th Avenue Theatre

1926 Fisher Radio Seattle

1926 United Airlines

1930 Washington Athletic Club

1934 Chateau Ste. Michelle Vineyards & Winery

1936 PEMCO Financial Services (PFS)

1946 Baugh Enterprises

1947 AlliedSignal Inc.

1947 Dames & Moore

1947 Group Health Cooperative of Puget Sound

1955 Holland America Line-Westours Inc.

1956 Benaroya Capital Company

1957 Aon Risk Services, Inc. of Washington

1959 Phil Smart, Inc.

1960 Overlake Hospital Medical Center

1962 Seattle Center

1966 Garvey, Schubert & Barer

1966 O'Brien International Inc.

1969 Mikron Industries

◆ JIM CORWIN

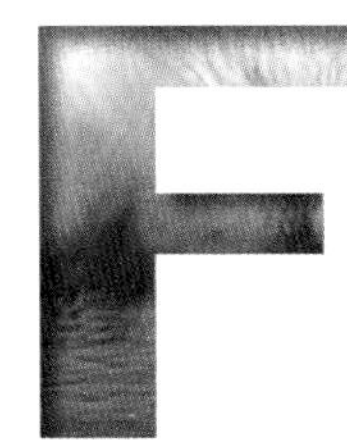

F**ounded in Seattle's University District in 1921, Continental Savings Bank is one of the oldest and largest residential and commercial real estate lenders in the Pacific Northwest. The locally owned, family company has built a thriving business by being innovative** and adaptable to the changing times. Today, it is a family of companies providing quality financial and real estate services, including retail banking, single-family residential and income property lending, real estate management, and insurance services in the Pacific Northwest and Hawaii. The company is recognized for its high standards of service, leadership, and integrity.

A Wide Range of Services

For more than 75 years, Continental has been meeting a variety of real estate financing needs in the community.

Its primary focus is lending money to families and individuals to purchase homes—from first homes to dream homes. To meet these very diverse needs, Continental offers a large number of loan types and special programs. It was one of the earliest lenders in the area to be approved to offer FHA and VA loans. Well known for their hands-on service, Continental loan officers work closely with home buyers, tailoring products to meet their special financing needs. "One of our greatest strengths is serving customers today while anticipating their needs of tomorrow," says Dick Swanson, president of Continental. "We continue to offer innovative new programs and more streamlined services for customers." For example, in the summer of 1996, Continental entered into a contract with the City of Seattle and began offering special home loans to city employees and employees of the Seattle Public Schools. For first-time home buyers, Continental has been the largest source of loans through the Washington State Housing Finance Commission's state bond program.

Continental literally builds communities by financing land acquisition and development and the construction of new homes. It is the fourth-largest single-family home construction lender in the state of Washington, providing loans to large and small builders and individual home buyers. For those who wish to renovate and remodel older homes, Continental has a variety of excellent programs.

Home buyers find the home purchase process especially smooth when they also take advantage of the services offered by Continental Escrow Company and Continental Insurance Services. Continental Insurance Services offers competitive home owners, life, automobile, and other property and casualty insurance coverage.

Continental's customers are very pleased that almost all of the loans that the company makes continue to be serviced by Continental. That means whenever customers have a question, there is someone in Seattle to help them.

Continental started by financing apartments and commercial buildings. These included many of the apartment buildings that are still providing homes to residents in the University District, Capitol Hill, and the Denny Regrade. It provided the funds to build the University Methodist Temple and the first Seattle Repertory Theatre, as well as many other commercial buildings. More recently, Continental has financed the Group Health Hospital and the Olive Tower for the nonprofit Seattle Housing Resources Group. Currently, the company is funding facilities for biotech firms, apartments, office buildings, and retail centers.

For more than 75 years, Continental Savings Bank has been meeting a variety of real estate financing needs in the community. Its primary focus is lending money to families and individuals to purchase homes—from first homes to dream homes.

To encourage commercial and apartment property owners to take full advantage of their investments, Continental's Real Estate Management Services provides complete professional management services. These include day-to-day property management, brokerage, and leasing.

With retail banking services a growing part of its business, Continental offers a wide range of deposit services combined with outstanding personal service—customers are pleased to be treated as special people, not as just a number. Continental's deposit services include checking accounts, ATM access, and traditional and specialized certificates of deposits. Continental Savings Bank is consistently rated in the highest categories for financial soundness by national rating organizations, so Continental's customers know that their deposits are safe.

Continental is the fourth-largest single-family home construction lender in the state of Washington, providing loans to large and small builders and individual home buyers (top).

Continental offers a wide range of deposit services combined with outstanding personal service (bottom).

Community Leadership

Continental's leadership in the community is demonstrated by its progressive loan programs and history of public service. Walter B. Williams, chairman emeritus of Continental Savings Bank, was awarded the First Citizen Award in May 1997 by the Seattle-King County Association of Realtors—the same award his father, W. Walter Williams, received in 1945. Continental also won the Washington Family Business of the Year award in 1996 in the large-business category. The Mortgage Bankers Association (MBA) of America gave a special award to Continental in 1989 for ". . . exemplary service in the provision of affordable housing. . . . Your actions honor the true public spirit and commitment of MBA members in communities across the United States." Continental was the only mortgage banking company to be presented this award.

Through its financial charitable contributions and personal staff involvements, Continental works with many nonprofits that provide shelter and housing for people with low to moderate incomes. Several of these include Common Ground, Community Home Ownership Center, Housing Partnership, Seattle Housing Resources Group, and UCEDA in Seattle's central area. Continental was also one of the founding members of the Washington Community Reinvestment Association, a consortium of banks in the state of Washington that pools money to finance low- and moderate-income apartments. Continental has always been a major supporter of United Way of King County.

Continental employs more than 450 people in its home office and branches. It is these committed, professional individuals who deliver the high quality of customer service for which Continental is well known.

Continental has grown steadily since it first started. Now, with its home office in downtown Seattle, the branches of Continental Savings Bank serve all of the Puget Sound area, eastern Washington, parts of Oregon, Idaho, and Hawaii, building better communities by helping people achieve their dreams of acquiring a home and realizing financial security.

For more than 70 years, the Four Seasons Olympic Hotel has been the Pacific Northwest's most elegant hotel and a meeting place for world leaders as well as Seattle's business, cultural, and civic community. Located on the original site of the University of Washington and now the heart of the city's business district, this grande dame property blends the splendor of another age with superb service and state-of-the-art amenities.

Originally called The Olympic, the hotel was built in 1924 after local citizens rallied around the idea that their up-and-coming city needed a grand hotel. Upon completion of the Italian Renaissance-style building, the *Seattle Times* reported that it was "an epochal accomplishment—a milestone in our civic life." The exterior of the hotel—accented with high, arched Palladian windows—is built out of buff-face brick with terra-cotta trim. With its elegant facilities and impeccable service, the 750-room Olympic had few rivals outside New York and Chicago.

A History of Service

Since The Olympic opened its doors in 1924, it has experienced an extraordinary existence. In 1929, for example, it added 300 "Willy Loman" rooms, named after the character in Arthur Miller's play *Death of a Salesman*, that were small and well suited for traveling salesmen and conventioneers. In the 1940s, William Boeing Sr., the aircraft manufacturer, and other prominent Seattle businessmen formed a men's club that occupied a series of rooms on the fourth floor.

The Olympic has hosted six U.S. presidents; Emperor Haile Selassie of Ethiopia; Crown Prince Akihito of Japan; and Prince Philip of England, the Duke of Edinburgh. Of the 17 world leaders attending the Asian Pacific Economic Conference (APEC) in 1993, 15 stayed at the hotel.

Over the years, the hotel experienced financial problems and a series of ownership changes. In the 1970s, when The Olympic was threatened with the wrecking ball, local citizens and state elected officials came to the rescue. The Washington State legislature passed a resolution that encouraged the board of regents of the University of Washington, which

Clockwise from left:
For more than 70 years, the Four Seasons Olympic Hotel has been the Pacific Northwest's most elegant hotel.

The Four Seasons Olympic Hotel blends the splendor of another age with superb service and state-of-the-art amenities.

The renovated building includes 190 deluxe rooms with added comfort and amenities.

still owns the land, to save the hotel. As a result, the regents signed a new, 60-year lease with Four Seasons ♦ Regent Hotels & Resorts, the world's largest operator of luxury hotels.

In 1982, the hotel completed a $60 million renovation that lovingly restored the original architecture, added modern comforts, expanded meeting and banquet accommodations, and reduced the number of guest rooms from 900 to 450—a project which doubled the space in each room. The renovated building includes 190 deluxe rooms, 196 Four Seasons Suites, 10 corner suites with sizable dressing and sitting rooms, and the spacious Cascade and Olympic presidential suites.

The Definitive Hotel Experience

The Four Seasons Olympic Hotel caters to the business traveler by providing a level of service and convenience that the staff calls "the definitive hotel experience."

Listed on the National Register of Historic Places, the hotel offers a timeless setting for today's business demands. The 12th-floor Business Center can handle any requests for typing/secretarial or personal computer needs for guests.

Each year, the hotel wins top national and international honors from the lodging industry for its superb service and state-of-the-art restaurants. The Georgian, a two-story, Renaissance-style dining room, was deemed by the *New York Times* to be the "most elegant dining spot in town," and features a Japanese-style breakfast, a children's menu, and health-conscious alternative cuisine dishes designed by the chef. The Garden Court is a majestic atrium with two-story Palladian windows where people can enjoy afternoon tea, lunch, and award-winning cocktails. Finally, Shuckers is applauded as the best seafood and oyster bar in the city.

The Four Seasons Olympic Hotel also offers some of the city's best shopping, featuring more than a dozen exclusive salons and luxury retail shops. The hotel is within minutes of more than 120 fine stores, as well as the Fifth Avenue Theatre, Seattle Art Museum, Pike Place Market and the waterfront, Washington State Trade and Convention Center, and many other downtown attractions. For guests from the Pacific Rim or European countries who stay at the Four Seasons, the hotel serves Japanese tea upon guests' arrival and provides around-the-clock concierge service from a multilingual staff of Japanese, French, Spanish, and German speakers equipped to handle last-minute essentials ranging from airline reservations to theater tickets. For clients needing translation of other languages, the hotel uses the AT&T translation service.

Children are also treated as special guests. Upon arrival, they receive a Four Season's gift of toys and *Four Seasons Kids*, a quarterly newsletter of special events and activities in town for children. All the hotel's restaurants offer children's menus, and every Sunday the Garden Court brunch offers a food station exclusively for the younger generation. And baby-sitting services can be arranged with a quick phone call to the Concierge Desk.

The Four Seasons Olympic Hotel is considered a priceless treasure by the Seattle community and, as such, gives back generously to the community. It supplies in-kind contributions and resources to auctions and fund-raising campaigns for a variety of respected organizations, including Children's Hospital, YWCA, Fred Hutchinson Cancer Research Foundation, Medina Children's Services, PONCHO, and Seattle Symphony.

The hotel boasts 10 corner suites with sizable dressing and sitting rooms.

The Garden Court is a majestic atrium with two-story Palladian windows where people can enjoy afternoon tea, lunch, and award-winning cocktails.

Guests of the hotel can maintain their exercise regimens in the on-site health club, which includes a lap pool and cardiovascular equipment.

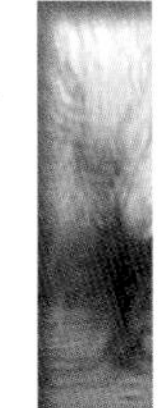
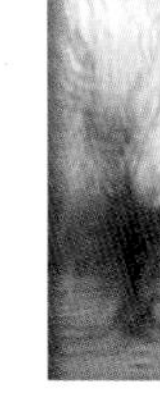

N 1979, A GROUP OF 43 BUSINESSES, FOUNDATIONS, AND INDIVIDUALS banded together to form The 5th Avenue Theatre Association, a nonprofit organization. Their aim was to save and restore The 5th Avenue Theatre, a vaudeville house and movie palace built in 1926 in downtown Seattle. Their mission led to the rebirth of one of the most remarkable, ornate theaters of our time, and the creation of a major performing arts center for the Pacific Northwest.

DICK BUSHER

The interior of The 5th Avenue Theatre is modeled after the Throne Room of the Forbidden City in Beijing. Built in 1926, the theater was originally a vaudeville house and reigned as one of Seattle's premier movie palaces for more than 50 years.

Renovating an Architectural Marvel

Celebrating the city's role in the 1920s as the Gateway to the Orient, The 5th Avenue Theatre re-creates one of ancient Imperial China's most stunning architectural achievements: the Throne Room of the Forbidden City in Beijing. In the center of the magnificent dome, a great dragon suspends a huge chandelier from its jaws, while the walls and ceiling display the pageantry and mystery of ancient China through murals, sculptures, and tapestries.

In designing the theater, architect Robert C. Reamer was acutely aware of two tragic events: the Great Seattle Fire in 1889 and the San Francisco earthquake in 1906. As a result, the interior contains very little wood; instead, it was sculpted from plaster and then carefully painted. The dome is completely suspended from the ceiling, so that in the event of an earthquake it can swing freely.

During the restoration, more than $50,000 was spent on vacuuming alone. The dome, walls, and columns were refurbished by the careful application of oil to bring forward the original luster of the paint.

The $2.6 million renovation was accomplished without any local, state, or federal funds, setting a precedent for theaters across the country. In 1980, The 5th Avenue became the first facility in the Pacific Northwest to receive the Heritage, Conservation, and Recreation Service Achievement Award from the Department of the Interior. On June 16, 1980, at the theater's grand reopening ceremony, the first lady of the American theater, Helen Hayes, declared, "The 5th Avenue is a national treasure."

"Business leaders had the keen foresight to preserve this jewel for the community," says Marilynn Sheldon, managing director of The 5th Avenue. "Seattle had already lost too many of its magnificent theaters to the wrecking ball. To restore this theater for this and future generations of Seattleites was the driving force behind the renovation."

An Institution for Cultural Enrichment

During the 17 years following its restoration, The 5th Avenue Theatre has operated as a nonprofit institution and has presented and produced more than 75 productions for more than 2,000 performances. Some 4.5 million people have attended productions, with annual attendance averaging more than 300,000.

In 1989, The 5th Avenue established The 5th Avenue Musical Theatre Company to produce and present the best in musical theater entertainment in a subscription series for Northwest audiences. Entirely self-supported through the sales of tickets, the nonprofit

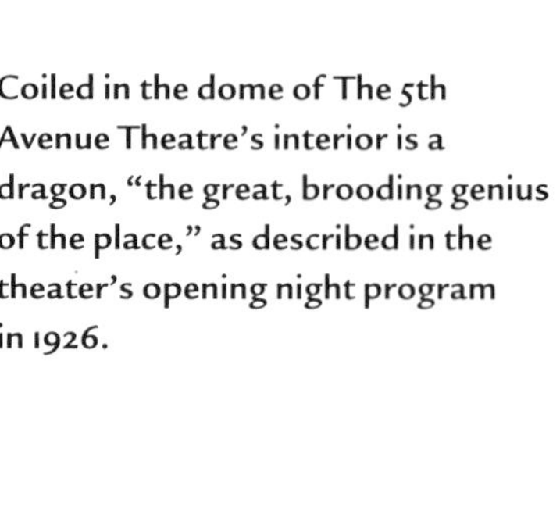

DICK BUSHER

Coiled in the dome of The 5th Avenue Theatre's interior is a dragon, "the great, brooding genius of the place," as described in the theater's opening night program in 1926.

▲▼ JOAN MARCUS

organization enjoys the patronage of more than 35,000 subscribers, the largest subscription audience in the Northwest.

Preserving and developing the American musical as an art form is central to the theater's mission, which is expanding the library of American musicals through the creation of new works. In 1996, The 5th Avenue Musical Theatre joined forces with Houston's Theatre Under the Stars and the Ordway Music Theatre of St. Paul to create New Musicals Studio/USA, a nonprofit consortium that brings together emerging composers and authors to create new musicals. Budgeted at more than $3 million for its first three years, New Musicals Studio/USA presents the work of lyricists, librettists, and composers as staged readings, then as workshop productions, and finally as fully staged musicals.

In addition to presenting national tours and producing its own musicals, The 5th Avenue makes its facilities available for concerts, lectures, films, and a variety of nonprofit events. Each year, it hosts the Seattle International Film Festival, Seattle Arts & Lectures Series, Seattle Choral Company, and Seattle Men's Chorus. In total, the theater is in use 75 to 85 percent of the time year-round.

Contributing to the Community

Educational outreach is a major thrust of The 5th Avenue's work. In 1994, it launched a pilot program titled Adventure Musical Theatre. Designed to travel to elementary schools, it introduces kindergarten and elementary-school-age children to American musical theater through the performance of an original musical, presented in a fun, imaginative, and interactive way. The program complements the Special School Matinee program, which provides a 90-minute, abridged performance of a full-length musical from the theater's season for students in grades four through 12. About 30,000 students from throughout the Puget Sound area attended school matinees between 1990 and 1996.

The 5th Avenue also contributes annually to the Seattle Times Fund for the Needy by offering half-price tickets for one performance of the holiday musical and donating the proceeds to support specific charitable organizations.

In 1993, the board of directors of The 5th Avenue Theatre Association established a $1 million endowment fund to benefit the cultural community in the form of grants that would increase educational opportunities for students to experience the performing arts. Administered by the Seattle Foundation, the Fund provides grants awarded for internships with performing arts organizations in Washington State.

The 5th Avenue is an active and vital member of the Seattle community—enriching cultural, artistic, and educational opportunities in the Puget Sound region through its philanthropic efforts and through its role as a center for the performing arts.

Tours of The 5th Avenue are available free to the public.

▶ THE 5TH AVENUE THEATRE

▶ CHRIS BENNION

Clockwise from top left:
The magnificent touring production of Rodgers and Hammerstein's *The King and I* played The 5th Avenue in 1997 with Hayley Mills as Mrs. Anna.

The Royal National Theatre's stunning 1994 production of Rodgers and Hammerstein's *Carousel* swept the Tony Awards that year and went on to dazzle the entire country with its national touring company. The 5th Avenue Musical Theatre Company was one of several regional musical theater companies that produced the tour.

Starring John Cullum in the title role, The 5th Avenue Musical Theatre Company's production of *Man of La Mancha* opened the 1995 season. This production went on to Honolulu.

Lauren Gaffney, Harv Presnell, and Daisy starred in *Annie Warbucks*, the sequel to *Annie*, the national touring musical that played The 5th Avenue for 11 sold-out weeks, beginning in July 1980 when the theater was first restored. *Annie Warbucks* was a production of the 1992 season and went on to open off-Broadway.

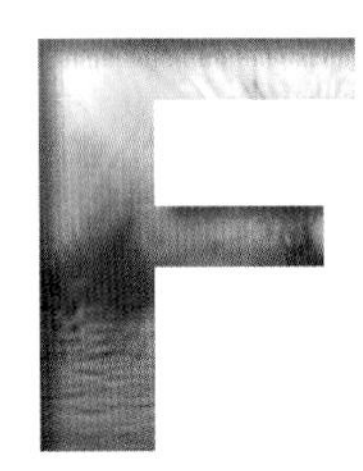

Fisher Radio Seattle is part of Fisher Broadcasting, which owns three very different and dynamic radio stations in Seattle: KOMO News 1000 (AM), 570 KVI (AM), and STAR 101.5 FM (KPLZ), as well as KOMO-TV 4 in Seattle and KATU-TV and KWJJ AM/FM in Portland. Additionally, Fisher owns Sunbrook Communications, a group of 18 radio stations in Montana and eastern Washington. With three distinctly different radio formats in the Seattle area, there's something for everyone under the umbrella of Fisher Radio Seattle.

Fisher Companies, a successful, family-owned timber and flour-milling business, entered the broadcasting business in 1926. Fisher Radio Seattle was created in May 1994 when KVI and KPLZ were acquired by Fisher Broadcasting Inc.

Notable for devoting significant resources to employee empowerment, Fisher Radio Seattle encourages employees to set goals beyond the normal boundaries of their jobs. The result is an employee-driven company that boasts an incredibly creative work environment and strong company loyalty. Fisher has realized its goal of hiring and retaining a diversified workforce that mirrors the community it serves.

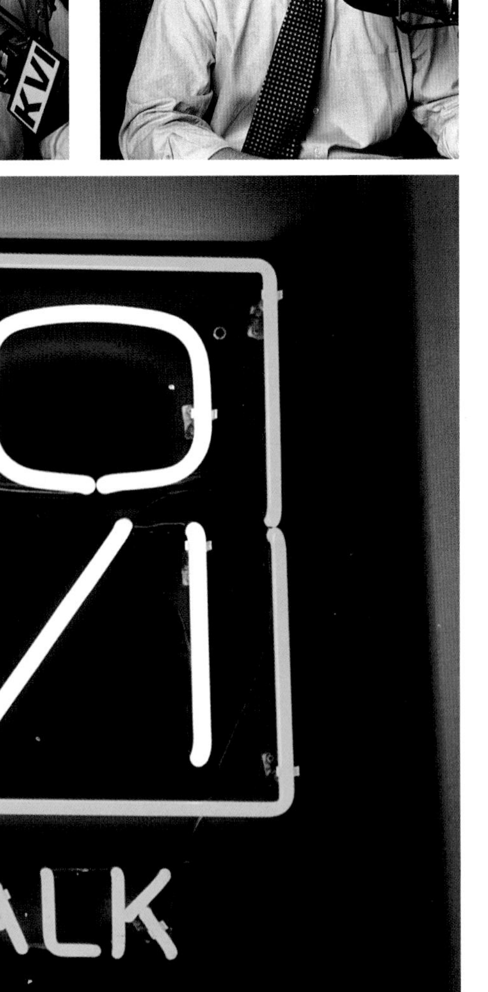

Clockwise from top left: Weekday mornings on KVI from 5 to 9, Kirby Wilbur combines the day's news and events with commentary and a historical perspective.

Seattle's best-known conservative media-personality, KVI's John Carlson anchors a fast-paced and informative show from 3 to 6 p.m.

KVI enjoys an immensely loyal following as it is the only talk-radio station in the Puget Sound region offering moderate and conservative viewpoints.

KOMO News 1000

KOMO News 1000, the flagship radio station of Fisher Broadcasting, is a long-standing voice in the Pacific Northwest. Providing a daily source of information for more than 70 years, KOMO News 1000 delivers award-winning news programming, University of Washington Husky Sports, popular talk shows, and useful educational features. Preceding KOMO-TV by some 30 years, the radio station backs its claim of understanding the Northwest by offering lively, informative programming that reflects the lifestyles and interests of people who call the region home.

As one of the premier AM radio stations in the country, KOMO News 1000 is current, relevant, and personable. The station tells the story behind the news, relating how today's events directly affect local residents. It speaks to an educated, current, middle majority and reflects a new, cosmopolitan Seattle without sacrificing the loyal listenership it has built over the years. With a 50,000-watt transmitter, KOMO News 1000 is one of the true giants on AM radio, reaching more than 300,000 listeners every week, from Oregon to British Columbia.

In addition to broadcasting interviews with local news makers and celebrities, the station boasts exclusive rights to the legendary Paul Harvey and ABC News. *Paul Harvey News & Comment* and *The Rest of the Story* draw thousands daily to the station. On Husky game days, the three-hour *Husky Tailgate* pregame show mixes game and sports information with liberal doses of humor and an irreverent look at local "Husky-mania." The station also enjoys exclusive broadcast rights to the opening day of yachting season in Seattle.

KOMO News 1000's *First Edition*, hosted by Rick Van Cise and Gina Tuttle, offers listeners four hours of information from 5 to 9 a.m. weekdays designed to enlighten and entertain. The program focuses on news, traffic, sports, weather, and family finances in addition to live interviews with news makers, celebrities, and special guests.

Weekday mornings from 9 until noon, Seattle's best-known psychologist hangs out her shingle. Dr. Joy Browne advises callers on relationships, stress, phobias, and a host of other challenges that life can bring. Browne's advice is fast, funny, and poignant, and confirms that sometimes common sense isn't all that common.

The award-winning KOMO *Noon News* keeps the Northwest on top of local, national, and world events. The cornerstone of the noon broadcast is *Paul Harvey News and Comment*. Harvey continues to be the number one news personality in American radio after more than a quarter of a century of delivering his unique perspective.

Bonnie Hart hosts from noon to 3 p.m. with a witty, insightful, and intelligent look at the day's events. With a generous dose of listener phone calls and special guests mixed in, the show is fresh and fast paced.

Afternoons feature four hours of news and information presented in a compelling and enlightening format. The perfect end to the workday, KOMO News 1000 provides listeners frequent traffic reports, weather forecasts, and tips on entertainment and upcoming events.

Weekday evenings, KOMO News 1000 offers *The Bruce Williams Show*, with advice on everything from how to start a business to solving a dispute with a neighbor. Late at night on the quirky, number-one-rated *Coast-to-Coast* with Art Bell, listeners discover some of life's oddities through Bell's unique perspective.

STAR 101.5 FM

STAR 101.5 plays "the best mix of the '80s and '90s"—a mix of the best music from the 1980s and today. The station reaches a diverse adult audience that numbers almost 400,000 each week. STAR's audience is nearly three-quarters female and attracts a loyal following from Bellingham to Olympia.

STAR 101.5 offers personalities and a music mix designed to make the workday and commute a little easier. Popular team Kent and Alan host the *Morning Show* weekdays from 5:30 to 10. Known for their friendly but pointed humor, Kent and Alan welcome listeners with a mix of local events, activities, weird trivia, and even

Bonnie Hart hosts KOMO News 1000 from noon to 3 p.m. with a witty, insightful, and intelligent look at the day's events (top left).

Providing a daily source of information for more than 70 years, KOMO News 1000 delivers award-winning news programming, University of Washington Husky Sports, popular talk shows, and useful educational features.

ideas on what to do with your kids on the weekends. On any given day, you'll get the opportunity to play the Battle of the Sexes or Rate-Your-Mate. Flo could stop by with one of her patented sports reports, you might catch Lorena the Psychic, or Kent and Alan's "News of the Stars."

Evenings, Jill Taylor spins the *Eighties at Eight*, an hour of the hottest hits from the 1980s along with special requests. The *Leeza Gibbons' Top 25 Countdown* on Saturday mornings and Sunday nights is a weekly countdown show from the former host of *Entertainment Tonight*. Saturday nights, it's time to disco, as listeners are transported back to when polyester was king with *Saturday Night Fever*. Sunday evening, *Backtrax USA* wraps itself around the look and sound of the 1980s.

STAR 101.5's community and listener involvement goes in numerous directions with, on average, a charity function every month. In 1993, STAR 101.5 launched the Starlight Foundation Auction and Golf Tournament to raise the money needed to grant wishes of children with life-threatening illnesses. The station has raised an average of $140,000 per year for the foundation.

The popular, one-of-a-kind roller-coaster wedding held every year at the Puyallup County Fair joins a couple in matrimony while riding an enormous roller coaster. Each fall and spring, the station honors a local teacher as Teacher of the Week, and throws a party for the honoree's class. STAR 101.5 also sponsors the Pet of the Week, which finds homes for animals from the Humane Society. The station goes all out at Christmas, giving away cash, participating in the annual holiday parade through downtown Seattle, offering safety reports on toys, and finding gifts for disadvantaged children.

Hot-Talk 570 KVI: A Conservative Voice

Hot-Talk 570 KVI is one of the greatest success stories in AM radio history. No other news/talk station has come so far so fast. KVI enjoys an immensely loyal following as it is the only talk-radio station in the Puget Sound region offering moderate and conservative viewpoints. Its issue-based, audience-driven format has given a voice to those disenfranchised by other media outlets. Broadcasting with 5,000 watts, KVI reaches some 260,000 listeners every week from Bellingham to Olympia with a perspective and an ideology that go beyond politics.

On the air since 1926, KVI grew to become a popular music station. Over the years, the growth of music stations on FM radio displaced a significant portion of the audience on the AM band. The search for a new format led KVI into the talk-radio arena where KVI picked up the Rush Limbaugh program. The response was unprecedented. KVI had hit a nerve and filled a void in radio programming for the region. Today, Limbaugh, America's highest-rated radio talk-show for adults, broadcasts on 570 KVI from 9 a.m. to noon and remains the Northwest's most listened-to talk show.

KVI has become the 1990s version of a town meeting, a place where people can go to make their voices heard. The station covers the most important issues that face the community, nation, and world. The cornerstone of KVI is debate, allowing talk-show hosts and callers a no-holds-barred forum to voice their opinions. By offering this unique feature, KVI has established itself as a two-way medium that is more than a place to listen—it's a place to be heard.

Listeners continually express their appreciation to the station for the news and information they claim they can't get anywhere else. As one listener said, "When I get on the air at KVI, I'm able to access my countrymen." That assessment speaks volumes about the grassroots level of participation in this radio station. Other listeners acknowledge that learning is the prime motivator for listening to KVI, adding that as

Known for their friendly but pointed humor, STAR 101.5 *Morning Show* hosts Kent and Alan welcome listeners with a mix of local events, activities, weird trivia, and even ideas on what to do with your kids on the weekends.

a source of historical perspective and in-depth news, KVI is unequaled.

Hot-Talk 570 KVI is home to a variety of voices. Weekday mornings from 5 to 9, Kirby Wilbur combines the day's news and events with commentary and a historical perspective. Wilbur is fondly described by listeners as "the type of guy you talk to over the back fence."

The time from 9 a.m. to noon is reserved for the one, the only, Rush Limbaugh. Bombastic and pointed, Rush takes no prisoners as he jousts with the political and ideological establishment.

The noon to 3 p.m. slot features Michael Medved, film critic for the *New York Post*, cohost of *Sneak Previews* on PBS, and author of numerous books. Medved offers enlightening insights on family, pop culture, and history. No stranger to the road, Medved has produced his show from major cities around the country.

Seattle's best-known conservative media-personality, John Carlson, anchors a fast-paced and informative show from 3 to 6 p.m. Carlson's *Live Wire* segment offers some of the station's most compelling programming: callers are given 30 seconds to sound off about whatever is on their mind. The result is rambunctious and riveting.

Weekend programming includes more diversity with Rabbi Daniel Lapin, Wayne LaPierre, and the *Ken Hamblin Show*. In addition, KVI regularly features special guests that have included William Bennett, Marilyn and Dan Quayle, Dick Armey, Lynn Nofziger, Newt Gingrich, and Bob Dole.

Making Its Voice Heard

As one of the last locally owned radio groups in the Northwest, Fisher Radio Seattle, Fisher Broadcasting, and the Fisher family are an integral part of the Puget Sound region. Year in and year out, the Fisher group demonstrates its commitment to the community through its programming and numerous civic programs. Fisher Radio carries out an extensive corporate giving program that supports, among other things, higher education, Children's Hospital, and other children's charities.

In 1986, Fisher Broadcasting established For Kids Sake, programming and events developed specifically for children. In pursuing quality children's programming on television and radio, the company collaborates with the Seattle Center (site of the Space Needle) and other local organizations. Fisher Radio Seattle takes advantage of its affiliation with KOMO-TV to jointly host certain programs, such as the annual food drive in November and the Fourth-of-Julivers street fair and fireworks show.

In these and countless other ways, Fisher Radio Seattle makes its voice heard in western Washington. And, with Fisher's commitment to excellence, the company stands ready to make an impact on the community for years to come.

STAR 101.5's community and listener involvement goes in numerous directions with, on average, a charity function every month.

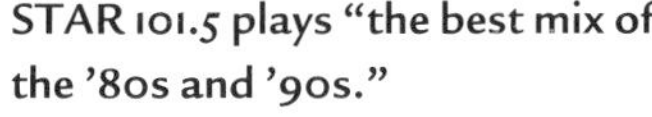

STAR 101.5 plays "the best mix of the '80s and '90s."

INCE ITS FIRST OPEN-COCKPIT BIPLANE HELPED TO DELIVER THE U.S. mail in 1926, United Airlines has been a pioneer of commercial aviation and a leader in airline service. United's history includes a number of industry firsts: the world's first flight attendant service in 1930; the first nonstop, coast-to-coast U.S. flight in 1955; implementation of the first nationwide automated reservations system in 1970; and, in 1990, the airline was the first commercial carrier to use satellite data communications in-flight.

United Airlines began its first scheduled service outside North America in 1983. Today, it is the largest air carrier in the world, flying to 139 destinations in 39 countries and two U.S. territories. With approximately 87,000 employees, it is also the world's largest majority employee-owned company.

Recognized as Seattle's hometown airline of choice, United has operated in the city since 1926, the same year it began a long-term relationship with The Boeing Company. Shuttle by United, launched in nine West Coast cities in 1994, includes 18 flights a day from Seattle to San Francisco. Offering an easy boarding process and low fares, the shuttle service continues to grow. United plans to expand in Seattle, as the company seeks new opportunities in both domestic and international markets. Furthermore, approximately 2,500 United employees currently make their home in Seattle.

SERVICE MAKES THE DIFFERENCE

United's business philosophy rests on the three pillars of safety, dependability, and competitive pricing. Offering unsurpassed global access and a simpler, more hassle-free travel experience, the airline has cultivated a philosophy of customer service built on insights gained from extensive customer surveys. As a result, United has invested in greater onboard comfort and added services.

"Moving into the future, we realize we have to differentiate our service in order to be the airline of choice worldwide," says Terry Brady, city manager of United Airlines' Seattle operations. "Our people make the difference. If we didn't have employees who understand customer service and strive to achieve it, we would not be where we are today."

A few years ago, United introduced an employee-driven style of management. As part of the cultural shift, frontline managers were empowered to lead customer-focused employee teams under the umbrella of city managers.

In early 1995, United launched the BOB Team, or "best of the best," in five cities to facilitate employee involvement and gather recommendations from the field. The BOB Team examines such processes as scheduling, operations, and customer service, and sets the wheels in motion to better those processes. Seattle was a testing station for the BOB Team and the first large city to adopt the program.

United's service has garnered kudos from many sources. It was voted the best airline in 1996 by *Travel and Leisure* magazine, and best in onboard service and in-flight safety by *Onboard Services Magazine*. It has also received numerous awards for serving the healthiest food, and its Mileage Plus program has won honors as the best overall frequent flyer program.

Hemispheres, United's onboard magazine, was named the best of 1,300 magazines for its cover design, photography, and editorial excellence, and America's best monthly travel magazine by the Society of American Travel Writers, the first time an in-flight magazine has won the coveted award.

In 1926, United Airlines began a long-term relationship with The Boeing Company, which provided United with B247s (left) and the modern B777 (right).

▲ STEWART HOPKINS PHOTOGRAPHY

A Presence in the Pacific Northwest

United is committed to having a major presence in the Pacific Northwest community, as demonstrated through United We Care. Employees rally around dozens of programs touching virtually all aspects of the community. Operating on an in-kind budget, United We Care is a corporate sponsor for major events and programs, such as the Northwest AIDS Walk, Urban League's All Achievers, Japanese American Society, Junior Achievement, Harborview Medical Center, Fred Hutchinson Cancer Research Center, and Children's Hospital.

United also sponsors Washington Junior Golf, Inner City Junior Golf, and Christmas in April, an annual home repair event. United employees helped make Seattle's Ronald McDonald House a valuable resource for families of children receiving medical treatment. As a proactive, preventive measure for missing children, United's Child I.D. program offers free fingerprinting and photographing at selected community events throughout the Puget Sound region.

United also partners with cultural and performing arts events and with sports teams in the region. It is a corporate sponsor of the Bumbershoot Festival, Corporate Council for the Arts, and PONCHO, an umbrella charitable group for performing arts organizations, as well as serving as the official airline for Summer Nights at the Pier, the Seattle Seahawks, Seattle Sounders, and Fred Couples Invitational. In conjunction with the Make-A-Wish Foundation, United sent approximately 65 kids on a Fantasy Flight to the North Pole from Sea-Tac Airport in 1996. The Seattle team continually assesses where it can leverage its time, money, and talent to make the greatest difference. And every year, United's Pride Day in July honors United employees and the dedicated work they do year-round.

United's history is one of innovation, leadership in its field, and service, both to its customers and to the communities in which its employees live and work. It is these qualities that have made it the largest airline in the world, and that ensure it will continue to grow and prosper into the 21st century.

Clockwise from top:

As a proactive, preventive measure, United's Child I.D. program offers free fingerprinting and photographing at selected community events throughout the Puget Sound region.

United We Care is a corporate sponsor for major events and programs, including the Northwest AIDS Walk.

Each year, United sponsors Take Your Community to Work Day, a mentoring program for high school students.

In 1930, on a downtown street corner once inhabited by wild grouse, a number of Seattle citizens erected a magnificent building dedicated to the advancement of amateur athletics and social activities. It turned out that they had built far more than even they had dreamed. ■ Everyone called it the WAC. To generation after generation, it has meant dreams of prowess and accomplishment coming true. To some, it was a gallery of pictures of men and women and great deeds, and the hope that one day they'd find their own image there. The WAC is the echoing gleam of crystal chandeliers illuminating the long hallways of the past; a child playing with alphabet blocks that spell out the future; or the rich scent of Thanksgiving turkey and rosemary, and the rustling of taffeta gowns. It is plump pillows and starched linens, and windows that open to let in the hum of the city and the smell of the sea.

Today, the WAC is the largest private club in America. It has become an unqualified success by adhering to its core values as a member-owned club. With 21 floors to serve the Club's more than 10,000 members worldwide, the WAC truly has something to offer everyone.

The WAC, Your Business, and Your Family

There's a good reason so many businesses and organizations prize their memberships in the Washington Athletic Club. For men and women, it's a part of a great network of common interest and purpose—the energy that has built the Northwest and influenced the world. It's a haven from the tensions of work and a reward for performance. WAC business programs, networking opportunities, and banquet facilities are the tools of leaders and future leaders.

Belonging to the WAC is a lifetime experience with lasting value. Some of its adult members still treasure their memories of getting started at swimming, racquetball, gymnastics, or karate when other kids couldn't find "a thing to do." And now their children create masterpieces for home refrigerators in WeeWAC's child care center while mom and dad get in a workout. From tyke to teen to almost-grown, the WAC offers a bountiful menu of sports, social opportunities, and belonging.

Athletic and Social Programs

Over the years, the WAC has nurtured a penchant for offering a full plate of creative athletic and social programs. Unmatched by any local gym, workout studio, sports club, school, or university, the WAC devotes five floors to fitness, exercise, competition, training, and helping members achieve their personal best. From basketball to ballet, from swimming to judo, the Club comes

In 1930, a number of Seattle citizens erected a magnificent building dedicated to the advancement of amateur athletics and social activities. It turned out that they had built far more than even they had dreamed—today's Washington Athletic Club (top).

Renowned for its personal style and intimacy, the Inn at the WAC offers members and their quests 130 elegantly appointed rooms and suites (bottom).

with the finest equipment and experts to help members reach their goals.

Continuing a tradition of unique social programming, the WAC hosts more than 250 special events each year. The WAC offers the best of times to broaden, entertain, and teach. At the WAC, a father discovers his daughter is a lady at an unforgettable Father/Daughter Banquet; enthusiasts and amateurs enjoy cigars and fine cognac at the Club's Main Event, a black-tie evening of boxing competition. The WAC is also about famous speakers, new fashions, and sampling a wine reminiscent of flowers. It's the Jubilee anniversary celebration each December, complete with tuxedos and gowns, casino-style gambling, dancing, and fine cuisine.

Fine Dining and Premier Accommodations

WAC restaurants bring something extra to the table. It can be felt in the tasteful comfort of Torchy's, the collegial warmth of Hagerty's Sports Bar, and the friendly casualness of the Sports Cafe. The WAC's restaurants, ballroom, and 16 banquet rooms have become a part of members' lives. They fit into shopping expeditions, business meetings, trips to town, conversation after the theater, and relaxing after work. The WAC also hosts wedding receptions and major business and social events of the season.

Renowned for its personal style and intimacy, the Inn at the WAC offers members and their guests 130 elegantly appointed rooms and suites with superior amenities, at a reasonable price. Located in the heart of downtown Seattle, the Inn at the WAC offers warm terry robes after a day of holiday shopping, as well as elegance and style for valued business guests. Guests may not remember that the newspaper was waiting at their door each morning, but they will remember that the Inn at the WAC takes away the trials of travel.

Beyond the Washington Athletic Club

The WAC is about more than what is contained within its walls. Members enjoy reciprocity at more than 170 clubs around the world. From Australia to Thailand, Hong Kong to Sweden, members will find a welcoming face and a home away from home.

The WAC is also proud to offer members privileges at several of the finest golf courses in and around the scenic Puget Sound area. So whether members are longing for the links or yearning for the beach, the Washington Athletic Club is the connection to rest and relaxation.

The WAC Mission

Stressing the ideals of service, quality, purpose, friendship, and personal growth, the WAC is a part of an attitude that characterizes this part of the world. It's a place to proudly bring others, to stay, to meet, to share ideas and a lifestyle. To many, belonging to the Washington Athletic Club is part of belonging in the great Pacific Northwest.

Clockwise from top:
Children create masterpieces for home refrigerators in WeeWAC's child care center while mom and dad get in a workout.

From handball to ballet, from swimming to judo, the Club comes with the finest equipment and experts to help members reach their goals.

The WAC's restaurants, ballroom, and banquet rooms have become a part of members' lives.

Founded in 1934, Chateau Ste. Michelle pioneered French varietal grape growing in Washington State, and has been winning acclaim for its classic European varietal wines since 1967. ■ Washington's oldest winery, Chateau Ste. Michelle's history dates back to just after the repeal of Prohibition when the state's bountiful fruit and berry harvests were vinified to produce the Northwest's first wines. By the 1950s, the company began planting classic vinifera grapes in the Columbia Valley, and buoyed by encouragement from wine writer Leon Adams and industry legend Andre Tchelistcheff, made its first varietal wines under the Ste. Michelle label in 1967. The wines awakened America to a new growing region.

Today, Chateau Ste. Michelle continues to be a leader in viticultural research and enjoys international regard for its world-class chardonnays, merlots, and cabernet sauvignons.

Classic Wine Making

Grapes are grown under the sunny skies of the Columbia Valley in eastern Washington, about 200 miles southeast of Seattle. The vineyards lie in the rain shadow of the Cascade Mountains, and the area's well-aerated soils, low rainfall, and warm summer temperatures yield blockbuster grapes. Long daylight hours during the growing season contrast with cool autumn nights to provide excellent structure, balance, and color intensity in the wines.

Under the inspired direction of wine maker Mike Januik, chardonnay, sauvignon blanc, and sémillon are barrel fermented and aged at the Woodinville chateau. Situated on 87 wooded acres 15 miles northeast of Seattle, the winery grounds were once the summer home of Seattle lumber baron Frederick Stimson, and now also serve as company headquarters.

Chateau Ste. Michelle makes its red wines in eastern Washington at Canoe Ridge Estate Winery, a state-of-the-art facility dedicated exclusively to small lot production. Keeping the wine in small barrels through aging gives the wine maker more options when it comes time to assemble the final blend.

Built in 1993, wine makers visited some of the best wineries in the world to benchmark a design for Canoe Ridge Estate Winery. To assure gentle treatment, a gravity flow system is used to minimize pumping, thereby reducing harsh tannins in the wines. Partial whole berry fermentation in specially sized tanks allows ideal cap depth-to-width ratios to extract maximum color and intensity from the fruit.

Situated on a steep slope overlooking the Columbia River, the winery is surrounded by the highly regarded Canoe Ridge Estate Vineyards and is within easy proximity of the winery's other vineyards. These include, among other prime sites, the Cold Creek Vineyard, planted in 1973. It is best known for its chardonnay and powerhouse

Clockwise from top:
Outdoor summer concerts, tours and tastings, and wine appreciation and cooking classes bring a quarter million people a year to the Woodinville winery.

Under the inspired direction of wine maker Mike Januik, merlot, cabernet franc, and cabernet sauvignon are made at Chateau Ste. Michelle's Canoe Ridge Estate Winery.

Situated on a steep slope overlooking the Columbia River is Chateau Ste. Michelle's Canoe Ridge Estate Vineyards.

cabernet sauvignon. Chateau Ste. Michelle's merlot from Indian Wells Vineyard, located at the base of the famed Wahluke Slope, has become one of the most sought after wines in the country.

The winery's commitment to quality has caught the attention of wine aficionados and critics alike. In 1996, *Wine & Spirits* magazine selected Chateau Ste. Michelle as a Winery of the Year, saying "Washington's leading producer succeeds with a vineyard focus."

Described by *Wine Spectator* as one of Washington's class acts, the magazine has named Chateau Ste. Michelle wines to its Top 100 Wines of the World list four times.

▸ JOHN RIZZO

Rooted in the Pacific Northwest

Chateau Ste. Michelle is actively involved in the Pacific Northwest's cultural and culinary scene. Outdoor summer concerts, tours and tastings, expansive grounds for picnics, dining, and wine appreciation and cooking classes bring a quarter million people a year to the Woodinville winery.

Complimentary guided tours and tastings are offered from 10 a.m. until 4:30 p.m. daily; no appointment is necessary. Reserve, single vineyard, and library wines are also available for tasting in the winery's Vintage Reserve Room; however, an appointment is required and a modest fee is charged.

In 1996, the winery introduced its first Artist Series Meritage, a Bordeaux-style red wine that pays tribute to internationally acclaimed glass artists, many of whom make their home in the area. Six pieces of glass art from celebrated artist Dale Chihuly were featured on the first Artist Series labels and are part of a permanent glass art collection at the winery.

Wines Take to the World Stage

Today, Washington's robust wine industry competes with ultra-premium wines from around the world, and Chateau Ste. Michelle's wines are usually found at center stage. The wines are exported to the United Kingdom, Germany, Sweden, Canada, the Far East, and other international markets. Its sister wineries include Columbia Crest, Domaine Ste. Michelle, and Snoqualmie in Washington state, and Villa Mt. Eden and Conn Creek in Napa Valley.

Combining the rich tradition and art of wine making with a dedication to research and innovation, Chateau Ste. Michelle continues to prove that the Columbia Valley is a world-class wine region.

Clockwise from top:
A well-stocked wine shop is just one of the features visitors to Chateau Ste. Michelle enjoy.

Chateau Ste. Michelle makes wines from classic European varietals grown under the sunny skies of the Columbia Valley.

Chateau Ste. Michelle is a leader in viticultural research and enjoys international regard for its world-class chardonnays, merlots, and cabernets.

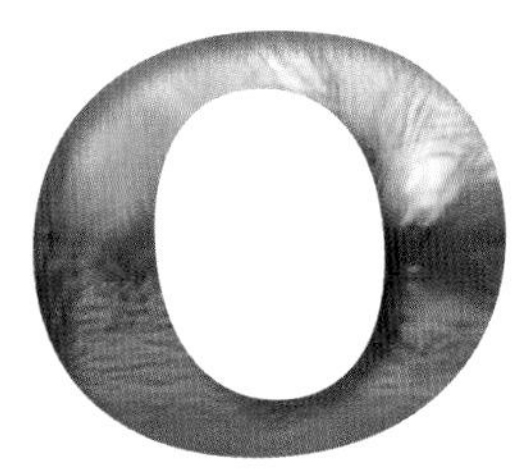

OVERLOOKING LAKE UNION, THE EASTLAKE OFFICES OF PEMCO Financial Services (PFS) are a familiar landmark to Interstate 5 drivers heading south toward Seattle's downtown, or north toward the University of Washington. The company's beginnings, however, were less conspicuous.

Seattle skyline from the shores of Lake Union.

Its history goes back to 1936, when Robert Handy, a 32-year-old high school math and journalism teacher, learned of a bill passed by the Washington State legislature allowing the establishment of credit unions.

The bill defined credit unions as nonprofit cooperatives whose primary purpose is to serve their members. Realizing that teachers would benefit from such a cooperative, Handy borrowed $5 from a friend to establish a credit union that would provide teachers "a safe place to save and a good place to borrow." On May 1, 1936, the Seattle Teachers Credit Union began. For several years Handy carried the business in his briefcase, earning only $25 a month for managing the credit union. In 1949, Handy built the first structure in the state to house a credit union; PEMCO Financial Services is still on that Eastlake Avenue site today.

Rapid Growth

By its fourth month of operation, the Seattle Teachers Credit Union had reached its $40,000 lending limit. Recognizing that most of the loans were for automobiles, Handy realized that teachers also needed affordable auto

Stanley O. McNaughton, president and CEO of PEMCO Insurance Companies, chairman of Evergreen-Bank, and treasurer-manager of Washington School Employees Credit Union (left).

PEMCO Financial Services serves more than half a million Washingtonians from its Seattle home office (right).

In 1949, founder Robert J. Handy built the first structure in the state to house a credit union (left).

From left: Hal Stover, Bob Ketcham, Joshua Green, Bob Handy, and Stan McNaughton celebrate Teachers State Bank's grand opening in 1971 (right).

insurance. As a result, Handy founded the Public Employees Mutual Casualty Companies (PEMCO) in 1949.

In 1952, the Seattle Teachers Credit Union, renamed Washington School Employees Credit Union, began serving school and college employees statewide. Today, that credit union is the third-largest in the state, serving 64,000 public and private school employees statewide.

Building on this foundation, Handy created Public Employees Mutual Insurance Company, now called the PEMCO Mutual Insurance Company, in 1951 to provide property and casualty insurance to the general public. In 1963, Handy established PEMCO Life Insurance Company, which sells life insurance primarily through credit unions. PEMCO Corporation, a computer services company, was established the same year to provide data processing services for more than 300 credit unions. In 1968, PEMCO Insurance Agency Inc. was formed to provide one source for collecting premiums. Soon after, Handy predicted the authorization of share-draft (checking) accounts for credit unions, which required bank services to be cleared through the Federal Reserve System. In 1971, a charter was granted for the Teachers State Bank, now called EvergreenBank, a commercial bank to serve credit unions, the general public, and small-business owners.

These seven institutions comprise PFS today; together, they serve well over half a million Washington residents. Reaching $1 billion in combined assets in 1996, the companies operate as one firm, providing financial services—money when you need it, anywhere, anytime, to anyone.

"I don't think there's another operation like ours anywhere in the country," says Stanley O. McNaughton, who is president and CEO of PEMCO Insurance Companies, chairman of EvergreenBank, and treasurer-manager of Washington School Employees Credit Union. "We are seven different companies that share common facilities and functions, human resources, marketing, communications, advertising, purchasing, data processing, printing and supply, and mail services. If you put all our customers and their families together, they would comprise the largest city in Washington."

The economies of scale achieved through this structure have proved invaluable. PEMCO Financial Services exceeds $1 billion in assets. McNaughton says that "when growth stops, death starts"; however, "growth is not always in size but should be in quality and strength."

Customer Service

Part of PFS' success has been its ability to combine the benefits of a large company offering complete financial services with the feel of the tiny credit union from which it emerged. The other key is in keeping a customer-focused philosophy. "Customers are not an interruption of our work, but the purpose. The only purpose of this organization is to serve customers. After the customers are served, we can serve our employees, our community, and our investors," McNaughton says.

PFS has had to adjust operations to accommodate such dynamic growth, while providing customers with the level of service they're accustomed to. "We finally reached a point," McNaughton explains,

PFS, like the Seattle skyline, has grown significantly since this 1965 photo.

"where we had to invest either in new automation or in more employees and a bigger building to put them in. Our growth was not only outdistancing our existing computer capability, but also hamstringing our customer services."

Today, technology is being installed and employees trained to offer greater convenience and more efficient service for the future. A common database will provide greater opportunity to create an office in every home where customers will have fingertip control of information and electronic money access.

Strong Leadership

In May 1996, McNaughton received the prestigious First Citizen Award from the King County Association of Realtors, recognizing him as one who exemplifies the spirit of community service. The 75-year-old leader has been at the helm of PFS since 1970.

Handy hired McNaughton in 1961 to address the issue of what kind of company PEMCO should be in 50 years. "Little did I realize at that time that I would spend the rest of my life making the plan come true. I was very fortunate," McNaughton says.

Handy had an individualistic character, a strong will, and a brilliant mind. But being outspoken, he needed help with his people skills. Among his first employees was Gladys McLaughlin, a dignified woman who was not afraid to challenge Handy when she thought he was wrong. A problem solver, she would listen to all sides of a disagreement before suggesting a solution. Handy and his staff appreciated her efforts as a major adviser. Hired in 1955, she worked at PEMCO for nearly 40 years before retiring.

Another who contributed greatly to PFS' successes was Bob Ketcham. Ketcham came to work in 1952, during PEMCO's formative years, and was one of its most versatile and valuable executives. He became an expert on financial matters and handled all construction responsibilities, including construction of the seven-story PEMCO Financial Center.

Bob Howisey was a college friend of Ketcham's who came to Seattle in 1947, following his discharge from the U.S. Navy. Ketcham suggested that Handy interview Howisey, and Handy liked him immediately. Howisey appreciated the way Handy would carefully think through an idea and then put the thought into action. Handy wanted information about recent advances in data processing; Howisey had experience with early IBM machines, and soon introduced PEMCO to the world of computers. Now, as the senior employee at PEMCO, Howisey recalls that a major responsibility of the executives was to help Handy identify the good ideas from the many he generated, and to convince him to drop the others. Howisey has been a part of every major decision made by the organization.

Hal Stover, another PFS founder, was a self-made man who got along with everyone.

Clockwise from top right: More than one-third of PFS' employees volunteer their time and efforts to make their communities a better place in which to live and work.

PEMCO joins the computer world in 1967. From left: Hal Stover, Gladys McLaughlin, an IBM representative, Bob Handy, Bob Howisey, Bob Ketcham, and Stan McNaughton.

PEMCO is Washington State's number one domestic insurer of private passenger automobiles.

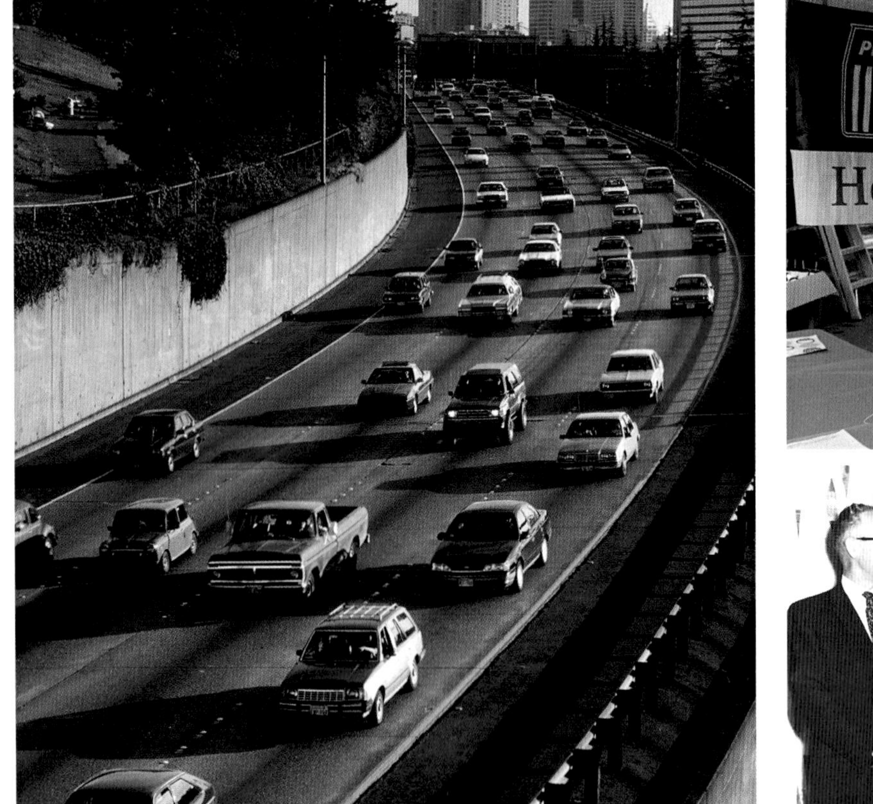

He became operating manager of the Credit Union—without ruffling Handy's sensitive feathers—and also helped form EvergreenBank. Stover received the Washington Credit Union League Person of the Year award for his work in the credit union movement.

Corporate Citizenship

Ketcham, McLaughlin, Howisey, Stover, and McNaughton all played significant roles in helping Handy shape the PFS companies. One thing each had in common was a commitment to corporate volunteerism. In a city known for its philanthropy, PEMCO has proved to be a corporate citizen with a big heart. Each year, 5 percent of the increase in net worth of PFS' combined seven institutions is donated to two foundations. Through the PEMCO Foundation, college scholarships are awarded to graduates of Washington State high schools. Teachers Foundation provides aid to tax-exempt organizations whose primary mission is to help disadvantaged individuals who, through no fault of their own, need help to become independent, productive citizens.

The company also devotes significant resources to finding innovative ways to expose young people to business. One example: PFS sponsors high school sophomores and juniors who attend Business Week, an award-winning summertime program in which students immerse themselves for seven days in the world of business: marketing, balance sheets, and computer simulations.

Community giving isn't practiced just by PEMCO's leadership. More than 300 of the company's 1,000 employees volunteer their time and efforts to make their communities a better place in which to live and work. Through business-education programs such as Junior Achievement, employees volunteer to teach students about America's free enterprise system. PFS also gives back to its employees, investing generously in training and benefits. This policy may account for its strong employee loyalty, reflected in an 8 percent turnover rate—a striking contrast to the 30 percent industry norm.

Says McNaughton, "A corporation is the greatest instrument ever created to do good. It creates wealth, it creates jobs, and it then uses that wealth to do good in the community. We challenge other companies to follow our lead and invest 5 percent of their profits back into their communities."

Building the Vision

"Share the vision, the benefits, and the recognition" is a theme reinforced throughout the seven PFS institutions. "Our employees are building cathedrals, not just laying bricks," says McNaughton. The PFS vision is one where the company can improve the quality of life for its customers, employees, and the community by providing ultimate convenience and service. Building on its solid foundation of customer service, public service, technological sophistication, and complete array of financial services, the PEMCO Financial Services vision will carry the company into the 21st century and beyond.

PFS offers services and products for all phases of its customers' lives.

PEMCO offers several special programs for its customers, including the PEMCO Safe Driver Plan and PEMCO Mariner Policy.

LICENSED THROUGHOUT THE WEST AS A CONSTRUCTION MANAGER and general construction contractor for the commercial sector and private industry, Baugh Enterprises is the largest, most respected employee-owned construction company based in the Pacific Northwest. It serves clients with offices in Seattle, where it started business in 1946, and in Beaverton, Oregon.

During its 50 years of operation, Baugh has built its reputation on customer service; the ability to create high-quality, efficient projects; and a belief in the importance of establishing long-term relationships. These relationships are important to the company and to its clients; a client may go five years or more between projects, but when the time arrives, the client contacts Baugh.

Baugh considers its real strength to be its people. Each individual is an asset—highly qualified, with hands-on experience. Throughout the Pacific Northwest, northern California, and Alaska, the construction firm has demonstrated expertise in every job, whether it calls for design/build coordination, budget estimates, or turnkey construction.

The majority of Baugh's work is in commercial and industrial construction, with particular emphasis on concrete, structural steel, mechanical piping for pulp and paper mills, high-rise offices, apartments, condominiums, hotels, hospitals and shopping centers, high-tech flex buildings, food processing, manufacturing plants, warehouses, and distribution complexes. Seismic retrofits, once a complicated and difficult discipline, are now a Baugh specialty. Steel, concrete, and new methods give added life to old structures.

A TEAM EFFORT

Baugh works with its clients on every step of a project, including the early stages where critical decisions have to be made. The company develops novel approaches for customers that benefit the owner while meeting project specifications. For maximum continuity and efficiency, the team assigned to each project follows it through from estimating to completion, servicing the client's needs and assuming responsibility for every aspect of the job. Whether a project is large or small, the team is in charge of the schedule, staff, and budget—everything the project needs to succeed.

Roughly 75 percent of Baugh's contracts are "negotiated priced," with cost savings split between the owner and contractor. By including the contractor on the design team, large cost reductions can be achieved with value engineering prior to determining the final price. Baugh also returns to clients considerable savings through superior construction performance. For example, Baugh handled the expansion of the Portland International Airport. Despite the complexity of the project, Baugh trimmed 14 months off the origi-

Clockwise from top:
The Benaroya Symphony Hall, located in downtown Seattle, comprises 185,000 square feet and will be the home for the Seattle Symphony Orchestra.

Baugh handled the expansion of the Portland International Airport, trimming 14 months off the original construction schedule and returning more than $4 million in value engineering and savings.

The Boeing Airplane 4-86 Wing Clean, Seal, and Paint Building has a 115,000-square-foot footprint in which aircraft wings are painted, processed, and finished in an assembly line format. More than 2,200 tons of structural steel are included in the building, which has clear-span trusses of 150 feet in length and 12 feet in depth.

▶ SOUNDVIEW AERIAL PHOTOGRAPHY

nal construction schedule and returned more than $4 million in value engineering and savings. The remaining 25 percent of its work volume is bid competitively for the express purpose of remaining current with cost and conditions in the marketplace.

By maintaining salaried superintendents to direct field workforces, Baugh performs a high percentage of work that is traditionally subcontracted in the industry, including concrete formwork, placement and finishing of concrete, structural steel and precast erection, rough and finish carpentry, and process piping. Project managers and field superintendents thrive on the challenge and the intensity, leading projects with precision, attention, and speed.

Turning Visions into Realities

In construction, brute force and high technology often mesh. Computers now produce more efficient schedules—weekly, daily, and even hourly. When pouring concrete in unstable weather, a worker's handheld Doppler weather radar gives the cue to pour, wait a little while, or try the next day. Improved pumps can now deliver concrete at 8,000 P.S.I. Still, in spite of technological advancements, the experience and skill of the workers remains the most important ingredient in any project.

Owners want their projects to be economical, but also effective and pleasing to the eye. In many cases, both can be achieved by using unique construction techniques that are also economical. The results are born of coordinated efforts, orchestrated and executed by the project team. Whatever the structure's purpose, its construction must be sound, its budget firm, and its schedules met. On every project, Baugh's workers must meet the challenges of construction on a daily basis—together.

A sample of the diversity of recent Baugh projects includes the retrofitting of a cement plant; the Portland International Airport expansion; the renovation of a pulp mill; the refurbishing of an art museum; and the construction of a huge concrete silo, a chapel for a private university, and a new building for the Seattle Symphony.

The owner who wants a new or revitalized building is responding to a need: a new store, a bigger facility, a more efficient plant. No one understands the practical needs of business and construction better than Baugh. For the past 50 years, Baugh has turned the visions of owners, architects, and entrepreneurs into realities. As Baugh heads into the next 50 years, it will continue to offer unmatched service, innovative solutions, and solid craftsmanship to its customers.

Clockwise from top left:
For the Intel facility in Dupont, Washington, approximately 100 acres of land were cleared for a 360,000-square-foot box plant and office structure. The project included installation of underground utilities; a steel joist roof system, with a 28-foot height; a cafeteria/restaurant; and interior production equipment installation. The entire project was finished in nine months.

Baugh provided civil, structural, mechanical, refractory, and electrical installation and civil structural design for the Ashgrove cement plant in Leamington, Utah.

The new Darigold cheese plant consists of 60,000 square feet of highly automated American cheese production. In addition to construction of the plant and cooler, Baugh installed all of the major process equipment and assisted vendors with start-up.

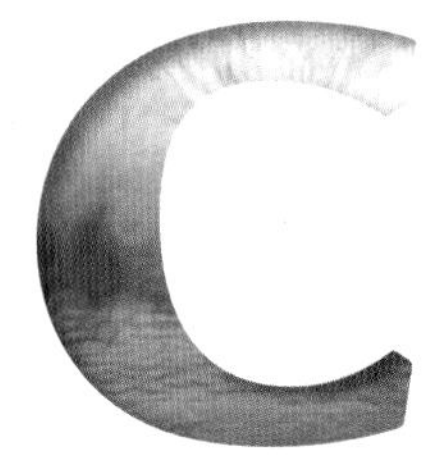

CELEBRATING ITS 50TH ANNIVERSARY IN 1997, THE ALLIEDSIGNAL Inc. operation in Redmond was one of the pioneering firms in the Northwest, and one of the first high-tech companies on the Eastside. Founded as United Control in 1947 by four former Boeing engineers, the company quickly established itself as a major supplier of electronic controls and accessory devices for military aircraft, missiles, and commercial transports. United Control later became Sundstrand Data Control, and moved from the University District to Redmond in 1963. AlliedSignal purchased Sundstrand in 1993, and today employs approximately 1,000 employees in the Puget Sound area.

With headquarters in Morristown, New Jersey, AlliedSignal Corporation is a $15 billion, international advanced-technology company with operations in more than 100 countries worldwide. Ranked among the 30 largest Fortune 500 companies, AlliedSignal is focused on three business areas—aerospace, automotive products, and engineered materials.

AlliedSignal Aerospace

As the largest aircraft equipment supplier in the world, AlliedSignal Aerospace, a division of the parent company, serves the aircraft equipment, defense, and space markets with a broad array of sophisticated systems, subsystems, components, and services. About 80 percent of its business is with U.S.-based customers, while the remaining 20 percent is international. Its extensive repair and overhaul facility in Redmond serves Boeing and the entire airline community.

With some 39,000 employees, AlliedSignal Aerospace makes more than 35,000 aerospace products, and offers nearly as many services for major airplane manufacturers in every air transport category. It is the world's leading independent supplier of turbofan engines, used in business aviation; airborne auxiliary power units that help start main engines and operate secondary power systems; air-conditioning and cabin pressurization systems; and actuation systems that operate primary and secondary control surfaces such as wing flaps, cargo doors, and landing gears.

Marketing products under such well-known brand names as Bendix, Garrett, and Bendix/King, AlliedSignal Aerospace is also a leader in the manufacture of turboprop engines, flight control systems, turbine engine starters, and weather avoidance radar. It operates in the forefront of landing systems technology, with its advanced wheels and carbon composite brake discs flying on the

Clockwise from top:
Celebrating its 50th anniversary in 1997, the AlliedSignal Inc. operation in Redmond, shown here in architectural renderings, was one of the pioneering firms in the Northwest, and one of the first high-tech companies on the Eastside.

Pilot Markus Johnson flight tests AlliedSignal's weather radar, traffic collision avoidance system (TCAS), and enhanced ground proximity warning system (EGPWS).

As world leaders in avionics, AlliedSignal plays a critical role in aviation safety. Every aircraft flying in the free world carries at least one early warning device manufactured in Redmond.

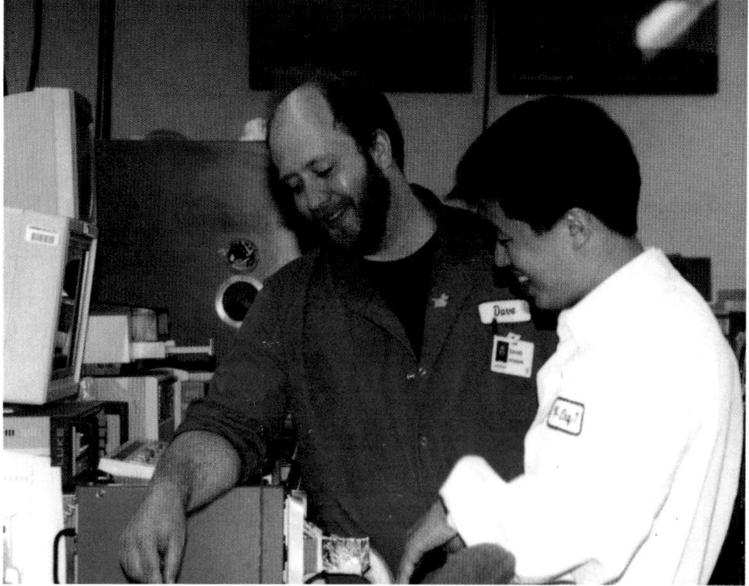

most advanced commercial and military aircraft in the world.

In addition to being the largest supplier to Boeing of equipment other than engines, AlliedSignal applies its technology wherever needed. It is the largest supplier of engines for smaller aircraft, and has played a major role in the U.S. space program, having supplied equipment for every manned spacecraft since the program's inception. AlliedSignal also supplies components and integrated systems for submarine weapons launch and control, and satellite command and control.

Avionics Specialists

As world leaders in avionics, AlliedSignal plays a critical role in aviation safety. With the increasing number of planes in the air, the issue of air safety becomes more and more critical. AlliedSignal leads the industry in traffic alert and collision avoidance systems. Its products help airline crews and passengers around the world reach their destinations safely and on time. Every aircraft flying in the free world carries at least one early warning device manufactured in Redmond.

"In Redmond, we're AlliedSignal's focal point for its efforts in aviation safety," says Frank Daly, vice president of flight safety avionics. "We're increasing our investments in advanced technology to address aircraft safety, and we work constantly with Boeing and others to understand how their needs and our technology can advance aviation safety." In early 1997, the Gore Commission on Flight Safety recognized AlliedSignal for its pioneering work in aviation safety.

AlliedSignal manufactures the industry's most advanced ground proximity warning system (GPWS), which helps pilots avoid mountains and other obstacles. In 1996, AlliedSignal took the GPWS to the next level of effectiveness with the release of the enhanced ground proximity warning system (EGPWS). Adding satellite-based location technology and a database of the world's terrain, the enhanced system shows the pilot where the aircraft is in relation to surrounding terrain and issues a "caution terrain" warning much earlier—60 seconds, rather than 30 seconds under the previous system.

EGPWS can also monitor the aircraft's rate of descent or ascent and issue a warning for incidents in which the pilot banks the aircraft too steeply, descends too steeply, or climbs too slowly. American Airlines is spending $25 million to outfit its entire fleet by 1999, and United Airlines, Alaska Airlines, and others are taking similar steps.

AlliedSignal Aerospace's Redmond site is perhaps best known as the world's largest supplier of black box flight data recorders. So named for its original color, the black box—which is, in fact, orange—includes both the cockpit voice recorder and the flight data recorder. Designed to record information to analyze serious aviation accidents in hopes of preventing them in the future, it covers enough parameters to make a detailed analysis of the problem.

AlliedSignal also manufactures a traffic collision alerting system and airborne weather radar, a state-of-the-art system that probes in front of the aircraft and delivers information on storm activity several hundred miles ahead, giving the aircraft plenty of time to avoid it.

Future Technology

With the future in mind, AlliedSignal is developing advanced sensing technology and computational devices that integrate all of these different technologies. "The next advance in safety avionics will involve the integration of safety units that will talk to one another. Components will share information in a central device called an integrated hazard avoidance system," says Don Bateman,

Clockwise from top left: AlliedSignal contributes $10 million annually to various nonprofit education, community, and cultural organizations. Participating in the annual United Way Kickoff Event are (from left) Norm Kline, general manager, Instrument Systems; Frank Daly, vice president of Flight Safety Avionics; and Don Warner, program manager.

A representative from China Northern Airlines receives training at AlliedSignal's training, repair, and overhaul facility in Redmond.

The enhanced ground proximity warning system (EGPWS) undergoes a final check at Redmond's state-of-the-art testing facilities.

AlliedSignal's chief flight-safety engineer and the man responsible for steering EGPWS through two decades of development. AlliedSignal is the only company producing such a product, and the company has a full-scale engineering development team devoted to the project.

In addition to its $5 billion aerospace business, AlliedSignal is one of the world's largest independent suppliers to the global automotive industry. The company produces braking systems; engine components such as filters, spark plugs, and turbochargers; and steering components. AlliedSignal also designs and manufactures seat belt and air bag restraint systems, and makes automotive replacement parts for distributors, installers, and retail outlets worldwide.

The Instrument Systems unit is part of AlliedSignal Aerospace's Electronic Systems division, and develops such products as bimetal thermal switches and precision accelerometers—which are used on virtually every commercial and military aircraft, and have been since the company's inception some 50 years ago. These products remain the backbone of Instrument Systems to this day, and the products can be found not only in aerospace applications, but also in energy exploration and diesel locomotives.

AlliedSignal's engineered materials businesses supply high-quality fibers, chemicals, and plastics worldwide for such diverse markets as carpeting, tires, apparel, seat belts, food and pharmaceutical packaging, and refrigeration, as well as advanced materials for the gas and electric utilities and electronics industries.

AlliedSignal Corporation supports its technology-intensive businesses through research, development, and engineering provided by some 16,000 scientists and engineers in 70 laboratories and technical centers worldwide. The company's efforts are reflected in the more than 27,000 U.S. and foreign patents held by the corporation, and its ranking among the top 10 patent recipients in American industry.

Among its research facilities is a $40 million Corporate Technology Center in Morristown, where the development of advanced materials such as ceramics, rapidly solidified alloys, advanced composites, and new fuel technologies offers potential product applications in each of the company's businesses.

At AlliedSignal Aerospace's Microelectronic Center, sophisticated computer-aided-design tools help create and produce proprietary integrated circuits. Other projects include programs for fault-tolerant flight and engine control systems, turbofan engines, and advanced silicon and microelectronic circuits.

By advancing its technology base, investing in modern facilities and methods, expanding into new markets, and implementing total quality management concepts to enhance its agility and flexibility as an organization, AlliedSignal is sharpening the competitive edge that ensures its future growth and success.

Clockwise from top right: AlliedSignal has supplied equipment for every U.S. manned spacecraft since the program's inception.

AlliedSignal's Redmond site is best known as the world's largest supplier of black box cockpit voice and flight data recorders.

AlliedSignal's Commercial Avionics Systems in Redmond manufactures the industry's most advanced ground warning system—EGPWS—which helps pilots avoid mountains and other obstacles.

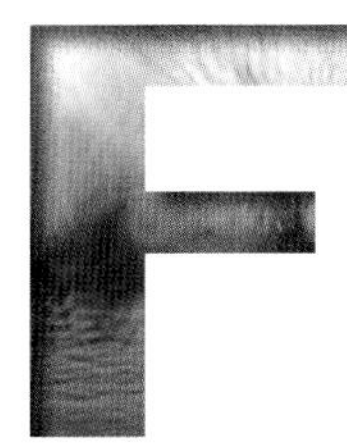

OUNDED IN 1959, PHIL SMART, INC. IS KNOWN AS THE Mercedes of Mercedes-Benz dealers in the Puget Sound area. Selling and servicing all Mercedes classes, from the entry-level C-Class to the luxury E-Class and S-Class models, and introducing the M-Class in 1997, its portfolio of these timeless cars continues to expand.

With close to 40 years in the business, Phil Smart, Inc. is well known for its service. "When the majority of car sales are repeat and referrals, the level of service has to be excellent," says Phil Smart Jr., president. "The added value customers receive when they buy a car from us starts with our excellent service. The sales staff first takes time to build a relationship with customers."

Excellent Service

Known for doing the right thing for the customer, Phil Smart, Inc. rates the highest scores among all Mercedes-Benz dealerships in the Puget Sound area on the nationally known consumer satisfaction index. A large percentage of customers are drawn to the dealership because of its reputation, and many of the company's 65 employees have worked at Phil Smart for more than 20 years. Continuity of leadership by a dedicated senior staff guarantees that the basic ideas on which the business was founded are never compromised. Each year, the dealership awards the PEPE Award to the employee who best embodies the positive, energetic qualities of the company.

Phil Smart's service department services an average of 75 cars a day—many of which have accumulated more than 200,000 miles. All servicing is performed in-house by senior technicians who receive ongoing factory training. Two senior technicians have achieved the level of Master Guild Technician, a category Mercedes-Benz of North America reserves for only the best of the best. The dealership added eight service stalls to its existing 18 in early 1997.

Recognizing that the customer makes a business a success, Phil Smart, Inc. believes in giving back to the community. Employees are active volunteers. Phil Smart Sr., who founded the business and passed the ownership to his son in 1980, was the first male volunteer at Children's Hospital. For the past 35 years he has worked on the rehabilitation ward one night a week, and has also been the official and only Santa Claus at the hospital for the past 23 years. He has spoken to some 25,000 people and traveled all over North America to talk about volunteerism. By sharing his time and talents with the community, Phil Smart Sr. sets a powerful example for others.

With $35 million in sales in 1996, Phil Smart, Inc. continues to grow, holding fast to its original success based on truth and integrity.

Phil Smart Sr. (left) and Phil Smart Jr. are owners of Phil Smart, Inc.—the Mercedes of Mercedes-Benz dealers in the Puget Sound area.

The exciting SLK is designed to be a sports car "for all seasons and reasons," thanks in large part to its standard retractable hardtop, standard ASR traction control, and a suggested manufacturer's retail price of $37,000.

Known for doing the right thing for the customer, Phil Smart, Inc. rates the highest scores among all Mercedes-Benz dealerships in the Puget Sound area on the nationally known consumer satisfaction index.

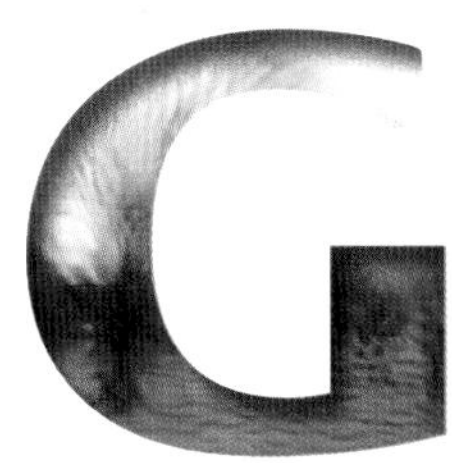

Group Health Cooperative of Puget Sound is recognized nationally as one of the pioneering health maintenance organizations in the country. Founded in 1947, it recently celebrated its 50th anniversary as the nation's largest consumer-governed health care organization. It serves more than 710,000 in the Pacific Northwest and is one of the state's largest employers.

Group Health's success proves that a nonprofit, consumer-governed health plan can prosper. It has grown to become what many consider the most successful cooperative in the country. Ranked among the best HMOs in the nation in *Consumer Reports, Newsweek*, and the National Research Corporations' *Healthcare Market Guide*, Group Health was among the first health care plans in the Northwest to be fully accredited by the National Committee for Quality Assurance.

With alliances and partnerships, Group Health continues to innovate for the future. In order to meet the needs of multistate companies in the Pacific Northwest and to improve members' ability to get care, it has increased its network of care providers and entered into a unique arrangement with Kaiser Permanente, the nation's largest HMO. Other choices offered to Group Health members and purchasers now include HMOs, point-of-service plans, and self-funded insurance options.

As one of the oldest and largest HMOs, Group Health operates and contracts with hospitals, specialty medical centers, and family health clinics across Washington and north Idaho. With a growing portion of its business in rural areas, Group Health contracts with more than 2,400 community physicians, group practices, and other care providers who meet its award-winning standards and medical protocols.

Patient Friendly and Cost Effective

Group Health is run by an 11-member volunteer board of trustees who are elected by the Cooperative's members. Serving on committees and working groups, members work with medical staff leaders and administrators to find ways to improve health services.

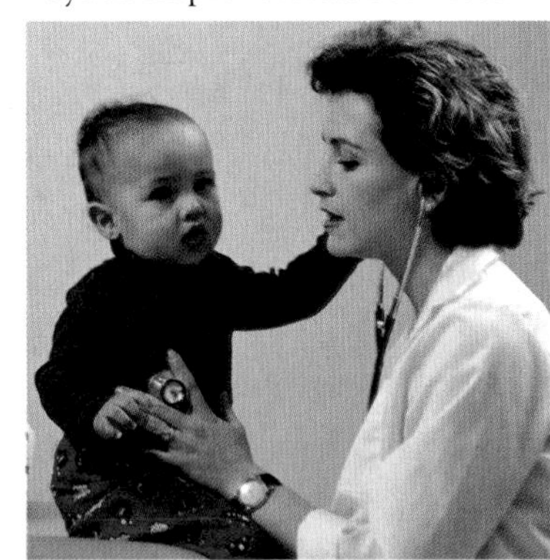

They also serve on local advisory groups to monitor the medical care and service, and to suggest improvements.

Consumer governance stems from a philosophy that having patients consult with nurses, doctors, and administrators leads to better information, analysis, and decision making, which results in better care. By drawing on their own experiences, from the AIDS patient who advises doctors and nurses working with other AIDS patients to the activists who lobby for new senior services, Co-op members make a difference.

Group Health strikes the delicate balance of providing quality, cost-effective medical care without neglecting the needs of patients. It is well known for its operational efficiency. For every dollar of premium collected, the Co-op returns more than 90 cents in the form of health care. Group Health contains costs by stressing preventive care and continually using new procedures that provide the best outcome at the lowest cost. Rather than micromanaging every case, the Co-op periodically reviews doctors based on patient satisfaction and clinical outcomes, and

While Group Health is known for its strong preventive care and health promotion focus, patients also receive cutting-edge specialty care, like coronary angiography (bottom left).

Group Health delivers care in many ways and settings: with its own staff in Group Health facilities (bottom right), and through a network of contracted providers and partners. No matter where care is delivered, doctors and health care teams make all health care decisions.

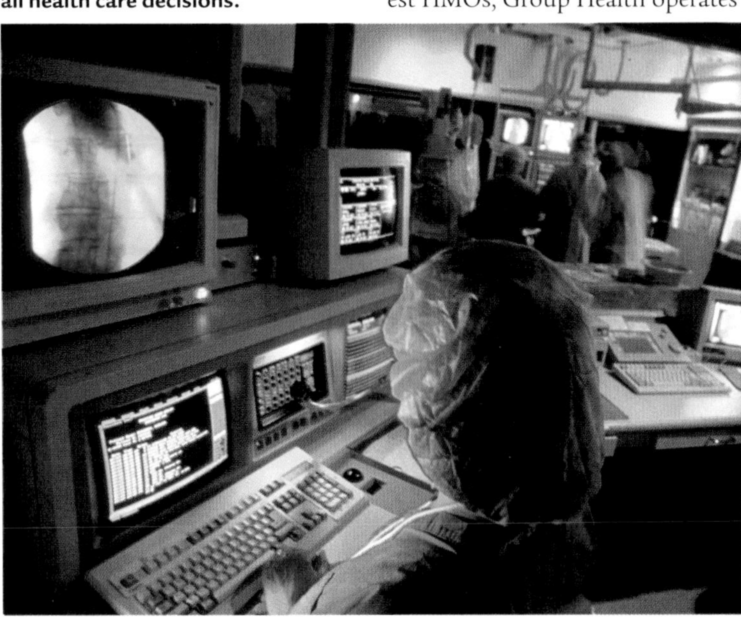

Doug Plummer

Walter Hodges

WALTER HODGES

doctors are trusted to make their own clinical decisions with their patients within an overall budget. The Co-op care network is made up of salaried physicians as well as independent contractors.

"Group Health has to survive as a business if it is to survive as a cooperative," says Phil Nudelman, president and chief executive officer of Group Health and current chair of the American Association of Health Plans. "We continue to find ways to improve care, service, cost, and choices for our purchasers and members. We must work to remain affordable for group and individual purchasers, but we must never sacrifice the quality of our care and service."

To keep costs low and patient satisfaction high, Group Health embraces a highly coordinated team approach. Health care teams are partnered with clinical improvement coaches and trainers. With a sophisticated information and clinical computer network, doctors and nurses can access clinical information—everything from patients' pharmacy profiles to the latest research-based clinical guidelines. Soon, doctors will be able to instantly compare a patient's profile with recommended care guidelines.

Group Health is among a handful of HMOs in the nation to perform research in health care. Its Center for Health Studies is a national research leader in primary care, prevention, geriatrics, mental health, and cancer care. It collaborates with the Fred Hutchinson Cancer Research Institute and the University of Washington to promote health and prevention, and operates the Center for Health Promotion to promote wellness among its members as well as the communities it serves.

WALTER HODGES

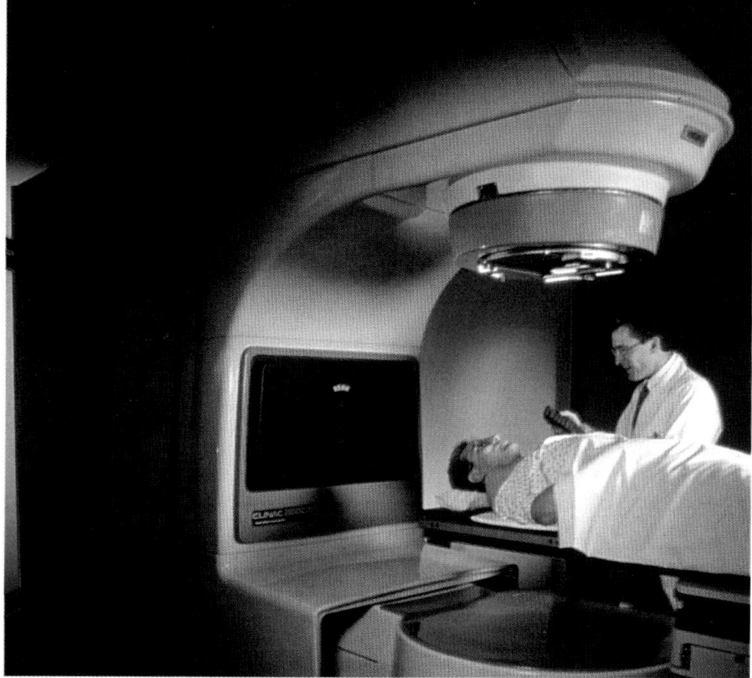

Group Health has over 30 neighborhood medical centers, like the Everett Medical Center (top right), located throughout the Puget Sound area. In all their medical and specialty centers, Group Health offers state-of-the-art diagnostic technology, in-house pharmacies, and 24-hour consulting nurse services.

Group Health has strengthened its focus on evidence-based and population-based medicine. By looking at patients in the context of other patients with the same condition, doctors now apply a far more methodical and systematic approach to treatment and management of chronic care. Over the past 25 years, for example, an increased awareness of senior health needs has improved care delivery for senior patients.

Group Health's mission goes beyond being a successful health maintenance organization. With the Group Health Foundation and through its community service activities, the Cooperative helps to promote public health in the communities it serves, focusing on improving infant mortality rates, childhood immunizations, health care for the homeless, and reducing violence. Additionally, it makes direct and in-kind contributions to organizations that further these services, and helps mobilize public and private efforts in these and other areas. For the past 50 years, Group Health has worked to improve the health and well-being of its members and of the Pacific Northwest. Today, it continues to innovate, leading the way as a national model for other health care providers.

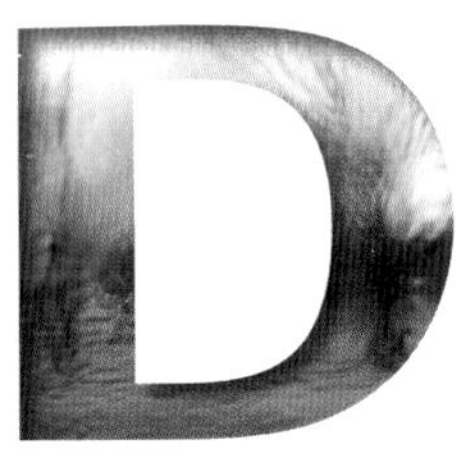

Dames & Moore is one of the Pacific Northwest's most prominent engineering and environmental consulting services firms. Today's Dames & Moore is part of the Dames & Moore Group, and is a $650 million company with more than 6,700 employees and 150 offices throughout the world. The firm specializes in providing comprehensive, integrated environmental, engineering, and construction management services that enhance the business, regulatory compliance, and technological commitments its clients must make on a global basis.

With close to 40 years of international experience, the scope and quality of Dames & Moore's services, coupled with its broad-based geographic operations, make the company unique among consulting companies.

◄ Soundview Aerial

Clockwise from top:
The Dames & Moore Group has been involved in the coordination of construction and rehabilitation projects at the University of Washington.

Dames & Moore serves Weyerhaeuser, the Bonneville Power Administration, several major developers, and many other clients in the Pacific Northwest.

BRW is managing construction of the renovation of the King Street Station building in Seattle, as well as coordinating construction of a commuter rail and bus access to the station.

Early Northwest Company

Founded in Los Angeles in 1938, Dames & Moore opened offices in Seattle and Portland in 1947. With additional Pacific Northwest offices in Boise, Tacoma, Spokane, Richland, Anchorage, Fairbanks, and Vancouver, British Columbia, Dames & Moore has the capabilities to successfully manage complicated, multidimensional projects throughout the region.

From the 1940s until the 1980s, Dames & Moore was a consulting firm focused on geotechnical engineering and environmental and geologic sciences. In the early 1990s, it began expanding its technical capabilities to become a full-service engineering and consulting practice. During this period, several Northwest companies, including Norecol Environmental Services of Vancouver, British Columbia, and Bovay Northwest, a Washington facilities engineering company, were acquired and integrated into the firm. Nationally, the firm was also adding to its capabilities by acquiring such firms as Walk-Haydel, a process engineering company; DecisionQuest, which specializes in litigation consultation; BRW, which specializes in development planning and transportation; and O'Brien Kreitzberg, the nation's foremost construction management firm.

The acquisition of BRW and O'Brien Kreitzberg, both of which have offices in the Northwest, has significantly enhanced the Dames & Moore Group's capability to offer fully integrated services in public works and transportation projects.

Known nationwide for its expertise in the development of livable communities, BRW specializes in planning and engineering services for infrastructure projects. In the Pacific Northwest, BRW has provided design and engineering services for many significant transportation and development projects, including the Tri-Met light-rail system in Portland, Oregon; the King Street Station intermodal terminal in Seattle; and a proposed Personal Rapid Transit System surrounding Seattle-Tacoma International Airport. BRW's Seattle-based staff led a team that performed planning, land use, and operational analyses of the light-rail, commuter rail, and regional bus program alternatives developed by the Regional Transit Authority for the new integrated transit system in the Seattle metropolitan region. BRW has also been involved with community planning for the Seattle Housing Authority and several of the region's medium-sized cities.

Clockwise from left:
Involved in major energy facilities throughout the Northwest, Dames & Moore is an active player in preparing pipeline and power plant permits, including those for the Olympic Pipeline.

BRW has provided design and engineering services for many significant transportation and development projects, including the Tri-Met light-rail system in Portland, Oregon.

The Space Needle at the Seattle Center rests on a foundation designed by Dames & Moore.

Another Dames & Moore Group company with a Seattle presence, O'Brien Kreitzberg, has served as construction manager for many local infrastructure and building projects. According to Regional Manager Vladimir Khazak, "O'Brien Kreitzberg provides construction management service for an array of complex projects." This is evidenced by the firm's work at wastewater projects in King and Kitsap counties, its coordination of construction and rehabilitation projects at the University of Washington, and its work at the historic King Street Station building in Seattle, where the company is managing construction of the renovation, as well as coordinating construction of a commuter rail and bus access to the station.

Environmental Contributions

Since the 1980s, Dames & Moore, the core business of the Dames & Moore Group, has been heavily involved in environmental and hazardous waste issues, in addition to its traditional geotechnical practice. It prepared the first Environmental Impact Statement under the comprehensive federal environmental law, known as NEPA. Involved in major energy facilities throughout the Northwest, Dames & Moore is an active player in preparing pipeline and power plant permits, including those for the Olympic Pipeline. Its staff has also been very active in support of major Seattle public projects.

The Space Needle at the Seattle Center rests on a foundation designed by Dames & Moore. More recently, the firm has been involved in the new federal courthouse and expansion of the Convention Center. Its expertise covers all aspects of hazardous waste management, ranging from process engineering and waste minimization to the design and implementation of protection and remediation programs for soils and surface and groundwater resources.

The firm is actively working to promote sustainable development in growing communities in Washington State through its water resources work. Because access to new water has been restricted by the state due to conflicting demands, Dames & Moore is working with its industrial clients who have large water rights and consumptive uses to become more efficient, creating surplus water for other uses, including sustainable community development.

Dames & Moore is also very active in the facilities engineering field. The company has completed projects for Boeing, as well as for clients in the emerging biotechnology and microelectronics industries in the Puget Sound area. The firm serves Weyerhaeuser, the Bonneville Power Administration, several major developers, and many other clients in the Pacific Northwest. Many of Dames & Moore's clients have worked with the company for more than three decades.

Committed to the Northwest

The Dames & Moore Group's long-term commitment to the Northwest is evidenced by more than 50 years of entrepreneurial work in the region. "We've developed a set of core values by which to run the company, where client service is the key value. We also constantly look for new ideas," says John Robinson, vice president and general manager of the Pacific Northwest Region.

The breadth of experience and talent of Dames & Moore's staff lends fresh perspective and far-ranging capabilities to its clients. Dames & Moore's commitment to Seattle and to the region, as well as its dedication to its clients, serves as a reflection of the firm's core values and diversity. Throughout the increasingly complex changes facing today's engineering industry, Dames & Moore has demonstrated its ability to offer the highest-quality planning, engineering, and consulting services available, while constantly adapting to the changing marketplace.

Since 1873, Holland America Line-Westours Inc. has been making its passengers' dreams come true. Once a principal carrier of emigrants from Europe to the United States, the premier cruise line operation is today sailing on luxury vacations in just about every ocean in the world.

Based in Seattle since 1983, Holland America and its sister companies—Windstar Cruises, Westmark Hotels and Inns, Gray Line of Alaska, Gray Line of Seattle, and Westours Motorcoaches—comprise a completely integrated tourism operation. Offering cruises year-round to the Caribbean from two ports—Tampa and Fort Lauderdale—and seven-day sailings to Alaska's Inside Passage and the Gulf of Alaska glacier route, Holland America also travels to Central and South America, Hawaii, Canada, New England, Europe, the Orient and South Pacific, and around the world. Most of its itineraries combine a luxury cruise with a land tour, which can range from a short adventure excursion to a full-itinerary tour of Alaska, the Pacific Northwest, or western Canada.

A Luxury Vacation

Deluxe by any standard, Holland America's midsize luxury ocean liners feature award-winning onboard service, larger than average staterooms, a complete program for children, and a "tipping not required" policy on each ship. Staffed by Dutch officers, the ships offer exquisite cuisine and service and can accommodate 1,200 to 1,500 guests.

Holland America understands that little things mean a lot to passengers. Passengers can banish their cares while enjoying wine tastings, deck sports, bridge and backgammon tournaments, string quartets and orchestras, horse racing and gambling, dance lessons, and even formal teas. The ease of a cashless society, as well as civilizing touches—such as fresh cut flowers and valuable antiques outfitting each ship—add to a rich experience.

With a variety of services that appeal to all ages, Holland America caters to a diverse clientele. Given that about 40 percent of its guests travel with their families, each ship is staffed with youth coordinators who manage age-appropriate activities for kids from five to 17 years in age. Holland America also provides children's menus, has special fares for kids, a complimentary ice cream bar, and other complimentary services.

Consistently rated among the top three cruise lines in the world, Windstar Cruises operates three four-masted ships. The 148-passenger vessels offer intimate, relaxing, and casually elegant cruises in the Caribbean and the Mediterranean, including the Greek islands and the French and Italian rivieras. Each Windstar ship also offers a two-table casino to entertain its guests.

Holland America Westours is Alaska's and the Canadian Yukon's largest and most experienced cruise tour operator, celebrating 50 years of service in 1997. It also has the most experienced motor coach operations in the Pacific Northwest, maintaining 150 deluxe motor coaches and super deluxe lounge coaches. Gray Line of

Clockwise from top:
Westmark Hotels operates 15 premium hotels in Alaska and the Yukon, offering personalized service for business and vacation travelers. Westmark Hotels is a wholly owned subsidiary of Holland America Line-Westours Inc.

Windstar's unique sailing ships can be seen in many of the oceans of the world. Offering sailings to Costa Rica, the French and Italian Rivieras, the Greek Islands, Turkey, the South Pacific, or the Caribbean, Windstar provides a luxury travel experience consistently rated as one of the best in the world. Windstar Cruises is a wholly owned subsidiary of Holland America Line-Westours Inc.

Deluxe by any standard, Holland America's midsize luxury ocean liners feature award-winning onboard service, larger than average staterooms, a complete program for children, and a "tipping not required" policy on each ship.

◂ Harvey Lloyd

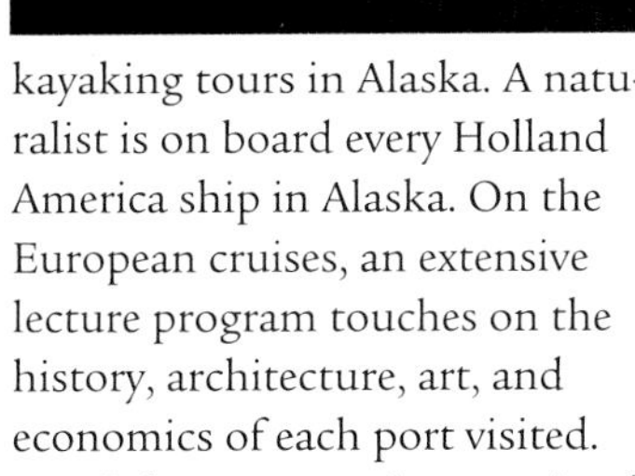

Seattle operates tours of Seattle; Mount Rainier; and Vancouver and Victoria, British Columbia. Gray Line of Alaska also explores the Alaska Highway and serves metropolitan areas in the Yukon and Alaska, including Anchorage, Tok, Fairbanks, and Skagway, as well as operating the deluxe McKinley Explorer scenadome railcars.

A Community Partner

Holland America Line-Westours employs more than 1,350 full-time, part-time, and seasonal workers in western Washington and does business with some 1,400 vendors statewide. The company estimates its direct economic impact to be more than $100 million. Holland America is a subsidiary of Carnival Corporation, traded on the New York stock exchange as CCL.

The company demonstrates its long-term commitment to the Puget Sound area as a major contributor to PONCHO, the local performing arts charity; the Seattle Aquarium; the Woodland Park Zoo; and the Washington Environmental Council.

Holland America is the official cruise line of the American Oceans Campaign, a title that recognizes the company's achievement in developing extensive environmental programs. The company exceeds Marine Pollution (MARPOL) Convention standards governing international regulations of processing and dumping at sea. It helped to fund a reef restoration project and a bird habitat conservation program in the Cayman Islands, and funded a $1.5 million raptor rehabilitation center in Sitka, Alaska. Holland America raises $100,000 each year for the Nature Conservancy and participates in its programs worldwide.

Holland America has been a world leader in ecosensitive tours, such as rain forest tours in Central America and walking and kayaking tours in Alaska. A naturalist is on board every Holland America ship in Alaska. On the European cruises, an extensive lecture program touches on the history, architecture, art, and economics of each port visited.

"The company is committed to delivering excellence and a quality travel product throughout its divisions," says A. Kirk Lanterman, chairman and CEO of Holland America Line-Westours. As evidence of its success in achieving this goal, Holland America has garnered the distinction of the Best Cruise Value Award from the World Ocean & Cruise Liner Society for five consecutive years, and earned the 1996 Onboard Service Overall Award from *Onboard Services* magazine.

Holland America will mark the passage of the 20th century with 127 years of experience. And the company will be making people's dreams come true for many years to come.

Clockwise from top left:
Gray Line of Seattle is the largest and most experienced tour operator in the Pacific Northwest. Offering a wide selection of excursion opportunities and convention services, the Gray Line of Seattle can satisfy the transportation needs of local businesses and convention and meeting planners, as well as visitors. Gray Line of Seattle is a wholly owned subsidiary of Holland America Line-Westours Inc.

The eight luxury cruise liners of Holland America Line represent the largest five-star fleet in the world today. These ships sail with itineraries that feature over 200 ports of call and are at home around the world.

Holland America Westours has the most experienced motor coach operations in the Pacific Northwest, maintaining 150 deluxe motor coaches and super deluxe lounge coaches, and 13 deluxe McKinley Explorer scenadome rail cars.

BENAROYA CAPITAL COMPANY IS A FAMILY-OWNED AND -OPERATED firm that includes a staff of 50 professionals experienced in property management and leasing. Founded in 1956, the Benaroya companies have been active in real estate development, and in acquiring quality real estate in prime locations.

Its portfolio reveals a strong preference for office buildings, light industrial facilities, and warehouse space, and also includes some retail properties.

Concentrating on the Local Market

Benaroya Capital restricts its business activities to the Puget Sound area, so that employees can be onsite whenever the need arises. This concentration on the local market strengthens the company's ability to cultivate long-term relationships with its tenants and provide extraordinary customer service.

Recent Benaroya Acquisitions

"We used to develop all of our properties," says Larry Benaroya, the son of the founder, who manages the company. "Now, we also acquire high-quality, existing buildings, which are often available at below replacement cost."

Indicative of its keen sense of the dynamics of the local marketplace, Benaroya Capital purchased the Metropolitan Park Towers in 1995. The twin towers, 18 and 20 floors tall, offer spectacular views of Lake Union, downtown Seattle, and the Olympic and Cascade mountains. Metropolitan Park is a fully leased office complex that stands to fare extremely well in the tightening office market. The acquisition also includes a permit-ready site for a third tower.

In 1996, Benaroya Capital purchased Park Place, a 21-story building on Sixth Avenue, in the heart of Seattle's central business district. Park Place is strategically located at the University Street on-ramp to I-5, and adjacent to Freeway Park. Park Place offers an abundance of parking and excellent views of Puget Sound and the Cascade Mountains.

Benaroya Capital is also a major player in redevelopment on the Eastside, with a string of recent acquisitions that include a 3.2-acre parcel in downtown Bellevue, several retail properties, the Northup North office complex near State Route 520, and another soon-to-be-announced office/industrial park.

Dominant Warehouse Developer

Since 1960, the Benaroya companies have been the dominant warehouse developer in the Puget Sound area. They have built award-winning business/industrial parks throughout the region, totaling millions of square feet.

Benaroya Capital continues to be active in purchasing and

Benaroya Capital's Park Place, a 21-story building in the heart of Seattle's central business district, is strategically located at the University Street on-ramp to I-5 and adjacent to Freeway Park. Park Place has excellent occupancy and an abundance of parking.

In 1995, Benaroya Capital acquired the Metropolitan Park Towers, a 650,000-square-foot office campus located at the Olive Street on-ramp to I-5 in downtown Seattle. "Met Park" offers spectacular views of Lake Union and the Olympic and Cascade mountains.

developing industrial property in the Kent Valley and on the Eastside. It recently purchased a site in Renton adjacent to the I-405 Freeway and built 440,000 square feet of industrial space. During construction, Park 405 was 100 percent preleased. The company has also acquired 52 acres in Kent at Van Doren's West, where it will construct 700,000 square feet of warehouse space in 1997. Later in 1997, the Benaroyas will begin construction of an additional 700,000 square feet of warehouse space in Kent along the East Valley Highway.

Benefits to the Community

Benaroya Capital and the Benaroya family strongly support numerous charitable organizations benefiting children, the elderly, the arts community, medical research, and educational programs. The family gives generously to causes they believe in, including a $16 million donation to the Seattle Symphony to underwrite the construction of a new symphony hall in downtown Seattle—the largest gift ever made to an arts project in the Puget Sound area. The Benaroya family also made a significant donation to Virginia Mason Medical Center, which is world renowned for its advances in diabetes research and treatment. The program is now called the Benaroya Diabetes Center. In this way, and in countless others, Benaroya Capital strives to enhance the quality of life in its home community.

In 1996, Benaroya Capital Company acquired Northup North, a series of five Class A office buildings in Bellevue, featuring an elegant parklike setting (left).

Benaroya Capital continues to be active in developing industrial property in the Kent Valley and on the Eastside (right).

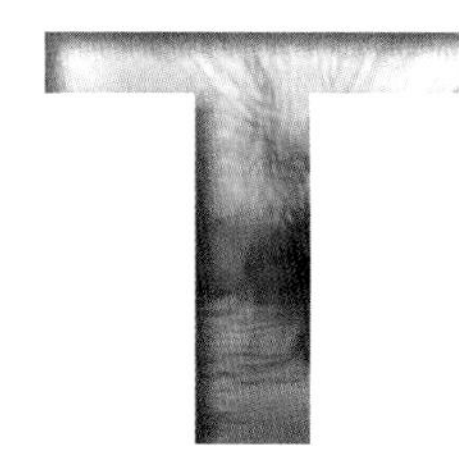

The Pacific Northwest is a region that has captured the imagination of the world. With a spirit of independence and ingenuity, industries of the Northwest have made significant contributions to global markets, science, and culture. Aon Risk Services, Inc. of Washington is involved on a daily basis with many of the companies on the leading edge of the region's growth and influence, because many of these companies are their clients.

Innovative, responsive, and client oriented, Aon Risk Services, Inc. of Washington is one of the premier insurance brokerages in the Pacific Northwest. With sister companies in Portland and Vancouver, Aon is poised to deliver solutions to the enterprises fueling the economic growth of the Pacific Rim and Cascadia.

Aon's prestigious clients include major national retailers, maritime enterprises, telecommunications companies, ports and airports, international hospitality companies, sports franchises, municipalities, and public and private construction projects, as well as personal insurance clients.

Offering Service, Experience, and Support

The array of services offered by Aon extends far beyond traditional brokering activities. Clients also benefit from Aon's ability to identify and assess risks, create advanced risk financing structures, turn risk data into information for decision making, facilitate advantageous claims settlements, assist in disaster recovery, and support risk management communications.

"Our first year with Aon Risk Services was 1996," says Doug Sutten, vice president of finance for Westin Hotels, "and we had very high expectations. Westin is the world's leading upscale hotel management company, and we are currently experiencing a period of accelerated growth and change. It is imperative that our broker have the depth of resources, and the experience, to handle complex international risk management issues. Aon has met and exceeded our expectations. The Seattle team has proven that they can deliver on their promise to provide superior resources and financially driven solutions to our company."

According to Aon Corporation Chairman and Chief Executive Officer Patrick Ryan, "The creative and innovative employees of Aon Risk Services in Seattle have made this one of the most successful offices in the Pacific Northwest, and in our company. They have succeeded through hard work, knowing their business, and providing the best products and services to clients." This success was recognized by Seattle's selection as Aon Group's 1996 Office of the Year.

The Aon Group

Aon Risk Services, Inc. of Washington is a subsidiary of the prestigious Aon Group, the fastest-growing international insurance brokerage and consulting services organization in the world. Aon, a Gaelic word meaning "oneness" or "unity," is exemplified by its wide array of services and the interdependent relationships between the subsidiary companies. Aon Group provides a broad range of insurance services, including retail brokerage, reinsurance and wholesale brokerage, alternative risk solutions, risk management consulting, and employee benefits and human resources consulting, through its directly owned global distribution networks. With nearly 700 offices in more than 80 countries in North and South America, Europe, Asia, and the Pacific, Aon Risk Services can access the people and the resources to deliver superior service to the most complex international clients.

Technology plays a critical role in Aon's ability to deliver quality service to its clients. "Our organization is a state-of-the-art example of the successful application of technology in the delivery of insurance services," states Dave Buelow, Aon Risk Services, Inc. of Washington's executive vice president and chief operations officer. "Because we are linked via the Knowledge Network, an international computer network between our offices around the world, we are capable of drawing upon an unparalleled array of resources in order to serve our clients." The company is electronically linked to a number of underwriters and

◀ Don Wilson

"The Seattle team has proven that they can deliver on their promise to provide superior resources and financially driven solutions to our company," says Doug Sutten (on left), vice president of finance for Westin Hotels.

clients, enabling more efficient and accurate communication. "The response to our technological capabilities has been phenomenal," Buelow comments. "Clients, underwriters, and employees appreciate the increase in productivity that our computer-based systems deliver."

Ryan anticipates further success as the company moves into the next century: "Aon's culture is one of dynamic growth; we do not rest on our past achievements." Recognizing the economic strength of the Pacific Rim, the Aon Corporation is aggressively expanding its operations throughout Asia. Aon was one of the first brokers to open a representative office in Beijing, and operates offices in Hong Kong, Indonesia, Japan, Malaysia, the Philippines, Singapore, South Korea, Taiwan, Thailand, Vietnam, Australia, New Zealand, and the Pacific Islands. In fact, Aon Group is the largest retail insurance brokerage operation in the Asia Pacific region. Aon is also the largest brokerage in Canada and the United Kingdom, and has an influential presence in continental Europe and Latin America.

▲▼ DON WILSON

Aon's leadership position in the marketplace has been solidified by strong organic growth and recent strategic mergers with the Bain Hogg Group PLC, and Alexander and Alexander Services Inc. Combined revenue exceeds $3.5 billion on a pro forma basis, and Aon now employs approximately 30,000 people worldwide. Significantly, employees of Aon own more than 30 percent of the company's common stock—a clear indication that confidence in the company's present and future performance is high.

In the Northwest, where quality of life is a distinctive element of the regional identity, Aon Risk Services, Inc. of Washington is committed to making a positive difference. The company has contributed time and resources to social service agencies, education and medical organizations, and the arts. With customary enthusiasm, Aon Risk Services, Inc. of Washington is an active participant in the effort to bring the Summer Olympics to Seattle in 2008.

Clockwise from top:
The Aon account team for the new Seattle Mariners baseball stadium project discuss construction issues.

Clients benefit from Aon's abilities to identify and assess risks, create advanced risk financing structures, turn risk data into information for decision making, facilitate advantageous claims settlements, assist in disaster recovery, and support risk management communications.

Innovative, responsive, and client oriented, Aon Risk Services, Inc. of Washington is one of the premier insurance brokerages in the Pacific Northwest.

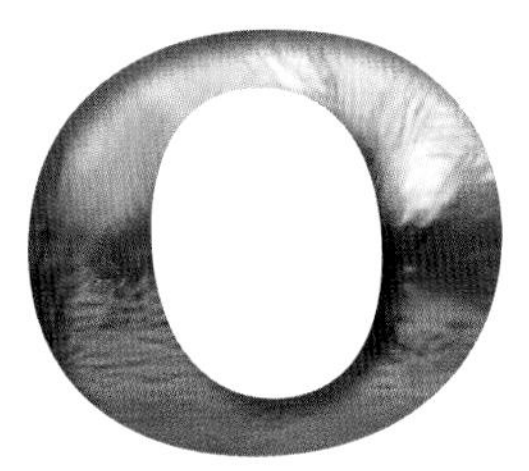

Overlake Hospital Medical Center was founded in 1960 to serve the health care needs of the Eastside community—from Bothell to Renton and from the Cascade Mountains to Lake Washington, including Mercer Island. Overlake's success since its founding almost 40 years ago rests to a great degree on its reputation for excellent medical services and its hands-on, practical approach to addressing the health care issues of the day. The community in turn shows its committed support through tremendous levels of volunteerism and active financial giving.

Licensed for 257 beds, Overlake is a nonprofit, non-tax-supported medical center that employs more than 1,500 people with facilities that are used by more than 700 physicians. As the premier Eastside hospital, Overlake leads the community in child-birthing, senior care, cancer care, emergency and trauma treatment, and psychiatric and surgical services.

A Full Spectrum of Care

Overlake's wide range of medical services and facilities ensures its prominent role in meeting the health care needs of the Eastside community.

Overlake is the only hospital on the Eastside to house a level III trauma center, a rating making Overlake second only to Harborview Medical Center in the Puget Sound region. The Emergency Center staff and board-certified emergency physicians provide advanced medical care for 36,000 patients each year.

Overlake Hospital Medical Center is also home to the Eastside's most comprehensive cardiac care program, and is the only Eastside facility licensed to perform open-heart surgery. The hospital's unique Reigert Chest Pain Center focuses on the early diagnosis and treatment of chest pain, saving lives while at the same time reducing costs.

Overlake's Childbirth Center, with its state-of-the-art child-birthing facilities and expert nursing care, was voted the best place to have a baby by readers of the *Eastside Parent* magazine in 1992 and 1994. The center's staff and physicians are specially trained and equipped to handle high-risk pregnancies and care for babies with special needs. An advanced monitoring system allows nurses to spend more time with patients, while computerized medical charts and advanced technology enable medical staff to detect any fetal distress. The innovative Postpartum Follow-up and Doula programs provide a free checkup for mother and baby one week after delivery, and allow for up to 12 hours of in-home assistance at a reduced rate for new mothers as well.

The Childbirth Center is but one part of Overlake's new Women's Hospital, a center of excellence offering a full line of women's services. The Women's Hospital and Childbirth Center at Overlake is the first of its kind in the state of Washington. The new Hospital recognizes and honors the unique needs of women by providing services and programs such as women's imaging, mammography, gynecology, education, personal development, health screenings, a women's library and conference center, and much more.

The cancer program at Overlake offers a full spectrum of care, from prevention to treatment and recovery. Core services include education programs and cancer screenings, on-site radiation and chemotherapy treatment, patient and family support groups, and hospice care—all provided in the 24-bed Richard E. Lang Oncology Unit. Overlake is also developing a comprehensive breast center that is dedicated to increasing survival rates among women with breast cancer through early detection and advanced treatment. The hospital has acquired or accessed some of the most advanced medical imaging equipment on the West Coast for cancer screening and

Overlake Hospital Medical Center operates the Eastside's only level III trauma center for serious or life-threatening emergencies.

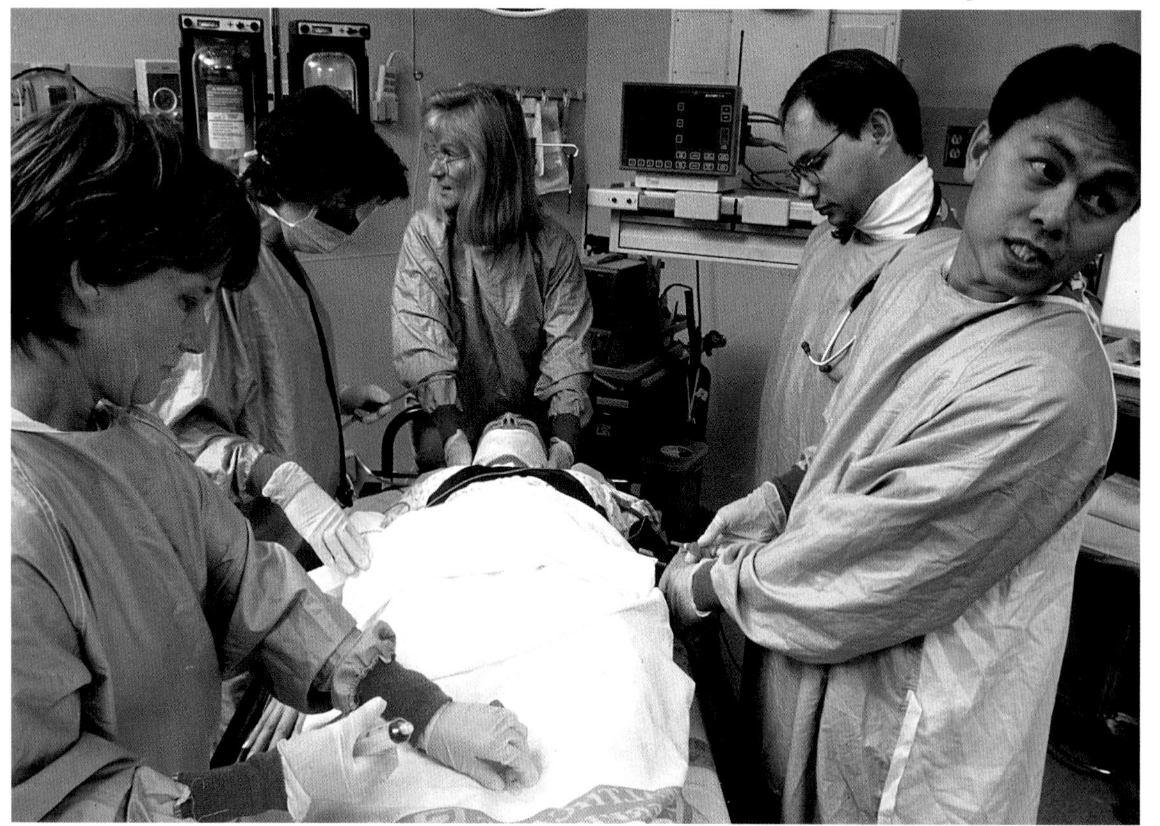

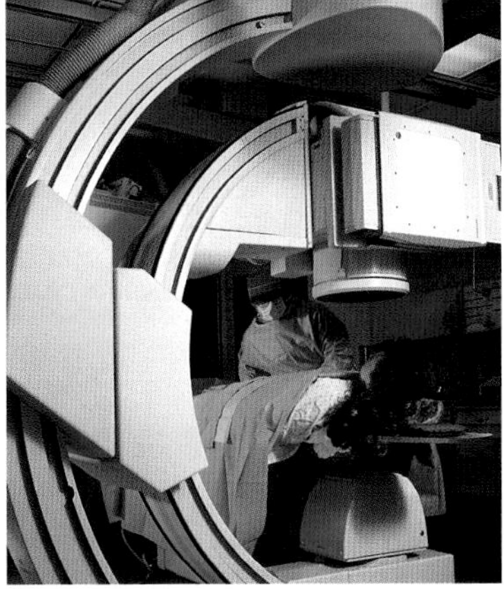

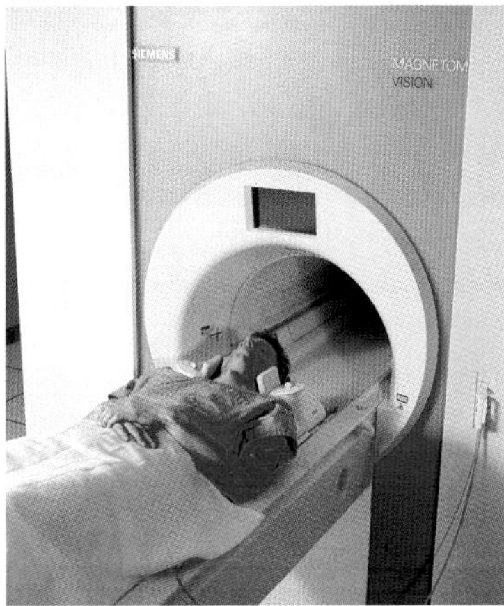

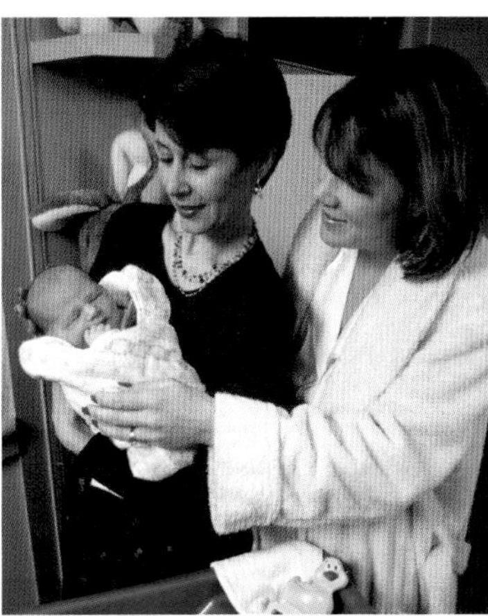

Clockwise from top:
Overlake Hospital Medical Center is a nonprofit, non-tax-supported community hospital, offering a full range of advanced medical services for the Eastside—from Bothell to Renton and from the Cascade Mountains to Lake Washington, including Mercer Island.

A partnership between Overlake Hospital and MotherCare of America has made it possible for Overlake mothers to receive at-home post-partum assistance in early infant care, light housekeeping, and family meal preparation.

Washington Imaging Services LLC—a joint venture between Overlake Hospital Medical Center, National Medical Development, and Overlake Magnetic Imaging—is home to one of the most advanced MRIs on the West Coast.

The Siemens Multistar TOP allows physicians to study a patient's circulatory system without surgery.

other uses. Overlake offers multiple support groups for cancer patients as well as for their family and friends.

Overlake also houses one of the few multiple sclerosis centers in the state and the Eastside's only inpatient and outpatient adolescent psychiatric treatment program.

Community Outreach Programs

In 1995, Overlake and other area hospitals launched Eastside Partners for a Healthier Community, an affiliation of the Seattle-King County Department of Health and more than 100 community groups and agencies. The program focuses on four areas: breast cancer detection; domestic violence, child abuse, and neglect; pregnancy, newborn risks, and healthier parenting; and adolescent health risk behaviors.

In 1993, the medical center created an Emergency Center Domestic Violence Program, and, more recently, a Domestic Violence Health Care Provider Training Program to meet the needs of childbearing families. These programs were developed in collaboration with local police and community organizations.

Overlake has also been holding annual women's health conferences for more than a decade. These events cover such topics as midlife issues, heart disease in women, and a holistic approach to stress management.

Overlake offers community members medical advice through the free Eastside Health Line, which is staffed by registered nurses 24 hours a day, seven days a week. Callers can also receive physician referrals through the Eastside Health Line.

Overlake publishes *Healthy Outlook*, a quarterly magazine containing articles on nutrition, innovative treatments, and health tips from physicians, nutritional specialists, exercise physiologists, and more. The publication also provides a schedule of workshops on topics such as planning for pregnancy, child safety, adult and infant CPR, heart disease, fitness and healthy lifestyles, nutrition, asthma management, living with diabetes, alternative medicine, and parenting strategies. Overlake's multifaceted Senior Care Program, created in 1987, sponsors dozens of courses and events for senior citizens that are listed in *Healthy Outlook*.

Since 1960, members of the Eastside community have turned to Overlake and found advanced medical services and uncompromising patient care. As the complex face of health care continues to change, Overlake's community spirit and focus will ensure the development of programs and services that continue to provide "Medical excellence every day™."

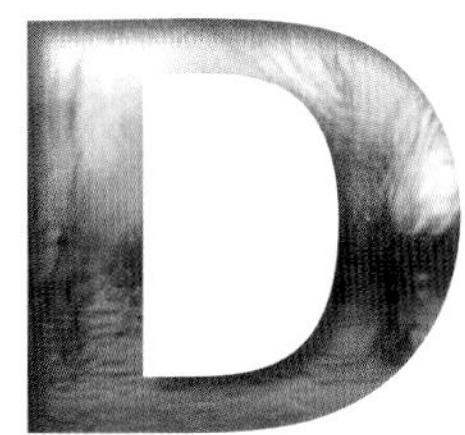

DINE, DANCE, SING, SCULPT, PAINT, PLAY, ACT, LEARN . . . IT all happens at Seattle Center, one of the greatest gathering places in the nation for the arts, entertainment, and leisure activities. Each year, 9 million visitors attend more than 1,500 cultural, educational, recreational, and entertainment events, and visit over a dozen attractions, making Seattle Center the fourth-largest visitor destination in the nation. Its world-class facilities and programming reflect the heart and soul of the community and draw people from all over the world to this 74-acre campus.

Serving as the region's premier entertainment venue, Seattle Center draws a mix of people of all ages and cultural backgrounds. "Seattle Center reflects the inclusiveness of the Northwest," says Virginia Anderson, Seattle Center director. "No matter what your interests, your age, or your culture—Seattle Center is a place for you. It's what draws people to the region and gives us our national preeminence."

And it has something for everyone—from an amusement park to a skateboard park; from the Opera House to the campus' hub, the Seattle Center House. The campus has never looked more inviting, and it sends a clear message of welcome.

Discovering the Unexpected

Hosting the World's Fair in Seattle was a dream fulfilled, and Seattle Center still embodies the original theme of the 1962 World's Fair—the 21st century. Older buildings have been renovated, while newer architecture has filled in the campus. A new sculpture garden and Peace Garden add to the ground's 20 acres of landscaping, which includes plazas, flower gardens, and fountains, plus the world's largest ivy-covered topiaries. People discover the unexpected when they visit Seattle Center, where more than 20 different venues reflect the enormous diversity of its offerings.

Newly renovated, the 17,500-seat KeyArena is the home of one of the premier NBA teams, the Seattle SuperSonics, along with being the region's favorite place for concerts, family shows, ice shows, and hockey. The circle-within-a-circle design of the International Fountain, rededicated to the public in 1995, symbolizes the region's vision of inclusiveness and attracts hundreds of people daily to its spectacular water and music shows. More than a few playfully join the show and get wet. Another popular attraction, the Seattle Center Monorail, is the first and only full-scale commercial monorail operating in the nation. Its twin trains carry up to 7,000 passengers per day between the city's downtown core and the Center. Each year, more than 2.5 million ride the train made famous by Elvis Presley in the film *It Happened at the World's Fair.*

Many other landmark attractions draw people to Seattle Center. Perched high above the city,

Seattle Center's popular International Fountain, with its serene mall and plaza, is a favorite spot for visitors and tourists to stroll around the park, picnic on the lawn, or cool off in the fountain's bowl.

◄ JEFFREY LUKE

▶ AUSTON JAMES

▶ STEVE MELTZER

Serving as the hub of the campus, Seattle Center House is an ideal place for community events and programs. Special concerts by the Seattle Symphony are among the hundreds of free and low-cost events held at the Seattle Center House (top left).

The Windstorm roller coaster, a popular ride in the Fun Forest Amusement Park, is one of dozens of rides enjoyed by all ages (top right).

Seattle's world-famous Space Needle provides incredible views while offering formal and relaxed dining to its visitors. The recently renovated Seattle Center House serves as the hub of the campus with a variety of food offerings and daily entertainment featured on its stage. The Fun Forest Amusement Park provides dozens of rides and a midway for the young and young-at-heart. New to the Center in 1999, the Experience Music Project will draw international audiences to this state-of-the-art interactive museum celebrating creativity and innovation in contemporary music.

Center Stage for the Performing Arts

What really matters is what happens *within* the buildings. The Pacific Northwest takes great pride and enjoyment in the performing arts, and Seattle Center is home to the best. The Seattle Opera, recognized internationally for its bold innovation and theatrical performances, draws audiences from around the world. It shares the Opera House with the Pacific Northwest Ballet, one of the nation's premier companies, which features an active repertoire of more than 70 works, and the Grammy Award-winning Seattle Symphony, which performs more than 100 concerts each year. Add to that the 300 talented musicians ages seven to 21 who perform in three orchestras as part of the

▶ STEVE MELTZER

Seattle Youth Symphony, and you get a feel for the full life of the Opera House.

Some of the nation's finest theater has grown and developed at Seattle Center. The Seattle Repertory Theatre, one of the largest and most respected professional nonprofit theater companies in the country, performs classic, contemporary, and original pieces in the Bagley Wright Theatre and on its second stage, the Leo Kreielsheimer Theatre. The nationally acclaimed Intiman Theatre Company presents award-winning plays at the Intiman Playhouse that focus on the enduring themes of great world drama, while The Group Theatre, the nation's most outstanding multicultural theater, showcases works that reflect and engage the diverse cultures of the local and international communities. The nationally award-winning Seattle Children's Theatre challenges and enthralls young patrons and

▶ JEFFREY LUKE

their parents with performances in the Charlotte Martin Theatre and their second stage, the Eve Alvord Theatre.

The Center also nurtures a flourishing visual arts culture in Seattle. The Northwest Craft Center is a unique gallery offering works by artists from throughout the West. Pottery Northwest has studio facilities and a gallery, and the Harrison Street Gallery in the Seattle Center House has exhibits reflecting the artistry of the Northwest.

The Best in Sports, Too

The spirit of the region is also expressed through the four sports teams that call Seattle Center home. The Seattle SuperSonics basketball team plays its home games in the KeyArena, along with the Seattle Thunder-

The Seattle Center Arts and Science Academy offers more than 300 middle school students the unique opportunity to study arts and sciences taught by the "best of the best" at a two-week summer program (bottom left).

The 17,500-seat KeyArena is the home of the Seattle SuperSonics basketball team and the region's favorite spot for concerts, family shows, ice-skating shows, hockey, and other sporting events (bottom right).

DAVID COOPER

JOHN TODD

Clockwise from top:
Pacific Northwest Ballet's annual presentation of the classic *Nutcracker* is a popular tradition for kids and adults alike. The world-renowned ballet company features an active repertoire of more than 70 works.

More than a dozen cultural festivals occur at Seattle Center each year, including the Chinese Arts and Cultural Celebration, an African-American culture celebration, and the Irish Festival, giving visitors a taste of the world.

Seattle Center is the place for great sporting events. Four sports teams call it home, including the Seattle SuperSonics, the Seattle Thunderbirds hockey team, the Seattle SeaDogs indoor soccer team, and the Seattle Reign women's professional basketball team.

birds, a member of the Western Hockey League, and the Seattle SeaDogs indoor soccer team (CISL). Playing in the Mercer Arena, a 6,000-seat venue, is the Seattle Reign, one of eight national teams in the women's professional basketball league (ABL). Seattle Center has also hosted a number of special sporting events, such as the Tour of World Figure Skating Champions, Canadian Hockey League Memorial Cup, 1990 Goodwill Games, and McDonald's Cup Gymnastics, as well as volleyball, boxing, tennis, and wrestling events.

Something for Everyone

Seattle Center has a broad range of world-class programming and public events, offering something for everyone. From Sonics basketball to artsEdge, the experimental arts festival, the Golf Show to the Children's Hospital Telethon, the Emerald City Cat Show to the Greater Seattle Bicycle Expo, the center's activities are as diverse as the large community it serves.

Its 18 meeting and exhibition spaces, along with its larger performance venues, host myriad programs and special events that keep the Center bustling year-round. It produces more than a dozen cultural festivals each year, including the Chinese Arts and Culture Celebration, Tibet Fest, and a major Native American pow-wow, giving visitors a taste of the world's cultures. Some people simply know Seattle Center as the place to go to experience Bumbershoot, perhaps the nation's largest arts festival; the Northwest Folklife Festival, a celebration of folk arts and culture; or the Bite of Seattle, to taste the region's culinary delights. The Center has also hosted national exhibits, including the *Son of Heaven* and the *Treasures of Tutankhamen*.

Through strong corporate support and entrepreneurial fervor, Seattle Center continues to expand its free public programming. It produces nearly 2,000 free activities and performances per year, such as the popular senior citizen dances held twice a week, Saturday Night Big Band dances, weekend events, and free outdoor concerts at the

STEVE MELTZER

STEVE MELTZER

AUSTON JAMES

Clockwise from top:
Northwest Folklife Festival, a celebration of folk art and culture, showcases community and international artists to more than 200,000 people over Memorial Day weekend. It is one of four major festivals that occur throughout the entire campus.

Thousands of kids have enjoyed Whirli-Balls, as well as dozens of other fun kid-size rides, exhibits, and hands-on workshops featured at Whirligig, Seattle Center's annual indoor spring festival for kids.

Graced by the Space Needle, the Seattle Center campus is dressed with thousands of festive lights for the annual KING 5 Winterfest holiday celebration. The wintertime festival offers indoor ice-skating, art workshops, concerts, and entertainment.

Mural Amphitheatre that attract crowds of up to 7,000 people.

Seattle Center offers hundreds of events and activities that enrich children's lives and excite them with the joy of learning. Small children delight in Whirligig, three weeks of indoor events and entertainment, as well as KOMO KidsFair, where 30,000 kids and family members enjoy a full day of free activities. In addition, almost 60,000 children participate each year in the week-long Seattle International Children's Festival, which brings companies from Asia, Europe, Africa, Australia, and the Americas to Seattle for six days of performances and entertainment.

Popular attractions for children include The Children's Museum, which fascinates kids with cultural exhibits, workshops, a child-sized neighborhood, and a drop-in art studio. The Pacific Science Center brings science to life, with more than 200 hands-on exhibits, demonstrations, laser shows, and IMAX® movies. And in 1998, the Science Center opens the new Boeing IMAX® Theater with 3-D technology.

Welcoming people from all walks of life, the Center emphasizes the noncommercial aspects of the holidays each year by offering the public numerous free activities. Attracting more than 350,000 people, the Center hosts the six-week-long KING 5 Winterfest, which offers indoor ice-skating, art workshops, concerts, and entertainment.

Seattle Center also takes a role in community activism. It filled a critical community need when it created the Peace Academy, a week-long leadership program for high school students, and established the Seattle Center Arts and Science Academy, a two-week summer program for 300 middle school children in which 22 programs are taught by professional artists and instructors.

A Great Place to Be

Altogether, there is no other place like Seattle Center. Thanks to strong public support, it will continue to meet the diverse needs of the community and enrich the lives of people with its innovative programs and facilities long into the 21st century.

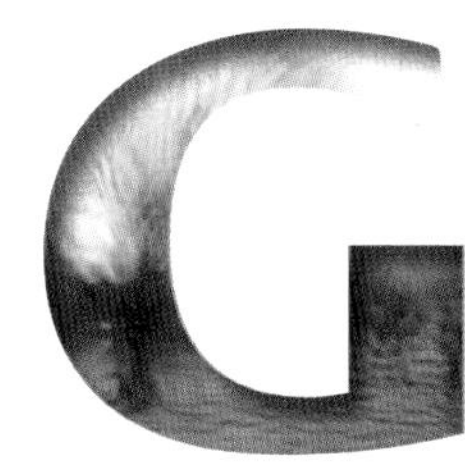

Garvey, Schubert & Barer was founded by three law school classmates in 1966, only two years after they graduated from the University of Washington School of Law. What the founders lacked in experience, they supplied in innovation. In 1972, the growing law firm was the first in Seattle to open an office in Washington, D.C., and a year later, one of the first to place a lawyer in Japan. Including the members of its Portland office, which opened in 1982, the firm now employs more than 90 lawyers.

Garvey, Schubert & Barer's innovative spirit filters through every aspect of the firm's activities. Offering a corporate culture that solicits and adopts ideas from any source, the firm resists hierarchy for the sake of hierarchy. Its sabbatical program applies to staff members and attorneys alike, and its internal committees include a cross section of staff members and associates, as well as owners and counsel.

Several years ago, Garvey, Schubert & Barer implemented a client audit program that invites clients to evaluate the firm's performance. Each audit is conducted by a lawyer at the firm who has not previously served the client; he or she conducts the interview and then makes recommendations for improving the firm's service. Based on feedback, the firm has accelerated electronic communications with clients, made other technological investments, and changed its billing format.

Ken Schubert, one of the firm's founders, describes the virtues of the program: "The client audit is an invaluable program that reflects our firm's orientation to service. It keeps the firm's lawyers in tune with client expectations, which differ considerably from client to client. Of course, I love hearing clients tell me that my firm is doing a great job. But we also like to hear if there is some room for improvement. It's foolish to sit in your office and worry about criticism. Instead, you have to get out, spend time with clients on your own nickel, and find out what you can do better. Clients are the most qualified people to provide that information."

Garvey, Schubert & Barer's diverse client list includes family-owned Ben Bridge Jeweler, Inc., which operates more than 50 stores in the western United States; China Ocean Shipping

Garvey, Schubert & Barer was an early major tenant of the Second & Seneca Building, which joined the Seattle skyline in 1991 (left).

K2 Corporation, a client of the firm for more than 20 years, is at the leading edge of ski manufacturing (right).

James Frederick Housel

Larry Prosor

(Group) Company, the national flag ocean carrier of the People's Republic of China; Data Dimensions, Inc., a publicly held consulting company and the leading provider of solutions to the inability of computers to properly interpret dates for the year 2000 and beyond; Foss Maritime Company, the largest tug and barge company in the Puget Sound area; K2 Corporation, a leading manufacturer of skis, snowboards, and in-line skates; PeaceHealth, a 4,800-employee health care system; Sir Mix-a-Lot, a double-platinum-selling rap artist; Stimson Lane, Ltd., the maker of Chateau Ste. Michelle and Columbia Crest wines; and Totem Ocean Trailer Express, Inc., one of the region's two principal carriers to Alaska.

A Wide Range of Services

The firm's attorneys represent these and other clients in a wide range of commercial transactions, including acquisitions, public offerings, tax-exempt bond offerings, licensing agreements, and international distribution of products. The firm's litigation practice is similarly broad, encompassing antitrust and intellectual property disputes, product liability and insurance defense, securities litigation, and many other areas.

Garvey, Schubert & Barer was an early entrant into the field of international trade, negotiating the 1979 resumption of shipping service between the People's Republic of China and the United States after a hiatus of nearly 30 years. The firm's international practice continues to concentrate on the Pacific Rim, with protection of intellectual property emerging as a critical international trade issue in the future.

In 1989, economic trends in the health care industry prompted Garvey, Schubert & Barer to form Whitman Garvey, Inc., a consulting affiliate that crafts business arrangements for health care providers. On appropriate projects, Whitman Garvey and Garvey, Schubert & Barer combine business and legal resources to develop comprehensive responses to challenges posed by consolidation of the health care industry.

As part of its practice, the firm has long embraced a commitment to public service. All attorneys are encouraged to devote 10 percent of their time to pro bono work. To reinforce the notion that public service is an integral part of their jobs and not merely an extracurricular activity, the firm modified its billing software to award billing credit for pro bono work toward the 10 percent goal. Public service work performed by lawyers at the firm tallied to more than $830,000 in 1995 and more than $950,000 in 1996.

The firm's largest public service clients include North and East King County Multi-Service Center, a shelter adopted by the firm in 1993 that offers transitional housing primarily to single-parent families headed by women; River Network, a program that purchases critical lands along rivers in Washington and Oregon and conveys the lands to public agencies for management; and the Northwest Women's Law Center, which advances legal rights for women. Attorneys at the firm also donate time to indigent clients, civil rights issues, Indian tribes, and numerous charitable organizations.

Recognizing the importance of a vibrant law school and faculty to the Seattle legal community, the firm established the first permanent endowed professorship at the University of Washington School of Law. Through the Garvey, Schubert & Barer Professorship in Law, the firm celebrates its roots and continues a cycle of energy and innovation.

JOHN RIZZO

The Columbia Crest winery is nestled in lush surroundings in Paterson, Washington. Garvey, Schubert & Barer is pleased to represent Stimson Lane, Ltd., the maker of Columbia Crest and Chateau Ste. Michelle wines.

A Foss tugboat assists a vessel owned by Totem Ocean Trailer Express. The firm provides a wide array of legal services to these maritime clients.

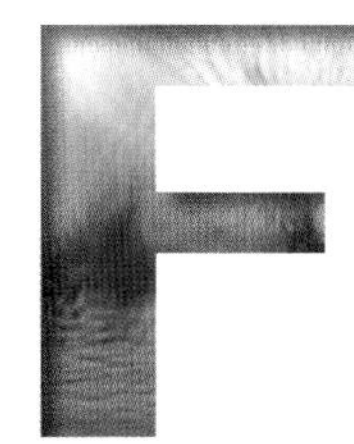

FROM SLALOM SKIS, KNEEBOARDS, WAKEBOARDS, AND TOWABLE inflatables, to such accessories as gloves, vests, ropes, and apparel, O'Brien International Inc. designs and manufactures the most complete line of towable water sports equipment in the world. Founded in Seattle in 1966, O'Brien dominates the towable water sports industry, a niche market that encompasses the hard and soft goods used in towing individuals behind boats and personal watercraft. Recognized for its exquisite product design and leading technology, O'Brien separates itself from the competition by introducing state-of-the-art products in each category.

Waterskiing originated in the United States in the early 1920s and has since become popular around the world. Curiously enough, the Seattle area is the hub of towable water sports development, with O'Brien playing the leading role in the expansion of waterskiing into jumping, trick skiing, kneeboarding, tubing, and now, wakeboarding.

While most of these activities are done for recreational purposes, many amateur and professional competitions exist in slalom skiing, jumping, kneeboarding, and wakeboarding, with O'Brien again having a leadership role.

Taking a business approach to a fun industry, the Redmond-based company has adopted a multiple product and distribution channel strategy, which makes O'Brien unique in its participation in all five channels of water sports distribution. With its technically superior products and commitment to service, O'Brien enjoys a significant market share in each channel, and has grown 33 percent since 1990.

TOM KING

Technological Advances Mean Superior Performance

O'Brien's G-4 skis are the most technologically advanced skis ever to hit water. The revolutionary rocker adjustment system allows skiers to customize the rocker to suit their style and maximize turning control and acceleration. The antidrift mini fin helps the ski hold an angle through the wake for greater tracking ability and truer line of acceleration. This attention to detail extends to variable sidewalls and tunnel configurations, and innovative blade design, which all contribute to make these skis the best of the best.

The largest and lowest-cost producer, O'Brien boasts the only multiple technology manufacturing facility in the industry, with expertise in compression molding, rotational molding, reaction injection molding, and honeycomb laminated composite manufacturing processes.

Through manufacturing refinements, product innovation, and the constant testing of new

Clockwise from top:
O'Brien's slalom skis cover the spectrum from junior size, entry level skis to high-performance, competition skis.

O'Brien leads the industry in towable inflatables and markets one- and two-person towables—both staples in the industry.

The company provides a research and development boat on nearby Lake Sammamish and another MasterCraft boat for use by employees wishing to test or just enjoy O'Brien products.

RICHARD MERZ

TOM KING

ideas, O'Brien has gained its significant market share. Its extensive research and development have led to some of the highest-quality, most cost-efficient, and best-designed products in the industry. The spoon-shaped Vortex kneeboard, unexcelled for surface tricks; the Low Rider kneeboard designed for explosive, big air flips; the G-series slaloms with their innovative flex and torsion control bar system; the Uro-Flex superlight wakeboard bindings; and the Evil Twin wakeboard design all point to the technical superiority of O'Brien's products.

▸ RICHARD MERZ

The hottest water sports category, wakeboarding is to waterskiing what snowboarding is to snowskiing. Riders stand sideways on these versatile boards, which are designed for turns, carving, and jumps—and for the advanced rider, flips and acrobatics.

O'Brien puts all its products through rigorous quality testing to ensure superior performance, durability, and consistency. The company's demanding product testing procedures are administered by a staff of seven engineers and teams of professional riders who test products on and off the water. The company provides a research and development boat on nearby Lake Sammamish and another MasterCraft boat for use by employees wishing to test or just enjoy O'Brien products.

O'Brien's products are endorsed by ski legend Andy Mapple, who holds five world records and has dominated waterskiing for the last 11 years. Mapple and five other record holders comprise the company's elite ski team.

The company's slalom skis cover the spectrum from junior size, entry level skis to high-performance, competition skis. More O'Brien G-series skis placed in the top five in more events at the 1996 U.S. National Championship than any other model of ski. O'Brien has also led the industry in towable inflatables for many years. The company markets one- and two-person towables—both staples in the industry.

The wakeboard market exploded in the early 1990s, and O'Brien quickly established itself as a leader. The hottest water sports category, wakeboarding is to waterskiing what snowboarding is to snowskiing. Riders stand sideways on these versatile boards, which are designed for turns, carving, and jumps—and for the advanced rider, flips and acrobatics. Beginners find wakeboarding easy to learn, and quickly progress to crossing the wake and doing jumps.

O'Brien took the ingredients that made it the top ski manufacturer and applied them to wakeboards. Innovations such as the ultrathin profile and shaved edges of the Evil Twin wakeboard set a new standard of excellence for equipment in this young sport. O'Brien's graphics convey the irreverence, intensity, and attitude of the Gen-X wakeboarder. Company sales of these products are expected to more than double in 1997.

Capitalizing on the strength of the product name, O'Brien enjoys a strong presence in both pro shops and general sporting goods stores. With aggressive international growth over the past few years, O'Brien distributes its towable water sports products worldwide. Employing 150 people, many of whom have worked for the company more than 20 years, O'Brien manufactures hard goods locally and sources inflatables, ropes, and other accessories from the Far East. O'Brien is the leading water sports company in Europe, Canada, Australia, South America, South Africa, and Japan.

The company's success is a result of its business commitment to a recreational industry. Says President Barry Tait, "Our commitment to be the best in quality, innovation, and technology is what drives our growth and makes us the household name in towable sports products worldwide."

▸ LEONHARDT GROUP

O'Brien G-series skis placed in the top five in more events at the 1996 U.S. National Championship than any other model of ski.

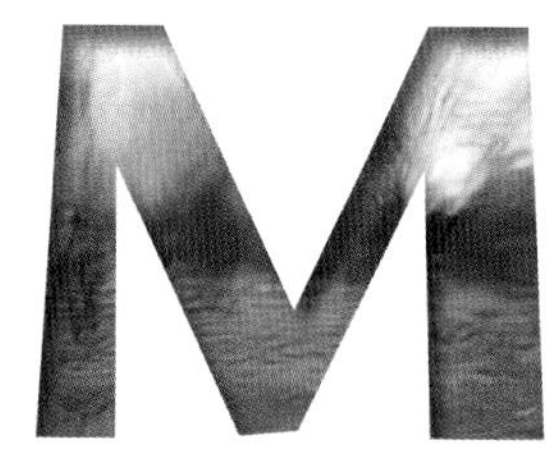

Mikron Industries is a Kent-based manufacturer of custom vinyl extrusions for the window and door industry. Founded in 1969, it is the leading developer of proprietary designs of polyvinyl extrusions for the window and door industry. ■ Under the guidance of Ron Sandwith, chairman and CEO, Mikron has become an industry leader by acting on new ideas, the biggest of which occurred in the mid-1980s. The company pioneered the use of custom vinyl as the main framing material for windows and doors installed in new construction, a specialization that emerged during the course of manufacturing vinyl extrusions for industries as diverse as aerospace, electronics, maritime, communications, and construction.

A Superior Product

As key industries worldwide expand their use of plastics in the products they manufacture, plastic extrusions have come to replace wood and metal in many applications—increasing the versatility, strength, and life of products while conserving energy and reducing manufacturing costs. In fact, rising energy costs and a tightening federal energy code drove the industry's growing use of vinyl. In new construction alone, the use of vinyl windows has grown from zero in 1985 to a projected 47 percent of total sales by the year 1999.

In addition to being a cost-effective building material, vinyl does not chip, peel, rot, crack, or rust. It is also an excellent insulator, making it very effective in places that experience harsh seasonal temperatures. And because vinyl is nonconductive to sound vibrations, it is a superb material for noise abatement along freeways and in urban areas.

Mikron's extrusions set the industry standard because they are weather and corrosion resistant, easy to operate, cost effective, and adaptable to the design elements of individual customers. As the largest extruder in the United States and the second largest in North America, Mikron has captured 75 percent of the sliding patio door market and a similar percentage of the vinyl window industry. The company attributes much of its steady growth over the past three decades to its commitment to continuous improvement, which embraces the goal of exceeding customers' expectations through innovative style, performance, and service.

Phenomenal Growth

The company's phenomenal growth—from $3 million in sales in 1984 to $82 million in 1996—is testament to the unsurpassed quality of its products. The company has also responded to demand for new color frames for windows and doors in both market sectors.

Clockwise from top:
Founded in 1969, Mikron Industries is a Kent-based manufacturer of custom vinyl extrusions for the window and door industry.

Mikron's modern, 300,000-square-foot plant in Kent is 10 times its original size.

Employing one of the most comprehensive computerized design and engineering systems in the industry, Mikron creates precise extrusion dies, or tools, made from superior stainless steel.

Mikron exports to Brazil, Argentina, Chile, and Australia, and is currently exploring new markets in Asia.

With just-in-time delivery service, Mikron is the first in the industry to operate state-of-the-art manufacturing plants on both coasts, enabling it to offer one- or two-day shipping service to most customers in North America. Its modern, 300,000-square-foot plant in Kent is 10 times its original size.

In 1994, Mikron opened a plant on 50 acres in Richmond, Kentucky, and has already broken ground to double the facility. With 600 employees, the two facilities operate 24 hours a day, 365 days a year, ensuring optimal product schedules and service. By streamlining inventory control and shipping methods, Mikron ships specialized customer parts with the shortest lead times in the industry.

Committed to Quality

Mikron's start-to-finish custom manufacturing process meets the specialized needs of window and door system manufacturers. From beginning to end, Mikron supports its customers in design, development, testing, and delivery of proprietary window systems. Mikron's design staff generates three-dimensional simulated drawings that meet client specifications and that utilize customers' input.

Employing one of the most comprehensive computerized design and engineering systems in the industry, Mikron creates precise extrusion dies, or tools, made from superior stainless steel. It then tests its finished extrusions for dimensional tolerance, shrinkage, durability, color, impact, and advanced weathering. Products also undergo independent tests for wind, water, and temperature resistance to make sure they meet stringent industry requirements.

One of the company's proudest accomplishments is in the area of recycling and ecosensitive manufacturing. Mikron begins by using environmentally safe materials that contain no heavy metals. It pays customers more than twice the market rate for the manufacturing scrap. Rather than ending up in a landfill, the returned vinyl is examined piece by piece to make sure only Mikron vinyl is recycled; then, it is ground into powder and a computerized compounder adds the ingredients lost in the first cycle. This win-win system ensures that nothing is wasted.

In 1991, Mikron began implementing the principles of the late Dr. W. Edwards Deming, whose enduring philosophies focus on continually improving product quality and service, helping employees develop pride in their workmanship, and adopting process thinking and the use of specialized control methods. Mikron has applied these principles both in-house and to its long-term partnerships with customers and suppliers. It also developed an extensive in-house training program and instituted quarterly profit sharing. Its team approach, flat management structure, and total quality management practices have resulted in higher production rates, lower scrap rates, and a very low employee turnover.

Mikron's commitment to quality has captured the loyalty of customers for three decades, and ensures its place as a industry leader for years to come.

Clockwise from top:
By streamlining inventory control and shipping methods, Mikron ships specialized customer parts with the shortest lead times in the industry.

To better serve customers in the east, Mikron expanded its operations in 1994 by opening a state-of-the-art facility in Richmond, Kentucky.

Mikron tests its finished extrusions for dimensional tolerance, shrinkage, durability, color, impact, and advanced weathering.

1970-1997

1971 Sabey Corporation

1971 Starbucks Coffee Company

1972 Bob Bridge Auto Center

1972 Harbor Properties, Inc.

1972 Shannon Electronics

1973 Insulate Industries, LLC

1975 Fred Hutchinson Cancer Research Center

1978 Cegelec ESCA Corporation

1978 Covenant Shores Retirement Community

1979 Expeditors International of Washington, Inc.

1979 Pinnacle Realty Management Company

1979 Watts-Silverstein and Associates

1980 The Crowne Plaza Hotel-Seattle

1982 Wall Data Incorporated

1983 Costco Wholesale

1988 Boullioun Aviation Services, Inc.

1989 Seattle Wash, Inc.

1990 ARIS Corporation

1990 Visio Corporation

1992 Heartstream Inc.

1994 Illinova Energy Partners

1994 Southwest Airlines

1995 AT&T Wireless Services

1995 Insignia Corporate Establishments (U.S.), Inc.

1996 Cavanaugh's on Fifth Avenue

GARY GREENE

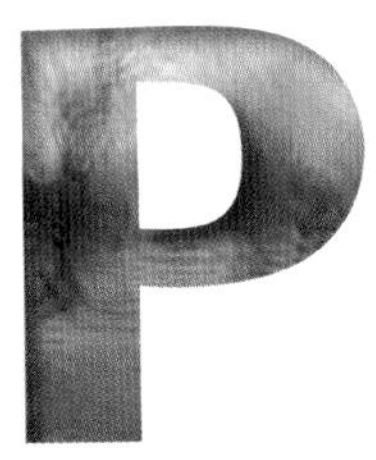

PROVIDING THE MARKET WITH INNOVATIVE COMMERCIAL, INDUSTRIAL, office, and retail properties, Sabey Corporation owns and manages more than 3 million square feet of diversified real estate. Founded in 1971 as a general contractor, Sabey Corporation has grown to a full-service real estate development company offering site acquisition, assistance in obtaining financing, complete design and construction services, office and warehouse space leasing, and property management. The company handles projects ranging from aerospace and corporate facilities to retail shopping centers and sports complexes.

While most people know of the company as developers, approximately 75 percent of its business is in redevelopment. "We're innovative recyclers," explains David A. Sabey, company founder. "We've been recycling for a long time and also saving a bit of Seattle's history in the process."

Identifying ways to turn underutilized real estate into successful developments—and at a lower per-square-foot cost—is Sabey's specialty. A combination of vision, construction expertise, and experience is required to understand what is possible, and to complete projects cost effectively. A team of in-house architects, engineers, and craftsmen use technological know-how, coupled with creativity, to increase a structure's value and usefulness.

Known for seeing opportunities where others don't, Sabey blends Pacific Northwest harmony with subtle nuances of its own. It is a company built on trust, where the management team understands one another and works well together in a dynamic environment. With more than 150 full-time employees, which more than doubles when seasonal retail and construction personnel are included, Sabey can respond quickly and creatively to opportunities.

A WIDE RANGE OF SERVICES

As one of the largest biotech developers and landlords in Seattle, Sabey has built and managed more than 300,000 square feet of lab space, including the facilities of Cell Therapeutics, Inc., PathoGenesis, Ostex International, ICL,

Sabey Corporation recycled a former Boeing "black box" into Riverfront Technical Park, a home for high-tech businesses. Sabey's architects and construction company redesigned the windowless office building by crafting a new facade, cutting in windows, and creating a dramatic entryway and office space with high-end finishes.

◄► J. FREDERICK HOUSEL

Smith Kline Beecham, NOAA, and GeneLex. Sabey's staff are experts in the highly unique build-out needs of biotech tenants, including the special construction, environmental, and management considerations that such projects pose.

Sabey preserved a bit of Seattle's history when it refurbished the Seattle Post-Intelligencer (P.I.) Building at 5th and Wall near downtown, now home to Group Health Cooperative, a national HMO model. In the process, Sabey saved a Seattle landmark, the giant, illuminated P.I. Globe, moving it to the new Seattle P.I. headquarters built by Sabey on Elliott Avenue West. While retaining the art deco character of the old building, Sabey breathed new life and purpose into the structure, the interior of which now forms a giant atrium that opens to skylights three stories above the ground floor. Sabey also transformed the Western Farmers Cooperative into the glass-encased Elliott Park Office Building, thus extending its life for another 50 years.

Sabey offers uncanny responsiveness to clients who need complex facilities constructed in short time frames. The 40-acre Oxbow complex located in South Seattle is a good example. The Boeing Company needed an 11-acre structure built in 90 days. Not only was it an enormous facility, but also a specialty "black" defense plant used for the top-secret engineering and manufacturing of the F-22A fighter and B-2 stealth bomber. Sabey completed the task on time and within budget.

When Boeing vacated the buildings, Sabey's trademark style of finding new uses for difficult properties once again came into play. Its construction arm, Sabey Construction, converted a high security aerospace building into a sophisticated and highly automated mail-sorting and distribution facility for the U.S. Postal Service. It also redeveloped another building on the Oxbow property into Riverfront Technical Park, a multitenant facility anchored by high-tech Internet and call center companies, including travel industry giant SatoTravel, CSG OpenLine, Boeing, and Exodus Communications. Both the original construction and the massive redevelopment project were built at a low cost per square foot and with record efficiency.

"The Oxbow redevelopment was a great project for us because it showcases our competitive advantage," notes Laurent Poole, Sabey executive vice president, referring to Sabey's integrated approach and ability to wear the hats of contractor, architect, developer, owner, and property manager.

Community Spirit

When Sabey Corporation raised the money and built the King County Aquatics complex for the U.S-Soviet Goodwill Games in 1990, it showcased the Seattle community to the world and offered a legacy to future generations. Located in Federal Way, 25 miles south of Seattle, the complex is the only Olympic-caliber swimming and diving facility in the Northwest. Used today for youth and masters events, it is viewed as one more stepping-stone toward Seattle's goal to host the 2008 Olympics. Sabey also renovated the University of Washington's Husky track in anticipation of the historic games, and is constructing a NCAA soccer stadium for Seattle Pacific University and the City of Seattle.

Sabey Corporation continues to give back to the community by underwriting community policing programs and donating to charitable foundations. David Sabey and other Sabey executives are active on the boards and committees of Bathhouse Theatre, University of Washington, University of Notre Dame Business School, Gonzaga University, and Eastern Washington University. In 1996, David Sabey was awarded the Department of Veterans Affairs Community Service Award for a project Sabey Construction built in Spokane. Sabey was one of the first companies in Seattle to provide on-site day care, in the P.I. Building, where Sabey's corporate offices are located.

▶ J. FREDERICK HOUSEL

▶ J. FREDERICK HOUSEL

For more than 25 years, the Sabey Corporation has built, leased, and managed property in the Pacific Northwest, and has perfected its style of "recycling"—redeveloping underused properties into profitable, successful ventures. With its staff's technical expertise and creative vision, Sabey will continue its tradition of success for many years to come.

Sabey Corporation built the international headquarters of The Pacific Institute with spectacular views across Seattle's Elliott Bay of the city skyline (top).

Sabey Construction converted a Boeing aerospace building into a sophisticated mail-sorting facility for the U.S. Postal Service (bottom).

Stand in line at a Starbucks café and you're likely to hear customers ordering everything from a simple decaf mocha to an extraordinary half-decaf, double-tall, 2 percent vanilla latte macchiato. Whatever the order, Starbucks Coffee Company fills it, setting the standard for espresso, cappuccino, and drip coffee, served up according to each customer's taste.

Named after the first mate in *Moby Dick*, Starbucks is a purist's paradise. You won't find flavored coffees like mocha almond fudge or chocolate vanilla—flavors added during the roasting process—because Starbucks insists on preserving the beans in their pristine form. Starbucks roasts each coffee to its individual flavor peak and then brews it to perfection. Its uncompromising standards demand that each espresso is made-to-order, drawn for 18 to 23 seconds, and served at once. Coffee is used in an exact proportion: two tablespoons per six ounces of water, to extract only the best flavors and avoid any bitterness.

North America's leading roaster, retailer, and brand of specialty coffee doesn't just promise a delicious cup of coffee. It promises respect, cool music, camaraderie, a tranquil corner, and a comfortable, bright place to recharge. In fact, it's the attention to design, lighting, ambience, and music that makes Starbucks locations such inviting places. The product, an environment that surrounds your senses, and the friendly servers—called *baristas*—behind the counter create a level of customer loyalty that any company would envy. The average customer visits Starbucks 18 times a month; 10 percent visit twice a day.

The Third Place

Seattle, the epicenter of the coffee tsunami, is the natural birthplace of America's favorite specialty coffee. Starbucks began business in 1971, selling coffee beans in Pike Place Market. At a time when canned supermarket coffee was the standard, selling fresh-roasted, whole beans in a specialty store was a revolutionary concept. It wasn't until 1987 that Starbucks began making coffee beverages in its stores.

Howard Schultz, chairman and CEO, likes to think of Starbucks as a "third place" in American communities—a place between

Clockwise from top:
Starbucks insists on preserving coffee beans in their pristine form, roasting each coffee to its individual flavor peak, and then brewing it to perfection.

Through a partnership with Host Marriott, Starbucks now has more than 70 airport kiosks.

The attention to design, lighting, ambience, and music makes Starbucks stores inviting places.

home and work where people from all walks of life can enjoy an uplifting environment while sipping superb coffee. He believes Starbucks cafés are natural descendants of the Italian coffee bars that captured his attention on a trip to Italy in 1983.

"I started walking through one Italian coffee bar after another in Verona and saw the connection between the people in that little city," says Schultz, who was director of retail operations and marketing for Starbucks at the time of the trip. "The culture of the country is based on the third place. It relies on the meetings in the coffee bar, the restaurant, or the piazza. It's unlike anything I had ever experienced. I said to myself, 'Where in America can you do this? It doesn't exist.' "

Schultz returned to Seattle and tried to persuade management, unsuccessfully, to adapt the authentic Italian espresso bar model for the American market. In pursuit of his dream, Schultz left Starbucks to form a new coffee company, Il Giornale. Three years later, he returned to Starbucks with a $3.8 million buyout offer and a plan to take his retail shops beyond the Pacific Northwest. At the time, Starbucks had 11 Seattle stores and less than 100 employees.

Losses doubled during the first couple of years as Starbucks invested in its expansion. But in 1991, sales jumped 84 percent, and the company broke into the black. Schultz named his first coffee blend Caffé Verona® after his touchstone, the old Roman colony.

▶ PRESENTATIONS NORTHWEST

Brewing Success

In less than a decade, Starbucks has elevated a pedestrian commodity to premium status. Today, Starbucks operates in nearly every major U.S. metropolitan area, serving more than 5 million people each week in more than 1,200 coffee bars. Starbucks is currently opening almost a store per day, and in 1996, opened five locations in Toronto in one day. It also launched its first overseas store in Tokyo in 1996, through a joint venture with an international partner, SAZABY Inc. In December of the same year, Starbucks entered the Singapore market.

Sustainable growth for Starbucks lies within its commitment to quality. Vertical integration gives the company complete control over the product—from selecting the finest quality arabica beans to roasting and distributing them through its locations. Starbucks has never sold franchises despite the cash appeal.

Retail stores account for 87 percent of the company's revenues, which exceeded $696 million in fiscal year 1996. The corporation anticipates that revenues will top $1 billion in fiscal year 1997. Starbucks also operates a national mail-order business and a specialty sales group that serves fine dining, food service, travel, and hotel accounts. The company's corporate headquarters is housed in the SODO district of south Seattle. It operates two roasting facilities in the Seattle

Today, Starbucks has become a gathering place within communities across North America, offering a place to meet, relax, or regroup and enjoy a cup of coffee. The stores pictured are in (clockwise from top) Friendship Center, Washington, D.C., and the Greenlake and University Village neighborhoods of Seattle.

▶ PRESENTATIONS NORTHWEST

area and a distribution and roasting facility in York, Pennsylvania, which opened in 1995 to serve its growing East Coast markets.

Lauded as one of the best-managed companies in the food business, Starbucks has enjoyed 350 percent growth since it went public in 1992. Despite an aggressive marketing plan, which consists of a goal of 2,000 locations by the year 2000, Starbucks is not a profit-driven organization, asserts Schultz. Instead, it's value driven. "Young businesses go through an imprinting process, just like raising kids. Our process has been to imprint the organization with strong values," he says.

Employee Perks

The 25,000 Starbucks partners, as employees are called, come first. "The relationship we have with our people and the culture of our company is our most sustainable competitive economic advantage," says Orin Smith, president and chief operating officer. The goal at Starbucks is to generate partner loyalty. To that end, all partners who work at least 20 hours a week receive full health and dental coverage, vacation days, and stock options in the Bean Stock program—benefits unheard of in the retail business.

Schultz is a firm believer that health benefits are a powerful lure for the kind of workers Starbucks wants to attract. Starbucks offers three managed care plans in which employees pay 25 percent of the premiums. In 1996, the cost of these benefits averaged $2,200 per worker, which, according to Senior Vice President of Human Resources Sharon Elliott, "more than pay for themselves." At a 1996 conference of business leaders, convened to discuss corporate responsibility, President Clinton applauded Starbucks for its progressive employee benefits.

New baristas, most of whom are students or recent graduates, receive 24 hours of training before they serve their first patron. The company demonstrates respect for its employees beyond benefits and training by seeking their opinions on complex and sensitive business issues. This attention to employees pays off: Starbucks boasts a fraction of the turnover rate of the average retailer and food service operator. And keeping employees happy translates into outstanding, personalized service.

Starbucks extended the concept of soothing beverages by introducing Infusia Teas—black, green, herbal, and iced teas—which are sold in retail locations.

Extending the Brand

In continually seeking innovative ways to serve its customers, Starbucks has created a number of partnerships with like-minded, people-oriented companies. Starbucks collaborated with Pepsi-Cola Company to develop and market a ready-to-drink bottled version of the popular Frappuccino® blended beverages.

Starbucks can be enjoyed in the sky on Horizon Airlines and United Airlines, both of which serve Starbucks coffee exclusively, or on the open sea wherever the ships of Holland America Line sail. In a partnership with Host Marriott, more than 70 Starbucks airport kiosks await the weary traveler. Starbucks has also formed alliances with Westin Hotels and Resorts; ITT Sheraton Hotels; Nordstrom; Star Markets; Barnes & Noble Book Stores; Toronto-based Chapters Inc. Book Stores; and most recently formed an alliance with U.S. Office Products to sell Starbucks coffee to offices throughout the United States.

Perfect Coffee Complements

Certain things in life go naturally with coffee, like music and ice cream. Two exclusive compact discs of jazz classics, jointly produced with Capitol Records on the Blue Note® label, were released in 1995 and 1996 along with their companion coffee, Blue Note Blend, creating a whole new product category. The Starbucks library of music continues to grow, from jazz to classical to holiday to blues, with new releases from popular labels making their debut quarterly.

Coffee and chocolate lovers took a deep breath when Starbucks released five super-premium ice-cream flavors—Italian Roast Coffee, Dark Roast Espresso Swirl, Java Chip, Caffé Almond Fudge, and Vanilla Mocha Swirl—in a joint venture with Dreyer's Grand Ice Cream, Inc. These tantalizing flavors made their debut in 1996 in grocery stores coast to coast, and quickly became the number one selling super-premium coffee-flavored ice cream in the nation. In November 1996, Starbucks introduced its first low-fat ice cream nationwide, Low-Fat Latte, and began introducing ice-cream bars into grocery stores in select markets.

Starbucks continually discovers new and exciting products by pushing the limits of the industry. What if a richly roasted coffee were added to a dark malt beer? Voilà. Double Black Stout, a joint venture with Redhook Ale Brewery, rolled out in 1996. Extending the concept of soothing beverages, Starbucks introduced Infusia Teas—black, green, herbal, and iced teas—which are sold in retail locations.

Full-Bodied Commitment

The Starbucks partnership with CARE, the worldwide aid and development organization, is another natural fit. As the largest North American corporate sponsor of CARE, Starbucks designs and funds projects in coffee-growing regions of the world. It's bringing safe drinking water and sanitation systems to more than 90 mountain villages in Guatemala, and helping drought-stricken Ethiopian farmers re-introduce the coffee plant to its birthplace, while generating income for 10,000 inhabitants. And it is helping reduce the infant mortality rate in Indonesia through its Village Maternal Health Project. Starbucks further supports these communities by donating $2 to CARE for every CARE sampler of coffees it sells.

Starbucks decided in 1995 to take its development efforts a step further. After a nine-month process, it adopted the Starbucks Commitment to Do Our Part, a framework for a code of conduct that embraces the goal of improving the quality of life of people in coffee origin countries. Recognizing that impacting conditions is a long-term commitment requiring the effort of many, the goals of the framework are implemented through yearly action plans of specific objectives and international programs. Starbucks commitment to improving the quality of life in the countries where they do business has also earned them the CARE International Humanitarian Award and the Council on Economic Priorities Corporate Conscience Award for International Human Rights.

Dedicated to supporting communities back home, Starbucks sponsors organizations that promote children's welfare, AIDS outreach, education, and environmental awareness. The company is also involved in a variety of community cultural events, including jazz and film festivals. And in January 1997, the company created the Starbucks Foundation, a nonprofit organization dedicated to giving back to the communities in which Starbucks does business.

In 1996, Starbucks celebrated its 25th anniversary of bringing the best cup of coffee to thirsty consumers. Indeed, Starbucks cafés have become the "third place" in communities nationwide, as well as worldwide. With its constant search for new and unique products, and its commitment to its employees and to the communities it serves, Starbucks Coffee Company will continue to inspire coffee drinkers for many years to come.

In a joint venture with Pepsi-Cola, Starbucks launched a ready-to-drink bottled version of the popular Frappuccino® blended beverage, available in supermarkets and at Starbucks locations.

Coffee and chocolate lovers took a deep breath when Starbucks introduced five super-premium ice cream flavors—Italian Roast Coffee, Dark Roast Espresso Swirl, Java Chip, Caffé Almond Fudge, and Vanilla Mocha Swirl—in a joint venture with Dreyer's Grand Ice Cream, Inc. New flavors and ice cream bars quickly followed, including the popular new Low-Fat Latte flavor.

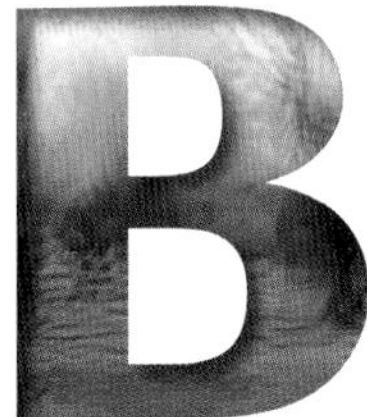

Bob Bridge Auto Center is the sixth-largest sales volume dealership in Washington, and falls in the top 5 percent of all auto dealers in the nation. Founded in 1972, the company sells and services new and used Toyotas, Pontiacs, and GMC trucks. ■ Bob Bridge's modern, six-acre facility features the highest-technology repair shop in Seattle. Twenty thousand customers entrust their car, truck, or van to Bob Bridge Auto Center every year. As cars become more and more complex, diagnosing the problem becomes the most difficult part of repair. The Auto Center's 26 technicians are skilled diagnosticians who are authorized to purchase any piece of diagnostic equipment that will help them in their jobs. And because consumer convenience is important, the service and parts departments are open long hours, Monday through Saturday.

The Auto Center employs 90 people, many of whom have worked together for 20 years. Its primary strength, according to President Bob Bridge, is the experience of the management team. If a customer goes 10 years between visits, he or she will likely be greeted by the same managers and staff members.

Bob Bridge operates under a sales pricing philosophy that sets it apart in the competitive industry. Bridge and his employees believe that new cars, trucks, and vans are nothing more than commodities, and each has a fair transaction price, which Bob Bridge posts weekly. Salespeople are then free to focus on the consumer's needs rather than on negotiating "the deal." Given that, on average, a two-car family will own 15 vehicles in a lifetime and will buy a new car every five years, it makes sense to have a business philosophy that earns customer loyalty.

Focusing on Customer Satisfaction

There are only two numbers to know when shopping for any new vehicle, according to Bridge. More than 20 years ago, Congress passed the Mulroney Law, which requires all manufacturers to put a sticker on every car window listing the manufacturers suggested retail price (MSRP). This figure states what the actual worth of the vehicle is—transportation costs

and all other factors being equal. Many consumers do not realize the MSRP for duplicate vehicles is the same regardless of dealer size and/or location. For that matter, all dealers, large and small, pay the same.

The second number, called the lease residual, estimates what the vehicle will be worth after a determined number of years. This number tracks the transaction prices of every vehicle, and is published in the ALG book and by banks everywhere. While some dealers may attach addendum stickers to a car, sticking to the MSRP and the lease residual gives the customer accurate comparison prices for any new vehicle. Says Bridge, "All you need to know are these two numbers to comparison shop with ease."

The industry's mistake, according to Bridge, is that it has focused on sales, rather than customer satisfaction. The salespeople at Bob Bridge Toyota, Pontiac & GMC are not hired for their closing expertise. Instead, their role is to show a customer the vehicles available and to see if they can meet the person's needs. When customers leave—whether or not they buy—thinking that they have had a great experience and obtained some valuable information, then a Bridge employee has successfully done his or her job.

Bob Bridge's philosophy of being straightforward has also made the dealership a leader in sales over the Internet. Of the 150 new cars or trucks it sold in September 1996, 30 were Internet sales. "Internet buyers are looking for the sales process Bridge's employees use every day with every customer," says Bridge.

Commitment to the Community

Each year, Bob Bridge displays its commitment to the city and region by budgeting approximately $20,000 to support a number of civic and youth programs in King County. The company looks for opportunities to sponsor events that make a difference in children's lives, such as underwriting a sixth-grade teacher and her class on a visit to Washington, D.C., or financing such local events as Renton River Days, a celebration held in conjunction with Seafair.

Prior to purchasing the dealership, Bridge worked for the Ford Motor Company. Overseeing dealership sales in many regions of the country, he felt particularly drawn to Seattle. "In 30 years of business, I've always been impressed by the superior work ethic of western Washington residents," says Bridge. "There's a pride in performing in your job here, and an orientation towards a high quality of life that shapes every Washingtonian. They are extremely loyal workers. I attribute my success directly to the extraordinary people I work with."

Bob Bridge Auto Center is the sixth-largest sales volume dealership in Washington, and falls in the top 5 percent of all auto dealers in the nation.

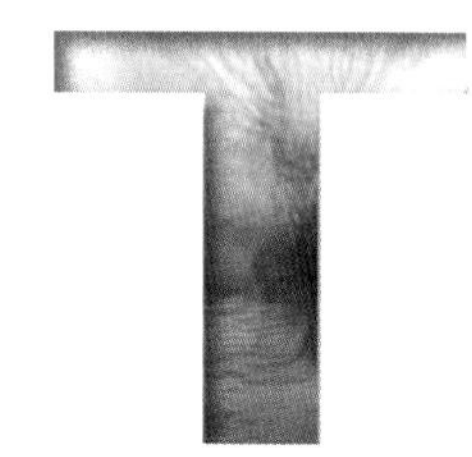

HE ELECTRONICS INDUSTRY HAS EXPERIENCED EXPLOSIVE growth in recent years, with the Pacific Northwest outpacing the national annual growth rate of 30 percent. Shannon Electronics, an industrial stocking distributor of electronic components based in Kent, Washington, is perfectly positioned to take advantage of this rapid growth and to become a regional leader of electronics distributors as the company approaches the next century.

Shannon distributes both imported and domestic parts, primarily to original equipment manufacturers (OEMs) along the Pacific coast. Shannon specializes in being a one-stop provider of electronic components and offers just-in-time inventory delivery, allowing customers to maintain lower levels of on-hand inventory. In addition to OEMs, Shannon has become a key distributor to numerous small- and medium-sized companies across Washington and Oregon, and has earned the reputation for maintaining one of the most highly trained sales staffs in the industry.

SERVICE, SUPPLIES, AND SKILL

As a stocking distributor, Shannon services a large number of customers operating in a wide variety of industries, specializing in those that work with audio and medical equipment, instrumentation, and industrial controls. The components purchased by these customers include potentiometers, relays, switches, capacitors, crystals and oscillators, inductors, coils, batteries, and surface mount components. Shannon is the only dedicated surface mount stocking facility in the Pacific Northwest.

Shannon also offers a range of value-added services, including kitting and auto replenishment. Kitting is a service where manufacturers employ Shannon to procure and assemble kits of electronic components that are used to construct a particular product. In providing auto replenishment services, Shannon monitors a customer's inventory and automatically restocks that inventory as needed.

"With the consolidation of the larger distributors over the last five years, and with the smaller OEMs turning to contract manufacturers for the assembly of their products, Shannon has a great opportunity to expand its business with smaller customers who are currently being pushed to the telemarketing desks of the national distributors," says Dick Thorp, founder and CEO of Shannon Electronics, who has more than 40 years of experience in electronics distribution. "By being very knowledgeable about our products and responsive to the concerns of manufacturers, we provide all of our customers with an excellence of service which makes us competitive at any level."

Shannon continues to emerge as a leader in the fast-paced, rapidly growing electronics distribution industry. At the end of 1996, Shannon's sales were running at a rate equal to \$6 million per year, and this rate is expected to double by the end of 1997. In recognition of this growth, Shannon was recently included as a member of the 1996 Washington Technology Fast 50, a list of the 50 fastest-growing technology-based companies headquartered within the state of Washington. Fueled by this growth, the company has expanded from being a distributor with a strictly local focus to being a regional one with offices in Washington, Oregon, and California.

With roots firmly established in the western United States, Shannon Electronics is primed for a future of success in a growing and dynamic market.

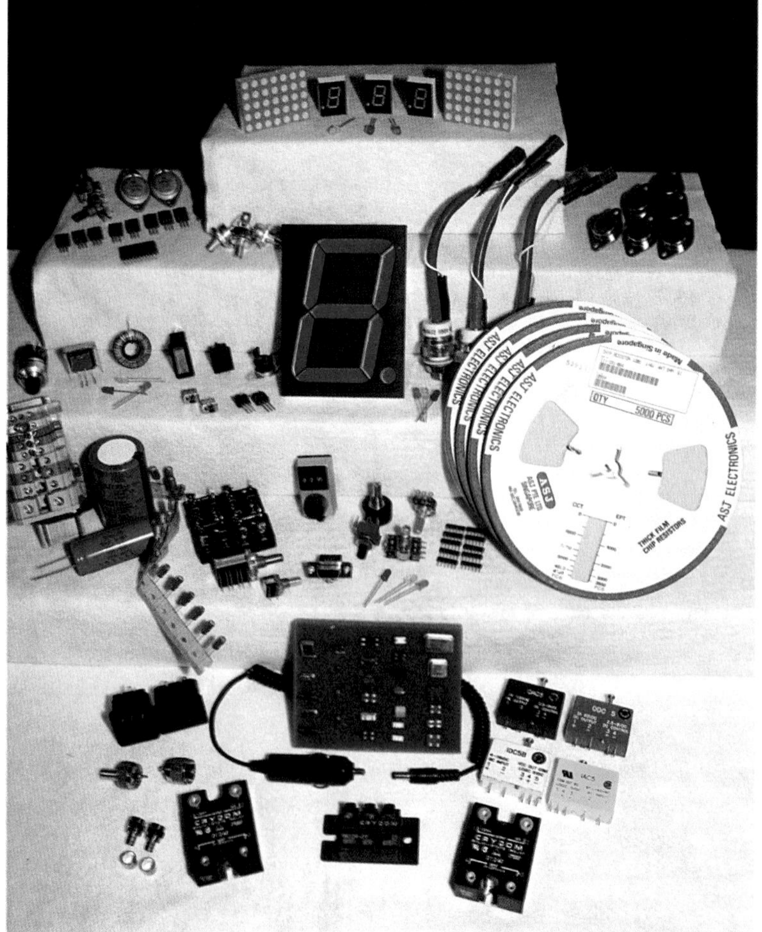

Shannon Electronics distributes both imported and domestic parts, primarily to original equipment manufacturers (OEMs) along the Pacific coast.

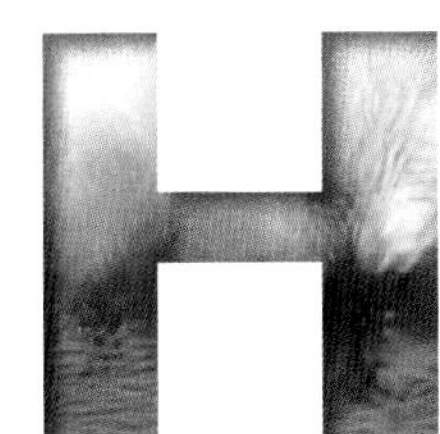

HARBOR PROPERTIES, INC. IS A FULL-SERVICE REAL ESTATE FIRM that has built a portfolio that includes office, retail, and residential properties. Formed in 1972, Harbor's roots trace back through predecessor corporations that built two of its greatest assets: the 1411 Fourth Avenue Building in 1929, and the Logan Building in 1958. Its real estate services include leasing, property management, security, tenant improvement, maintenance, and account management. Harbor's restoration of historic buildings, and construction of new ones, has attracted exciting new shops, restaurants, condominiums, offices, and cultural venues to the city. Harbor also has played a pivotal role in bringing numerous projects developed by others to the downtown area, including the Seattle Art Museum, Watermark Tower, and Waterfront Place.

Believing in a Renewed Downtown

Harbor's projects have centered around the revitalization of the downtown area, particularly on First and Western avenues. Once a grand and vibrant pedestrian corridor bordered by Pike Place Market, Pioneer Square, and the waterfront, by the early 1970s, the area had badly deteriorated. Harbor Properties began acquiring and renovating neglected and abandoned properties that were built around the turn of the century.

Harbor Steps Park and Apartments was the culmination of this development effort. Part of a multiphase project, the 16,000-square-foot staircase park extends between First and Western avenues and includes eight cascading fountains, sweeping steps, and a central courtyard. The $6 million public amenity offers a pedestrian link between the waterfront and downtown business core, where one can relax and enjoy the bustling waterfront.

The award-winning apartment tower at Harbor Steps includes 169 apartment homes that set a new standard of luxury for downtown residential properties. Harbor Steps East, the second phase of the development project, includes 285 apartment homes, a boutique inn, and a large, elevated, landscaped courtyard connecting with the west tower via two sky bridges. The revitalization project has been a catalyst in attracting additional residential developments downtown and creating a neighborhood that mixes old and new, subsidized and market-rate, ownership and rental, and youth hostel and extended-stay housing.

Harbor also owns and operates the Stevens Pass Ski Resort. Located in the Cascade Mountains two hours from the city, Stevens Pass is one of the state's oldest operating ski resorts and one of its most efficiently operated. The expertise of a real estate company gives Stevens Pass a competitive advantage among regional day ski areas. Opened in 1937 and purchased by Harbor in 1976, Stevens Pass continues to expand ski operations and services, with eight new chairlifts, two new lodges, a ski school, the Stevens Pass Nordic Center, and a new, high-speed quad lift. Working closely with the National Forest Service and the Washington Department of Ecology, Stevens Pass has successfully expanded with minimal impact on the surrounding mountain ecosystems.

The hallmark of Harbor is the care and maintenance of its properties. As a firm that builds to own, not to sell, Harbor invests in long-term care. The company's involvement goes beyond property management to consider urban design that truly benefits a neighborhood.

Clockwise from left:
Part of a multiphase project, the 16,000-square-foot Harbor Steps Park extends between First and Western avenues and includes eight cascading fountains, sweeping steps, and a central courtyard.

Located in the Cascade Mountains two hours from the city, Stevens Pass is the state's oldest operating ski resort and one of its most efficiently operated.

Harbor's projects have centered around the revitalization of the downtown area, including ownership of the 1411 Fourth Avenue Building.

▸ DAVID CUMMINGS

▸ SCOTT F. WICKLUND

▸ PATRICK BARTA

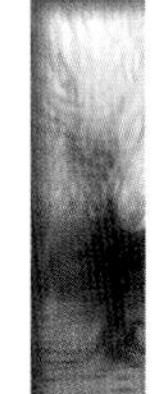

INSULATE INDUSTRIES, LLC HAS BEEN THE LEADER IN THE VINYL window industry since its 1985 introduction of Insulate Windows, the first vinyl window for new home construction on the West Coast. Founded in 1973 by Garry Wamsley and Annette Edwards, the Auburn-based company manufactures and sells windows, doors, and other vinyl-extruded products for manufacturers in the building industry. With a state-of-the-art facility located 20 minutes south of Seattle, the independently owned company of 600 employees has built a national reputation for service.

With the foresight to see that aluminum windows would not meet the stricter energy codes for new home construction, Insulate Industries began extruding its own vinyl in 1990, becoming the first integrated extruder/manufacturer on the West Coast and one of only a handful nationwide.

Energy efficient and environmentally friendly, vinyl windows are one of the most innovative products to enter both the new construction and home improvement markets in recent years. Because vinyl is less conductive of temperature, cold cannot pass through it and heat cannot escape. Vinyl is comparable to wood, much more efficient than aluminum, and completely recyclable. The color of the frame will not fade or peel, so it never needs painting, and it's resistant to damage from the sun, humidity, and other weather elements, making it maintenance-free for a lifetime. These qualities have made vinyl the fastest-growing window material on the market today.

Value, Efficiency, and Custom Styling

The value and efficiency of the Insulate windows and doors product line have made Insulate Industries the technological leader. From single hung and casement windows to awning, slider, and garden windows, from bays and bows, skywalls and skylights to patio, swing, and oversized doors, Insulate Industries' deep and broad product offering is distinctive in the marketplace.

Engineered to the highest-quality standards demanded by professionals, Insulate Windows can be combined in a variety of specialty shapes to create a sophisticated, custom look to fit any home. In addition to manufacturing to standard sizes, Insulate Industries custom builds to order, as well as selling open frames. The 200 Series windows are durable single-hung and slider windows, while the 400 and 500 Series offer the most quality features in slimline windows in the industry, and include casements, awnings, and picture windows.

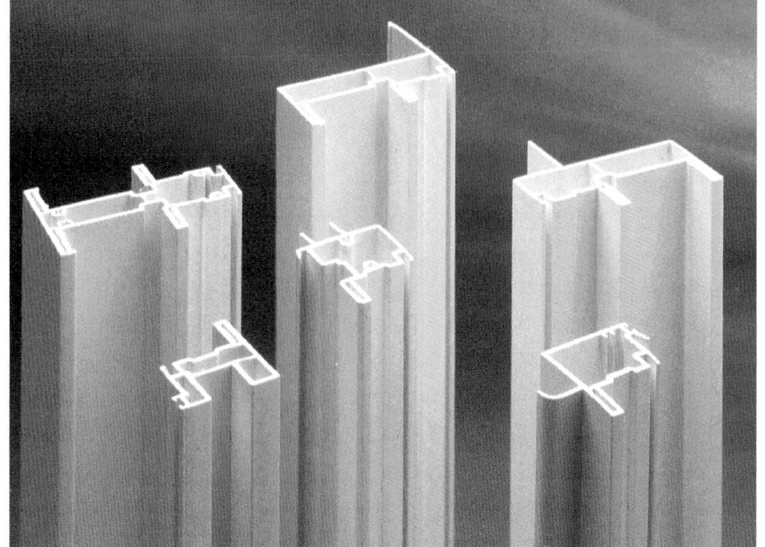

Clockwise from top:
Insulate Industries extrudes, manufactures, and delivers premium vinyl windows and doors throughout the Northwest.

Insulate's extrusions are constructed from a vinyl compound that minimizes the expansion and contraction of the window by reflecting ultraviolet and radiant heat rays. Each extrusion is designed with multiple hollow chambers to ensure energy efficiency.

The leader in vinyl window and door technology, Insulate Industries fabricates its own line of vinyl windows and doors, and provides extrusions to other manufacturers.

With the introduction of the 700 Series casements and awnings in 1996, architectural details like radius and gable top casements and operating octagon awnings are possible without the hassle and cost of mixing and matching wood, aluminum, and vinyl windows to get the desired features. The 700 Series offers a variety of elegant styles in an extended range of sizes that exceed industry standards.

Insulate Industries primarily sells finished products in markets west of the Rocky Mountains, including Alaska, Washington, Oregon, Idaho, Montana, California, Nevada, New Mexico, and Hawaii. Through a variety of export distribution channels, the company serves Pacific Rim markets and Russia, and is pursuing new markets in Korea, Vietnam, and China. Export sales account for a growing share of the company's annual sales and are expected to double in 1997 as demand increases in Asia for Western-style building products.

Tripling its size in the last five years, Insulate Industries retains its position as the industry leader by constantly developing technological innovations to improve the superb energy performance of its windows. In 1997, it set a new industry standard in sound buffering with its sound transmission control windows. The company also introduced the J-channel, a channel placed on the exterior of the window so it can receive house siding, and the second generation of the fresh air passive ventilation system—the Insulair Vent. The firm continues to respond to customer demand for more color choices, with a gray cap stock option complementing standard white and almond.

In January 1996, Insulate Industries formed a fifty-fifty joint venture with CertainTeed Co., which manufactures a variety of building materials from its 35 plants located throughout North America. Insulate Industries will benefit from CertainTeed's industry experience and leadership while broadening its resources to meet customer demand for new products.

Clockwise from top:
Insulate Windows' quality assurance department ensures the integrity of all its vinyl windows and doors, allowing the company to guarantee customers a lifetime of dependable operation.

The 700 Series by Insulate Windows offers vinyl casements and awnings in an extended range of sizes and architectural shapes seen previously only in wood windows.

Insulate Windows' variety of shapes, sizes, and grid styles are combined to give a home unique, impressive curb appeal.

Service Plus Quality

"Exceptional service is a big reason for our rapid growth and loyal customer base," says Edwards, president of Insulate Industries. "We have the best lead time in the industry, with a turnaround of seven to eight business days. Back orders are unusual, and orders are delivered on time, in full, and in excellent condition. In a spirit of partnering with customers, we've made ordering product easy with an electronic quoting program, in which customers can submit orders in a Windows 95 format."

Insulate Industries' fleet of factory-trained service technicians repair all products on-site. The company offers responsive after-sale service and a lifetime warranty on all products to original owners.

The firm employs a total quality management approach to ensure a zero-defects quality process and complete safety. Because growth can create problems, managers learned long ago that answers are found in the trenches. They regularly turn to employees to find ways to improve production and solve problems, incorporating their ideas into product development.

With its constant innovation, quality product, and excellent service, Insulate Industries continues to set the standard in the vinyl window industry.

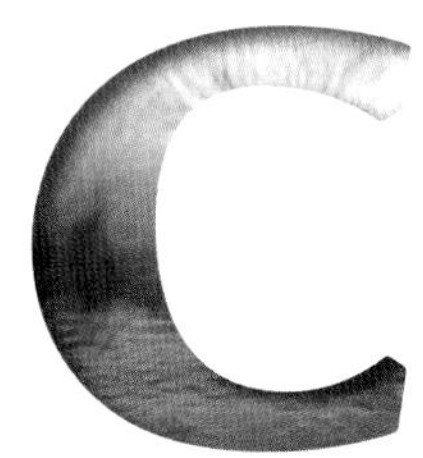

CANCER IS A FAMILY OF DISEASES THAT STRIKE ONE IN THREE people; the current rate of cancer survival, although improving, is only about 50 percent. ■ The Fred Hutchinson Cancer Research Center exists to improve those odds. By developing new knowledge, often in association with other area institutions, and sharing it with professionals, hospitals, other researchers, and the general public, the Hutchinson Center plays a unique and important role within the region's health care system, coming ever closer to its goal of eliminating cancer as a cause of human suffering and death.

A LIVING MEMORIAL

The Center is named for a homegrown baseball sensation named Fred Hutchinson, who pitched 11 years for the Detroit Tigers and managed the Cincinnati Reds. Tragically, the man known for his tenacity, winning determination, and courage died of lung cancer in 1964 at age 45.

Fred's brother, noted Seattle surgeon Dr. William Hutchinson, worked for years to establish a living memorial to his brother. In 1971, the National Cancer Act made federal matching funds available for cancer research, and in 1975, the Hutchinson Center opened. Today, the Center conducts research from three downtown-area sites, including expanded facilities at South Lake Union.

In addition to competitively awarded federal research funding, the Center also receives crucial support from private contracts, grants, and generous philanthropic contributions. Private contributions are key to the Center's recruiting of scientists with new ideas and its purchasing of state-of-the-art equipment.

The Center has a significant impact on the region's economy, spawning flourishing biotechnology companies in the Puget Sound area, including Immunex, Genetic Systems, CellPro, and Cell Therapeutics. In addition, over the next several years, the Center will continue its phased unification of research facilities at South Lake Union. The new campus exemplifies the Center's stature as a major employer of 2,200 individuals, more than 500 of whom hold master's and/or doctoral degrees.

ADVANCING KNOWLEDGE, SAVING LIVES

During 1995, its 20th anniversary year, the Center chose as its slogan Advancing Knowledge, Saving Lives. The Center carries out that vision through pioneering research in four scientific disciplines: basic sciences, clinical research, public health sciences, and molecular medicine.

In the Basic Science Division, laboratory scientists seek to understand the fundamental life processes that underlie the causes of cancer. Using state-of-the-art equipment, they unravel the cell to look for answers to such questions as how cells work and what causes a cell to become cancerous.

The painstakingly incremental process of the Center's basic sciences research has been rewarded with important developments. For instance, the late Dr. Harold Weintraub and his colleagues discovered the gene that directs a cell to become a muscle. That discovery and other observations helped to define how early embryonic cells turn into specialized cells in tissues and organs throughout the body, giving clues

Clockwise from top right: The Hutchinson Center's new, expanding campus will eventually unite all its scientists at one location at South Lake Union near downtown Seattle.

The Fred Hutchinson Cancer Research Center is named for the standout major-league pitcher and manager. Fred's brother, Dr. William Hutchinson, founded the Center after Fred died of cancer at the age of 45.

Special events, such as a celebrity baseball game hosted by TV stars Casey Sander (catching) and Richard Karn (batting), are among the many ways the community helps fund the vital research at the Hutchinson Center.

to understanding how human cells malfunction and become cancerous.

Scientists in the Clinical Research Division work with patients in a research setting, seeking better ways to diagnose and treat cancer, particularly blood-related cancers. Center scientists developed the bone marrow transplant, a technique that is now saving thousands of lives worldwide.

One of the first senior scientists to join the Center, Dr. E. Donnall Thomas, won the Nobel prize in medicine in 1990 for this technique, the newest established treatment of cancer, which stands alongside chemotherapy, surgery, and radiation. Marrow transplantation has increased the cure rate for certain types of leukemia to more than 80 percent. Today, this technique is performed more than 10,000 times each year worldwide and is used to fight a growing number of diseases, including breast and ovarian cancer and sickle-cell anemia. Other studies include stem cell therapy, a major advancement based on marrow transplantation technology, as well as immunotherapy and genetic engineering. As the site of the largest bone marrow transplant program in the world, the Center pursues scientific advances in molecular pharmacology, immunology, and infectious diseases.

Researchers in the Public Health Sciences Division focus on prevention. The division includes the nation's first and largest program devoted to cancer prevention research—an important activity, given that an estimated 80 percent of all cancers may be preventable.

The division also serves as the clinical center for the Women's Health Initiative, a $625 million, 15-year national program sponsored by the National Institutes of Health to find ways to prevent chronic diseases in women.

Translating knowledge generated in the laboratory into new cancer treatments is the goal of the scientists in the Molecular Medicine Division. Formed in 1994, the division devotes much of its research to gene therapy—the introduction of genes into cells to supply functions that are deficient in the cells, with the hope that those cells can go back into the patient to cure a specific gene defect. This research can provide the basis for curing not only cancer, but AIDS, cystic fibrosis, and other diseases.

Partners in Caring

The Hutchinson Center collaborates with many public and private institutions in Seattle to advance cancer research and treatment and train new scientists. Each year, for instance, 20 graduate students enter a graduate program in molecular and cellular biology, a joint program of the Center and the University of Washington (UW). Center scientists hold joint appointments at UW schools, and pediatric specialists serve on the medical staff of Children's Hospital and Medical Center.

The Center's commitment to finding new and better ways to fight cancer provides a ray of hope that one day no one need know the pain of cancer.

Clockwise from top left: Researchers in the Public Health Sciences Division focus on preventing cancer in large populations.

The Hutchinson Center's Dr. E. Donnall Thomas (left) received the 1990 Nobel prize in medicine from King Carl XVI Gustaf of Sweden for his pioneering work in bone marrow transplantation.

Laboratory scientists at the Hutchinson Center, such as Dr. Dusty Miller, unravel the mysteries of the human cell and explore promising new treatments.

The Hutchinson Center performs more life-saving bone marrow transplants than any institution in the world.

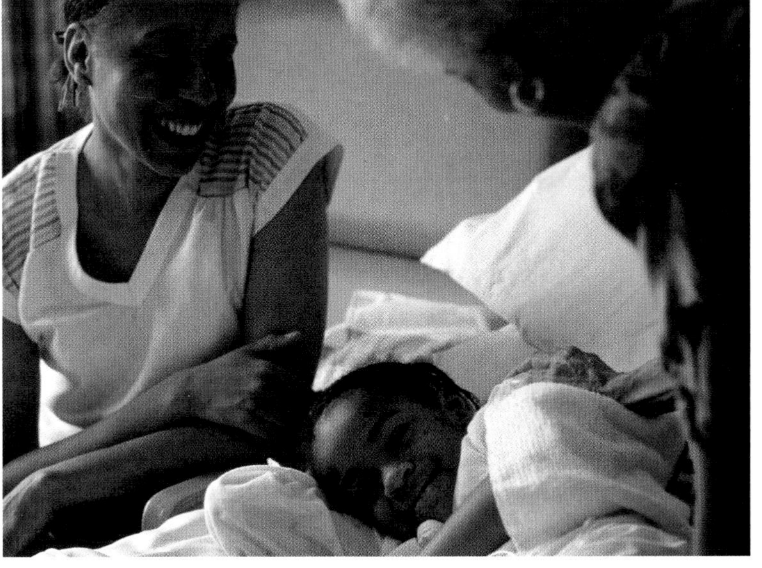

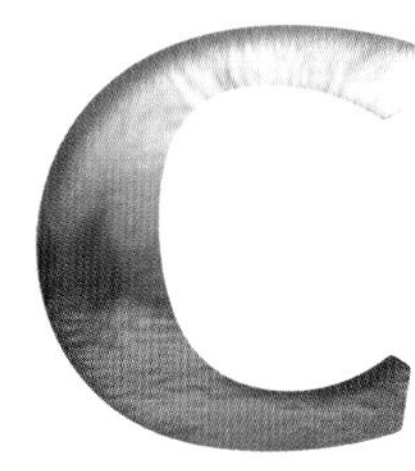

Cegelec ESCA Corporation became one of the first software companies on the Eastside when its 12 founders relocated from Palo Alto to Bellevue, Washington in the late 1970s. Today, Cegelec ESCA is one of the top three suppliers of power control systems and services in the United States, with a customer base that represents one-third of the largest U.S. electric utilities. A $32 million company with 250 employees at its Bellevue headquarters, it is the eighth-largest software company in the Puget Sound region.

As a subsidiary of Paris-based Cegelec, the company is part of the Alcatel Alsthom Group. Alcatel companies form one of the largest multinational groups in the world and are key players in many industries. Among its many contributions to technology, Alcatel Alsthom counts the installation of the world's largest switching base and the design and construction of TGVs (high-speed trains), cruise ships, power plants, and complete telecommunications networks and satellite systems.

Technology and Business Solutions for Change

Cegelec ESCA markets its real-time power system solutions directly to utilities in the United States, Canada, Mexico, Australia, and New Zealand. At the foundation of Cegelec ESCA systems is a set of products called the energy management platform (EMP). Used by utilities in their control centers to manage the generation, transmission, and distribution of electrical energy, EMP has put Cegelec ESCA at the forefront of the industry. Its integrated, modular design streamlines system installation and enables utilities to install what they need, when they need it, rather than completely overhaul their systems. Cegelec ESCA also licenses some of its software for integration into real-time systems for the nuclear, aerospace, telecommunications, transportation, oil, gas, water, and process control industries.

According to Alain P. Steven, president and CEO, Cegelec ESCA has become an industry leader by focusing on the needs of utility customers faced with a rapidly changing industry, and by partnering with them to provide what they need over the long haul. Cegelec ESCA's teams work together to incorporate computer technology advances to create software products for energy management systems. They find ways to improve systems, which leads to streamlining operations and lowering costs.

Cegelec ESCA's newest market is growing rapidly as the U.S. electric utility industry prepares for federally mandated deregulation, which is radically changing the structure of the industry and the needs of the electric utilities. To accommodate these new demands, utilities require new technologies and cost-effective ways of keeping them current. Cegelec ESCA systems have suc-

The Public Power Corporation control center for Greece's national power grid uses Cegelec's EMP as its energy management system.

The *Sun Princess* sits docked at Pier 68 in Seattle, en route to Los Angeles from Vancouver, British Columbia. The electrical propulsion system was supplied by Cegelec.

Ron Wurzer Seattle Times

cessfully met these needs. The company provides state-of-the-art systems that, through continual upgrading, never become obsolete. This approach to system enhancement lets Cegelec ESCA and its customers adjust quickly to changing demands.

▶ PHILLIPE GUIGNARD

Supporting the University of Washington

Cegelec ESCA relocated to the Seattle area from Palo Alto because its founders were impressed by the region's high quality of life and the outstanding electrical engineering program at the University of Washington (UW). In recognition of this excellent program, in 1982, Cegelec ESCA and the university cofounded the Electrical Energy Industry Consortium within UW's electrical engineering department. Chaired by Cegelec ESCA, the consortium provides funding to support student scholarships and fellowships. Today, approximately 40 percent of Cegelec ESCA's engineers and programmers are UW graduates. Several also teach at the university.

▶ SCOTT E. BUFKIN

▶ RICHARD G. SHAW

The Cegelec World Presence

Cegelec ESCA and its parent company, Cegelec, enjoy strong synergy. Currently, Cegelec ESCA and the Cegelec division ERE-D both provide energy management systems based on EMP, thereby making it available to the worldwide electric utility market. In the coming years, explains Steven, Cegelec ESCA will draw on the expertise of its parent company to expand into the power generation and other energy-related fields.

Cegelec is a $4 billion company with 35,000 employees and operations worldwide. It's among the top three companies in industrial controls and is Alcatel's prime contractor for all telecommunications and energy projects.

As an electrical contractor, Cegelec designs, installs, commissions, and maintains installations in more than 80 countries. It also conducts logistics studies and manages such complicated projects as fluid-flow networks, environmental engineering, smart cabling, and security systems. Cegelec applies its expertise in power and process control to such areas as drive systems, process automation, and instrumentation and supervision systems.

Cegelec's activities in the United States are far ranging, explains Brian Pope, Cegelec corporate vice president. It is currently a single-source systems vendor for the U.S. Navy's new polar icebreaker. As a supplier to the U.S. Navy, Cegelec also has a development contract to provide future propulsion systems for navy ships. Marine propulsion is one area where Cegelec is building leadership in the Puget Sound region. It is building and installing the first electric propulsion system ever used in merchant ships and fishing vessels, and was recently awarded propulsion contracts on two new ships for locally based Holland America.

Cegelec is also doing business in the U.S. aircraft industry. For example, in 1996, Cegelec installed a new drive system for The Boeing Company's 52-year-old transonic wind tunnel at Boeing Field. Possibly the largest drive system in the Puget Sound region, the $20 million renovation enables the wind tunnel to produce air speeds of nearly 800 miles per hour and extends its use by 50 years.

"Cegelec is committed to Washington State and the Puget Sound area," says Pope. "We plan to continue to expand our Northwest base. It's a two-way relationship, actually. Many companies here have recognized our leadership, showing their confidence by making Cegelec the company of choice."

Clockwise from top:
Operators sit at consoles below the map board at the control center for Pennsylvania Power and Light Company in Allentown.

Cegelec is a worldwide supplier of turnkey projects for electric power generation, transmission, and distribution.

Cegelec ESCA Corporation headquarters is in Bellevue, Washington.

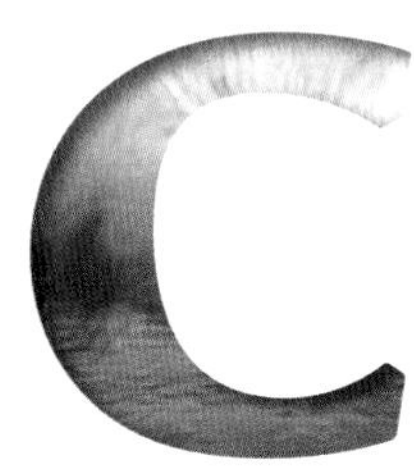

Covenant Shores is a 12-acre retirement community on the northern shores of Mercer Island. Located just 10 minutes from downtown, its scenic waterfront campus includes 700 feet of lakefront property and a 51-slip marina. Established in 1978, Covenant Shores is part of Covenant Retirement Communities, a long-standing organization—with 100 years of ministry—which is owned by the Evangelical Covenant Church. Since its inception, Covenant Retirement Communities has grown to include 13 nonprofit retirement communities in seven states.

Residents come from all denominational backgrounds and meet a minimum age requirement of 62 years; there is no maximum age limit for residents. The one-time entrance fee and low monthly fees provide a continuum of care throughout a resident's lifetime. As a continuing care community, people can make decisions during their independent years that will carry them through later years when changes may occur in their health situation. Having these services in place is designed to give residents peace of mind.

Clockwise from top:
Located just 10 minutes from downtown, Covenant Shores' scenic waterfront campus includes 700 feet of lakefront property and a 51-slip marina.

Independent residents enjoy a daily meal of fine cuisine served in the lakefront dining room or on the large deck overlooking Lake Washington.

Covenant Shores offers a wide choice of living accommodations and floor plans, from modest studios to 1,800-square-foot apartments—many with waterfront views.

Something for Everyone

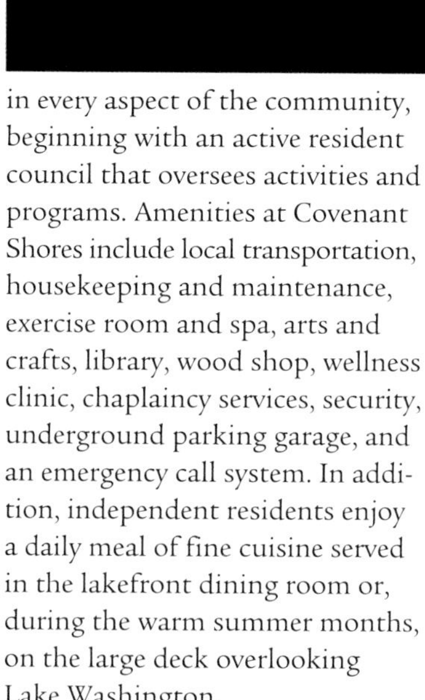

Covenant Shores not only offers its 250 residents a community of friends and neighbors, but also many opportunities for personal development that they might not have living alone. Through its diverse activity program, people can participate in many interests: painting, sailing, woodworking, walking, line dancing, shuffleboard, singing, exercising—the list of activities is as diverse as the residents themselves. And with priority access to the marina, residents can moor everything from a small canoe to 40-foot sailboats. Residents also enjoy day trips to museums, plays, and new restaurants, as well as overnight visits to Vancouver and other destinations in the Pacific Northwest.

An enormous amount of resident involvement is evident in every aspect of the community, beginning with an active resident council that oversees activities and programs. Amenities at Covenant Shores include local transportation, housekeeping and maintenance, exercise room and spa, arts and crafts, library, wood shop, wellness clinic, chaplaincy services, security, underground parking garage, and an emergency call system. In addition, independent residents enjoy a daily meal of fine cuisine served in the lakefront dining room or, during the warm summer months, on the large deck overlooking Lake Washington.

Recognizing that one size does not fit all, Covenant Shores offers a wide choice of living accommodations and floor plans, from modest studios to 1,800-square-foot apartments—many with waterfront views. The campus expanded in the 1990s to add 100 independent apartments and assisted living quarters. In 1997, it expanded its on-site health care services with the opening of the Health Center, a skilled nursing facility that accommodates 43 people.

Approximately one-third of the residents come from outside the Seattle area in order to be close to their families. Residents can also transfer from another Covenant retirement community.

The Covenant Church benevolence fund demonstrates the Christian mission of the community; in more than 100 years, no one has ever left a Covenant retirement community because he or she could no longer afford to stay.

"We often hear people say, 'Our only regret is we wish we had moved in sooner,' " says Ronald Bergstrom, administrator of Covenant Shores. "I think many of our residents had no idea what a full, rich, active life they could have in their retirement years."

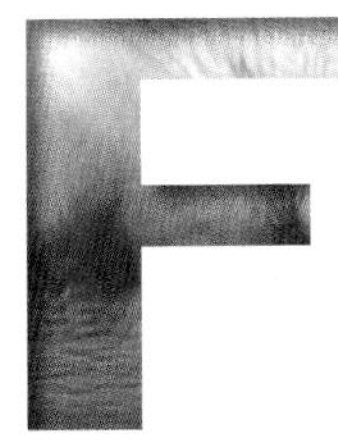

FOUNDED IN 1980, WATTS-SILVERSTEIN AND ASSOCIATES IS A multimedia communications firm that combines multiple disciplines under one roof. The company introduces or helps to position new products, communicates success stories, designs sales and presentation aids, writes keynote speeches, and creates educational tools. Watts-Silverstein helps clients define their goals, plan the steps to achieve them, and even measure the return on their investment. No other company in the Northwest, and few in the country, can offer its scope of services.

COLLABORATIVE CREATIVITY

Adept at bringing in people who can rally around a concept, Watts-Silverstein calls its problem-solving process collaborative creativity. The company's system is based on the belief that creativity is enhanced when team members reach a consensus and then brainstorm that idea together. Watts-Silverstein's extraordinary team of people is drawn from the diverse fields of event management, public relations, software production, digital graphic design, marketing, advertising, ntertainment, journalism, and even medicine.

Pragmatically creative, Watts-Silverstein pioneered corporate events for product launches, brought computer-controlled slide shows to the Northwest, and is again in the forefront of the industry in its use of digital media, which includes CD-ROM, Internet, digital versatile disc (DVD), and computer graphics.

With core values stemming from cofounders Charlie Watts and Bruce Silverstein, Watts-Silverstein has brought a business savvy to the creative process. Proven systems of managing cost and meeting deadlines on budget provide an additional edge. "What separates our work is our collective experience and a completely objective position, which is a very positive thing for clients," says Watts.

Over the years, Watts-Silverstein has built a long list of loyal clients worldwide. It had the good fortune to grow along with five or six client companies that have become industry leaders. The firm has worked with Nintendo since it opened its first U.S. office in 1981, and with Microsoft since it was a company of 35 employees. Longtime local clients also include Starbucks Coffee Company, SAFECO, Paccar, Kenworth Truck Company, Alaska Airlines, Weyerhaeuser, and dozens of other corporate leaders in the Northwest. The firm has also developed many smaller projects for start-up companies.

National clients include Walt Disney Company, AT&T, Intel Corporation, Georgia Pacific, Jantzen, Inc., and Allied Signal. Watts-Silverstein has worked on every continent in the world except Antarctica. Its computer-based graphics have won top industry awards year after year, and many of its projects throughout the Americas, Australia, Asia, India, and Europe have been recognized at film festivals and design competitions.

Watts-Silverstein and Associates remains very committed to the Northwest community. Every year, the company launches numerous pro bono projects, creating events and presentations for organizations like the Woodland Park Zoo's Elephant House, Cystic Fibrosis, Philchuck Glass School, United Way, and Children's Hospital and Medical Center, and targeting causes such as drug use education and campaigns against teenage drinking and driving. Says Silverstein, "We feel very much a part of the Northwest."

Clockwise from top right: Watts-Silverstein introduces or helps to position new products, designs sales and presentation aids, writes keynote speeches, and creates educational tools.

The company helps clients define their goals, plan the steps to achieve them, and even measure the return on their investment.

Watts-Silverstein's system is based on the belief that creativity is enhanced when team members reach a consensus and then brainstorm that idea together.

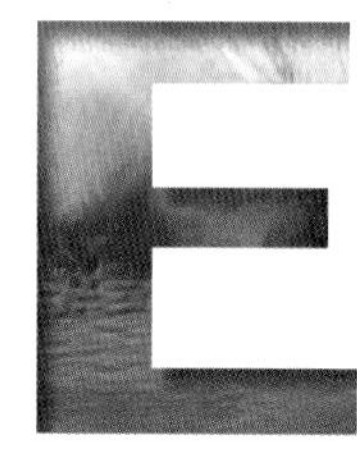

Expeditors International of Washington incorporated in 1979 to pursue the innovative idea of consolidating customs clearance and freight forwarding into one business. The company quickly gained a leading share of the nation's market for importing air freight from the Far East, in addition to exports and clearance.

Today, the global logistics company serves clients worldwide with air and ocean freight forwarding, ocean freight consolidation, customs clearance, cargo insurance, duty drawback, distribution, and value-added logistics. Its broad range of services and sophisticated systems integration serves customers wanting a seamless international transportation and distribution operation. Expeditors is not a small-package, courier, or domestic delivery company, but instead deals in international transportation and distribution of freight weighing 100 pounds or more.

In the industry, Expeditors has earned high marks for its integrity, stability, and focus. Locally, it has been called "the biggest, most successful overlooked public company in the Puget Sound region," even though the worldwide organization has more than 126 offices and international service centers and 3,200 employees spanning five continents. Expeditors responds to its clients' need for financial viability, geographic representation, electronic capability, experienced personnel, and competitive pricing—all of which adds up to reliability.

Roughly 70 percent of the company's revenue comes from air freight, while customs brokerage and ocean freight make up the balance. Rather than owning ships or planes, Expeditors opts to contract with multiple commercial airlines and ocean freighters to negotiate the best routing, pricing, and flexibility for customers. "We're a travel agent for freight without owning any equipment," says Peter J. Rose, chairman and CEO of Expeditors. "And that keeps us flexible."

Meeting Customer Needs through Diversification

While sticking to its core competencies, Expeditors has diversified to meet the needs of its custom-

Each Expeditors office holds training sessions for its employees on topics ranging from letters of credit to updates of the company's computer software.

Peter J. Rose, chairman and CEO of Expeditors International of Washington, Inc. (www. expd. com)

ers, which range from small businesses to multinational corporations. Ocean freight consolidation services smooth the flow of goods for U.S. customers buying from multiple vendors in the Far East. Value-added logistics services range from in-transit assembly to processing merchandise returns. From warehouses around the world, Expeditors collects and merges shipments, making sure the inventory arrives at the right place at the right time.

Because Expeditors also moves information around the world, the company sees itself as being in the communications business. In the early 1980s, Expeditors began developing a state-of-the-art electronic data information system to link the Seattle headquarters with branch offices, and customers with their shipments. From the factory floor to the retail shelf, clients can dial in anytime to trace their shipments globally in real time. By removing the burden of day-to-day monitoring of shipments—as well as collecting, analyzing, and entering tracking information—customers are free to focus on running their businesses.

Expeditors has grown by opening offices rather than acquiring companies. In 1981, the company reached a milestone when it opened offices in Hong Kong, Taiwan, Singapore, Chicago, San Francisco, and New York. After going public in 1984, Expeditors continued to expand into new markets and broaden its range of services. In 1994, offices were opened in Finland, Spain, Sweden, and South Africa, and agency agreements were signed in Russia, Hungary, and Croatia. Expeditors became the first foreign freight forwarder to be licensed by the Chinese government. The company's most recent growth has been in the Near and Middle East and the Indian subcontinent. Traded on NASDAQ under the symbol EXPD, Expeditors recorded $730 million in revenue in 1996.

"I don't think we're an American company. We're an international company," says Rose, who is Canadian. Expeditors' sensitivity to foreign cultures has led to certain strategic decisions that have paid off handsomely, including hiring locals familiar with the market to run each branch office.

Fostering the Entrepreneurial Spirit

Expeditors has managed to sustain continuity and a sense of family while growing exponentially—something many companies struggle with. Considered highly unusual in the industry, Expeditors nurtures a sense of ownership and entrepreneurial spirit among employees through a decentralized management style. Branch offices are responsible for their financial performance, and under an incentive program receive a percentage of their region's profits each month. The result: District managers run the company and top management provides support.

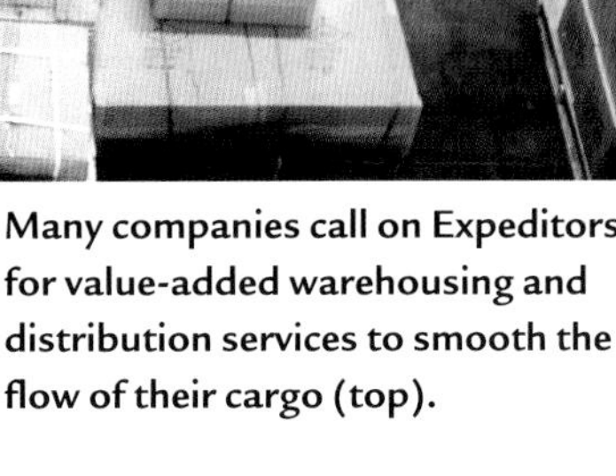

Many companies call on Expeditors for value-added warehousing and distribution services to smooth the flow of their cargo (top).

Expeditors' proprietary computer software, exp.o, gives customers immediate information about their shipments, enabling them to gain more control over their business (bottom).

The in-house quality program at Expeditors is something Rose is particularly proud of. The company has gone far beyond its ISO 9002 certification to train and promote the professional development of its employees. All employees receive a minimum of 52 hours of in-house training on such subjects as computing, sales skills, and geography.

Employees can also choose a career path, and the company will finance their participation in accredited programs. If an employee wants to learn Spanish, or any other skill relevant to the business, he or she is given a green light. Expeditors has one of the highest licensed broker/employee ratios in the industry, which ultimately benefits customers. The firm also actively seeks opportunities to promote women. This kind of support encourages employee retention, a truism revealed in the employee turnover rate, which is less than half the industry average.

The headquarters of Expeditors supports Junior Achievement and Fred Hutchinson Cancer Research Institute, of which Rose serves on the board. Each branch office contributes to community programs of its own choosing. With satisfied employees, customers, and neighbors, Expeditors is a tremendous success in all realms.

Pinnacle Realty Management Company is an international real estate investment management firm providing a wide range of realty services, including the acquisition, disposition, rehabilitation, property management, financing, and repositioning of select real estate assets located primarily throughout the United States. Pinnacle's clientele represents investors from nearly a dozen countries, including Germany, China, Canada, and Japan. Its professional executive staff brings depth and diversity to its complementary services, which are focused to preserve and enhance the value of the assets it represents.

"Pinnacle is unique in the real estate industry," says President and CEO Stan Harrelson. "No company is structured quite like it. By combining expert knowledge of the local industry with strategic investment planning, we marry exceptional investment, management, and disposition capabilities with a forward-thinking, value enhancement approach to each asset we represent." Vertically integrated to respond to ever changing investor needs, Pinnacle continually seeks greater customer efficiencies through partnered relationships on behalf of its many clients.

Pinnacle's international client base includes more than 250 institutions, pension funds, private partnerships, foreign clients, sole owners, and government housing groups. By offering expert guidance in every aspect of real estate investment management, Pinnacle's staff seek to first understand the needs of the owners they represent, and then fit the pieces of the real estate puzzle together to enhance their clients' success.

"The defining characteristic of Pinnacle," according to Chairman and Founder John Goodman, "is its talented people." As Goodman explains, "We're driven by an entrepreneurial spirit, a long-term vision, and a customer service culture that's focused on delivering results." Pinnacle's multileveled investment managers have an average of 10 years' experience in the field and more than six years with the company.

Harrelson emphasizes, "There are two kinds of real estate management companies. There are those that manage predominantly for their own account, and there are those that manage predominantly for the accounts of others, or third parties. What it boils down to is choice." As one of only two nationally recognized third-party fee managers in the United States, Pinnacle manages the assets of others for a fee and does not own any of the real estate that it manages.

Clockwise from left:
The Pinnacle Realty Management Company's international headquarters is located in the historic Pioneer Square district in downtown Seattle.

Stan Harrelson, Pinnacle president and CEO

John Goodman, Pinnacle chairman and founder

◄► Stewart Hopkins

◄ Stewart Hopkins

"Other property managers who own real estate sometimes fall into a trap of worrying too much about their own investments instead of their clients," says Northwest Regional President Ward McLain. As solely service providers, this third-party relationship allows Pinnacle's staff to focus entirely on understanding and servicing the needs of the client.

Strategic Growth

Through strategic acquisitions, Pinnacle built a powerful national infrastructure for delivering service and responding to the ever changing investment needs of its clients. Many of these acquisitions have developed from forming partnerships with innovative local firms. In 1994, Pinnacle partnered with Phoenix Realty Group, the wholly owned real estate subsidiary of Phoenix Home Life, a 142-year-old mutual life insurance company headquartered in Hartford, Connecticut. The partnering of the two firms' staffs, infrastructures, resources, and talents has allowed Pinnacle to deliver innovative and collaborative investment management services to its clients.

Performance Creates Success—Success Creates Growth

The staff at Pinnacle believe that property management is about performance—that is, the ability to position each asset the company represents in the marketplace to maximize its potential value. Performance is what every investor looks for, and it is what makes Pinnacle different. "Our goal," says Harrelson, "is to be a superior customer service organization. Responsive client service is the foundation that allows Pinnacle to deliver market-leading asset performance for its customers. It's that simple."

With an expanding management portfolio exceeding $5.9 billion in 1997, Pinnacle's size offers clients significant strategic advantages. However, Pinnacle's goal is not to be the largest in the industry, but to be good enough to be chosen not only by potential clients but by potential partners, vendors, residents, tenants, and employees.

Taking great pride in the quality of work performed for clients, Pinnacle's real estate teams spend significant time trying to perfect and meet a diverse level of client demands with a multitude of specialized services. Pinnacle has stayed on the crest of innovation with a national computer network and a sophisticated electronic data communication delivery system. Bolstered by multimillion-dollar annual investments in technology advancements, the Pinnacle Management Information System offers clients immediate access to critical market information and links the company's offices nationwide, as well as its clients, into this ever changing database of information and opportunities. "It's an important piece of Pinnacle's infrastructure that enables us to deliver performance," says Harrelson.

Many clients have been with the company since 1979, when John Goodman founded Goodman Financial Services, later renamed Pinnacle Realty Management Company. The company started in the multifamily residential management business, and by 1985, it managed nearly 5,000 units in the Puget Sound area. It branched out to other northwestern cities, including Portland, Oregon, and Richland, Kennewick, and Pasco, Washington, and eventually expanded outside of the northwest region into Phoenix, Las Vegas, and several cities in California. Responding to client demands, Pinnacle expanded nationwide in the late 1980s, becoming a major real estate firm in such markets as Atlanta, Chicago, Dallas, Orlando, and Washington, D.C.

By 1997, with a continually expanding presence in 36 states, Puerto Rico, and Canada, Pinnacle has achieved a level of national prominence in residential property management as the second-largest fee manager in the country. In the northwest region, where the firm was founded, Pinnacle stands out today as the largest property management and brokerage firm in the Pacific Northwest.

With its international headquarters located in the historic Pioneer Square district in downtown Seattle, Pinnacle reigns as the only major West Coast residential property management company. Northwest branch offices

Clockwise from top:
Members of the Northwest Region property management staff perform on-site inspection, an important part of Pinnacle's customer service.

Pinnacle's executive staff continually seek new ways to improve operations.

The Pinnacle Management Information System offers immediate access to critical market information and links the company's offices and clients nationwide.

▶ STEWART HOPKINS

▼▲ STEWART HOPKINS

are located in Portland, Oregon; Spokane and the Tri-cities area in Washington; and Boise, Idaho; as well as Vancouver, British Columbia. Pinnacle's diverse operations in the Puget Sound area span Olympia to Everett and Silverdale to Issaquah and are highly representative of the company's operations in other regions of the country.

Wide Range of Services

Responding again to client requests, Pinnacle developed a national brokerage network to assist its many and varied clients in the acquisition and disposition of real estate assets. Pinnacle offers full-service asset brokerage by managing transactions ranging from a single-tenant property in secondary and tertiary markets to the largest institutional properties located in major metropolitan statistical areas. Pinnacle's strong presence in the industry and its international relations enable it to access a large pool of qualified buyers, sellers, and investors.

"Our people understand buildings and the markets they're in. Pinnacle's unique combination of management and brokerage expertise enables it to maximize a seller's value," notes Director of Brokerage Services Greg Beckel. This unique partnership of property management staffs and brokerage staffs enables Pinnacle to underwrite properties accurately, as well as identify and capture opportunities quickly.

Many real estate brokers tend to apply a one-size-fits-all approach to brokering. As Harrelson stresses, "Pinnacle's partnerships with clients enable it to understand the client's specific needs, differentiate properties, and deliver to owners more accurate insight into a prospective building's future performance opportunities."

Pinnacle brokers have been the dominant apartment brokers in the Pacific Northwest for many years. For the past several years, Pinnacle has ranked among the top three commercial brokerage firms in this same region. Nationally, Pinnacle offers brokerage expertise in all major cities where the company provides management expertise. By the mid-1990s, Pinnacle's brokerage operations had grown in Arizona, California, Florida, Georgia, Texas, and the Washington, D.C., metropolitan areas. Consistent with the Pinnacle philosophy and vision to be an industry leader, Pinnacle brokers are not just salespeople; they are investment analysts representing Pinnacle's clients in solving their various real estate investment needs.

Residential and Commercial Management and Leasing Services

Although Pinnacle began as a residential management firm, it diversified in the 1990s to become a dominant player in commercial management and leasing. At the beginning of 1997, Pinnacle's commercial portfolio included retail, office, and industrial properties located throughout the United States, thereby placing it among the top commercial management companies in the country. Its national commercial infrastructure includes marketing, leasing, construction management, maintenance, landscaping, executive management, owner/tenant relations and services, operating controls, and market analysis.

Pinnacle's multiple specialties allow it to serve its clients' varied real estate investment management needs. In many instances, Pinnacle manages for one client multiple assets of different types located in multiple states. For example, one client may have residential properties in Washington State, commercial properties in Oregon, properties being rehabilitated in Georgia, and properties being acquired in Florida—all handled by local market specialists from Pinnacle's real estate staffs. "We have to think like the owner and understand the investor. Investors' needs are usually not limited to one type of real estate asset located in only one market," says McLain. "We believe in these partnered relationships because time and again, their payoff to our clients is high performance."

Is there a focus on client relationships? "When I started the company, we were set up to do what the client needed," says Goodman. "What Pinnacle has become is an extension of that. In the past, property management was our mainstay, but today it's a lot more. Property management is one part of the process of an investor's relationship with an asset. As we continually earn more trust with new clients, they often ask us not only to find projects for them to acquire, but also to then manage, lease, refinance, and reposition in the marketplace. Along the way, we did whatever it took to enhance the value of their assets."

◄► STEWART HOPKINS

Pinnacle's clientele represent investors from nearly a dozen countries, including Germany, China, Canada, and Japan (left).

Pinnacle diversified in the 1990s to become a dominant player in commercial management and leasing (right).

Facilities and Risk Management

As buildings built decades ago need improvements, Pinnacle, through its affiliated entity Phoenix Corporate Services, is playing an increasing role in commercial facilities management, overseeing the physical aspects of a business, such as plant management, maintenance, and employee health safety. This in turn frees companies to focus on their core business operations.

Pinnacle also offers risk management services, from property liability and casualty to employer risks. Pinnacle staffs assist clients in selecting property insurance, performing site reviews, and handling other insurance details.

Pinnacle Plus

An important part of having a successful income-producing property is having happy and excited residents and tenants. Pinnacle regularly focuses on developing new and innovative services for these groups. One example is Pinnacle Plus, a program created in 1996 where residents and tenants having a Pinnacle Plus card receive special discounts on a myriad of products and services offered by local merchants in the area where the assets are located.

Success in the Public Housing Arena

In 1994, Pinnacle expanded its management services to public sector housing in response to the increased privatization of government housing. Employing new approaches to repositioning public housing and developing interactive resident programs, the company quickly built a national leadership reputation for transforming troubled residential properties into desirable communities.

In 1997, Pinnacle emerged as the largest single provider of public housing management services in the United States. With major public housing management assignments located in Seattle; Miami; San Bernardino; Chicago; San Juan, Puerto Rico; and expanding markets in between, Pinnacle continues to offer private sector services in response to a public sector movement to partner with leading real estate service providers to provide a higher quality of housing for its public residents. Pinnacle brings a customer sensitivity to public housing management, believing in a holistic approach that merges the physical facilities with the social needs of residents.

Whispering Pines, composed of 10 buildings with a total of 246 units, is a public housing community located in Snohomish County, about 15 minutes north of Seattle. A former haven of crime and the object of years of neglect and mismanagement, Whispering Pines represents a national success story in public/private collaboration in public housing rehabilitation. Based on the strength and experience of Pinnacle's management program and its proven track record in turning around properties with prolonged maintenance and management neglect, the Snohomish Housing Authority selected Pinnacle to manage the property. The firm performed a massive renovation project to provide housing for low- and moderate-income people. The renovation not only resulted in a drastic reduction in crime, but it helped forge a community where residents take pride in their surroundings and responsibility for keeping them safe and livable.

Pinnacle—"Putting the Pieces of Success Together"

In both the public and private sectors of residential and commercial real estate, Pinnacle has achieved great success through the combination of expert knowledge of the industry, strategic investment planning, a wide range of specialized services, and a solid customer service culture. Says Harrelson, "The most important thing is that our Pinnacle staffs keep the role of the company in perspective. We don't let our egos get in the way of our customers' belief in what we're going to do for them. We're there for them. It's this alignment of purpose with the client that's critically important. You have to match what your client wants with market performance." These traits assure that Pinnacle will continue its phenomenal growth for many years to come.

In 1996, the company introduced Pinnacle Plus, a program in which residents and tenants of Pinnacle properties receive special discounts on a myriad of products and services offered by local merchants (left).

John Goodman and Stan Harrelson have built Pinnacle into an international firm offering expert services, including acquisition, disposition, rehabilitation, property management, and financing (right).

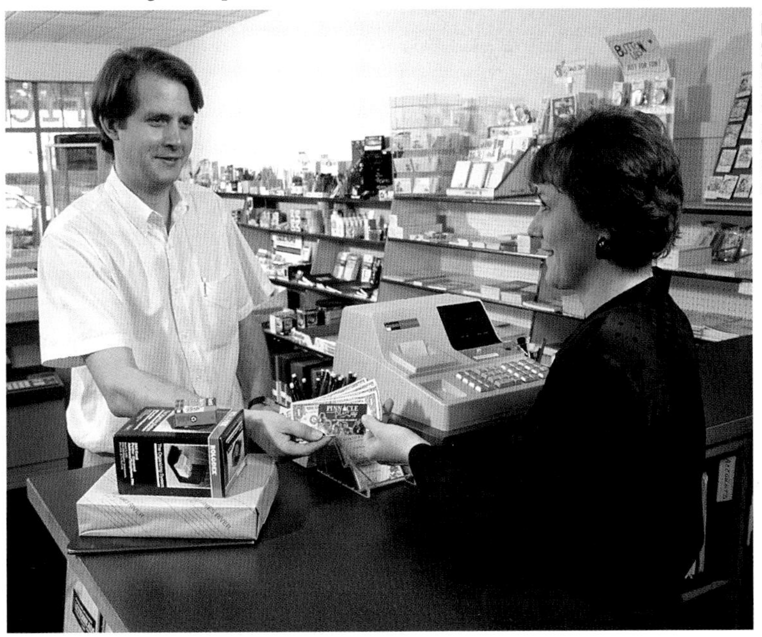

◀▶ Stewart Hopkins

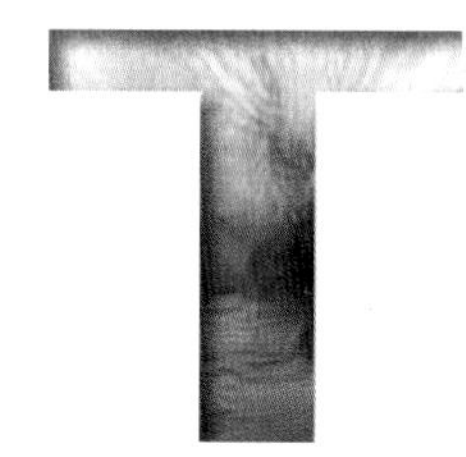

The Crowne Plaza Hotel-Seattle is located in the heart of downtown Seattle and caters to the upscale business and leisure traveler. Established in 1980, it belongs to a family of 150 hotels that enjoy a national reputation for high-quality service. Crowne Plaza Hotels and Resorts are found in major U.S. cities and several overseas locations. The newest hotels to wave the Crowne Plaza flag are the pristine San Francisco Parc Fifty Five Hotel and the St. Anthony Hotel, a national and state historic landmark located in San Antonio.

The Latest in Modern Accommodations

In 1995, Crowne Plaza Hotel-Seattle underwent a full refurbishment. Each of its 415 gracious guest rooms is furnished with a king-size bed or two double beds, remote TV, cable and on-command pay movies, two telephones, clock radio, full-length mirror, iron and ironing board, and a sitting area for guests to relax and take in the sweeping views of the Cascade Mountains or Puget Sound.

The exclusive club floors house guest rooms and three suites where guests enjoy a private lounge, complimentary continental breakfast and evening hors d'oeuvres, and turndown service. The three presidential suites—Olympic, Cascade, and Rainier—command spectacular panoramic views from the 34th floor.

The Crowne Plaza Hotel-Seattle is located in the heart of downtown Seattle and caters to the upscale business and leisure traveler.

The Crowne Plaza Hotel-Seattle enjoys repeat clientele from groups and individual travelers, as well as corporate, civic, and government business groups. It houses most of the Major League Baseball teams when they come to town, and many travelers who embark from Seattle on ocean cruises with Holland America.

Fitness and Fine Dining

Crown Plaza guests take pleasure in a number of first-class amenities—including complete exercise facilities, whirlpool, sauna, valet parking, dry cleaning, and no-smoking floors. The helpful concierge can book tours, make dinner or airline reservations, offer suggestions for sight-seeing and cultural events, and more. Photo binders displaying menus of local restaurants are available for those wishing to explore some of the world-class dining the city has to offer. Visitors needing to work can take advantage of computers and clerical support available on-site, plus fax, photocopy, and teleconferencing services. And, as a convenience to its international clientele, Crowne Plaza accepts foreign currency and uses Holidex worldwide reservations.

The hotel's excellent service and convenient downtown location—four blocks from the Washington State Convention and Trade Center, and within walking distance of major shopping and cultural interests—has made it the hotel of choice for many visitors. It's a 15-minute walk to Pioneer Square and the Pike Place Market and Waterfront; 15 minutes from the Seattle Center and Space Needle via the Monorail; and 15 minutes from the Kingdome.

Shuttle service on the Gray Line brings guests to the hotel's front door, making door-to-door service from the airport a 25-minute ride. Local and national companies regularly hold meetings at the

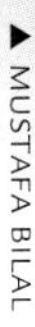

Its glassed canopy and natural light make the award-winning City Views a welcoming place to relish breakfast, lunch, or dinner.

hotel and book their out-of-town business clients or company personnel there as well.

Business meetings or luncheons at the hotel are simple to arrange. With one phone call, guests can book the appropriate space at the hotel to fit the function and the mood, and leave all the details to the hotel staff. This one-stop shopping for planning events has received accolades from users. Nine meeting rooms, including an executive boardroom and elegant dining room, can be tailored to meet the needs of groups of 10 to 400 people. Guests with epicurean tastes appreciate the artistically catered menus.

Creativity is the Crowne Plaza's trademark. For special events that call for a "fresh" touch, the white-canopied outdoor patio makes the perfect setting, whether it's a reception, wedding, award ceremony, or holiday party. The patio pavilion is open from April through October to catch the last of the crisp, sunny fall days.

The hotel's extraordinary service regularly garners positive feedback. Employees, empowered to get things done, can handle any guest's needs, from the routine to the extraordinary. Crowne Plaza demonstrates its commitment to spending the time and resources to develop a corporate culture that centers on service. For managers and line employees, training is ongoing. Such attention to employee development has paid rich dividends in the form of high employee loyalty and low turnover. Employees actively participate in the hotel's community outreach program, which supports Children's Hospital and Orion Youth Center.

The sunlit City Views is among Seattle's favorite restaurants for outstanding regional fare. In addition to serving the freshest Northwest cuisine, it offers a Mediterranean menu with daily pasta specials, a healthy alternatives menu, a "salad inventions" menu, and a complete children's menu. Its glassed canopy and natural light make the award-winning City Views a welcoming place to relish breakfast, lunch, or dinner. The Lounge displays a long list of microbrews on its board and serves specially priced Happy Hour hors d'oeuvres. And in pure Seattle style, an espresso cart on the ground floor provides lattes and espresso throughout the day and evening.

Visitors to Seattle can count on the Crowne Plaza to offer all the amenities required for a comfortable, successful stay.

Business meetings or luncheons at the hotel are simple to arrange. With one phone call, guests can book the appropriate space at the hotel to fit the function and the mood, and leave all the details to the hotel staff.

ALL DATA INCORPORATED, LOCATED IN KIRKLAND, IS a multinational corporation that develops, markets, and supports software products that assist individuals and organizations in using their business information assets to achieve competitive advantage. The company is known for customer focus, value-added solutions, and technology leadership.

There was a time not long ago when companies relied on massive computer mainframe systems to meet their information needs. Most enterprises have since shifted to a model known as client-server computing, in which clients (desktop computers) access information from multiple sources (servers). With increasingly flattened organizations and cross-functional approaches to business processes, client/server systems have empowered people at all levels to access and use information.

As technology becomes more complex, the need becomes even greater for a simple, straightforward way to get information into the hands of the business user. Wall Data® products deliver information from virtually anywhere to the business user's desktop—simply and seamlessly—and provide a powerful set of tools for organizing data in ways that enhance individual productivity. As one customer put it, "It's the fastest way to get to anything that's not on your personal computer."

SOFTWARE THAT SETS THE STANDARD

Wall Data currently offers products under four brands. RUMBA® software provides easy access to computer applications and data residing on personal computers, servers, multiple host mainframes, and minicomputers in enterprisewide information systems. SALSA® software allows users to create custom business applications using simple drag-and-drop templates. ARPEGGIO™ software lets users publish enterprisewide information via corporate networks, intranets, or the Internet. ONESTEP® Service Programs provide a comprehensive set of service offerings to Wall Data's business software users.

Part of the philosophy driving these products is to engage the business user in a fun, friendly way. The result—software that sets the standard for ease of use and works "the way people think." "We champion the business user by simplifying working with data," says Founder and President John Wall.

Wall Data's number one priority is customer satisfaction. In 1994, the company created ONESTEP Service Programs, which offer customers centralized technical support, on-line resources, software upgrade insurance, and training for users at all levels. Wall Data trains every employee on processes to better serve customers and continually improve results to meet a goal of 100 percent customer satisfaction.

RUMBA software provides easy access to computer applica-

Wall Data Incorporated, located in Kirkland, can also be found on the World Wide Web at www.walldata.com.

KEITH BROFSKY

tions and data residing on personal computers, servers, multiple host mainframes, and minicomputers in enterprisewide information systems. Wall Data has licensed more than 5 million copies of its RUMBA software to more than 11,800 organizations to date.

RUMBA software is helping organizations in a wide variety of industries to enhance productivity and turn data into business information assets. Using RUMBA, a physician, for example, can remotely access medical files from another hospital, or records from other patients with similar histories. As a result of RUMBA's value in medical environments, two or three hospitals in the United States and Europe join the family of users every month.

Every business has to keep track of many things. What if users could create an application uniquely suited to them without having to program it? That's what Wall Data's SALSA software is all about. It can be used to create applications for corporate tasks such as equipment and inventory management, customer information tracking, and employee benefits tracking. The SALSA approach drastically reduces the time and expense of creating a custom software application.

Ready-to-run SALSA Intranet applications are also available separately. These complete applications can be automatically deployed to users via the corporate network or intranet, and can be changed using SALSA for the desktop. Examples of SALSA Intranet applications include Employee & Vendor Directory, Service Request Tracker, Time Sheet Manager, and Computer & Equipment Tracker.

Wall Data's most recent family of products, ARPEGGIO software, allows organizations to unlock information from across the enterprise and publish it in any form required by the business user. Business users are consumers of information. They don't want to take the time to learn how to extract information from a corporate database; they simply want the information they need to get their job done delivered to them in an easy-to-digest format. The ARPEGGIO software line is the ideal tool for pulling data from a variety of sources and publishing it to the business end user quickly and painlessly.

ARPEGGIO™ Live! software extends the information publishing metaphor to the World Wide Web. It allows organizations to instantly publish real-time information and applications over corporate intranets and the Internet to business users with a Web browser. ARPEGGIO Live! opens up an organization's existing business information assets to a much broader range of users—all with minimal investment in installation, training, and support.

Since its founding in 1982, Wall Data has grown from 39 to more than 750 employees and to $139 million in revenues. The company went public in 1993 after building a strong base for its products in North America and Europe. It has since expanded to Asian and Latin American markets. The firm is traded on NASDAQ under the symbol WALL.

While maintaining marketplace leadership, Wall Data contributes to the community in many ways. Working strategically with the Washington Software Association, it sponsors programs that bridge the technology gap for students, teachers, and parents in communities at risk. It also funds children's programs at the Seattle Repertory Theatre and initiatives for K-12 schools and universities. The company's dream is to create a model for how a school and business community can work together to deliver technology that empowers education.

John Wall, founder and president, Wall Data Incorporated (left)

Part of the philosophy driving the company's products is to engage the business user in a fun, friendly way. The result—software that sets the standard for ease of use and works "the way people think" (right).

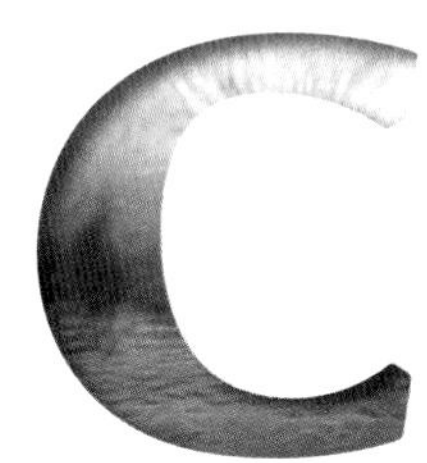

Costco Wholesale is a phenomenally successful chain of cash-and-carry membership warehouses that sell high-quality brand-name and private-label merchandise at low prices. The eighth-largest retailer in the United States, Costco sells $19 billion in goods and services each year from more than 250 warehouses worldwide.

The company was formed out of the 1993 merger of The Price Company and Costco Wholesale Corp., whose founders pioneered the membership warehouse concept in the late 1970s. Uniting an already strong regional presence—Price Company was based in San Diego, and Costco had opened its first warehouse in Seattle just south of the Kingdome in 1983—the companies each brought roughly $7 billion in sales and 100 stores to the table, doubling their purchasing power and securing Costco Wholesale's position as the industry leader.

Today, Costco Wholesale enjoys a strong North American presence, with 198 stores in 23 states, 55 Canadian locations from Vancouver Island to St. John's, and 13 warehouses in Mexico. It has also opened warehouses in the United Kingdom, Korea, and Taiwan, and anticipates operating 292 warehouses by fiscal year 1998, including increasing its presence in New York City and Atlanta.

An Idea That Saves Money

Nonexistent in 1976, warehouse clubs have mushroomed to a $40 billion annual business, and sales have grown a robust 17 percent each year since 1987. Warehouse clubs eliminate many of the costs traditionally associated with retail. As such, they can provide the most cost-effective means of distributing a limited selection of high-value merchandise in a wide variety of product categories. Payroll, occupancy, and advertising costs run roughly three times below that of department stores and supermarkets, a savings that can be passed on to the customer. The mark up on a product runs anywhere from zero to 14 percent, which is consistent for all stores, and Costco Wholesale won't carry a product if it can't save customers money.

Costco Wholesale's warehouses, which average 127,500 square feet, also keep labor costs to a minimum through an innovative system of distribution and packaging. Rather than using a traditional distribution center, Costco Wholesale receives merchandise from the manufacturer directly to each location, or ships directly to each warehouse from one of numerous North American cross-dock depots. Instead of stacking goods on shelves, merchandise remains on pallets, which are transferred directly onto the warehouse floor.

By offering high-value items at the lowest possible price, Costco Wholesale has enjoyed meteoric growth. Its warehouses average $77 million in sales each year, nearly double that of its competitors. The company offers its 25 million cardholders the best value on a limited selection of high-quality merchandise, including such luxury items as expensive wine, microbrewery beer, and designer jeans, and such regional merchandise as ethnic foods and specialized sporting gear.

Costco Wholesale seeks to find those crossover items that are ideal for both small businesses and households, and frequently offers two sizes of an item to meet their respective needs. Approximately 70 percent of the products

Costco Wholesale sells high-quality brand-name and private-label merchandise at low prices (left).

Costco Wholesale's warehouses average 127,500 square feet (right).

The company offers its 25 million cardholders the best value on a limited selection of high-quality merchandise, including such luxury items as expensive wine, microbrewery beer, designer jeans, and electronic devices.

sold at a Costco Wholesale warehouse are always available. Another 15 percent are "treasure hunt" items—high-end merchandise that is only sold for a short time, including Alaskan king crab legs, fancy cigars, and racing bikes—which add excitement and an element of surprise to members' shopping experiences. The remaining 15 percent is seasonal merchandise, such as camping equipment, lawn mowers, and back-to-school items.

In 1986, Costco Wholesale began selling fresh bulk foods, which now account for 10 percent of the sales mix.

Continued Growth through New Ideas

In 1986, Costco Wholesale began selling fresh bulk foods amid industry skepticism. Not only did sales soar, but the fresh foods also brought members back to the store more frequently. Food and sundries now account for 64 percent of the sales mix. In 28 of its locations, the company is currently testing expanded fresh food sections, which include an assortment of prepared roasted chickens and other take-home meals, truffles and fancy cakes, salads, deli trays, and soups. New ideas such as these have propelled the company's growth over the years.

In 1993, Costco Wholesale rolled out its private label, Kirkland Signature, which saves shoppers 15 to 50 percent on products that equal or exceed the quality of the leading national brand. Bearing the Kirkland Signature are packaged ground beef patties, color print film, ultrathin diapers, shampoo and conditioner, and other items.

Despite its size, Costco Wholesale nimbly responds to new product ideas. The company has built vendor loyalty by living by the deal, and treating vendors as partners. In turn, it asks vendors to consistently and voluntarily quote the lowest possible prices on all items. When a business buys $60 million in olive oil and $120 million in household batteries each year, it's granting vendors enormous purchasing power.

Always seeking new ways to save members money and better serve them, Costco Wholesale has launched a new credit card program for its customers. The company also began distributing a monthly magazine, *The Costco Connection*; a mail-order catalog; and *Passport*, a booklet of weekly coupons mailed each summer to current and prospective members that offers additional discounts on a variety of merchandise.

Costco Wholesale has continued to expand its successful ancillary businesses, including its pharmacies, optical centers, photo-processing labs, and gasoline stations. Today, approximately 70 percent of the warehouses have pharmacy and optical departments. This one-stop-shop approach is just another example of Costco Wholesale's commitment to meeting the needs of its customers—today and for years to come.

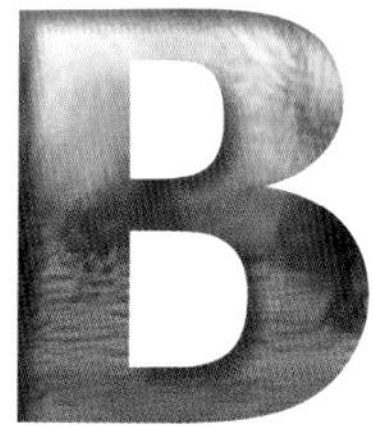

Bellevue-based Boullioun Aviation Services, Inc. is engaged in the acquisition, lease, and sale of new and used commercial jet aircraft to airlines worldwide. In addition to its core leasing activities, the company provides asset management services to airlines and financial investors, including fleet management, aircraft remarketing, technical advisory services such as aircraft inspections and appraisals, and asset-backed lending.

Called "creating the virtual airline" by British Airways, leasing enables airlines to focus on transporting customers rather than managing assets. "Buying and holding onto assets for 25 years doesn't necessarily offer airlines the flexibility that is critical in responding to changing market needs," says Robert Genise, president and CEO of Boullioun. "As an operating lessor, we have the ability to move aircraft around while also offering airlines a cost-beneficial alternative to owning aircraft directly."

These benefits have fueled a dramatic growth in aircraft leasing over the last 10 years. While airlines will continue to own a majority of their aircraft, by 2000, an estimated 35 percent of aircraft deliveries worldwide will be leased.

Rapid Success

The cyclical and capital-intensive nature of the aircraft operating lease business requires sophistication and significant financial resources. A subsidiary of The Sumitomo Trust & Banking Co., Ltd. since 1994, Boullioun commenced its current operations in 1988 and is rapidly becoming one of the top players in the international aircraft lease market, with a growing portfolio of commercial jet aircraft on lease to airlines around the world.

Boullioun, because of its increasing size, can acquire aircraft at attractive prices. These aircraft are then pooled for funding purposes. Both the acquisition price and funding costs impact how the company prices leases to customers. Boullioun assumes all of the asset risks on the aircraft it leases; however, it utilizes its diverse portfolio and customer base to minimize the risks of its investments. If a particular asset turns out to be weak, the effect is mitigated by the rest of Boullioun's portfolio and the company's ability to re-lease the aircraft. In contrast, an airline committed to a particular aircraft type that becomes unpopular will have difficulty removing the planes from its fleet when required.

Pointed toward the Pacific and with business roots in the United States and Europe, Boul-

Brant Photographers, Inc.

Members of Boullioun's senior management team are (standing, from left) Owen Roberts, executive vice president of marketing; Joel Hussey, senior vice president of finance and administration; (seated, from left) Myron Anton, executive vice president of technical services; and Robert Genise, president and chief executive officer.

lioun is highly representative of the focus and future of Seattle. With expected assets exceeding $1 billion in 1998 and potential growth to $1.5 to $2 billion by 2000, Boullioun attributes its meteoric growth in the specialized industry of aircraft leasing to its success in building long-term relationships and tailoring transactions to fit customers' needs.

"It's imperative that when we do business with an airline, they walk away feeling that they got a fair deal. Long-term relationships are built on satisfied customers. That's the approach our team takes," says Genise, who has 26 years of experience in leasing and finance of international aircraft and other equipment.

In the last few years, Boullioun has built a very capable, experienced team of people. The operating lessor's worldwide staff of 46 includes 23 professionals in marketing, finance, engineering, accounting, and law, as well as technical experts who inspect and evaluate aircraft prior to purchase and monitor each aircraft's condition while on lease to customers.

Customers range from very large to very small airlines, and include British Airways, Singapore Airlines, LAN Chile, Istanbul Airlines, China Southern, China Airlines, Virgin Express, America West, TAP Air Portugal, China Xinhua, and Carnival Airlines.

Developing Foreign Markets

Boullioun is pushing into the Asian market aggressively, both from Seattle and through a joint venture, Singapore Aircraft Leasing Enterprise (SALE), which Boullioun formed in 1994 with the prestigious Singapore Airlines. From its initial activities as an arranger and manager of operating lease transactions, SALE has developed into a full-scale lessor that acquires, owns, and leases a growing portfolio of primarily widebody aircraft to the burgeoning market in Asia. Boullioun performs the marketing and technical services for the joint venture, which will expand to serve global markets. The combined portfolio of SALE and Boullioun consists of 737s, 747s, 757s, 767s, 777s, A320s, and A321s—a total of 63 aircraft plus options.

In addition to SALE, Boullioun operates an office in Singapore that handles the Asia Pacific region, as well as an office in London that covers Western and Eastern Europe and the Middle East.

Boullioun also is investing significant time and energy in developing the South American market, where a number of airlines have become entrepreneurial in their management practices. Recognizing that air travel stimulates business and the economy, many countries have expanded point-to-point air service within the continent.

In late 1996, Boullioun purchased nine additional 737 aircraft from The Boeing Company, bringing its total annual order of the world's most popular twin jet to 17 aircraft. Boullioun also acquired one new and two used 737s from other sources. Airlines in North America, Europe, and China will take delivery of the 20 aircraft by mid-1998.

While expanding its operations throughout the world, Boullioun hasn't lost sight of the local community. The company supports the United Way, including participating in its Day of Caring, and also embraces the local performing arts and a variety of charitable organizations. Through an annual matching program, Boullioun encourages employees to give back to the community and reinforces a high level of volunteerism. And with its phenomenal level of success in the highly competitive and technical industry of aircraft leasing, Boullioun will be an integral part of the Greater Seattle community for many years to come.

▸ WATANABE PHOTOGRAPHY

▸ WATANABE PHOTOGRAPHY

Placing orders for 17 new 737 300s and 400s in 1996 has made President and Chief Executive Officer Robert Genise a familiar figure at Boeing facilities (top).

"Ordering the right airplanes in the right configurations is critical to our ability to lease them throughout their projected lifespan," says Genise (bottom).

EATTLE WASH, INC., AS THE NAME IMPLIES, IS THE AREA'S leading garment dyer and processor of men's, ladies', and children's sportswear. Originally, the company was started by Mike Mendelsohn as a sideline to an existing laundry operation. It soon became evident that the process of taking white garments and applying fashion colors and finishes was a big hit with area sportswear distributors and retailers. Mendelsohn, along with partners Darrell Allen and Jim Milgard, decided to expand the business into its own building and further diversify by adding its own garment sewing (Astro Design) and packaging facility (Image Concepts).

Seattle Wash, Inc. started with one 35-pound-capacity dye machine. Since then, it has grown to 28 machines that range from special sample machines to computer-driven dye machines for large production runs. The company manufactures, dyes, and packages finished products directly for retailers, as well as on a contract basis for other sportswear companies.

Flexibility, Speed, and Innovation

Based on the philosophy of delivering flexibility in color and style with shorter lead times, Seattle Wash performs contract dyeing services for approximately 300 customers. Its customers range in size from small boutiques to the largest retailers in the world, including major apparel clubs, department stores, and mail-order retailers. The company ships nationwide, as well as to Japan, Canada, and Mexico.

Seattle Wash fulfills a niche role in providing quick response to color changes in the market. In the sportswear business, imported goods must be ordered three to six months in advance, and colors are decided upon at the same time. Retailers suffer when the popular colors sell out early. By bringing in undyed clothing from overseas, the color and finish can be applied as the current market demands, thereby providing a quick turnaround for customers.

Seattle Wash is the major dyer in the Pacific Northwest, and is one of the largest garment dyers on the West Coast. It dyes cotton, cotton-lycra, nylon, and polyester woven fabrics. The company also provides special treatment dyeing, such as stone washing, acid washing, rain washing, and tie-dyeing.

On the cutting edge of working with new fabrics, Seattle Wash continually develops new products, such as dyeing synthetics and creating special finishes to achieve silky textures. The company pioneered a new field of working with enzyme and supersoft finishings

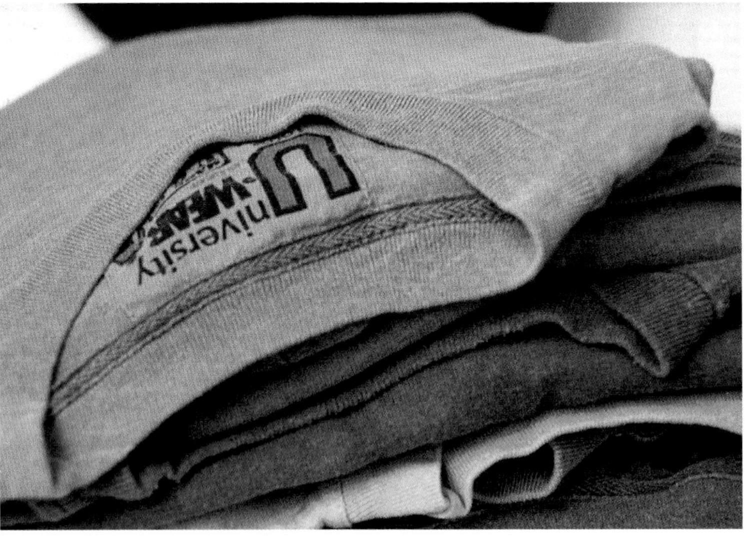

ROBERT PINTER

Seattle Wash, Inc. provides special treatment dyeing, such as stone washing, acid washing, rain washing, and tie-dyeing.

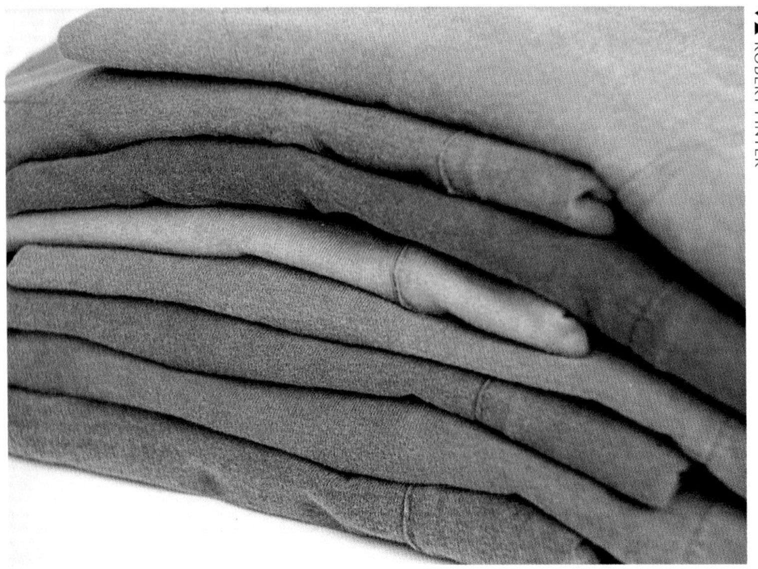

ROBERT PINTER

for mixed fabrics and 100 percent cotton. Using new technologies, Seattle Wash can dye mixed fabrics in the same machinery, while achieving a higher level of environmentally friendly processing.

Seattle Wash also works heavily with cotton-lycra blends, and rayons that require special handling in dyeing. The firm is one of the few dyers in the United States to be approved to dye Tencel®, an up-and-coming fabric that has become popular in Japan. The company is pioneering finishing and dye techniques for newly developed hemp clothing.

"We're successful because we haven't relied on other people's ideas. We are not just a contract dye and sewing operation. We're constantly developing new ideas and processes, and manufacturing our own products, including private label," says Mendelsohn, who now serves as company president.

ROBERT PINTER

Mike Mendelsohn, Darrell Allen, and Jim Milgard (from left)

ROBERT PINTER

Colorworks, Astro Design, and Image Concepts

Seattle Wash, responding to its need to service customers in the mid-mountain region, recently purchased Colorworks, a state-of-the-art garment dyer in Salt Lake City. The addition of these 32 machines makes Seattle Wash one of the largest garment dyers in North America.

Seattle Wash has established a subsidiary, Astro Design, to design and manufacture garments. The garments are built to compensate for fabric shrinkage to ensure proper fit after dyeing. Astro Design also offers pattern and grading services, full cutting service, relabeling, and sample production.

The company has also responded to the market need for simple "package-priced" garments, including fabric selection, sewing, dyeing, custom packaging, and financing. Image Concepts was established to handle this demand, and a distribution center was opened.

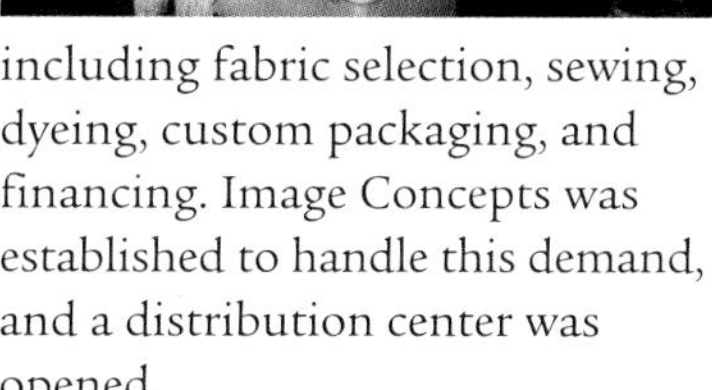

Seattle Wash and its subsidiaries offer a wide range of garment services, including correcting dye jobs done by other companies that are not up to standard, full pattern-making services, garment quality testing and consulting, laboratory color matching, and color samples for retailers to use in coordinating colors throughout a department.

"Our growth has occurred as a result of our ability to prove to our customers that we can respond to their changing needs," notes Allen, president of Image Concepts.

As Seattle Wash continues its fast-paced growth, it invests its profits back into the company and its employees. Seattle Wash believes in giving back to its employees, all of whom receive full benefits, including a 401(k) plan. The company also gives back to its local community by supporting a number of community efforts through in-kind contributions, and demonstrates its commitment to the global environment by using all organic, environmentally friendly dyes in its processing.

ROBERT PINTER

Seattle Wash is the major dyer in the Pacific Northwest, and is one of the largest garment dyers on the West Coast. It dyes cotton, cotton-lycra, nylon, and polyester woven fabrics.

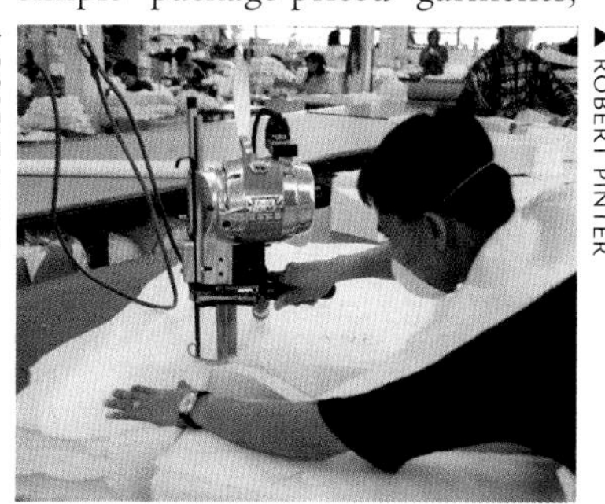
ROBERT PINTER

ROBERT PINTER

ROBERT PINTER

The company has responded to the market need for simple "package-priced" garments, including fabric selection, sewing, dyeing, custom packaging, and financing.

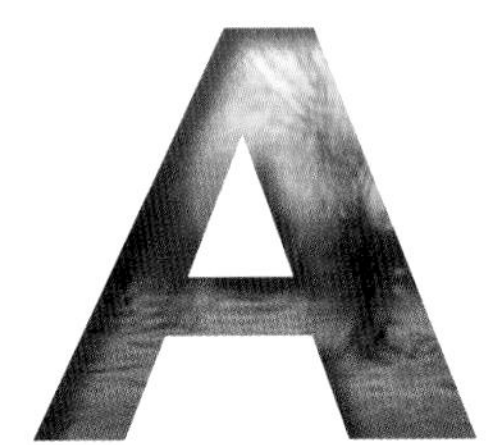

RIS Corporation, an information systems consulting, training, and software development company, provides business solutions to Fortune 1000 companies and government organizations worldwide. Founded in 1990 by President and CEO Paul Song, ARIS enables clients to strategically use client/server and Internet technology to improve their operations and competitive position.

The company's focus, says Song, is people: developing long-term relationships with customers, employees, partners, and vendors through respect, uncompromising integrity, and fiscal responsibility. Spurred by Song's leadership and energy, the privately held company has grown to 11 offices and more than 400 employees since 1990.

With corporate headquarters in Seattle; two training centers in Bellevue, Washington; and one in Portland, ARIS boasts a strong Northwest presence that is complemented by offices in Denver; Washington, D.C.; Dallas; Tampa; and the United Kingdom. ARIS has worked with such diverse clients as Boeing, Weyerhaeuser, Standard Insurance, NIKE, and the IRS.

According to Song, who earned a master's degree in computer science from MIT, ARIS arrived on the business scene at the right time with the right expertise. The company's meteoric rise reflects the trend among American enterprises to outsource information systems development rather than maintain large, internal information systems departments. With the rapid pace of technological change, companies find it more cost effective to outsource to experts in relevant technologies.

New Technology

ARIS has quickly earned a reputation in the industry for successfully completing complex consulting projects. Such systems include those that augment inventory management, financial accounting, manufacturing, and management systems.

In 1994, the company teamed with Tektronix, a manufacturer of color printers and measuring instruments, to embark on one of the largest implementations of Oracle applications in the world. As Tektronix grew, it implemented approximately 38 computer information systems and 100 product families spanning operations in 56 countries. Tektronix wanted to consolidate its systems into one. ARIS implemented a customized solution that saved the company money while easing the flow of information among its business divisions. This empowered Tektronix to embark on strategic initiatives that were previously impossible—initiatives critical to its long-term competitiveness.

ARIS also works with organizations to customize system solutions using existing technologies. Breaking new ground, ARIS recently completed a custom-integrated mobile application, using Oracle Mobile Agents for the Excise Group of the Internal Revenue Service. The new system, called ExFON, provides IRS field agents with real-time, mobile access to a wealth of pertinent information stored in a database at their headquarters. Previously relying on paper files, faxes, and phone calls, these remote agents are now substantially more efficient and accurate with instant mobile access to diesel fuel excise tax records and the ability to issue penalties to offenders in just minutes.

As one of the largest technical training providers in Microsoft BackOffice, Oracle, and Internet technologies, ARIS has helped to pioneer innovative training methods such as on-line training. With this training method, students

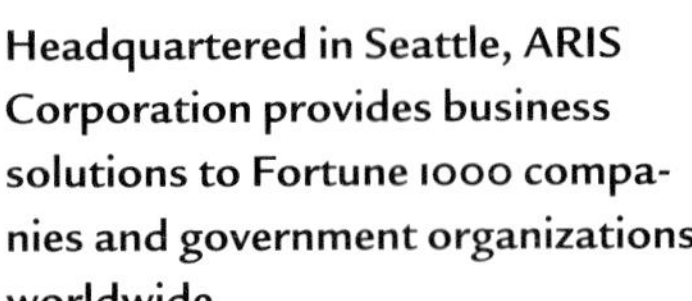

Headquartered in Seattle, ARIS Corporation provides business solutions to Fortune 1000 companies and government organizations worldwide.

ARIS Education provides comprehensive technical training solutions through public and private instructor-led and computer-based training to enhance clients' capabilities and increase employee expertise.

work at their own pace while interacting with a teacher and other students via Internet chat sessions, user forums, and E-mail. Additionally, ARIS Education provides comprehensive technical training solutions through public and private instructor-led and computer-based training to enhance clients' capabilities and increase employee expertise.

Augmenting its technical training and consulting, Noetix Corporation, a wholly owned subsidiary of ARIS, develops leading-edge software applications for Oracle relational databases and Java database connectivity to provide customers with immediate access to the latest advances in technology. In 1997, ARIS released DFRAG 5.0, a sophisticated database defragmentation and space-management utility product, as well as NoetixGenerator, which works with Oracle Discoverer.

Paul Song, president and CEO of ARIS Corporation

Focus on People

The corporate culture and can-do attitude are what distinguish ARIS in the marketplace. "High stress contributes to a 43 percent turnover rate for the information service technology industry," says Song. "We're proud to have a turnover rate in the teens, and, in fact, the lowest in the industry. We've bucked the trend by providing people a great place to work, one that encourages new ideas and career growth.

"People have asked me," he continues, " 'What's the key to your success?' I tell them it comes down to one thing: If you want to look good, surround yourself with people who make you look good. Our products and services reflect the synergy created when you put good people together."

In the face of enormous growth in the industry, Song anticipates that the challenge for ARIS will be to maintain its culture, spirit, and focus while continuing to expand. The company plans to grow at about 65 percent in revenues annually over the next three years, while opening additional offices in Europe and the United States. Song expects to meet this challenge with the same dedication and energy that has led ARIS to its current market-leader position.

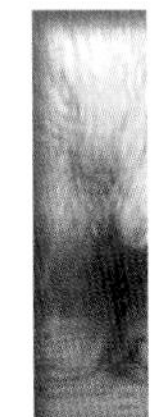

N TODAY'S INFORMATION-INTENSIVE BUSINESS WORLD, VIRTUALLY every business process and communication is enhanced by visuals or graphics. However, the drawing tools necessary to create these graphics are typically fragmented. Visio® Corporation develops tools that replace multiple specialized products with a single business graphics solution that spans the needs of an enterprise.

Started in 1990 by two founders of Aldus Corp. and a lead PageMaker developer, Visio is a second-generation software company that understands how to build great products and strong customer support. Its drawing engine not only set the standard for creating, storing, and exchanging drawings and diagrams in business, but also make possible lower purchasing and deployment costs, volume licensing advantages, streamlined support and training, and the ability to share drawings across applications and work groups. The tool has been widely used. Sales for this publicly held company have rocketed from $7 million in fiscal year 1993 to $60 million in fiscal year 1996.

A Multitude of Uses

Visio's drawing engine is simple enough to use for everyday diagrams, powerful enough for sophisticated two-dimensional technical drawings and engineering schematics, and extensible enough to be a mission-critical component of client/server development. Novice users can take advantage of predrawn drag-and-drop SmartShapes® symbols, or use wizards to automatically create a range of layouts. More experienced users can customize shapes and drawings. And those more comfortable with spreadsheet or database formats can enter data into templates, then let Visio build the drawing for them.

Visio products are ideal for drawings and diagrams that use standard symbols or parts. One tool does all the jobs—whether it's flowcharts, block diagrams, relationship diagrams, organizational charts, geographic and directional maps, marketing and financial charts, project schedules, network maps, or office layouts. Visio's product line includes Visio Standard, Visio Professional, and Visio Technical.

Business and technical professionals often need drawings that can be dynamically revised and linked with data. Visio takes advantage of the advanced capabilities of Microsoft Windows by seamlessly integrating Visio drawings with Windows desktop applications, such as Word, Excel, and PowerPoint.

Corporate and third-party developers can license Visio to create their own graphics-based solutions. Visio leverages OLE technology and development tools like Microsoft Visual Basic

Clockwise from top:
Visio Corporation was founded in 1990 and shipped its first Visio product in 1992. Today, with more than 1 million users, Visio Corporation markets three products aimed at different users: Visio Standard, Visio Technical, and Visio Professional.

Visio is often used in the field to update a project, sketch out an idea, or close a sale.

Visio Corporation is headquartered in Seattle, and sells its products in nine languages and in 35 countries around the globe.

so developers and technical professionals can create a wide range of custom and line-of-business solutions. Visio backs its products with on-line help, extended technical support, and developer training classes.

Visio products can be used to create a wide variety of drawings, including space plans, time lines, flowcharts, directional maps, network diagrams, and more. All drawings contain predrawn drag-and-drop SmartShapes® symbols.

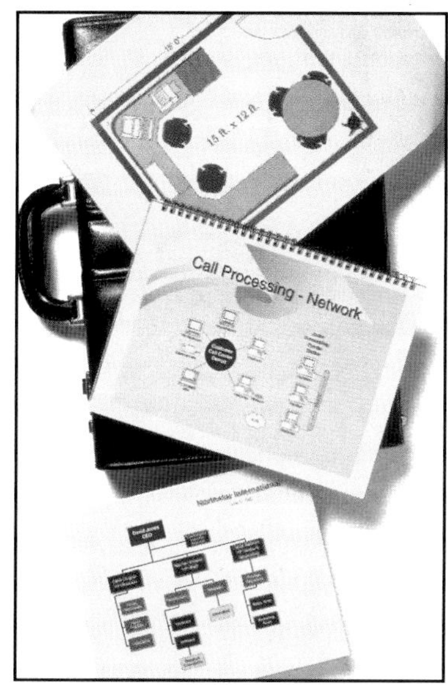

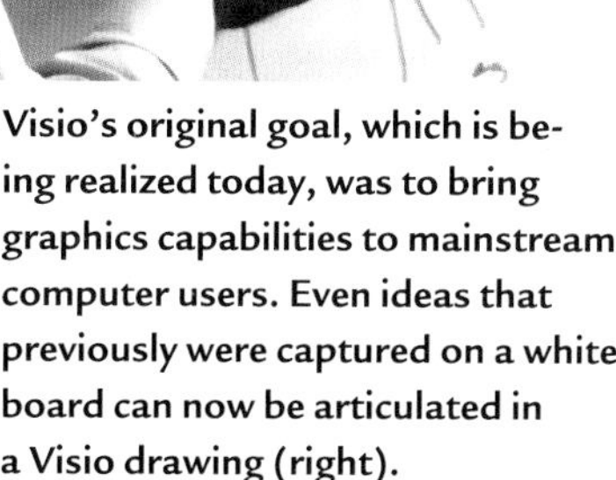

Visio's original goal, which is being realized today, was to bring graphics capabilities to mainstream computer users. Even ideas that previously were captured on a white board can now be articulated in a Visio drawing (right).

Visio's simple drag-and-drop Windows approach provides users of all types and skill levels the ability to produce a wide variety of professional drawings and diagrams (left).

Real-Life Applications

Visio is also a great tool for any organization whose sale of a product involves a drawing. Time and time again, Visio has helped companies make the sale, proving itself to be a valuable asset for solving real customer problems.

For example, Fluor Daniel Inc., a global engineering and construction firm, standardized its operations with Visio because it was the only product that all 7,000 of the company's employees could easily use, and the only one that could simultaneously track and document work processes for ISO 9000 certification compliance. Fluor Daniel had already made extensive use of AutoCAD from Autodesk, but found it too complex to be used by many nontechnical employees within the company. Visio not only preserved the investment in AutoCAD drawings, but also extended new drawing capabilities across the enterprise and reduced support and training by replacing several other drawing programs.

Amoco Corporation's Worldwide Exploration Business Group, which plans complex oil exploration and development projects, had been using sophisticated project planning software, but found it too inflexible to handle on-the-fly changes and too complex for preplanning work. Since standardizing on Visio, Amoco has trimmed planning costs and streamlined planning processes. Project teams now use Visio's flowcharting and organization charting to plan, schedule, and prioritize tasks; highlight decision points; describe alternative plans; and define milestones.

The ease of use, breadth of application, and superior technology of Visio's products have propelled the company into worldwide markets in North America, Europe, Asia, and Latin America. Visio has sales offices in the United Kingdom, France, Germany, Australia, and Miami, and a service center in Dublin. It serves multinational companies with product versions in English, German, French, Spanish, Dutch, Swedish, Chinese, and Japanese.

Rooted in Seattle

Visio's goal is to become the standard for drawing and diagramming on the Windows PC. With ambitions this large, Visio is headquartered in Seattle to capitalize on the talent pool and entrepreneurial energy created by the presence of Microsoft and other software manufacturers and vendors in the area.

"The sense of what's possible is larger in Seattle," says Jeremy Jaech, president and CEO of Visio Corp. "It's a huge achievement to take a technology and apply it across a whole spectrum. We've capitalized on the talent in the area to make this happen."

Visio has 160 employees in Seattle and another 75 in Europe and the Pacific Rim. The company prides itself on hiring people with experience in creating high-volume, commercially successful software products. This has resulted in a more mature workforce and a family-oriented corporate culture for the company.

Despite being a young company, Visio has launched a charitable giving program that donates 1 percent of its profits to environmental and social causes, and to the arts in the form of direct grants. As the company continues to grow in the years to come, it has pledged to increase its contributions to these causes, proving once again that Visio Corporation is a valuable asset to all sectors of the population.

UDDEN CARDIAC ARREST, THE LEADING CAUSE OF DEATH IN the Western world, claims more than 350,000 American lives each year, largely because lifesaving treatment—an electrical shock to the heart known as defibrillation—does not reach victims within the first few critical minutes. Timely defibrillation is the single most critical factor in rescuing an individual from ventricular fibrillation, in which the heart's normal electrical signals become disorganized and erratic.

Survival rates from ventricular fibrillation can exceed 70 percent if defibrillation is administered—but the chances of survival decrease by approximately 10 percent with each minute of delay. Presently, fewer than 25 percent of all emergency first-response vehicles deployed through ambulance and fire services, and fewer than 1 percent of police cars, are equipped with defibrillators, due in large part to the devices being heavy, maintenance intensive, difficult to use, and expensive. As a result, defibrillation therapy often arrives too late, resulting in a survival rate from sudden cardiac arrest of fewer than 5 percent in the United States.

In an effort to improve these survival rates, Heartstream Inc., founded in Seattle in 1992, developed the ForeRunner™ automatic external defibrillator (AED), a four-pound device the size of a hardcover book, which delivers a powerful electric shock to jolt the heart back to normal function. The ForeRunner AED uses voice and text prompts to instruct the care-giver throughout its use. It automatically analyzes the patient's heart rhythm; if a shock is required, the device instructs the user to press a single button to deliver it. It will not permit a shock to be delivered if it is not necessary. Using the ForeRunner AED, emergency personnel, including medical technicians, police, firefighters, flight attendants, and security guards, can rapidly and reliably deliver defibrillation therapy.

ForeRunner represents a breakthrough in automatic external defibrillation technology. The device is easy to use, virtually maintenance free, small, lightweight, durable, and inexpensive, yet delivers the most advanced electrical therapy.

REGULATORY CLEARANCE

Heartstream began shipping ForeRunner products in November 1996, after receiving clearance from the U.S. Food and Drug Administration. ForeRunner makes the implementation of early response programs practical in communities, industrial settings, and other public and private facilities. In 1997, it became the first AED to be carried on a U.S. airline, when American Airlines ordered some 300 devices.

"The in-flight use of the ForeRunner AED represents a significant milestone in our efforts to put defibrillation technology in the hands of trained people who reach victims of sudden cardiac arrest first," says Alan Levy, president and CEO of Heartstream.

The American Heart Association estimates that up to 100,000 lives could be saved each year in the United States alone by the widespread deployment of a defibrillator like the ForeRunner AED, and has advocated the deployment of hundreds of thousands of such devices. In its efforts to make this lifesaving technology more widely available, Heartstream received its CE mark under the European Medical Device Directives Annex II process in 1996 to market its products in the European Economic Area, and approval by the Canadian Standards Association to market ForeRunner in Canada, ensuring that immediate help for cardiac arrest victims will be available in countries throughout the world.

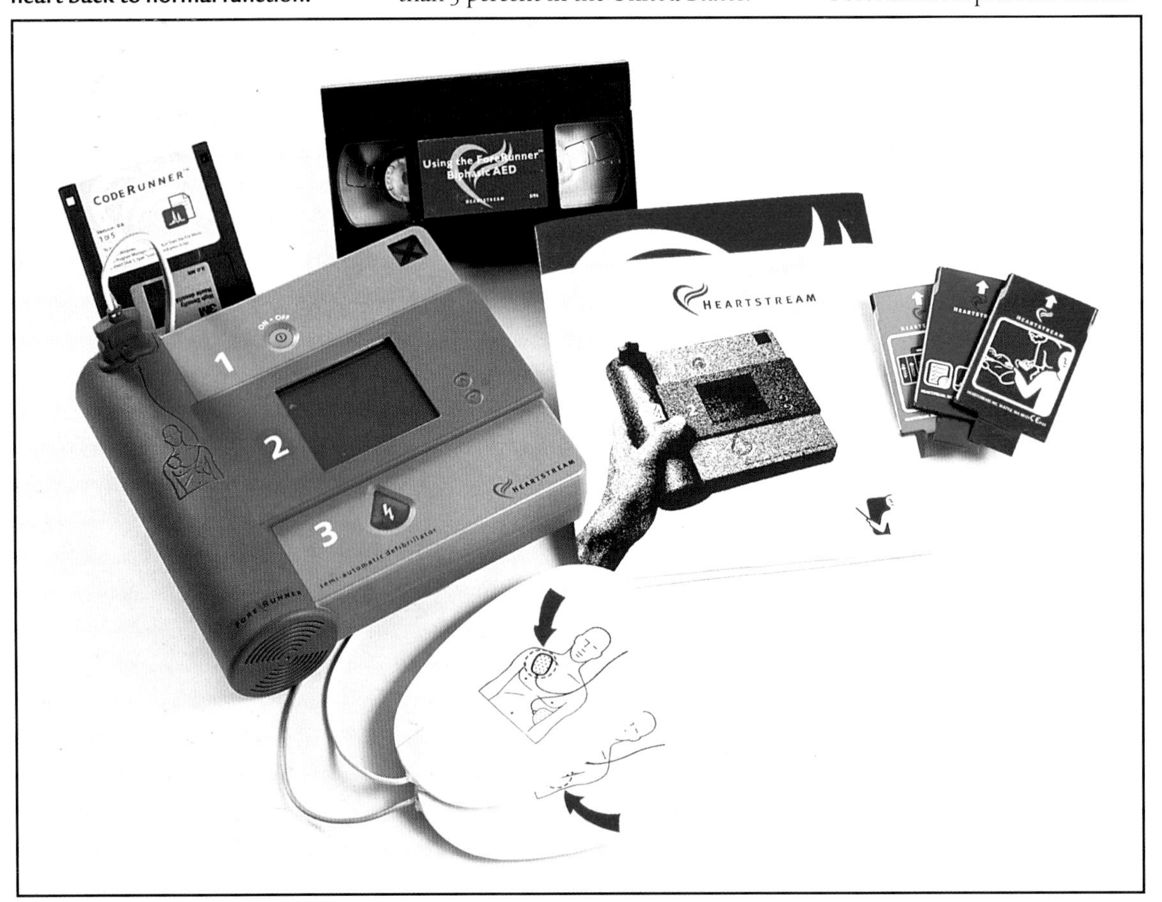

In an effort to improve cardiac arrest survival rates, Heartstream Inc. developed the ForeRunner™ automatic external defibrillator (AED), a four-pound device the size of a hardcover book, which delivers a powerful electric shock to jolt the heart back to normal function.

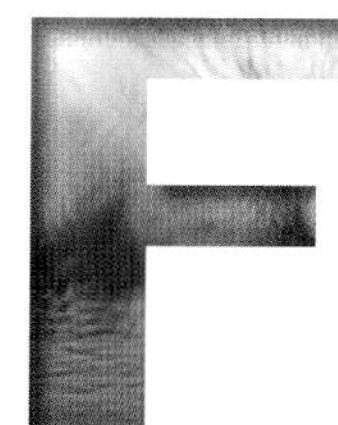

From its headquarters in Dallas, Southwest Airlines operates out of 50 cities coast to coast—from Providence to Fort Lauderdale, San Diego to Seattle, and just about everywhere in between. Southwest began service in 1971 with three planes; today, it is the fifth-largest U.S. airline based on customers carried. Southwest has more than 2,200 flights each day and more than 24,000 employees nationwide, and is the only major shorthaul, low-fare, high-frequency, point-to-point carrier in the United States.

Many airlines seek to benchmark their performance against Southwest, a company that has come to be seen as an icon of employee motivation and customer service. Southwest is proud of its many firsts in the industry: It was the first major airline to offer electronic ticketing, first to develop a Web page, and among the first to accept ticketing over the Internet. It was also the first to offer employees profit sharing.

For the past five years, Southwest has earned the "Triple Crown" for the best on-time performance, best baggage handling, and fewest customer complaints, according to U.S. Department of Transportation consumer reports. In addition, Southwest boasts a clean safety record—without a single crash—and was named the world's safest airline by *Condé Nast Traveler*.

Led by its unorthodox chief executive, Herb Kelleher, Southwest has pioneered a unique corporate culture in the industry, garnering the distinction of being one of the top 10 companies to work for in America according to the Robert Levering and Milton Moskowitz book *The 100 Best Companies to Work for in America*. The desire of each employee to do his or her best rests at the core of the Southwest spirit, and is what gives the company its competitive edge.

National Scope, Local Presence

Seattle is a very important market for Southwest Airlines, where it began service in June 1994 with eight flights a day. Service has grown to 32 flights a day, including nonstop service to Spokane, Las Vegas, Boise, Salt Lake City, Oakland, Reno, San Jose, and Sacramento. In addition, Southwest flies directly to Burbank, Los Angeles, Ontario, and San Diego, California; Kansas City; and Phoenix. Southwest is the largest carrier in California and is Boeing's largest 737 customer worldwide.

Many of Southwest's 125 employees working at Sea-Tac Airport, as well as pilots and flight attendants who make their home in Seattle, invest their time and talent in community programs, such as Southwest's Adopt-a-School program. Employees work with students at Maple Elementary in south Seattle. In 1996, Southwest treated 120 of these kids who live in the airline's flight path to a 20,000-foot-high spin around Seattle.

Southwest is the official airline of Seafair, the Mariners, and the SuperSonics, and donates 5,000 Mariners tickets to associations such as local Boys and Girls Clubs each year. As Southwest's national charity of choice since 1985, Ronald McDonald House receives millions of dollars and countless volunteer hours generated by the airline each year.

Southwest is a rapidly growing company boasting an unprecedented record of profitability in the industry—24 consecutive years. With its emphasis on service, value, and innovation, the airline will continue to be a vital part of the Pacific Northwest for many years to come.

▸ Pam Francis

Clockwise from top:
Herb Kelleher is an unconventional CEO of an unconventional airline. He chain-smokes, dresses in costume, drinks Wild Turkey bourbon, and created a sensation in Dallas when he arm-wrestled the chairman of an aviation company over a legal issue.

One of Southwest's customer service agents displays the airline's legendary POS—Positively Outrageous Service. For the fifth consecutive year, the Department of Transportation's *Air Travel Consumer Report* listed Southwest as having the best on-time performance, best baggage handling, and fewest customer complaints of all major airlines.

When Southwest Airlines first started in 1971, it wanted to be known as a fun and absolutely outrageous company. Southwest outfitted its flight attendants in orange hot pants, lace-up go-go boots, and wide, hip-slung belts.

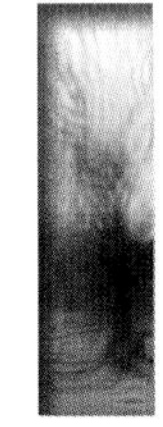

In an era when the energy industry is going back to its roots—to a time when customers had a choice, and entrepreneurial shops tailored products and services for clients—Illinova Energy Partners is making quite a name for itself. And it is doing it the old-fashioned way—by providing customized energy solutions to fit the unique needs of its wholesale and retail customers.

Since its inception in 1994, Illinova Energy Partners has climbed into the ranks of the top 10 power marketing organizations in the country; it is the third-largest in the western United States, with expected sales of approximately $600 million in 1997. The company is part of an international corporation, Illinova, a Fortune 1000 company with combined assets of $5.7 billion, which gives it the financial strength to cover a broad array of energy, energy service, and risk management products. Illinova has been in the electric and natural gas business for more than 100 years. This experience, combined with the financial strength to cover products and with talented employees drawn from around the country, has contributed to the rapid rise of Illinova Energy Partners.

The Illinova family also includes Illinova Generating, an independent power producer that invests in, builds, and operates independent power projects worldwide; Illinois Power, which delivers electricity, natural gas, and energy products to 600,000 customers in Illinois; and two partnerships—Tenaska Marketing Ventures, which enables Illinova to market natural gas supplies, and North American Energy Services, which operates and maintains power projects. With holdings in nine countries and offices in 12 U.S. cities, including Seattle, Illinova helps businesses improve productivity and profitability.

Crafting Energy Solutions

Illinova Energy Partners' first step is to listen and learn about a client's operational needs. It then analyzes a customer's energy use and acts as an extension of its staff to manage, and, if necessary, finance energy projects. Illinova then leverages its capabilities and experience to craft bankable energy solutions, which range from energy services and energy supply to resource management and development of independent power projects and financing packages. It manages energy supply portfolios in a way that reduces risks while saving time and money. Illinova's customer-focused approach to solutions means there is no bias toward a particular fuel source, equipment manufacturer, or vendor.

Illinova Energy Partners follows in the tradition of the early utility companies, which were market-focused shops that tailored energy solutions for their customers. Pictured at right is a utility company located in the Midwest circa 1920.

"Deregulation of electricity is the driving issue now," says Robert Schultz, president of Illinova Energy Partners. "We provide energy information and energy products to businesses, plus offer a range of energy services that help clients improve their operations or save money. In this way, businesses are prepared to extract savings today and have a strategy for saving in the new marketplace."

In the Pacific Northwest, Illinova's bulk power customers include Seattle City Light, Puget Power & Light Company, Washington Water Power, Bonneville Power Authority, Pacificorp, and public utility districts in Chelan, Grays Harbor, Grant County, and Snohomish County, Washington, to name a few.

Evaluation Is Key

A leader in providing customer-focused risk management product design, Illinova Energy Partners helps clients evaluate their position in two key ways. The first is by employing The Utility Manager, the EQ Service Bureau, or EQ Energy Audits, a combination of software and hands-on service that provides management information on all utilities—electricity, solid waste, water, natural gas, recycling, and sewer—and helps clients assess and control utility costs. Illinova's partner with The Utility Manager is Utility Cost Management, an Olympia-based company that owns the program.

With these energy information services, customers can tell where utility resources are going, their costs, and uses that need attention. The software can also be used to benchmark, check billings, budget, analyze performance, build consumption pattern and forecast purchasing requirements.

With information generated by The Utility Manager, Illinova can manage the interface between customers and their present utility to help customers get the most from the rate they're on, or, in some cases, negotiate a better rate. Northwest customers using the state-of-the-art software include, among others, Microsoft, Weyerhaeuser, Safeway, University of Washington, Best Western, and Seattle Public Schools.

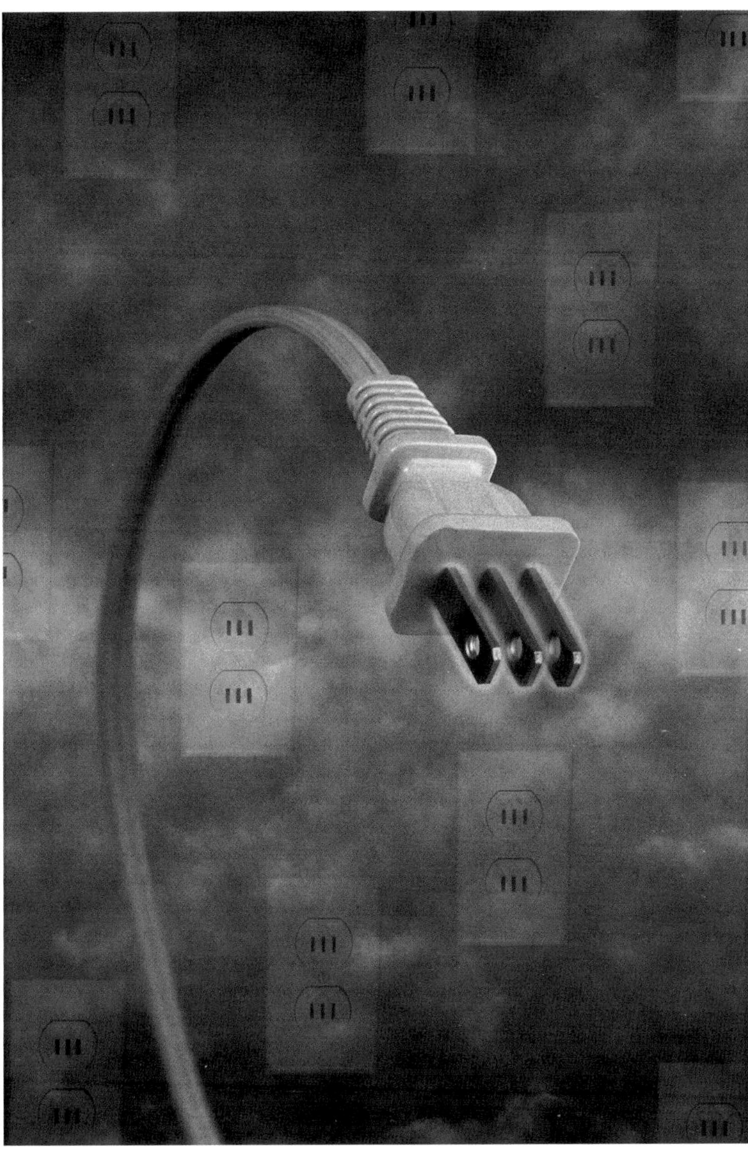

Illinova's portfolio of service covers a broad array of energy, energy service, and risk management products.

A second key evaluation tool is the EQ Service Bureau—a service bureau approach to managing utilities, streamlining the accounting process, and forecasting purchasing needs. With its 47 verification checks, the EQ Service Bureau assures billing accuracy and locates savings opportunities. In addition, EQ Service Bureau helps reduce accounting costs and headaches.

The third key evaluation tool offered by Illinova Energy Partners is the EQ Energy Audit, which involves inspection of a customer's facilities to identify ways to increase energy efficiency and reduce energy costs. Each audit report includes a complete energy inventory and a range of recommendations, cost options, and payback periods.

Illinova is a single contact for improving energy efficiency, upgrading equipment, or outsourcing operations. In addition, the company relieves budget pressures and distractions from a client's core business by providing customer service, turnkey engineered solutions, project management, system operation, and flexible financing tools. Experienced staff can design, engineer, acquire equipment, and manage construction of energy-related projects, as well as plan, design, and install energy management systems to maximize productivity and minimize energy costs. Illinova also offers expertise in gas distribution systems and devices.

Together, Illinova's portfolio of services helps customers develop their energy consumption and supply strategies, and then extract financial benefits from both the supply and demand sides of their energy requirements equation.

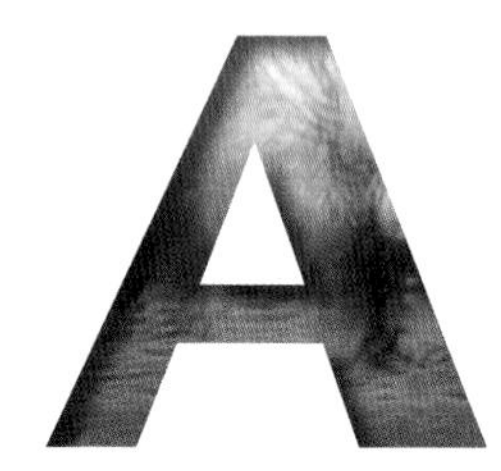

PREMIER PROVIDER OF WIRELESS VOICE, ADVANCED messaging, aircraft communications, and wireless data services in the United States, AT&T Wireless Services became a wholly owned subsidiary of AT&T after a merger between McCaw Cellular Communications of Kirkland and AT&T, the world's leading provider of communications services and products. Today, more than 41 million people use wireless services, and some 35,000 people sign up for new service each day.

As part of doing business, AT&T Wireless Services believes in building communities one step at a time, and looks for community partnerships in which employees can play a large role. The company strategically focuses dollars, time, and technology to support community groups and nonprofit organizations, focusing on public safety, emergency preparedness and response, special needs populations, education, youth at risk, and cultural diversity.

Around the world, AT&T Wireless Services employs 12,000 people who apply their ideas and energy to making a difference in the communities in which they work. "The key to the success of our community programs is our dedicated employees," says Steve Hooper, CEO. "When the community calls, our employees eagerly answer."

Service in Seattle

AT&T's 3,000 employees in the Seattle area regularly answer that call. During the annual AT&T Day of Caring, hundreds of employees take off a half-day of work to make improvements in neighborhoods from Woodinville to Tacoma. In 1996, the company began giving all employees one paid workday off each year to devote to their community. Over the years, it has worked hand in hand with many citizen groups and local law enforcement agencies, including Crime Stoppers, Community Policing, and Washington State Patrol, to create safer neighborhoods.

AT&T New Year's at the Needle earns accolades from around the region.

AT&T also devotes significant resources to creating or cosponsoring programs that bring pleasure to residents and increase their sense of community. Each summer, for example, the company puts on AT&T Summer Nights at the Pier, a six-week concert series on Seattle's Elliott Bay that has become a citywide favorite, with nearly 60,000 people enjoying 17 concerts in 1996. Since 1993, special benefit concerts have raised more than $200,000 for Seattle Public Schools and the American Red Cross.

The AT&T Family Fourth of July lights up more than Lake Union. Whether sitting in Gas Works Park, in a boat on the lake, or in a neighborhood across town, thousands of people gather on Independence Day to enjoy the most spectacular pyrotechnics show ever launched in Seattle. And after the party is over, nearly 100 AT&T employees from around western Washington paddle out in kayaks and canoes to clean up the debris.

Every year, AT&T cosponsors the Seattle-to-Portland Bicycle Classic, during which more than 10,000 bikers pedal 180 miles. After completing the first leg of the two-day trek, many bikers go straight to the AT&T Calling Center to make free cellular calls to update friends and family.

The Seattle Mariners and AT&T team up every season in the program Home Runs that Help. For every home run the Mariners

hit during the season, AT&T contributes $100 to King County Big Brothers.

AT&T also gears up for the winter holiday season. Twice a year, at Christmas and Valentine's Day, employees throw a party for their friends at the Wallingford Senior Center. They come bearing gifts and cellular phones, which seniors use to call loved ones across the country.

Inspired by Intiman Theatre's 1996 holiday season production of *Having Our Say*, AT&T joined with the theater to ask senior citizens and youths between the ages of nine and 18 to share a story about a senior who had made a significant impact on their life and community. The response was overwhelming. Hundreds of essays poured in, and a panel of distinguished community leaders selected 150 essays to display in the theater lobby. The author of each story received two tickets to the play, and the top 10 honorees received signed, limited edition posters from the play, as well as profiles in the local media.

And finally, AT&T rings in each new year with AT&T New Year's at the Needle, a grand fireworks display launched from the Space Needle at midnight before a crowd of 40,000. Thousands more watch from nearby neighborhoods, while others enjoy the spectacle on television.

Local children and seniors crafted a 2,700-square-foot American flag for the AT&T Family Fourth Celebration (top).

AT&T employee volunteers bring cheer to local senior centers during the holidays with free cellular phone calls nationwide (bottom).

Ready When Needed

AT&T is also there when a special need arises. Proving that communication is invaluable during a crisis, when western Washington suffered severe flooding in 1996, AT&T joined forces with its longtime nationwide partner, the American Red Cross, to supply 50 local volunteers, plus cellular phones, pagers, and free airtime, to perform damage assessment and help staff emergency shelters.

"The American Red Cross is fortunate to be blessed by the gifts of time and talent provided by the employees of AT&T Wireless Services," says Elizabeth Dole, national executive director of the American Red Cross. "It has helped us develop a sophisticated communications network, and its gifts of technical expertise and cellular equipment have increased our ability to quickly respond to the urgent needs of disaster victims."

These are just a few of the dozens of programs sponsored each year by AT&T to support and build communities. Both in small and large ways, they make a difference in the lives of people living in the Puget Sound region.

WITHIN WALKING DISTANCE OF MAJOR SHOPPING, entertainment, and tourist attractions, Cavanaugh's on Fifth Avenue caters to Seattle business and pleasure travelers wanting first-class, comfortable surroundings. Located in the heart of the city's bustling downtown, it is one of Seattle's newest hotels, featuring 300 guest rooms and suites that command outstanding views of the mountains and city. Half of the rooms have water views.

Cavanaugh's is located in the former U.S. Bank building between Union and Pike streets, the site of the old Hotel Georgian from Seattle's early days. The hotel and conference center are part of a mixed-use development that includes restaurants and retail and professional office space. Situated next to Nordstrom, two blocks from the Convention Center and three blocks from the entrance to the Pike Place Market, Cavanaugh's is the first facility in the revitalized downtown core to convert from a commercial property into a hotel.

KNOWN THROUGHOUT THE NORTHWEST

As the newest of eight hotels owned and operated by Goodale & Barbieri Companies in the inland Northwest, Cavanaugh's immediate success in Seattle is in part a product of an established, loyal clientele from Montana, Idaho, and elsewhere in Washington where Cavanaugh's is a familiar name, known for its high standards of guest service.

"Our guests' reactions have been overwhelming, as they have been asking us for many years when we were going to open a Cavanaugh's in Seattle," says Lori Main, the general manager of Cavanaugh's on Fifth Avenue. An 18-year veteran with Cavanaugh's who came to Seattle after managing its Kalispell, Montana, hotel, Main says, "It's a natural fit, a friendly company coming to a friendly city."

The hotel opened in May 1996, one month ahead of schedule, with few people aware that more than 80 tons of debris (80 percent of which was recycled) were removed from the site through nondisruptive construction techniques. The former bank offices were redesigned into 257 spacious and 40 smaller rooms, all with a queen- or king-size bed. The needs of business

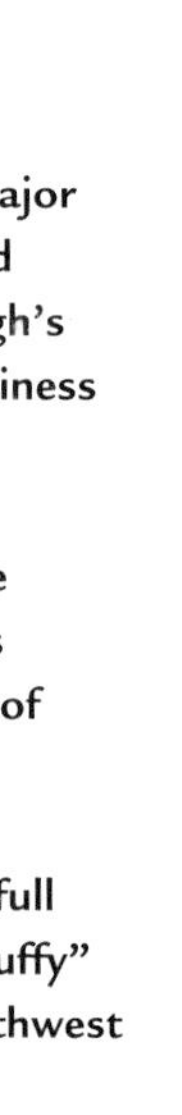

▼▲ J. CRAIG SWEAT

▼ J. CRAIG SWEAT

Clockwise from left:
Within walking distance of major shopping, entertainment, and tourist attractions, Cavanaugh's on Fifth Avenue caters to business and pleasure travelers.

Cavanaugh's, a familiar name throughout the Northwest, is known for its high standards of guest service.

The Terrace Garden serves a full menu all day of "fresh, not fluffy" fare, including the finest Northwest seafood available.

travelers were kept in mind during the remodeling, with such added conveniences as coffee and coffeemakers, full-length mirrors, and extra lights in the bathrooms. Two phones in each room handle incoming calls and modems, and most rooms offer honor bars.

Other amenities at Cavanaugh's on Fifth Avenue include meeting and banquet facilities, which can accommodate groups of 10 to 600 people, located primarily on one floor, and all with windows. A 180-car underground parking garage was redesigned for out-of-the-weather drop off and pick up of guests. The Terrace Garden Restaurant and Lounge, and the aerobic fitness center, are on the fifth floor. The hotel also offers 24-hour room service and a concierge staff to meet guests' needs.

The Terrace Garden boasts the largest outdoor deck in Seattle, which faces west to the Olympic Mountains. The restaurant serves a full menu all day of "fresh, not fluffy" fare, including the finest Northwest seafood available. The chefs are encouraged to try new cuisines and presentation ideas, and the menu changes frequently.

Private Ownership

Goodale & Barbieri Companies (G&B) was founded in 1937 as a family-owned, diversified real estate development and management company with a portfolio of more than 6.8 million square feet in Washington, Idaho, and Montana. Private ownership contributes to the down-home, natural fit of Cavanaugh's hotels in the Northwest.

In Spokane, Cavanaugh's Inn at the Park is considered eastern Washington's finest lodging facility. It opened in 1983 with a 4,000-square-foot skyline ballroom. It complements Cavanaugh's Fourth Avenue, in the city's heart, and the resort-style Cavanaugh's River Inn on the Spokane River. Other Cavanaugh's locations include Kennewick and Yakima, Washington, and Kalispell, Montana.

Goodale & Barbieri also specializes in commercial redevelopment. It played a vital role in the redevelopment of downtown Spokane, including River Park Square and the securing of the first Nordstrom located outside the Puget Sound area. In Kalispell, G&B manages the 26-acre, mixed-use Kalispell Center Mall, which is connected to a 132-room Cavanaugh's. This 1986 development earned G&B the Certificate of National Merit from the U.S. Department of Housing and Urban Development.

For more than 20 years, G&B has been the leader in providing quality low-income housing to the inland Northwest. On behalf of Catholic Charities, it has developed and managed low-cost housing for the elderly in Spokane, Pullman, and Walla Walla, Washington.

In addition to real estate interests, G&B owns a dairy, a ticket agency, and an entertainment company. In the spring of 1996, G&B became 50 percent owner of the Moose Lake Company, a Montana-grown retail company specializing in outdoor clothing and merchandise. The Moose Lake Company joined Cavanaugh's on Fifth Avenue with a new, 8,000-square-foot store located on the Fourth Avenue side of the building. With all of these interests and its convenient location in each of the cities, Cavanaugh's Hotels has positioned itself to handle all meeting, travel, and entertainment needs of the customer.

J. Craig Sweat

J. Craig Sweat

Clockwise from top:
The Terrace Garden boasts the largest outdoor deck in downtown Seattle.

The needs of business travelers were kept in mind during the remodeling, with such added conveniences as coffee and coffeemakers, full-length mirrors, and extra lights in the bathrooms.

The hotel opened in May 1996, one month ahead of schedule, with few people aware that more than 80 tons of debris (80 percent of which was recycled) were removed from the site through nondisruptive construction techniques.

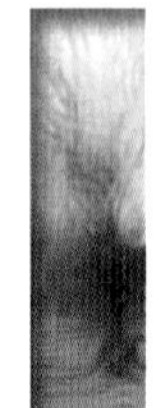

Insignia Corporate Establishments fills a special niche in the high-end office market: It provides office space and support services for small businesses of one to 10 people who want prestige at an affordable price. Whether a company needs a single office or a multiple-office suite, Insignia offers variable term leases that give tenants maximum flexibility to expand or contract, thereby virtually eliminating the risk normally associated with long-term leases.

Since Insignia opened its first suite of offices in 1990 in Calgary, it has added to its portfolio in Calgary and expanded to Vancouver, British Columbia, and Seattle. Future plans include expansion to other cities in the western United States.

Full-Service Accommodations

Located on the 38th floor of the First Interstate Center in downtown Seattle, Insignia's offices command superior views of Elliott Bay, Mt. Rainier, and the city. Each tenant enjoys personalized telephone answering service, full signage in the building and elevator lobbies, and its company logo on its own front door. Each location features an elegantly appointed reception area; a stocked kitchen; a multifunctional, high-speed photocopier; an integrated voice mail system; and dedicated modem and fax lines. There are also boardrooms and conference rooms that can accommodate anything from a private meeting for two people to a seminar for 50.

In addition, a furnished, fully equipped guest office is available to a tenant's clients or out-of-town company personnel. Tenants can furnish the individual offices themselves or rent fine, custom-designed furniture from Insignia. On-site secured storage is provided for archived files or promotional materials that are not needed on a daily basis. Daily maintenance and janitorial services provide a comfortable and clean environment.

An Insignia receptionist answers the telephone, greets visitors, and manages mail, courier, and package receipt. The company also makes available administrative or secretarial support, such as word processing, filing, proofing, research, and assembling of promotional materials, as well as an administrative staff that can handle bookkeeping, spreadsheet services, database management, desktop publishing, and notary services.

Located on the 38th floor of the First Interstate Center in downtown Seattle, Insignia's offices command superior views of Elliott Bay, Mt. Rainier, and the city.

◀ Larry Evensen, Imaging Northwest

Flexibility

The risk of being locked into personal covenants is one of the most difficult issues for start-up companies. Insignia removes that risk with a simple two-month deposit and eliminates the up-front capital costs involved in setting up an office.

"We've been successful because we give small tenants the ability to lease in a world-class building at significant savings and with flexible lease terms," says Ken Gordon Jr., Insignia president. "We can save businesses anywhere from 30 to 50 percent when comparing our concept to a stand-alone lease."

Should an Insignia tenant ever need an office away from home, Insignia's suites in downtown Calgary, Toronto, and Vancouver are always available as a place to work, hold meetings, or obtain support services. This service makes Insignia well suited for national firms, which account for a majority of its tenants. Such high-tech firms as Microsoft, Novell, Lotus, Powersoft, Sybase, and Sentex Corporation, as well as personal consultants, boutique law firms, and international trading companies find Insignia's flexibility ideal.

GREG PROBST

Susan Alworth, originally from Duluth, Minnesota, moved to Seattle in 1986. A graduate of the University of Montana, she specializes in scenic photography of the Pacific Northwest and other travel destinations, as well as people and event photography. Alworth's images have appeared in *Balloon Life* and *Where Magazine-Seattle*, in publications for the Seattle-King County Convention & Visitors Bureau, and in Landmark calendars.

Janice Bell, a native of Washington State, attended the University of Colorado, Boulder and the University of Puget Sound, Tacoma. The owner of JCB Enterprises, she has traveled to Asia, Thailand, Korea, Africa, Russia, Mexico, Europe, and many parts of the United States to photograph the people, land, and wildlife of these regions. Bell's work has appeared in *Young Children* magazine, the *Lakewood Journal*, brochures for several nonprofit organizations, and another Towery publication, *Tacoma: Tomorrow's City . . . Today*.

Chris Bennion is a freelance photographer from Connecticut who has lived in Seattle since 1975. A graduate of Stanford University, Bennion specializes in performing arts and corporate photography. His previous clients include the Seattle Repertory Theater, Seattle Opera, Intiman Playhouse, Seattle Symphony, Liaison International Stock Photography, A Contemporary Theatre, and Empty Space Theatre.

Benjamin Benschneider, originally from Colorado Springs, moved to Seattle in 1979. Currently, he is a staff photographer for the *Seattle Times*.

Alan Berner is a native of St. Louis who moved to Seattle in 1981 by way of Tucson. A graduate of the University of Missouri with bachelor's degrees in philosophy and photojournalism, he is currently a staff photographer for the *Seattle Times*. Berner has been named Regional Photographer of the Year three times by the National Press Photographers Association (NPPA), and has received a Nikon/NPPA Documentary Sabbatical Grant.

Anthony P. Bolante is a photographer for the *Eastside Journal*. A native of Honolulu, he has lived in the Seattle area since 1994.

Bob Brooks, a resident of Halifax, Nova Scotia, is the owner and operator of Bob Brooks Illustrative Photography. A specialist in photojournalism as well as sports, news, and stock photography, he has won more than 50 international awards, including a Master of Photographic Arts medal from the Professional Photographers of Canada and a Commemorative Medal for the 125th Anniversary of Canadian Confederation. Brooks has covered a variety of assignments, from the International Figure Skating Championships to various Olympic Games, and his work has been published in *Life*, *Time*, *National Geographic*, *Sports Illustrated*, *Fortune*, and *Newsweek*, among other magazines.

Jim Corwin earned a bachelor of arts from the University of Washington and a degree in photography from Everett Community College. He spent 12 years working for photo labs in the Seattle area before opening his own business in 1990. A native of Portland, Oregon, Corwin specializes in travel, nature, people, and sports photography, and he has worked for such clients as The Boeing Company, Safeway, U S West Communications, GTE, and Microsoft. His work has been published in *National Geographic Traveler*, *Audubon*, *Mother Earth News*, and *Business Week*.

Hermine Dreyfuss, a freelance photographer, has traveled throughout the United States and to four continents, capturing images of everyday life. She is the owner of the Custom Wardrobe, Inc. in Washington, D.C., where she currently resides. Dreyfuss' images have been featured in leading U.S. and international publications as well as in *The Lure of the Loom: Traveling with Textiles*. Additionally, her *Kyrgyzstan: Nomadic Culture* exhibit is currently on display at the World Bank in Washington, D.C.

Robert Esposito is a native of Pittsburgh who moved to Seattle in 1988. The owner of Panorama Designs, he specializes in stock photography; mechanical drafting/checking for clients using AutoCAD, a computer-aided drafting program; and coordinating music and images from up to nine slide projectors. Having cataloged more than 30,000 slides, Esposito has won several awards in competitions sponsored by

◀ JIM BATES

area camera clubs, and his work can be seen in *American Magazine*, *American History*, *Washington CEO*, and *RV West Magazine*.

Natalie Fobes is a Seattle-based freelance photographer specializing in environmental photography, as well as images of people and places. Her love of photography has taken her from the Chukchi reindeer camps of Siberia to the cloud forest of Guatemala, and her images have appeared in *National Geographic*, *Audubon*, *Smithsonian*, and *Time* magazines, as well as in the book *Passage to Vietnam*. Fobes' 10-year project *Reaching Home: Pacific Salmon, Pacific People* was published in 1994 and won the Pacific Northwest Booksellers Award in 1995. A Pulitzer Prize finalist and the recipient of the Edward J. Meeman Award from Scripps-Howard, she recently cofounded the Blue Earth Alliance, a nonprofit organization dedicated to helping photographers document endangered cultures and environments.

William B. Folsom, owner and operator of the McLean, Virginia-based William B. Folsom Photography, Inc., has a stock photography file of more than 37,000 images on such subjects as the U.S. armed forces, aviation, high technology, and North American animals. In addition to more than 75 cover photographs for such publications as *Time*, *Civil War Times Illustrated*, Delta Air Lines' *Sky*, and *Washington Flyer* magazines, Folsom has contributed to nearly 30 books, including *Algonquians of the East Coast* and *Smithsonian Guide to Aviation*.

Robert Fried has traveled on assignment to more than 50 countries. A graduate of the State University of New York with a degree in anthropology, he specializes in travel and editorial photography for advertising, corporate, and education markets. Fried's pictures have been published extensively in the travel/tourism industry, international magazines, guide/picture books, encyclopedias, and calendars, and his clients include American Express, *GEO* magazine, the *Los Angeles Times*, *National Geographic Traveler*, the *New York Times*, *Travel & Leisure*, UNICEF, and World Book. He currently lives north of San Francisco and enjoys growing tomatoes.

Greg Gilbert, a native of Olympia, moved to Bainbridge Island in 1967. A former student of the Art Center College of Design in Pasadena, he has been a staff photographer for the *Seattle Times* for more than 30 years. A general interest photographer, Gilbert was named an NPPA Photographer of the Year in 1971, and his work has appeared in *Life* and *Time* magazines. In 1986, he flew around the world in 34 hours in a record-breaking flight.

Michael J. Glaze owned his first camera at age six and has loved taking pictures ever since. He has worked as a real estate photographer in the Los Angeles area, has specialized in wedding photography, and is currently a freelance and stock photographer who travels the globe to capture images for travel and international publications. In the Emerald City, Glaze teaches basic photography for the Mountaineers Annual Nature Photography course, critiques and judges photography as a member of the Seattle Photographic Society, and covers the scenes in and around Seattle.

John Coulter Gossett is a photographer who has an eye for the outdoors. The Pacific Northwest's beauty and evolving cities drive his passion to capture its people and landscapes on film. An outdoor adventurist, he enjoys kayaking, mountain biking, and fly-fishing. Currently, Gossett lives in Salt Spring Island, British Columbia, and works for Tsunami Photography.

▶ SEATTLE TIMES / TOM REESE

Gary Greene, involved with photography since 1974, started his own photography and graphic design business, Gary Greene Artworks, in 1984. He specializes in outdoor photography, concentrating primarily on Pacific Northwest scenes. Greene's work has been published by the National Geographic Society, Hallmark, U S WEST Communications, the Environmental Protection Agency, Hertz, Impact Photographics, and the Automobile Association of America, as well as in *Petersen's Photographic Magazine*, *Popular Photography* magazine, and *Oregon Coast* magazine. An accomplished fine artist and art instructor, he has authored three books: *Creating Textures in Colored Pencil*, *Capturing Flowers with Colored Pencil*, and *Flower Photos for Painters*.

Brian Groppe, a graphic designer whose work focuses primarily on book and poster design, has been creative director for Towery Publishing, Inc. since 1986 and is principal art director for the company's Urban Tapestry Series. A 1979 graduate of California College of Arts and Crafts in Oakland, Groppe's work has been published in *Print* magazine's *Regional Design Annual*. His professional honors include a silver award in *Photo/Design* magazine's 1992 Annual Poster Design Contest, Addy awards in 1994 and 1995 for the book covers for *Chicago: Second to None* and *Chaos & CyberCulture*, and a 1994 Addy for the *Memphis in May International Festival Fine Art Poster*. Groppe is currently the art and photography editor for OneKey, an Internet search engine. He lives in Memphis with his wife, Susan, an Orff music specialist, and their two daughters.

◀ JIM BATES

Gary Hayes is a freelance photographer from the Pacific Northwest. Specializing in travel and nature photography, he has worked with such clients as Microsoft, Holland America Westours, Cunard Cruise Lines, and the Seattle Crowne Plaza. Hayes' images have appeared in *Alaska Airlines Magazine*, *USA Today*, and *Business Monthly*. He has served as editor of *Photomedia* magazine and as chapter president of the American Society of Media Photographers.

Hillstrom Stock Photo, established in Chicago in 1967, is a full-service stock photography agency. The company's files include images of architecture, agriculture backgrounds, classic autos, gardens, and high-risk adventure/sports.

Tim J. Johnson, a specialist in still life, product, corporate, and outdoor photography, works for Strode Photographers. With a bachelor of fine arts from Art Center College of Design in Pasadena, California, Johnson has worked with such clients as Frank Russell Company, Maersk Line, Tree Top, and Insulate Industries. He also enjoys scenic and mountain photography, and counts breathtaking aerial photo shoots among the great events of his professional career. Johnson's images were featured in *Tacoma: Tomorrow's City . . . Today*.

Dan Lamont, a lifelong Seattleite, is a freelance photographer who specializes in the coverage of environmental and land-use issues for such international magazines as *Time*, *Life*, *Forbes*, and *Der Spiegel*. With a bachelor of arts in documentary photography from the University of Washington, Lamont has an extensive list of corporate and nonprofit clients. He is the recipient of awards from the Society of Professional Journalists and the Seattle Design Association, as well as of the Tempodrome Award, which is bestowed in Germany.

Fred Lyon is a self-proclaimed "unstoppable explorer with a gentlemen's sensibility, sharing his curiosity of the world through the medium of photography." A Time-Life photographer whose work has appeared in such magazines as *Time*, *Life*, *Fortune*, *Sports Illustrated*, and *People*, he has photographed five U.S. presidents as well as numerous celebrities and captains of industry. Lyon's vineyards in California have served as subject matter for many images in his comprehensive collection of wine-related photography. Paying homage to his hometown, Lyon's *The Bridges of San Francisco: Perceptive Photographs by Fred Lyon* exhibit is housed at the Chicago Art Institute.

Kevin McGowan, originally from Milwaukee, is a commercial photographer for Strode Photographers in Tacoma. His work has been displayed in the Everson Museum of Art in Syracuse, New York, and he has received awards from the Professional Photographers Association of Washington. McGowan has worked with such clients as the Roman Meal Company, STL International, and the American Plywood Association. He particularly enjoys shooting travel, nature, and lifestyle images.

Richard T. Nowitz, chosen as the 1996 Travel Photographer of the Year by the Society of American Travel Writers, maintains a portfolio of images culled from his assignments with *National Geographic World*, for which he has been a contract photographer since 1992. Nowitz has been the principal photographer for Insight travel guides on Israel, Egypt, Cairo, Jerusalem, Wales, and London, and his work has been published in *Condé Nast Traveler*, *Endless Vacation*, *National Geographic Travel*, *Smithsonian*, *Time*, and *U.S. News & World Report*.

Pedro Perez, originally from California, moved to the Seattle area in 1996. A graduate of California State University at Fresno, he is a photographer for the *Seattle Times*.

Tom Reese, a native of St. Louis, holds a bachelor's degree in journalism from the University of Missouri, Columbia. His images have appeared in the *Everett Herald*, *Columbia Daily Tribune*, *Kansas City Times*, and *St. Louis Suburban Journal*. Reese moved to Seattle in 1983 and is currently a photographer for the *Seattle Times*.

Steve Ringman, a street photographer for the *Seattle Times*, specializes in capturing emotional stories on film. He has twice been named the NPPA Photographer of the Year and has received the San Francisco Bay Area Press Photographer of the Year award five times. A native of Mount Vernon, Washington, he graduated from the Brooks Institute of Photography in Santa Barbara with a bachelor of fine arts in photography. Ringman currently lives in Issaquah with his wife of 20 years and their two children.

Dean Rutz, a native of Palatine, Illinois, moved to Seattle in 1988. A graduate of Indiana University, he has worked as a staff photographer for the *Washington Times* and the *Palm Beach Post*. Currently, Rutz is a photo editor for the *Seattle Times*.

Stefan Schulhof, a member of Professional Photographers Association of British Columbia, Professional Photographers of Canada, and Canadian Association of Photographers & Illustrators in Communications, is an award-winning photographer whose work can be seen in *Visions in View* and the *Vancouver Sun*. His clients include BBDO Advertising, B.C. Telephone, Canadian Helicopters, Coldwell Banker, *Forbes* magazine, and Westin Hotels. Schulhof was born in Dublin and moved to Canada at age four.

John Stamets specializes in architectural photography and panoramic photojournalism. A native of Ohio, he is a graduate of Yale University. Stamets contributed to *Portrait of a Market*, which was published by Real Comet Press in 1987. Additionally, he has completed 25 projects for the Historic American Buildings Survey. Currently, Stamets works part-time for the University of Washington Department of Architecture.

Teresa Tamura is a photojournalist for the *Seattle Times*. With a bachelor's degree in journalism from Idaho State University and a master of fine arts in photography from the University of Washington, Tamura has worked for the Twin Falls *Times-News*, the San Fernando Valley and San Diego editions of the *Los Angeles Times*, and the *Morning Call* in Allentown, Pennsylvania.

Kurt Thorson was born in the San Juan Islands in 1952 and spent much of his childhood there. From 1975 to 1978, he studied painting and drawing at the Cornish College of the Arts, where he won a Mark Tobey scholarship. Following a period of world travel after graduation, he returned to Waldron Island for 10 years to live on the Nature Conservancy Preserve. Thorson has used his unique background to approach photography with an artist's eye for form and balance as well as a craftsman's demand for quality. His work has been published by the Sierra Club, World Wildlife Fund, *GEO* magazine, and National Wildlife Federation.

Steve Warble, the director of orchestras for the Barrington, Illinois, public school system, developed an interest in photography as a result of his numerous journeys to national parks and wilderness areas throughout the United States and Canada. He is the owner of Elgin, Illinois-based Mountain Magic Photography, which specializes in stock photo sales and decor photography, and his work has been featured in dozens of magazines, calendars, books, and commercial and environmental displays.

Alex Waterhouse-Hayward, a native of Buenos Aires, was a high school teacher in Mexico City for 20 years before moving with his wife and children to Vancouver, British Columbia. He has been an editorial photographer specializing in people ever since. Waterhouse-Hayward has freelanced for numerous Canadian magazines and is a regular contributor to the *Globe and Mail*. His work has appeared in *InterView*, *Time*, *People*, *Entertainment Weekly*, *Esquire*, *I-D*, *Arena*, *Spin*, *Vanity Fair*, *Future Sex*, and the *Los Angeles Times*.

Gregory Williams, a lifelong resident of Savannah, graduated from the Savannah Technical Institute with a degree in photography and has studied under renowned nature photographer John Earl. A freelance photographer, Williams specializes in landscape, unique architecture, and abstract photography, and many of his images are used in chamber of commerce guides across the nation. He is the winner of several regional Sierra Club photo contests, and in 1996, mounted an exhibit titled *Savannah and the Georgia Coast*.

Ron Wurzer is originally from Southern California, where he attended California State University, Fullerton. Currently living in Seattle, he is a staff photographer for the *Seattle Times*.

▶ SEATTLE TIMES / MARK HARRISON

Other photographers and organizations that have contributed to *Seattle: Pacific Gem* include Robin Bartholick, Stephanie Boyar, Linda Coan, Johnny Closs, David Cooper, Rick Dean, Nick Gunderson, Mark Harrison, Ben Kerns, Jim Lott, Rod Mar, Pacific Northwest Ballet, Greg Probst, David Sailors, Meryl Schenker, Seattle Symphony, the *Seattle Times*, Gary Settle, Mike Siegel, Harley Soltes, Betty Udesen, and Barry Wong.

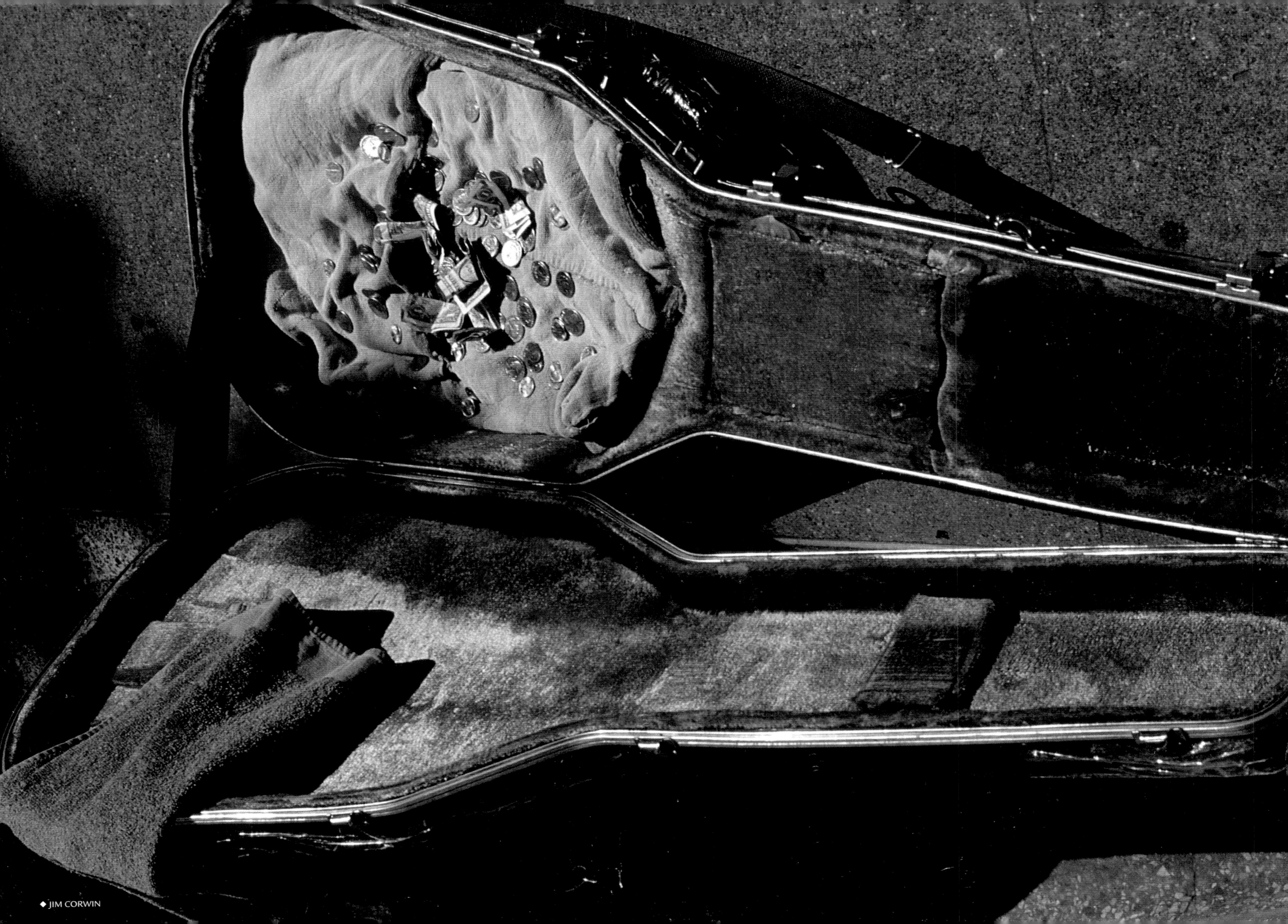

◆ JIM CORWIN

◆ JIM CORWIN